Praise for

A CALL TO ACTION

"When reading *A Call to Action*, I got the sense that this is a man who has spent nine decades advocating for women and will continue to do so until his last breath. He is a man on a mission, listing twenty-three challenges he and The Carter Center are determined to work on for the betterment of women. He demonstrates how he used his influence throughout his lifetime to push women's rights forward. . . . Carter's book overwhelms as well as inspires."

—*Huffington Post*

"Women's studies scholars and readers interested in international human rights may find these accounts of discrimination and abuse disturbing but should be challenged to respond to Carter's call for action."

—*Library Journal*

"*A Call to Action* reinforces [Carter's] dedication to wiping out injustice—and his ability to move others to join his cause."

—*St. Louis Post-Dispatch*

"A tour de force of the global abuse and manipulation of women, including statistics that will stun most readers with details that cannot be ignored. . . . The scope of the material is astounding. . . . Mr. Carter's *A Call to Action* should not only be required reading in America, but should also serve as the template for a complete reinterpretation of the religious views behind our treatment of each other, to discover what he claims is the true meaning behind the miracle of creation."

—*Pittsburgh Post-Gazette*

"*A Call to Action* ends with a list of recommendations to ameliorate the condition of women and girls worldwide, such as having more women in higher public office and involving religious scholars to give a more forward-looking interpretation to their faiths. It is this commitment to a progressive religious outlook that makes Carter almost a lone voice in U.S. politics."

—Progressive.org

"[Carter] wrote his book with deep knowledge, insight and compassion. . . . Indeed, it is time to wake up."

—*Morning Call* (PA)

"*A Call to Action* enhances [Carter's] role as elder statesman and human rights warrior by focusing entirely on the enslavement, degradation, and torture that women endure around the world. . . . An important book that should serve as a reference guide and instructional manual for dealing with the atrocities against women."

—*The Daily Beast*

A CALL TO ACTION

Women, Religion, Violence, and Power

JIMMY CARTER

Simon & Schuster Paperbacks

New York   London   Toronto   Sydney   New Delhi

SIMON & SCHUSTER PAPERBACKS
A Division of Simon & Schuster, Inc.
1230 Avenue of the Americas
New York, NY 10020

First Simon & Schuster Paperbacks edition March 2015

SIMON & SCHUSTER PAPERBACKS and colophon are
registered trademarks of Simon & Schuster, Inc.

For information about special discounts for bulk purchases, please
contact Simon & Schuster Special Sales at 1-866-506-1949 or
business@simonandschuster.com.

The Simon & Schuster Speakers Bureau can bring authors to your
live event. For more information or to book an event, contact
the Simon & Schuster Speakers Bureau at 1-866-248-3049 or visit
our website at www.simonspeakers.com.

Interior design by Claudia Martinez

Manufactured in the United States of America

10   9   8   7   6   5   4   3   2   1

The Library of Congress has cataloged the hardcover edition as follows:

Carter, Jimmy, 1924–
A call to action : women, religion, violence, and power /
Jimmy Carter.
pages   cm
Includes index.
1. Women's rights. 2. Women's rights—Religious aspects.
3. Women—Social conditions—21st century. 4. Women—
Violence against. 5. Sex discrimination against women. 6. Sex
role—Religious aspects. 7. Human rights. I. Title.
HQ1236.C375   2014
323.3'4—dc23   2014007266

ISBN 978-1-4767-7395-7
ISBN 978-1-4767-7396-4 (pbk)
ISBN 978-1-4767-7397-1 (ebook)

To Karin Ryan,

and the countless women and girls
whose abuse and deprivation she strives to alleviate

CONTENTS

═══

A CALL TO ACTION

INTRODUCTION

All the elements in this book concerning prejudice, discrimination, war, violence, distorted interpretations of religious texts, physical and mental abuse, poverty, and disease fall disproportionately on women and girls.

I saw the ravages of racial prejudice as I grew up in the Deep South, when for a century the U.S. Supreme Court and all other political and social authorities accepted the premise that black people were, in some basic ways, inferior to white people. Even those in the dominant class who disagreed with this presumption remained relatively quiet and enjoyed the benefits of the prevailing system. Carefully selected Holy Scriptures were quoted to justify this discrimination in the name of God.

There is a similar system of discrimination, extending far beyond a small geographical region to the entire globe; it touches every nation, perpetuating and expanding the trafficking in human slaves, body mutilation, and even legitimized murder on a massive scale. This system is based on the presumption that men and boys are superior to women and girls, and it is supported by some male religious leaders who distort the Holy Bible, the Koran, and other sacred texts to perpetuate their claim that females are, in some basic ways, inferior to them, unqualified to serve God on equal terms. Many men disagree but remain quiet in order to enjoy the benefits of their dominant status. This false premise provides a justification for sexual discrimination in almost every realm of secular and religious life. Some men even cite this premise to justify physical punishment of women and girls.

Another factor contributing to the abuse of women and girls is an acceptance of violence, from unwarranted armed combat to excessive and biased punishment for those who violate the law. In too many cases, we use violence as a first rather than a last resort, so that even deadly violence has become commonplace.

My own experiences and the testimony of courageous women from all regions and all major religions have made it clear to me that as a result of these two factors there is a pervasive denial of equal rights to women, more than half of all human beings, and this discrimination results in tangible harm to all of us, male and female.

My wife, Rosalynn, and I have visited about 145 countries, and the nonprofit organization we founded, The Carter Center, has had active projects in more than half of them. We have had opportunities in recent years to interact directly among the people, often in remote villages in the jungles and deserts. We have learned a lot about their personal affairs, particularly that financial inequality has been growing more rapidly with each passing decade. This is true both between rich and poor countries and among citizens within them. In fact, the disparity in net worth and income in the United States has greatly increased since my time in the White House. By 2007 the income of the middle 60 percent of Americans had increased at a rate twice as high as that of the bottom 20 percent. And the rate of increase for the top 1 percent was over fifteen times higher, primarily because of the undue influence of wealthy people who invest in elections and later buy greater benefits for themselves in Washington and in state capitals. As the conservative columnist George Will writes, "Big government *inevitably* drives an upward distribution of wealth to those whose wealth, confidence and sophistication enable them to manipulate government."

Yet although economic disparity is a great and growing problem, I have become convinced that *the most serious and unaddressed worldwide challenge is the deprivation and abuse of women and girls*, largely caused by a false interpretation of carefully selected religious texts and a growing tolerance of violence and warfare, unfortunately following the example set during my lifetime by the United States. In addition to the unconscionable human suffering, almost embarrassing to acknowledge, there is a devastating effect on economic prosperity caused by the loss of contributions of at least half the human beings on earth. This is not just a women's issue. It is not confined to the poorest countries. It affects us all.

After focusing for a few years on the problem of gender discrimination through our human rights program at The Carter Center, I began to speak out more forcefully about it. Because of this, I was asked to address the Parliament of the World's Religions, an audience of several thousand assembled in Australia in December 2009, about the vital role of religion in providing a foundation for countering the global scourge of gender abuse. My remarks represented the personal views of a Christian layman, a Bible teacher for more than seventy years, a former political leader.

I reminded the audience that in dealing with each other, we are guided by international agreements as well as our own moral values, most often derived from the Universal Declaration of Human Rights, the Bible, the Koran, and other cherished texts that proclaim a commitment to justice and mercy, equality of treatment between men and women, and a duty to alleviate suffering. However, some selected scriptures are interpreted, almost exclusively by powerful male leaders within the Christian, Jewish, Muslim, Hindu, Buddhist, and other faiths, to proclaim the lower status of women and girls. This claim that women are inferior before God spreads to the secular world to justify gross and sustained acts of discrimination and violence against them. This includes unpunished rape and other sexual abuse, infanticide of newborn girls and abortion of female fetuses, a worldwide trafficking in women and girls, and so-called honor killings of innocent women who are raped, as well as the less violent but harmful practices of lower pay and fewer promotions for women and greater political advantages for men. I mentioned some notable achievements of women despite these handicaps and described struggles within my own religious faith. I called on believers, whether Protestant, Catholic, Coptic, Jew, Muslim, Buddhist, Hindu, or tribal, to study these violations of our basic moral values and to take corrective action.

No matter what our faith may be, it is impossible to imagine a God who is unjust.

ZAINAH ANWAR,

FOUNDER OF SISTERS IN ISLAM, MALAYSIA

In the following pages I will outline how I learned more and more about these issues, as a child, a submarine officer, a farmer, and a church leader during the civil rights struggle, as a governor and a president, as a college professor, and in the global work of The Carter Center. During the nine decades of my life I have become increasingly aware of and concerned about the immense number of and largely ignored gender-based crimes. There are reasons for hope that some of these abuses can be ended when they become better known and understood. I hope that this book will help to expose these violations to a broader audience and marshal a more concerted effort to address this profound problem.

I will explore the links between religion-based assertions of male dominance over women, as well as the ways that our "culture of violence" contributes to the denial of women's rights. I maintain that male dominance over women is a form of oppression that often leads to violence. We cannot make progress in advancing women's rights if we do not examine these two underlying factors that contribute to the abuse of women.

In August 2013 I joined civil rights leaders and two other American presidents at the Lincoln Memorial to commemorate the fiftieth anniversary of Martin Luther King Jr.'s "I Have a Dream" speech, delivered there in 1963. As I looked out on the crowd and thought about the book I was writing, my thoughts turned to a different speech that King made, in New York City four years later, about America's war in Vietnam, in which my oldest son was serving. King asserted, "I knew that I could never again raise my voice against the violence of the oppressed in the ghettos without having first spoken clearly to the greatest purveyor of violence in the world today—my own government." King went on to ask that we Americans broaden our view to look at human freedom as inextricably linked with our commitment to peace and nonviolence.

Using this same logic, it is not possible to address the rights of women, the human and civil rights struggle of our time, without looking at factors that encourage the acceptance of violence in our society—violence that inevitably affects women disproportionately. The problem is not only militarism in foreign policy but also the resort to lethal violence and excessive deprivation of freedom in our criminal justice system when rehabilitation alternatives could be pursued. Clearly, short-term political advantages that come with being "tough on criminals" or "tough on terrorism" do not offer solutions to issues like persistent crime, sexual violence, and global terrorism.

I realize that violence is not more prevalent today than in previous periods of human history, but there is a difference. We have seen visionary standards adopted by the global community that espouse peace and human rights, and the globalization of information ensures that the violation of these principles of nonviolence by a powerful and admired democracy tends to resonate throughout the world community. We should have advanced much further in the realization of women's rights, given these international commitments to peace and the rule of law. Instead many of the gains made in advancing human rights since World War II are placed at risk by reliance on injury to others as a means to solve our problems.

We must not forget that there is always an underlying basis of moral and religious principles involved. In August 2013 Pope Francis stated quite simply that in addition to the idea that violence does not bring real solutions to societal problems, its use is contrary to the will of God: "Faith and violence are incompatible." This powerful statement exalting peace and compassion is one on which all faiths can agree.

In June 2013 The Carter Center brought together religious leaders, scholars, and activists who are working to align religious life with the advancement of girls' and women's full equality. We called this a Human Rights Defenders Forum. Throughout this book I have inserted brief statements from some of these defenders that offer a rich array of ideas and perspectives on the subject.

1 | MY CHILDHOOD

I grew up west of Plains, Georgia, in the relatively isolated rural community of Archery, where about fifty African American and two white families lived, ours and that of the foreman of a repair crew for the Seaboard Airline Railroad. Then and even now there is a spirit of chivalry in the South, and I was taught to respect all women. My mother, a registered nurse, was often away from home at all hours, especially when she was on private duty, serving in her patient's home for twenty hours a day. She would come home at 10 o'clock at night, bathe, wash her uniform, leave a written list of chores and instructions for me and my sisters, and return to her patient at 2 A.M. When this was her schedule, my parents hired one or two black women to prepare meals for us and care for the house. Even in those times of racial segregation, my father ordained that we treat these women with deference and obedience, and I never knew of a time when they failed to deserve this high regard.

I stayed in the house as little as possible, preferring to be with my father working in the fields or the woods, at the barn or blacksmith shop, or with my friends on the creek and in the forest when there was no work to be done. I was immersed in an African American culture, with my black playmates and fellow field workers.

My heroine was Rachel Clark, whose husband, Jack, cared for my family's livestock and farm equipment and who rang the farm bell an hour before daylight to rouse everyone for the day's work. In *Always a Reckoning*, my first and longest poem is "Rachel." I describe her as having "an aura like a queen" and never being called on by white people for menial personal service such as cooking, washing clothes, or doing housework. She and I were bonded in many ways, as she taught me how to fish, how to recognize trees, birds, and flowers, and how I should relate to God and to other people. Rachel was famous for picking more cotton and shaking and stacking more peanuts than anyone else, man or woman. There was a quiet but intense contest in the field each day at harvest time when pay was based on accomplishment, and she was always the best. This was a source of great prestige in our agricultural community. I would work beside her as she picked two rows of cotton to my one and sometimes helped me stay even with her as we moved back and forth across the field. I relished the nights I spent with Rachel and Jack, sleeping on a pallet on their floor. I was not aware of distinctions among people based on race or sex in those early and innocent days of my life.

My basic attitude toward women was not changed when I was only six years old and acquired my first knowledge of adult sexual and racial relationships on my daily visits to the nearby town of Plains. The peanut crop on our farm matured during summer vacations from school, and my father permitted me to go into the field, pull up a small wagonload of peanut plants by their roots, and haul them to our yard. There I plucked about ten pounds of the mature pods from the vines, drew a bucket of water from the well, carefully washed away the clinging dirt, and kept the green pods overnight in a pot of salty water. Early the next morning I boiled the peanuts, divided them into twenty small paper bags, and then toted them in a basket down the railroad track about two miles to Plains, where I sold them for a nickel a package.

I would arrive there early every morning for weeks, except Sundays, and go in and out of the grocery stores, blacksmith shops, stables, gas stations, the post office, and farm warehouses until my basket was empty. The traveling salesmen and other men ignored me as though I were a piece of furniture, and would gossip, tell dirty jokes, and give lurid accounts of their sexual exploits as though I were not there. Having been taught to respect my mother and all other women, I was surprised to learn which wives around the town were said to be unfaithful, which girls were "putting out," how often the men went to the whorehouses in the nearby city of Albany, and how much it cost. What surprised me most was that many of these white men preferred black women, when other interracial social contact was completely taboo. These were things I never discussed with either of my parents.

I began to realize for the first time that I lived in a community where our Bible lessons were interpreted to accommodate the customs and ethical standards that were most convenient. There was no such thing as divorce because we lived by the admonition in Mark 10:7–9, "For this reason a man will leave his father and mother and be united to his wife, and the two will become one flesh. So they are no longer two, but one. Therefore what God has joined together let man not put asunder." It was well known, however, that some men were living with unmarried women and some with the wives of other men. My godmother, the head nurse at the hospital, was married to one man but lived with another, a senior medical doctor in town; they had a baby who was named after me. Two farmers who lived near each other swapped their entire families, wives and children, and so far as I know lived happily ever after without worrying about such details as marriage licenses.

I was caught up in an even more generic misinterpretation of the Holy Scriptures concerning racial inequality, which has affected my entire life. I came to realize that rationalization is a human trait, of which we are all guilty at times. I certainly do not like to admit that any of my deeply held beliefs are in error, and when any are challenged I seek every source of evidence to prove that I am right. The ultimate source of authenticity for my fellow religious believers was the Holy Bible, which provided the foundation for our Christian faith. The Hebrew text of the Bible, the New Testament, and the Koran, plus ancient interpretations, are complex combinations of history, biography, and the teachings and actions of those we revere. Many devout people consider these texts to be inerrant—incapable of containing error—despite the fact that some verses directly contradict others in the same holy book, and some ancient statements, such as descriptions of stars falling from the sky to the earth, are contrary to scientific knowledge. The overall messages or themes of the scriptures can be discerned, however, and they almost invariably espouse the moral and ethical values of peace, justice, compassion, forgiveness, and care for the destitute and those in need.

We can forget or ignore these principles if their violation is to our social, economic, or political benefit. I experienced this for almost three decades of my life, when I was part of an American society that espoused the "separate but equal" ruling of the U.S. Supreme Court. Although it was apparent to everyone that the practical application emphasized *separate* rather than *equal*, the legal system of racial segregation prevailed until the civil rights laws were adopted in the mid-1960s.

The segregation laws were observed throughout Georgia, the rest of the Deep South, and to some degree in all other states, and in my early years I never knew them to be questioned. It is difficult now for me to believe that no serious objections were raised when my only friends and playmates and their families went to a different church than ours, attended inferior schools, and could not vote or serve on a jury. When one of my black friends and I went to a movie in the county seat we rode in separate cars on the passenger train and sat at separate levels in the theater. These were practices in which I was complicit. Distinguished religious leaders visited our Plains Baptist Church on occasion to preach sermons based on selected scriptures about how it was God's will that the races be separated, and they even mentioned with pride how far we had progressed since slavery had ended in the United States—although forced servitude was obviously condoned by the biblical texts they quoted.

I have a hazy memory of the first time I was conscious of segregation in my own life, when I was about fourteen, and later I wrote a poem about it called "The Pasture Gate." I was returning with two friends from working in the field, and when we got to the gate between our barn lot and the pasture they stood back to let me go through first. I thought there might be a wire to trip me—we frequently played such pranks on each other—but later I surmised that their parents had told them that, as we were now older, we were no longer to treat each other as equals.

Not yet seriously questioned or rejected by many secular and religious leaders is a parallel dependence on selected verses of scripture to justify a belief that, even or especially in the eyes of God, women and girls are inferior to their husbands and brothers.

⁐∞⁊

If women are equal in the eyes of God, why are we not equal in the eyes of men?

ZAINAH ANWAR,
FOUNDER OF SISTERS IN ISLAM, MALAYSIA

There has long been a distinction in societal attitudes toward men and women who engage in extramarital sex. In the summer 2013 issue of *Christian Ethics Today* is an article by a young Canadian woman who, at nineteen, was a devout unmarried Christian, stigmatized by her pastor when he learned she had participated in a sexual act. Before an assembly of young people, this spiritual leader decided to teach her a lesson by analogy; he passed around a glass of water and had each person spit in it, then asked, "Now who wants to drink this?" Now happily married and with three children, her declaration that she is not "damaged goods" and unworthy of a decent husband is intended to reassure the four out of five evangelical Christian women who have had sex before marriage that they are acceptable in the eyes of God and should not be defamed.

I read her statement with some discomfort, but with a realization that it was both true and helpful. My hometown was and still is deeply religious. We have eleven churches to serve a total population of fewer than eight hundred, and they are still the centers of our social life. When I was a teenager it was rare for boys and girls to sleep together unless it was assumed by them and their families that they were soon to be married. There were just two or three girls who were known to be willing to depart from these standards, but it was considered normal among boys to take advantage of any sexual opportunity. Rosalynn and I were deeply in love, and we decided to wait until after our wedding to consummate our marriage. It would have been completely out of character for her to do otherwise, but I was always reluctant to let other young men know that I was a virgin, feeling that it was somehow a reflection on my manhood.

I have come to realize that societal standards—at least in the Western world—are much different from what I knew as a youth, but there is still a sharp difference between those that apply to boys and those that apply to girls. I still believe that abstinence is the best choice for both, but condemnation and disgrace are not appropriate, and there should not be any distinctions in rules of behavior for males and females.

2 | COMMITMENT TO PEACE AND WOMEN'S RIGHTS

I was serving as an officer in the U.S. Navy during the latter days of World War II and the first years of peace and was fascinated, even then, with political affairs. I followed closely the formation of the United Nations and kept a copy of its Charter and by-laws on the ship with me. There was a consensus among political leaders and the general public of all nations that the time had come for an end to devastating wars and a common commitment to seek peaceful alternatives to inevitable disputes. The dominant players and permanent members of the United Nations Security Council were the five major nations that had been victorious and were determined to establish insurmountable impediments to armed conflict and to ensure that Germany, Japan, and Italy, the defeated aggressors, would be pacified. The stated purpose of the United Nations was "to promote cooperation in security, economic development, social progress, human rights, civil liberties, political freedom, democracy, and lasting world peace." Leaders also considered it imperative to take common action to prevent a repetition of horrible human rights crimes, most notably the Holocaust and the deaths of millions of others who could not escape the consequences of ethnic or racial hatred.

During those halcyon days these same leaders moved to provide a permanent international foundation of justice and equality for all people. The United Nations Charter committed all member states to promote "universal respect for, and observance of, human rights and fundamental freedoms for all without distinction as to race, sex, language, or religion." The next step was more specific, and, with special leadership in the American delegation from former first lady Eleanor Roosevelt, the organization produced the thirty simple and clear articles that fulfilled the bold and challenging expectations of the Charter.

The Universal Declaration of Human Rights was ratified in 1948 by a vote of 48 to 0. There were eight abstentions, including from the Soviet bloc, which objected to the right of citizens (especially Jews) to emigrate from their home country, and South Africa, whose all-white apartheid government did not consider black people deserving of equal status. It is significant that there were no objections raised to the guarantee of equal rights for women and girls, except that Saudi Arabia, which also abstained, opposed the provision guaranteeing equality within marriage. Eight Islamic governments voted in favor of the Declaration. There is no possibility that these same commitments could be made today, as memories of the devastation of world war have faded, the five permanent members are often at odds and no longer as dominant, and there is more polarization within regions and individual countries.

It is helpful to examine the document in some detail to understand the universal commitment to equal status between men and women in all walks of life. The full text can be found on the Internet. Every word applies to women as well as men, but I have excerpted and emphasized phrases that apply directly to the subject of this book. Some of them are surprising in their specificity and relevance now.

> PREAMBLE. Whereas recognition of the inherent dignity and of the equal and inalienable rights *of all members of the human family* is the foundation of freedom, justice and peace in the world, . . .

Whereas the peoples of the United Nations have in the Charter reaffirmed their faith in fundamental human rights, in the dignity and worth of the human person *and in the equal rights of men and women* and have determined to promote social progress and better standards of life in larger freedom . . .

Article 1. *All human beings* are born free and equal in dignity and rights.

Article 2. Everyone is entitled to all the rights and freedoms set forth in this Declaration, *without distinction of any kind,* such as race, color, *sex,* language, religion, political or other opinion, national or social origin, property, birth or other status.

Article 4. No one shall be held in slavery or servitude; slavery and the slave trade shall be prohibited in all their forms.

Article 5. No one shall be subjected to torture or to cruel, inhuman or degrading treatment or punishment.

Article 16. (1) Men and women *of full age,* without any limitation due to race, nationality or religion, have the right to marry and to found a family. They are entitled to *equal rights as to marriage, during marriage and at its dissolution.*

(2) *Marriage shall be entered into only with the free and full consent of the intending spouses.*

Article 21. (3) The will of the people shall be the basis of the authority of government; this shall be expressed in periodic and genuine elections which shall be by *universal and equal suffrage* and shall be held by secret vote or by equivalent free voting procedures.

Article 23. (2) Everyone, without any discrimination, has the right to *equal pay for equal work.*

Article 25. (2) *Motherhood and childhood are entitled to special care and assistance.* All children, whether born in or out of wedlock, shall enjoy the same social protection.

Article 26. (1) Everyone has the *right to education*.
(3) Parents have a prior right to choose the kind of education
that shall be given to their children.

These were clear and unequivocal commitments made by the world's
leaders to be binding in perpetuity. It is shameful that these solemn international agreements, later ratified by national legislative bodies, are
being violated so blatantly. Some people may even find them outdated
and naïve. It must be presumed that even the authors of the Declaration realized at the time that many of the world's religious leaders,
who remained remarkably silent, did then and always would exempt
themselves and their compliant followers from the granting of these
guaranteed equal rights to women and girls.

War and violence against women not only have similar social, cultural, and religious supports, they are mutually reinforcing. These supports allow societies to tolerate conditions
in which a third of women and girls can be treated violently,
without mass outcry and rebellion. When we challenge the
attitudes and norms that enable violence against women, we
also are helping to confront the conditions that support war.

REV. DR. SUSAN BROOKS THISTLETHWAITE,
PROFESSOR OF THEOLOGY AND FORMER PRESIDENT,
CHICAGO THEOLOGICAL SEMINARY

It is a tragedy that this declaration of guaranteed equal rights for
all people has not been realized and that there has also been a general and growing acceptance of warfare and violence instead of peace.
The concept of the United Nations Security Council as the primary
arbiter of disputes and of individual nations resorting to armed combat only as a last resort and to protect themselves has been subverted

by divisions among the five permanent members, each of whom has strong regional alliances and interests and a veto over any final decision.

More than any other nation, the United States has been almost constantly involved in armed conflict and, through military alliances, has used war as a means of resolving international and local disputes. Since the birth of the United Nations, we have seen American forces involved in combat in Afghanistan, Bosnia, Cambodia, the Dominican Republic, El Salvador, Greece, Grenada, Haiti, Iraq, Korea, Kosovo, Kuwait, Laos, Lebanon, Libya, Nicaragua, Panama, Serbia, Somalia, and Vietnam, and more recently with lethal attacks in Pakistan, Somalia, Yemen, and other sovereign nations. There were no "boots on the ground" in some of these countries; instead we have used high-altitude bombers or remote-control drones. In these cases we rarely acknowledge the tremendous loss of life and prolonged suffering among people in the combat zones, even after our involvement in the conflict is ended.

Some of these military actions may have been justified in the defense of our nation or its vital interests, but the tragedy is that their easy adoption, sometimes without the consent or knowledge of the public or most members of Congress, has made the resort to violence a natural and even popular facet of foreign policy. Some devout Christians have been in the forefront of advocating warfare even when the choice was hotly debated among the general public. "An eye for an eye" has become more important to them than the teachings of Jesus as the Prince of Peace.

When America is questioned about its military involvement throughout the world, the increasingly natural and common answer is, "We need to show our strength and resolve and to take military action when necessary to achieve our goals." Without debating the political need, peaceful alternatives, or the ultimate success or failure of these military adventures, the previously firm commitment to peace and human rights by the United Nations and its strongest member has been largely abandoned. Our neglect of these obligations increases the suffering of the innocent and defenseless.

I am grateful to see our withdrawal of U.S. forces from Iraq, but we are negotiating now to retain between eight thousand and twelve thousand NATO troops in Afghanistan until 2024. The primary impediment to an agreement is our insistence that these troops be immune from prosecution under Afghan law for any crimes they may commit. If the troops remain, their peacekeeping role should be combined with a concerted effort by the United Nations and others to negotiate amicable settlement of disputes.

3 | THE BIBLE AND GENDER EQUALITY

The relegation of women to an inferior or circumscribed status by many religious leaders is one of the primary reasons for the promotion and perpetuation of sexual abuse. If potential male exploiters of women are led to believe that their victim is considered inferior or "different" even by God, they can presume that it must be permissible to take advantage of their superior male status. It is crucial that devout believers abandon the premise that their faith mandates sexual discrimination. Islamic scholars assure me that there is no justification for this discrimination in the Koran, but there are specific verses in the Holy Bible that can be interpreted on either side of the issue, and some ascendant male leaders in all faiths take advantage of the interpretation most beneficial to them. There are now about 7 billion people in the world, and more than 2 billion are Christians. Since many fundamental beliefs about human relationships are common to all major religions, I will assess this issue at some length, from a Christian's point of view.

I have been quite active in my local church and in the Southern Baptist Convention, both before and after I held public office. Like my father before me, I am a deacon and a Bible teacher and have volunteered as a layman to work as a missionary in several states to explain my Christian faith and invite people to become followers of Jesus Christ as their personal savior. These have been some of the most gratifying experiences of my life. I began teaching Bible lessons when I was eighteen years old, as a midshipman at Annapolis. I continued to do so as a farmer, governor, and president, and still fulfill this pleasant duty in my church in Plains whenever I am home on Sundays, about thirty-five times a year. There are usually several hundred visitors who come to hear me teach, representing most of the states and often ten or twenty foreign countries. About a fifth are Baptists; the others are mostly Protestants and Catholics, but there are also some Jews, Muslims, Buddhists, Hindus, and others who do not profess a religious affiliation or belief. I try to apply the lesson texts, about equally divided between the New Testament and the Hebrew text, to modern-day circumstances and events, and encourage open discussion between me and the audience. At times there are disagreements, and I learn a lot about different points of view concerning issues that divide believers.

These points of contention are not between Muslim and Christian, Catholic and Protestant, or Baptist and Episcopal, but are almost always within our own individual faiths or denominations. The schism among Baptists is one example. There have always been theological disputes, but now the most contentious are those that involve everyday life. In the time of the early Christian Church followers questioned whether it was acceptable to eat meat that had been offered to idols, if one had to become a circumcised Jew first before accepting Christ as savior, which apostle spoke with the most authority, and whether Jesus could be both human and divine. Now the debates are more about the status of homosexuals, the use of contraceptives, when it is permissible to resort to abortion, and if some verses in the Bible can be in error or applicable only to the time when they were written. One of the most prevalent and divisive issues is whether or not women are equal to men in the eyes of God.

After intense debates leading up to the annual Southern Baptist assembly in 2000, the newly chosen leaders and a majority of voting delegates made several decisions that caused me concern, relating to the interpretation of the scriptures. I had no doubt about the sincerity and good intentions of the participants, but my wife and I began to question whether our beliefs were compatible with those adopted and later mandated by the Convention. The change that was most troubling to us was an emphasis on a few specific Bible verses about the status of women and how they would be applied in practical terms, including one that called for wives to be "submissive" to their husbands. Let me quote the passage:

> Be subject to one another out of reverence for Christ. Wives, be subject to your husbands as you are to the Lord. For the husband is the head of the wife just as Christ is the head of the church, the body of which he is the Savior. Just as the church is subject to Christ, so also wives ought to be in everything to their husbands. Husbands, love your wives, just as Christ loved the church and gave himself up for her, in order to make her holy by cleansing her with the washing of water by the word, so as to present the church in splendor, without a spot or wrinkle or anything of the kind—yes, so that she may be holy and without blemish. In the same way, husbands should love their wives as they do their own bodies. He who loves his wife loves himself. For no one ever hates his own body, but he nourishes and tenderly cares for it, just as Christ does for the church, because we are members of his body. For this reason a man will leave his father and mother and be joined to his wife, and the two will become one flesh. This is a great mystery, and I am applying it to Christ and the church. Each of you, however, should love his wife as himself, and a wife should respect her husband. (Ephesians 5:21–33)

It seems to me that the first sentence introduces a balanced and equal relationship in marriage, but I understand how male supremacists base their claim on some selected phrases.

When I was a child, the most revered Baptist was Lottie Moon, who had been one of our early missionaries to China. She gave much of her food to poor people and died of starvation. Even now, the financial contribution of Baptist congregations for evangelistic work in foreign countries is given in the name of this woman. In every sense of the word, she was the leader in evangelism, a fundamental commitment of my faith. Although a number of female Baptist pastors had been called by local congregations to serve their churches for many years, in 2000 official actions of the more conservative Southern Baptist Convention leaders soon made it clear that Southern Baptist women would no longer be serving as deacons, pastors, or chaplains in the armed forces, or even as professors in some Convention seminaries if there were male students in the classroom. I felt that another ancient principle was being violated with this decision: the premise that each local Baptist congregation was autonomous and that a majority of those voting in conference had the authority to decide who could join as members and who would serve God as lay leaders or the church's pastor.

Rosalynn and I decided to end our relationship with the denomination to which I had been loyal during the first seventy years of my life, but to remain active in our local Baptist church congregation, which was more traditional in its beliefs. For the same reasons, a substantial number of individual Baptists and entire church congregations made the same decision. There is an obvious need and desire among Baptists to resolve these disagreements, and some progress has been made, but one of the most obvious and persistent differences is whether to accept women in positions of leadership if they are elected by a local congregation. In our own Maranatha Baptist Church we enjoy having both a man and a woman as pastors, and at this time half our elected deacons (including the chair) are women.

Later I will describe how people of other faiths disagree on this issue, but let me first explain why, in my opinion, Jesus Christ was the greatest liberator of women in a society where they had been considered throughout biblical history to be inferior. Even wives and widows of prominent and revered men had few legal rights. It is well known to those familiar with the Bible that, to enhance his own well-being, the patriarch Abraham gave away his wife, Sarah, to live in the harem of the pharaoh of Egypt and later attempted to give her to the heathen king Abimelech, claiming both times that she was not his wife but his sister. Men could possess multiple women (King Solomon had three hundred wives and seven hundred concubines), but a woman could be punished by stoning to death if she had more than one sex partner.

There is one incontrovertible fact concerning the relationship between Jesus Christ and women: he treated them as equal to men, which was dramatically different from the prevailing custom of the times. The four Gospels were written by men, but they never report any instance of Jesus' condoning sexual discrimination or the implied subservience or inferiority of women. In a departure from earlier genealogies, Matthew even includes four gentile women (all of whom had extramarital affairs) among the ancestors of Christ: Tamar, Rahab, Ruth, and Bathsheba. The exaltation of and later devotion to Mary, as Jesus' mother, is a vivid indication of the special status of women in Christian theology.

There are too many examples from the earthly ministry of Christ to describe here, but two or three are illustrative. Despite the strict prohibition against a Jewish man dealing with women in public, Jesus had no hesitancy about conversing at the community well with a Samaritan woman who was a pariah both among Jews and her peers because of her ethnicity and lascivious behavior. She accepted him as the promised Messiah and took his message back to her village—the first example of an evangelical witness. Jesus also rejected the double standard of punishment for adultery, by granting both a pardon and forgiveness to a guilty and condemned woman. Christians remember the story of how Jesus dealt with this ancient but then still prevailing command:

And the scribes and Pharisees brought unto him a woman taken in adultery; and when they had set her in the midst, they say unto him, "Master, this woman was taken in adultery, in the very act. Now Moses in the law commanded us, that such should be stoned: but what sayest thou?" This they said, tempting him, that they might have to accuse him. But Jesus stooped down, and with his finger wrote on the ground, as though he heard them not. So when they continued asking him, he lifted up himself, and said unto them, "He that is without sin among you, let him first cast a stone at her." And again he stooped down, and wrote on the ground. And they which heard it, being convicted by their own conscience, went out one by one, beginning at the eldest, even unto the last: and Jesus was left alone, and the woman standing in the midst. When Jesus had lifted up himself, and saw none but the woman, he said unto her, "Woman, where are thine accusers? Hath no man condemned thee?" She said, "No man, Lord." And Jesus said unto her, "Neither do I condemn thee: go, and sin no more." (John 8:3–11)

The Gospel of Jesus Christ has at its center the ending of domination of every kind. For some Christians to use the Gospel to compromise the human rights of women and others borders on the obscene. Propagated with appeals to idealized heritage, immutable sacred history, and paternalistic care for the religiously ignorant, their rights-denying actions must be exposed for what they are—formal policies for the retention and augmenting of power by those men who already have it. The ethic of Jesus Christ proclaims the radical equality of human value. The ending of the subordination of women—and of all who are dominated—is critical to the building of the reign of God on earth as it is in heaven.

DR. ALISON BODEN,

DEAN OF RELIGIOUS LIFE, PRINCETON UNIVERSITY

Perhaps more significant was the fact that women traveled with Jesus' entourage and that their spiritual and financial support within his ministry was accepted. It may be that his closest confidante was Mary, the sister of Martha and Lazarus, whom he visited often in Bethany and who seemed to be one of the few people who understood that he would be crucified and resurrected. She anointed his feet with perfume a few days before his death, as Jesus said, "It was intended that she should save this perfume for the day of my burial" (John 12:7). Mary Magdalene, one of his loyal followers, had the honor of visiting his empty tomb; Jesus then appeared to her and instructed her to inform all the other disciples, who were hiding in fear in a secret place, that the Savior was risen from the grave.

There are a few selections from Saint Paul's letters to the early churches that, taken out of historical context, seem to indicate his departure from Jesus' example and show a bias against women by directing that they should be treated as second-class Christians. I do not maintain that these troubling scriptures are in error or that there are contradictions between different portions of the inspired word of God, but it is necessary to assess the local circumstances within troubled early church congregations and interpret Paul's instructions to "brothers and sisters" who were confused and disorderly. Paul is not mandating permanent or generic theological policies when he directs that women worship with their heads covered, keep their hair unbraided, dress modestly, and never adorn themselves or speak in a worship service. In a letter to his disciple Timothy, Paul expresses a prohibition against women teaching men, but we know, and he knew, that Timothy was instructed by his mother and grandmother. It is also difficult to understand how Paul's close friend Priscilla is revered for having been a teacher of Apollos, one of the great evangelists of that day, so that he could more accurately reveal that Jesus was indeed the long-awaited Messiah.

To resolve the apparent disharmony between Jesus and Paul, I refer to some of Paul's remarks. In his letter to the Galatians, he states, "But now that faith has come, we are no longer subject to a disciplinarian, for in Christ Jesus you are all children of God through faith. . . . There is no longer Jew or Greek, there is no longer slave or free, there is no longer male and female; for all of you are one in Christ Jesus." (Galatians 3:25-28) In his letter to the Romans, Paul thanked twenty-eight outstanding leaders of the early churches, at least ten of whom were women: "I commend to you our sister Phoebe, a deacon of the church at Cenchreae. . . . Greet Priscilla and Aquila, who work with me in Christ Jesus. . . . Greet Mary, who has worked very hard among you. . . . Greet Andronicus and Junia, my relatives who were in prison with me; they are prominent among the apostles, and they were in Christ before I was. . . . Greet Philologus, Julia, Nereus and his sister, and Olympas, and all the saints who are with them." (Romans 16) It is inconceivable to me that Paul would encourage and congratulate inspired women who were successful deacons, apostles, ministers, and saints and still be quoted by male chauvinists as a biblical source for excluding women from accepting God's call to serve others in the name of Christ. Paul has not separated himself from the lesson that Jesus taught: that women are to be treated equally in their right to serve God. Devout Christians can find scriptures to justify either side in this debate. The question is whether we evangelical believers in Christ want to abandon His example and exclude a vast array of potential female partners, who are equally devout and responding to God's call.

To a substantial degree, the argument justifying male dominance is based on two reports in Genesis of God's creation of human beings that may seem somewhat contradictory. It was the sixth day of creation when, as described in Genesis 1:26–27, "God said, 'Let us make humankind in our image, according to our likeness. . . .' So God created humankind in his image, in the image of God he created them; male and female he created them." Then, in the second chapter of Genesis, God first created man and later decided that he needed a partner. "So the Lord God caused a deep sleep to fall upon the man, and he slept; then he took one of his ribs and closed up its place with flesh. And the rib that the Lord God had taken from the man he made into a woman and brought her to the man. . . . Therefore a man leaves his father and his mother and clings to his wife, and they become one flesh." Both of these scriptures emphasize the mutuality and equality of worth of male and female, but many Christian and Jewish fundamentalists use the second selection as a basis for their belief in the superiority of men because man was created first. This belief is combined with the allegation that Eve should be held solely accountable for "original sin" because she accepted the forbidden apple from the serpent, tasted it, and gave it to Adam.

My inclination is to consider more seriously the policies of the early Christian Church, after Jesus Christ came to explain the meaning of more ancient texts and to let us know more personally the true nature of God, who exemplifies a combination of justice, mercy, forgiveness, and love. The question of patriarchy is addressed quite clearly in Saint Paul's 1 Corinthians 11:11–12: "You need to learn, however, that woman is not different from man, and man is not different from woman. Woman may come from man, but man is born of woman. And both come from God."

There is no need to argue about such matters, because it is human nature to be both selective and subjective in deriving the most convenient meaning by careful choices from the thirty-one thousand or so verses in the modern Christian Bible. If men with religious authority wish to remain in power, they can accept the version they prefer.

It is ironic that women are now welcomed into ascendant positions in all major professions and other endeavors but are deprived of the right to serve Jesus Christ in positions of leadership as they did during his earthly ministry and for about three centuries in the early Christian churches. It is inevitable that this sustained religious suppression of women as inferior or unqualified has been a major influence in depriving women of equal status within the worldwide secular community as spelled out in the Universal Declaration of Human Rights.

It is likely that Christians and people of other faiths who represent the purest and most admirable qualities of their beliefs are those who devote their lives to service among people in need. When we have gone into the isolated villages throughout Africa to try to control or eliminate debilitating diseases, we have found that the Islamic mullahs, Christian priests, or other spiritual leaders are often providing the only rudimentary medical care available to the community. In the absence of medical training and modern treatment capability, they are dealing with cases of AIDS, encroaching blindness, worms within or emerging from bodies, extended stomachs and stunted growth of children, grossly enlarged arms and legs, open wounds, and broken bones. The religious leaders are the ones most trusted by the people, and, with no confusing theological debates as an impediment, they deal with fellow believers as equal to each other and deserving of blessing from whatever superior being they revere. Their commitment to serving others is inspirational.

In my presidential inaugural address I promised to promote human rights around the world, and later I used the imprisonment and murder of Ugandan people by President Idi Amin as a horrible example of abuse of those rights. The dictator retaliated by ordering all Americans in his country to assemble in Entebbe and threatened them with death or expulsion. I was in a quandary about how to respond, until I learned that he claimed to be a Muslim and was very proud of having made a pilgrimage to Mecca. I called the king of Saudi Arabia to seek his help and was relieved to hear almost immediately an announcement from Amin that the Americans would be permitted to leave Uganda unharmed. The majority of them, who were Christian missionaries, sent me notice that not one of them was accepting this offer but that all would remain at their assigned posts with their families, despite the continuing threats to their lives.

For many generations, religious missionaries have provided a connecting link between worshipers in more affluent communities and less fortunate people who are suffering from hunger, disease, and oppression. There is no distinction between men and women, either among the benefactors or those who receive the benefits of their ministry. It is impossible to overestimate their dedication and the positive impact of religious organizations like the Catholic Relief Services, Heifer International, the International Islamic Charitable Organization, and dozens of others. Religious and secular organizations provide more assistance to needy people than the contributions of governments and they combine financial help with devoted service. They form close personal ties in local communities and recognize the special suffering of women and children from deprivation and abuse, though they are sometimes constrained in their good works by laws and religious tenets that perpetuate sexual discrimination. I serve on the finance committee of our small church in Plains, and 10 percent of our total annual budget is earmarked—without discussion or debate—for the work of Baptist missionaries overseas. We collect a special additional offering each year for those providing benevolent services within the United States. In addition to the personal service of thousands of missionaries, religious groups in the United States contribute more than $8 billion annually for benevolent purposes in these projects overseas.

During the year that I ran for president, Jerome and Joanne Ethridge volunteered to serve as foreign missionaries from our local church. After intensive training in French they were assigned to serve in Togo, a small country in West Africa. Jerome had worked in the fields of an agricultural experiment station near Plains, and neither he nor Joanne had ever addressed an audience even as Bible teachers, so they had a formidable task in spreading the gospel in about a third of the country. Their assigned area was northeast of a river that was almost impossible to cross during the extended rainy season. Instead of preaching to the people, the Ethridges decided to ascertain their greatest needs and attempt to meet them.

Joanne immediately began to learn the local language, Ifè, and was soon teaching the women how to read and write. At the same time, she worked with biblical scholars who were writing the New Testament in the language. As they traveled from village to village, they observed that few of the people had a supply of clean drinking water and depended instead on stagnant ponds that filled during the rainy season. The water became increasingly unfit as the ponds slowly dried up during the rest of the year, and waterborne diseases were prevalent. Baptists in North Carolina donated a well-drilling outfit, and Jerome went to each village and, with local help, bored holes down to the aquifer and installed a pump. This was a slow process, so Joanne usually went to the villages ahead of Jerome, to prepare the people for her husband's arrival and to teach the rudiments of health care to the women. The Ethridges would say simply that they were providing these services in the name of Jesus Christ. When they had enough converts, they helped to organize a local church congregation. Jerome told me that one of their biggest problems was to induce the men to treat women as equals, not having to cover their heads and encouraging them to speak during worship services, and to teach both boys and girls about their new faith.

After working for several years and bringing fresh and healthy water to more than eighty villages, they decided to build a bridge across the raging river. They sent the well-digging equipment to a missionary in nearby Ghana, and Baptists back home agreed to provide reinforcing bars and cement for the bridge. Neither had ever built anything of the kind, but with the help of volunteers they began their project. Rosalynn and I visited them on one of our trips to the area soon after the bridge was finished. It was heavily used by the previously isolated people, who could now reach the rest of their country throughout the year. When Jerome and Joanne retired after twenty-three years in Togo there were more than five thousand new Christians in the area, and their eighty churches each had a local minister. Based on the example set by Jesus, the men and women acted as equals in His service.

Despite sharp differences of opinion about the role of women in positions of religious leadership, people of faith offer the greatest reservoir of justice, charity, and goodwill in alleviating the unwarranted deprivation and suffering of women and girls. This includes popes, imams, bishops, priests, mullahs, traditional leaders, and their followers who search for ideals and inspiration from a higher authority.

The principle of treating others the same way one would like to be treated is echoed in at least twelve religions of the world. "Others" transcend gender, race, class, sexual orientation or caste. Whoever and whatever the "other" is, she has to be treated with dignity, kindness, love, and respect. In African communitarian spirituality, this is well expressed in the Ubuntu religious and ethical ideal of "I am because you are, and since we are, therefore I am"—a mandate based on the reality of our being interconnected and interdependent as creation. Therefore pain caused to one is pain shared by all.

FULATA MOYO, PROGRAM EXECUTIVE,
WOMEN IN CHURCH AND SOCIETY,
WORLD COUNCIL OF CHURCHES

4 | FULL PRISONS AND LEGAL KILLING

As governor, I began to see more clearly that the tacit acceptance of bias, discrimination, and injustice creates an underlying tendency toward violence or abuse in a society, and a culture that results in the disproportionate suffering of women and others who are unable to defend themselves. This harm is magnified when ascendancy of the powerful is combined with religious beliefs that exalt one group of people at the expense of others.

When our family moved into the governor's mansion we found that the servants there, all black, were trusted inmates from the women's prison, and we learned of their unjust treatment under the law. One of our cooks asked to borrow $250, showing me a letter that indicated she could be released with this payment to the local court in her hometown. I investigated the case and found that her husband had been an abusive drunkard who stayed at home only on her paydays as a licensed practical nurse; he beat her and took almost all the money. One day she fought back and killed him with a butcher knife. She nevertheless was sentenced to prison until she paid a fine of $750. As an inmate she had been able to raise only $500 during her past four years in prison. I had the state attorney general intercede, and the woman was set free within a few days.

Rosalynn and I met a woman while vacationing on Cumberland Island, off the Georgia coast, who reported that her mother had borrowed $225 to put up bail for her son, who was charged with a minor crime. She was illiterate and had put her mark on what she understood was a promissory note with her five acres of land as collateral. When she went to repay the loan she was told that she had signed a warranty deed and had sold her land. I went to the Camden County courthouse and found that the report was true, but there was a pending legal case and it would be improper for a governor to intercede. The Georgia Supreme Court later ruled against the woman, and she lost her property.

Another case involved a young woman named Mary Fitzpatrick, who was visiting a friend in the small town of Lumpkin, Georgia. A man was killed in a gunfight, and as the only visitor in town Mary was accused of the crime and taken to jail. She first met her court-appointed lawyer as they entered the courtroom for the trial, and he advised her to plead guilty, with a promise of light punishment. Instead she received a sentence of life imprisonment. Mary demonstrated extraordinary talent in all her assigned duties during our four years in the governor's mansion, and as the newly elected president I obtained permission to act as her parole officer and to take her to the White House with us. In the meantime, the trial judge in Lumpkin had become a member of the Supreme Court of Georgia, and he agreed to have the evidence reexamined. Mary's innocence was proven, and she received a full pardon.

I began to visit the state prisons and found terrible discrimination against poor, black, and mentally handicapped people. Some had been in solitary confinement for several years. I employed a professional criminologist, Ellis C. MacDougall, as the director of Georgia state prisons and initiated an overhaul of our policies. Working with Director MacDougall's guidance, I explored ways to decrease the number of imprisoned citizens. We gave sentenced persons a thorough physical and mental examination to learn their past experience and inherent capability and to ascertain the best education and training programs in prison to prepare them for a productive life. We depended on early release and work-release programs as jail terms neared an end, and I recruited a large corps of probation officers from among members of the Lions, Kiwanis, Rotary, and other service clubs. These volunteers spent a day or two in Atlanta with me and the prisons director and went through an intensive training course. They pledged to accept just one prospective probationer or parolee as a personal responsibility, visited the prisoner's family before release, and promised to find or provide a full-time job for the person in their charge. These volunteers worked closely, of course, with professional probation officers.

These same efforts were being made by other state leaders, and during our annual governors' conferences we shared experiences and competed to determine who had most reduced our prison populations. At a gathering of Georgia's former governors in 1995, Rosalynn asked one of the most recent about his greatest success in office. He proudly replied, "We built enough prison cells to reach from the state capitol to my home town." The construction and operation of local and state prisons has now become a valuable economic asset, especially in more remote rural areas where other industries are scarce.

There is an inevitable chasm between societal leaders who write and administer criminal laws and the people who fill the jails, often unnecessarily. The cumulative effect of this gap is a lowering of barriers against discrimination and violence that affects racial minorities, women, the mentally handicapped, and others who are naturally more helpless and vulnerable. We who are more privileged are not deliberately perpetuating our status at the expense of others, but we rarely wish to confront or be involved in the problem. Exalted commitments to peace and human rights are abandoned as we accept and rationalize the privileges we enjoy. The prison system is just one clear example.

At that time, in the 1970s, only one in a thousand Americans was in prison, but our nation's focus has turned increasingly to punishment, not rehabilitation. During the past three decades extended incarceration of people convicted of drug use and other nonviolent crimes has replaced an emphasis on rehabilitation with job training and restoration of citizens' rights after the convicted have paid their debt to society. There are now more than five times as many American inmates in federal, state, and local prisons as when I was president, and the number of incarcerated black women has increased by 800 percent! An ancillary effect is that this increased incarceration has come at a tremendous financial cost to taxpayers, at the expense of education and other beneficial programs. The cost of prosecuting executed criminals is astronomical. Since 1973, California alone has spent roughly $4 billion in capital cases, leading to only thirteen executions, amounting to about $307 million spent for the killing of each prisoner.

Although the number of violent crimes has not increased, the United States has the highest incarceration rate in the world, with more than 7.43 per 1,000 adults imprisoned at the end of 2010. With only 4.5 percent of the world's population, we claim 22 percent of the world's prison population. Many of these prisoners, some now incarcerated for life, have never been found guilty of a violent crime but have been convicted of drug-related offenses. The American Civil Liberties Union reported in November 2013 that there are now 3,278 persons in federal and state prisons who are serving life sentences without parole—for nonviolent crimes! Not surprisingly, 65.4 percent of them are black. I gave a major address about drug use while president in 1979 and called for the decriminalization of marijuana, but not its legalization, with an emphasis on treatment and not imprisonment for users who were not involved in the distribution of narcotics. This proposal was well received at the time, but the emphasis was placed on punishment and not rehabilitation after I left office.

Despite the proliferation of excessive imprisonments, the number of pardons by U.S. presidents has also been dramatically reduced. I issued 534 pardons in my four-year term, and in their eight-year terms Ronald Reagan issued 393, Bill Clinton 396, and George W. Bush 189, but in his first term Barack Obama issued only 23.

⤬

As a "Nun on the Bus" I heard the struggles of ordinary
people. I learned that to be pro-life (and not just pro-birth)
we must create a world where all people have their basic
needs met. This is justice. Governments hold the responsibility of enacting laws that ensure living wages and safety nets
for people who fall through the cracks of the economy. In
the United States, both federal and state policy makers must
end political gridlock and enact just laws that ensure that
all people have access to the basics: food, shelter, education,
healthcare, and living wages. These are pro-life programs.

SISTER SIMONE CAMPBELL OF NUNS ON THE BUS

In October 2013 the United Nations special rapporteur on violence
against women, Rashida Manjoo, reported a substantial increase in
the proportion of women being incarcerated globally compared to men,
and stated that conditions of their imprisonment are more severe than
those faced by men. She explained that women often are subjected to
incarceration for crimes committed under coercion from men who exercise abusive authority over them, especially in the pursuit of illegal
drug trafficking or other criminal enterprises. "Moral crimes," such as
sex outside of marriage, are additional reasons for incarcerating women
that do not affect men, and they face stringent evidentiary rules that
even result in punishment of rape victims. Conditions in prison can
also be more severe for women, as they face increased risk of sexual
assault. Manjoo also addressed the issue of young children living in
prisons with their mothers, as well as the situation of women who are
primary caretakers of children and the devastating effects of their detention on children left behind.

The special rapporteur stated, "Current domestic and international
anti-drug policies are one of the leading causes of rising rates of incarceration of women around the world. . . . In a context of scarce resources and, given that most women offenders rarely pose a threat to

the public, it is imperative that States consider alternatives to women's incarceration."

Another significant and extraordinary response to crime in the United States and other countries is the death penalty. The Carter Center takes a firm stand against capital punishment, and I often send a letter to foreign leaders under whose authority people are sentenced to death. Rosalynn and I also intercede with U.S. governors and others who may be able to commute the ultimate punishment to life imprisonment.

In a case before the U.S. Supreme Court while I was governor in 1972, *Furman v. Georgia*, the justices issued a de facto moratorium on capital punishment throughout the United States because there were no clear and consistent legal grounds for its imposition. An important question was whether the death penalty was a violation of the U.S. Constitution, which prohibits "cruel and unusual" punishment. When all the states complied with new standards, the Court permitted the resumption of executions in 1976 as a result of *Gregg v. Georgia* and similar cases from other states. There were just three state executions in the United States while I was governor and president, one in 1977 and two in 1979, but there have been 1,359 since 1980. It is interesting that there have been only three executions by the federal government since 1976.

The United States is the only country in NATO or North America that still executes its citizens, and Belarus and Suriname are the only exceptions in Europe and South America. In fact, the Charter of Fundamental Rights of the European Union specifically prohibits the death penalty among any of its members. Even with a strongly conservative U.S. Supreme Court, there have been encouraging signs that decisions made in other Western democracies and changing American public opinion are having an effect. In 2002 the Court ruled that an "intellectually disabled" person could not be executed; in 2005 the death penalty was not permitted for criminals under the age of eighteen; and in 2008 it was prohibited for rape if no death was involved.

Unfortunately, individual states are still permitted to define "intellectually disabled," and some of them, including Georgia and Florida, make it almost impossible to legally meet the criteria, so that people who are severely handicapped are killed.

It is clear that there are overwhelming ethical, financial, and religious reasons to abolish this brutal and irrevocable punishment. Although a majority of Americans express support for the death penalty if asked simply if they wish to abolish it altogether, definitive recent polls show that, when given a choice, only 33 percent of Americans would choose the death penalty for murder, while 61 percent would prefer a punishment other than the death penalty. The highest number supports a life sentence without parole plus restitution to the family of the victim. Just 1 percent of police chiefs believe that expanding the death penalty would reduce violent crime. This change in public opinion is steadily restricting capital punishment in state legislatures and the federal courts.

One argument made by proponents of the death penalty is that it is a strong deterrent to murder and other violent crimes, but evidence shows just the opposite. Whereas the last execution in Canada took place in 1962, in 2011 there were 598 murders in Canada and 14,610 in the United States. In fact, the homicide rate is nearly three times greater in the United States than in any Western European country, all without the death penalty. Southern states carry out over 80 percent of executions but have a higher murder rate than any other region. Texas has by far the most executions. Looking at similar adjacent states, there are more capital crimes in South Dakota, Connecticut, and Virginia (with death sentences) than in neighboring North Dakota, Massachusetts, and West Virginia (without death penalties). There has never been any evidence that the death penalty reduces capital crimes or that crimes increased when executions stopped. In fact, in a study conducted by Professor Gary Potter at Eastern Kentucky University, it was found that homicide rates increase before, during, and immediately after executions. This demonstrates that more people become victimized by lethal violence when the state kills. Here is an excerpt from Potter's testimony to the Health and Welfare Committee of the Kentucky legislature in March 1999:

> Studies of capital punishment have consistently shown that homicide actually increases in the time period surrounding an execution. Social scientists refer to this as the "brutalization effect." Execution stimulates homicides in three ways: (1) executions desensitize the public to the immorality of killing, increasing the probability that some people will be motivated to kill; (2) the state legitimizes the notion that vengeance for past misdeeds is acceptable; and (3) executions also have an imitation effect, where people actually follow the example set by the state. After all, people feel if the government can kill its enemies, so can they.

It is logical that any increase in societal violence will increase the incidence of violence against women. When the state acts in a brutal and lethal manner, this conveys to the community that violence is acceptable.

And tragic mistakes are prevalent. DNA testing and other factors have caused 143 death sentences to be reversed since I left the governor's office. Some devout Christians are among the most fervent advocates of the death penalty, contradicting Jesus Christ and misinterpreting Holy Scriptures and numerous examples of mercy. We remember God's forgiveness of Cain, who killed Abel, and the adulterer King David, who arranged the killing of Uriah, the husband of Bathsheba, his lover. Jesus dramatically forgave an adulterous woman sentenced to be stoned to death and explained away the "eye for an eye" scripture. There is a stark difference between Protestant and Catholic believers. Many Protestant leaders are in the forefront of demanding the ultimate punishment, while official Catholic policy condemns the death penalty.

Perhaps the strongest argument against the death penalty is extreme bias in its use against the poor, minorities, and those with diminished mental capacity. Although homicide victims are six times more likely to be black than white, 77 percent of death penalty cases involve white victims. Also, it is hard to imagine a rich white person going to the death chamber after being defended by expensive lawyers. This demonstrates a higher value placed on the lives of white Americans. The prevalence of punishment instead of a chance for rehabilitation is another vivid indication of societal resort to violence, which sets an unintended basis for violence against those who are relatively defenseless.

One hundred forty-three countries have abolished the death penalty by law or in practice, and the United Nations General Assembly has adopted resolutions in 2007, 2008, and 2010 calling for a global moratorium on executions, with a view to eventual abolition. Our country is not in good company in its fascination with the death penalty; 90 percent of all executions are carried out in China, Iran, Saudi Arabia, and the United States.

⚜

If the idea is to end violence in society, then killing is certainly not the answer.

DIVYA IYER, SENIOR RESEARCHER AT
AMNESTY INTERNATIONAL IN INDIA

As everyone knows, young people are bombarded with "normalized" violence through highly realistic video games that take the player through many hours of simulated combat and criminal behavior. In addition, movies, television, magazines, and music videos are full of demeaning depictions of women. These games and media make us less sensitive to violence and the debasement of women, so we are more inclined to accommodate them in real life.

Despite these disturbing trends toward a more violent global society, it is reassuring that our most notable heroes, even in more modern times, have remained the champions of peace, including Mahatma Gandhi, Mother Teresa, Martin Luther King Jr., and Nelson Mandela.

5 | SEXUAL ASSAULT AND RAPE

Although I am not a lawyer, I have been involved in the drafting, passage, and implementation of laws on almost every conceivable subject as a legislator, governor, and president. I was closest to law enforcement while governor, riding always in the front passenger seat of a State Patrol car and often assuming the duties of a radioman. There were a few times when I approved the driver's request to run down a speeding vehicle or to investigate a suspicious incident that we witnessed.

While Rosalynn and I were living in the governor's mansion we had a young out-of-state college student stay with us for a brief period early in the fall semester, until she could get settled in a dormitory. After attending class for a few days she came home one night and woke us, crying, to report that she had been raped. We called a doctor to examine her; he found several serious bruises on her arms and around her genitals and prescribed a sedative so she could get some sleep. The next morning I asked our guest if she knew her rapist, and she replied that he was a fellow classmate with whom she had decided to go on a date. At my urging, she agreed that I report the crime, and when I arrived at my office I called the state's attorney, reported the incident, and asked that he proceed with legal action.

He reported late that afternoon that he was having some difficulty, and I was infuriated to learn that the local officials were reluctant to make a legal issue of the case. I directed them to come see me. Quite apologetically, the officials said that this was a fairly common occurrence on university campuses, that the attacker always claimed that sex was consensual, and that any case brought against a white male student had very little chance of success. In addition, the young woman would be forced to testify in a highly publicized trial and would be cross-examined about every detail of the events during the date night and any other sexual experiences she might have had in the past. He added that it was the general policy of the two dozen colleges and universities in the Atlanta area to resort to counseling of both parties instead of a court trial. With permission of our young guest, I discussed the issue with her parents, and they decided that she should enroll in a different college.

I have been a distinguished professor at Emory University for the past thirty-two years, and in addition to teaching and lecturing I meet regularly with the president, deans, and other professors to discuss mutual interests of The Carter Center and Emory. I told the president about our guest at the governor's mansion and deplored the policy of many universities to resort to counseling of both victim and rapist and to punish or expel a male student only in egregious cases or when there was clear proof of repetitive offenses. He expressed concern at how infrequently the survivors of sexual assault choose to go down the hard road of legal recourse and explained that Emory had recently established a new policy to deal with this problem, with a separate process for sexual assault.

Administrators, faculty, and student leaders at Emory are evolving plans to promulgate more widely the warnings of and penalties for sexual abuse, train a permanent cadre of one thousand sexual assault peer advocates, encourage immediate reporting of abuse by victims and bystanders, provide private and professional counseling for victims, and decide what legal steps to take against students found guilty of rape. With the help of experts like Dr. David Lisak, a forensic consultant, Emory and other universities are learning how they can increase students' confidence in an effective administration of justice. Dr. Lisak's research focuses on "the causes and consequences of interpersonal violence—motives and behaviors of rapists and murderers." It has been estimated that one in five female students is sexually assaulted in American universities, but most people do not know that most of these crimes are premeditated and committed by a few men. This problem is perpetuated by the reluctance of rape victims to report the crime and to identify the perpetrator, who is almost always known to the victim before the attack. One of the reasons for this reluctance is a lack of clear procedures and support structures on the campus, and many college administrators are reluctant to address the problem because of the potential stigma to the institution if there is an increase in reported sexual assault cases. Another group reluctant to resolve cases of sexual assault is other men who witness or learn about the attack and know who the rapists are. They have to be convinced of its seriousness, become acquainted with campus policy, and be willing to support the victim instead of the criminal.

A report funded by the U.S. Justice Department found that more than 95 percent of students who are sexually assaulted remain silent, a much larger proportion than among the general public. The report's analysis, conducted at the State University of New York in New Paltz, revealed that an institution of that size, with about eight thousand students, would be expected to have more than 1,700 female victims of rape or sexual assault during the eleven years of the study. However, only six students reported a sexual assault to the office responsible for initiating proceedings, and only three cases resulted in a campus hearing—with one male student expelled.

The tragedy is that most on-campus rapes are perpetrated by serial rapists, who can safely assume that their crimes will not be revealed. In a New England study published in 2002 in the journal *Violence and Victims*, 120 rapists were identified among a sample of 1,882 students.

Of those, seventy-six were serial rapists who had each, on average, left fourteen seriously scarred victims. Their collective tally included 439 rapes and attempted rapes, 49 sexual assaults, 343 acts of sexual abuse or violence against children, and 214 acts of battery against intimate partners. In most cases their crimes were planned and premeditated. Why would any institution want them to remain as students? One answer comes from the *Hopkins Undergraduate Research Journal* of March 2012, which reported that one in three college assaults that get reported are committed by student athletes, who are often popular and influential.

Despite institutional unwillingness to deal forcefully with these crimes, there is increasing legal pressure to do so from an unexpected source. Title IX of the Education Amendments to the Civil Rights Act became effective in 1972 and is widely known for its prevention of discrimination against female students in campus sports. In 2001 the law was interpreted by the Department of Education to apply to sexual harassment, and now schools are required to designate a coordinator for Title IX and to take "immediate and appropriate steps to investigate or otherwise determine what occurred and take prompt and effective steps to end any harassment, eliminate a hostile environment if one has been created, and prevent harassment from occurring again." The threat of having federal funds withheld is a powerful incentive for an institution to comply, and I hope the U.S. Department of Education will put maximum pressure on schools at all levels to establish policies that are firm and clear. With proper leadership at the presidential level, universities can prevent deans and other officials from responding to a report of rape simply by suggesting the victim get counseling or take some time off or by telling her that legal proceedings are likely to embarrass her and result only rarely in punishment for the rapist.

Emory University is moving rapidly to evolve a balanced and effective policy of dealing with the problem of sexual assaults on its female students, and the student body seems to be supportive. This is one comment about an early progress report that appeared in the student newspaper:

"Emory has failed to enact sanctions that are capable of deterring would-be perpetrators. In the context of the existing sexual misconduct policy, there are no written sanctions listed for perpetrators. Creating a more stringent policy does more than just add another line to the University's sexual misconduct policy. It will raise awareness of the intolerable nature of sexual assault and start to reduce the number of attacks on our campus. Ultimately and most importantly, we can create an environment that makes it more likely for victims to come forward and take action against those who have sexually assaulted them, as well as put in place a strong deterrent against such crimes being committed in the first place."

It's time for all people of faith to be outraged. It's time for our Christian leaders to stand up and say that women, made in the very image of God, deserve better. And it's time for us in the faith community to acknowledge our complicity in a culture that too often not only remains silent, but also can propagate a false theology of power and dominance. There is a growing understanding that women must be central to shaping solutions. . . . There is a new generation of young leaders determined to ensure the bright future of all people regardless of gender.

JIM WALLIS,

AUTHOR, FOUNDER AND EDITOR OF

Sojourners MAGAZINE

When I was serving in the Naval Reserve Officers Training Corps program at Georgia Tech, as a midshipman at Annapolis, and on battleships and submarines, it was understood that the role of women in the military was limited to service in the continental United States and that their duties would be in medical professions, communications, intelligence, science and technology, and as storekeepers. For all practical purposes, they were given equal status in January 2013, when the secretary of defense announced that the ban on women serving in combat roles would be lifted. The most recent report is that women now make up 14 percent of U.S. military personnel, with more than 165,000 enlisted and 35,000 women serving as officers.

I was pleased when the decision was made while I was president to appoint women as Naval Academy midshipmen with equal status. Rosalynn and I are usually invited to spend a few nights with the superintendent during visits to the campus for my class reunions, and we have listened with close attention to descriptions of how much progress has been made in successfully assimilating women midshipmen, now about 22 percent of the total student population, into life in the enormous Bancroft Hall dormitory, in public activities, in the classrooms, and on ships.

I have learned, however, that my alma mater has the same basic policy concerning sexual assaults as other institutions of higher education, and this permissive policy is now being questioned since a female midshipman alleged that she was gang-raped by three football players during a party at an off-campus house in April 2012. The female cadet said she got drunk at the party and passed out. She had little recollection of what had happened but learned about the alleged assault from friends and social media. She said she felt tremendous pressure not to report the incident. After she did bring the case to naval authorities, she stopped fully cooperating with them, still fearing a backlash. Later, her lawyer explained that she "was ostracized and retaliated against by the football players and the Naval Academy community." She was punished for underage drinking while her accused assailants were allowed to keep playing football. The Naval Criminal Investigative Service closed the initial investigation.

The female cadet sought legal help and the Navy reopened the investigation. In August 2013 an official hearing was conducted, with the purpose of making a report to the Academy superintendent, who would then decide whether to put the case into the hands of prosecutors and law enforcement officials in military court. As I was writing this on a Saturday morning during the hearing, the news media reported that the twenty-one-year-old female midshipman had requested a respite for the weekend after being cross-examined for more than twenty hours during the past three days, enduring waves of hostile questions from lawyers of the accused. The officer presiding over the hearing denied her request, stating that he couldn't excuse her as long as she was physically able to testify. She explained that she had refused to cooperate with investigators at first because she was scared of what might happen to her and because she didn't want her mother to find out that she had been raped. The previous day's interrogation had focused on her technique in performing oral sex. "How wide did you open your mouth?" the lawyer asked. He claimed it was a linchpin of his client's defense, as were questions about her previous love affairs and the type of underwear she wore.

No court-martial has begun against any of the football players yet, but charges in the sexual assault case were dropped against two of the football players, one in January 2014 because he had not been read his rights before questioning. At the same time, it was reported by the Pentagon that during the past year the Air Force Academy had reported forty-five cases of sexual assault, with fifteen reported cases at the Naval Academy and ten at West Point. Senator Kirsten E. Gillibrand, Democrat of New York, released a statement on January 10 saying that "the prevalence of sexual assault in the military and the crisis of underreporting continue to extend to the academies, and that is tragic and heartbreaking."

This almost inconceivable procedure at the U.S. Naval Academy—with prosecution of the alleged rapists entirely up to the commanding officer—demonstrates vividly why victims of rape in the military are so reluctant to report the assaults. In addition, the U.S. Justice Department utilizes this fear of reporting abuse as a means to excuse the Department of Veterans Affairs from paying rape victims when later medical claims are made. As reported by Ruth Marcus of the *Washington Post* in October 2013, U.S. appellate judges have ruled in several cases that female victims, after release from the military, are not eligible for financial help for psychiatric or other damages unless they had reported the crime immediately after it occurred. Despite the fact that the military acknowledges that most rapes and other serious sexual assaults are never reported to authorities and that severe permanent damage, including post-traumatic stress disorder, often requires treatment for victims in later years, these rulings specify that failure to make a timely report of these crimes can be used as evidence that they did not occur. Marcus summarizes, "In short, we know these incidents are not reported, yet if you don't report them, you're out of luck."

Lawmakers in Congress have proposed taking the decision-making power to press charges in sexual assault cases out of the military chain of command and putting it into the hands of prosecutors and law enforcement professionals. This question was raised after the Department of Defense estimated that there were about 26,000 instances of unwanted sexual contact in the military in 2012 (up from 19,000 two years earlier), but, according to Pentagon statistics, only about 3,200 assaults were reported and 300 prosecuted, which is about 1.2 percent of known cases. This tiny number of prosecutions, and much fewer convictions, can be compared with about 37 percent of prosecutions for similar crimes in the civilian court system.

I know from personal experience in the Navy that commanding officers are responsible for ensuring appropriate protection and care of victims, as well as for investigating and holding accountable those who have committed crimes. I also know that it reflects negatively on commanders' leadership capabilities if such misconduct is known to exist among their subordinates. It was reported to Congress that two male officers among the rare offenders convicted by courts-martial of sexual assault were given clemency by three-star generals. Instead of accepting the proposal to remove total control of military commanders from prosecution, Congress passed legislation in December 2013 that will tighten responses to cases of rape and sexual assault by ending the statute of limitations, barring military commanders from overturning jury convictions, making it a crime to retaliate against people who report such crimes, mandating dishonorable discharge or dismissal of anyone convicted of such crimes, and giving civilian defense officials more control over prosecutions.

This is notable progress, but the problem is much more serious among American troops than is generally acknowledged. According to a report by National Public Radio in 2010, "a survey of female veterans found that 30 percent said they were raped in the military. A 2004 study of veterans who were seeking help for post-traumatic stress disorder found that 71 percent of the women said they were sexually assaulted or raped while serving. And a 1995 study of female veterans of the Gulf and earlier wars, found that 90 percent had been sexually harassed." It was reported more recently that some women employees of civilian contractors serving in a war zone must sign an agreement that forbids them from suing if they are raped by a fellow worker.

The lesson to be learned from all this is how prevalent the rape of women is in universities and the military, two of the most appreciated and revered sectors of American society, where sexual equality is guaranteed and our respected government professes to honor the highest standards of justice. We can only imagine how much worse the situation can be in nations where women are officially derogated and where civil war zones are known to be completely lawless.

Earlier I asserted that the normalization of violence committed by the state encourages violence in society, and this idea especially applies to young people in the military and in universities. If our military is called upon to commit unjustified violence, this will influence the thinking and behavior of highly impressionable service members and college students, who are just beginning to live independently and exert themselves in a highly charged environment. If their government easily chooses violence and punishment to solve problems, they will internalize this choice, which will influence how they deal with each other and make their own way in the world.

There is sometimes encouraging public concern about excessive leniency in civilian courts toward rapists and a lack of concern about victims. It has been demonstrated in Montana, when a fifty-four-year-old teacher, Stacey Rambold, raped one of his fourteen-year-old students, who subsequently committed suicide. Rambold was initially ordered to complete a sexual offender treatment program. However, when Rambold violated the terms of the program, he was brought back to court for sentencing by District Judge G. Todd Baugh. At the sentencing hearing, the judge stated that the rape victim was "older than her chronological age" and was "probably as much in control of the situation" as her rapist, and sentenced Rambold to fifteen years, but suspended all but thirty days to be served in prison. The judge's action is alleged to have violated a Montana state law specifying a minimum of two years' imprisonment for this offense. Members of the National Organization for Women filed a complaint with the Montana Judicial Standards Commission, which has the power to sanction jurists. Petitions with over 140,000 signatures accompanied their complaint calling for removal of the judge from the bench. This altercation has not yet been resolved.

Rape trials are extremely sensitive, and care must be taken in making any kind of executive declaration. One unexpected impediment to the all too rare prosecution of accused rapists in the military occurred when President Barack Obama, as commander-in-chief, made a justified comment in May 2013 that those who commit sexual assault should be "prosecuted, stripped of their positions, court-martialed, fired, and dishonorably discharged." Almost immediately more than a dozen pending cases of sexual assault were challenged by both judges and defense lawyers on the grounds that there had been "unlawful command influence," prejudicing the chance for a fair trial for accused rapists. A former judge advocate general of the Army and dean of a law school in Kansas said, "His remarks were more specific than I've ever heard from a commander-in-chief. When the commander-in-chief says they will be dishonorably discharged, that's a pretty specific message. Every military defense counsel will make a motion about this." As predicted, during the following month charges were dismissed and judges ruled against discharge in cases at Shaw Air Force Base in South Carolina, at Fort Bragg in North Carolina, and in two cases in Hawaii. There have been defense motions with the same allegation in a number of other cases on which final judicial decisions have not yet been made. I remember similar cases that involved the same jurisdictions when I was in the White House, but not being a lawyer I was warned repeatedly by my legal advisors against any interference, no matter how well-intentioned, that might prejudice a jury.

These continuing and largely unresolved sexual crimes in the universities and military branches of America are vivid and disturbing indications of how far we still have to go in protecting some of our most vulnerable citizens. There is a strong reluctance by responsible leaders to admit that such abuses exist within their institutions, and many victims are hesitant about becoming involved in seeking justice, with the prospect of further embarrassment and failure to see the perpetrators punished. Full use of Title IX restraints in educational institutions and action by the Congress regarding abuses in the military can help to reduce these offenses and set an example for other nations.

6 | VIOLENCE AND WAR

One of the first projects adopted by The Carter Center was to identify and honor the world's foremost contributor to human rights each year. An accompanying award of $100,000 was made possible by the generosity of Dominique de Menil, an heiress of the fortune derived from the world's largest petroleum services company, Schlumberger Limited. The ceremonies for the Carter-Menil Human Rights Prize were usually at The Carter Center or the Rothko Chapel in Houston and included an address by Nelson Mandela or another invited guest. I had this honor for the first ceremony, and Dominique asked that I speak about war being the greatest cause of human suffering and abuse, especially of women, children, and others who are innocent and defenseless.

This brought back memories of my early career and my inauguration week at the White House, when Rosalynn and I had a series of receptions for special groups. We were most favorably impressed when the commissioned and noncommissioned military officers came through the receiving line. I was not surprised that, unlike other guests, their comments frequently referred to a hope or prayer for peace. As a naval officer I had been fully prepared for armed combat and believed that by participating in deterring military action against my country I was helping to maintain peace. I had given a lot of thought, both then and when I was serving in elective public office with enormous influence, to the conditions under which it would be appropriate to go to war. My training in military history taught me that in more modern warfare, when there are no clearly defined battle lines in combat as there were in the American Civil War or World War I, it is impossible to discriminate between military and civilian casualties.

When is a war justified? I attempted to answer this question in my speech at the Nobel Peace Prize ceremony as the United States was preparing to launch a second war in Iraq. I did not know at the time that the American president and the British prime minister had decided almost a year earlier to find a justification for the invasion of Iraq. In March 2003, with the invasion imminent, I wanted to address the military action by reiterating the ancient Christian standards for armed combat, and I prepared this op-ed for publication in the *New York Times*:

Just *War*, or a *Just* War?

Profound changes have been taking place in American foreign policy, reversing consistent bi-partisan commitments that for more than two centuries have earned our nation's greatness. These have been predicated on basic religious principles, respect for international law, and alliances that resulted in wise decisions and mutual restraint. Our apparent determination to launch a war against Iraq, without international support, is a violation of these premises.

As a Christian and as a president who was severely provoked by international crises, I became thoroughly familiar with the principles of a just war, and it is clear that a substantially unilateral attack on Iraq does not meet these standards. This is an almost universal conviction of religious leaders, with the most notable exception of a few spokesmen of the Southern Baptist Convention who are greatly influenced by their commitment to Israel based on eschatological (final days) theology.

The preeminent criterion for a just war is that it can only be waged as a last resort, with all non-violent options exhausted. It is obvious that clear alternatives do exist, as previously proposed by our leaders and approved by the United Nations. But now, with our own national security not directly threatened and despite the overwhelming opposition of most people and governments in the world, the United States seems determined to carry out military and diplomatic action that is almost unprecedented in the history of civilized nations. The first stage of our widely publicized war plan is to launch 3000 bombs and missiles on a relatively defenseless Iraqi population within the first few hours of an invasion, with the purpose of so damaging and demoralizing the people that they will change their obnoxious leader, who will most likely be hidden and safe during the massive bombardment.

Weapons used in war must discriminate between combatants and non-combatants. Extensive aerial bombardment, even with precise accuracy, always results in great "collateral damage." The American field commander, General Franks, is complaining in advance about many of the military targets being near hospitals, schools, mosques, and private homes.

Violence used in the war must be proportional to the injury suffered. Despite Saddam Hussein's other serious crimes, American efforts to tie Iraq to the 9/11 terrorist attacks have been unconvincing.

The attackers must have legitimate authority sanctioned by the society they profess to represent. The unanimous vote of approval in the Security Council to eliminate Iraq's weapons of mass destruction can still be honored, but our announced goals are now to achieve regime change and to establish a Pax Americana in the region, perhaps occupying the ethnically divided country for as long as a decade. For these objectives, we do not have international authority. Other members of the U.N. Security Council have so far resisted the enormous economic and political influence that is being exerted from Washington, and we are faced with the possibility of either a failure to get the necessary votes or else a veto from Russia, France, or China. Although Turkey may still be enticed by enormous financial rewards and partial future control of the Kurds and oil in Northern Iraq, its Democratic parliament has at least added its voice to the worldwide expressions of concern.

The peace to be established must be a clear improvement over what exists. Although there are visions of a panacea of peace and democracy in Iraq, it is quite possible that the aftermath of a successful military invasion will destabilize the region, and that aroused terrorists might detract from the personal safety of our people and the security of our nation. Also, to defy overwhelming world opposition will threaten a deep and permanent fracture of the United Nations as a viable institution for world peace.

The heartfelt sympathy and friendship offered to us after the 9/11 terrorist attacks, even from formerly antagonistic regimes, has been largely dissipated, and increasingly unilateral and domineering policies have brought our country to its lowest level of international distrust and antagonism in memory. We will surely decline further in stature if we launch a war in clear defiance of U.N. opposition, but to continue using the threat of our military power to force Iraq's compliance with all U.N. resolutions—with war as a final option—will enhance our status as a champion of peace and justice.

Despite this and other pleas for constraint, we launched a war based on false premises that devastated Iraq, had no beneficial results, and greatly strengthened radical forces in Iran and throughout the region. A total of 4,487 U.S. soldiers have been killed and, according to the British *Lancet*, over 600,000 Iraqis, most of them civilians, had died by June 2006. U.S. armed forces continue to be engaged in a war in Afghanistan that is now in its thirteenth year.

There are times when the international community can work in concert to prevent atrocities and when the use of military force is justified. In Libya in 2011 and again in eastern Congo in 2013, concerted global action, approved by the UN, was taken when atrocities were occurring or threatening.

Mothers and women have suffered serious consequences from the war in Iraq. Increased rates of birth defects have, according to our research, been caused by chemical and radiological contaminants derived from depleted uranium munitions. This affects the future of everyone in our city. The international community must recognize the existence of the problem, acknowledge its size and impact, and offer effective solutions. We need immediate measures to clean the environment and provide necessary resources for the diagnosis and treatment of the many cases of congenital deformity (heart defects) that are occurring. Then the international community must focus on the most important goal of preventing more wars and banning the use of prohibited weapons.

DR. SAMIRA ALAANI,
PEDIATRICIAN, FALLUJAH HOSPITAL, IRAQ

In 2002 the U.S. president announced a military doctrine of "preventive" war, which justifies armed attack or invasion of another country if it is believed that we might be threatened sometime in the future. The "war on terror" was initiated in response to the horrendous attack on the World Trade Center and Pentagon on September 11, 2001, and has no end in sight. We have assumed the right to incarcerate foreign nationals at Guantánamo and within the United States for indefinite periods (possibly for life) without a trial or legal charges being brought against them.

Another example of this unprecedented assumption of unilateral authority to take military action is the execution of suspected evildoers, even American citizens, in foreign countries by drones or Special Forces. Human Rights Watch investigated a series of U.S. drone attacks in Yemen and reported in October 2013 that a disturbing number of the people killed were civilians. At the same time, Amnesty International assessed attacks in Pakistan and estimated that there had been as many as 374 drone strikes since 2004. These two human rights organizations reached a similar conclusion: that hundreds of civilians have been killed and that the United States may have violated international law and even committed war crimes. A separate investigation by UN officials found that 2,200 people have been killed by U.S. drones in Pakistan during the past decade, of whom at least six hundred were either civilians or noncombatants. The nonpartisan New America Foundation, which has a reputation for careful analysis, reports that between 336 and 391 civilians have been killed in Pakistan and Yemen. After these revelations, a pledge was made by the president that new policies would be implemented to make civilian casualties almost impossible. But a drone strike in Yemen in December 2013 targeted an eleven-vehicle convoy—many more vehicles than Al Qaeda would typically use—that turned out to be a wedding party traveling to the bride's home. Top Yemeni officials acknowledged that civilians were killed and awarded compensation to the victims' families: about $110,000 and 101 Kalashnikov rifles! Such compensation seems to imply that although each death is a tragedy, the total number is not as important as trying to balance America's status as a champion of human rights with deterring terrorist activity.

This is not a new problem. Secret efforts by the United States to kill foreign leaders was a burning issue while I was running for president in 1976, centered on a U.S. Senate committee study conducted under Senator Frank Church (one of my opponents). Because of aroused public condemnation of the practice, President Gerald Ford prohibited assassinations by any agent of the United States, and I later strengthened this directive. It was clear to me that such a program of assassination, except in cases where the action was absolutely necessary to prevent an imminent attack against our nation, was both immoral and counterproductive.

As information becomes available about the "targeted killing" program, mostly carried out by drone strikes, we are learning that the results may be the opposite of what our government hopes to achieve. Two Yemeni citizens traveled in 2013 to Washington, D.C., one to testify before a Senate Judiciary Committee and the other to meet with policymakers. They both came to seek answers about drone strikes that devastated their villages and families. Faisal bin Ali Jaber was the uncle of an imam who was meeting with Al Qaeda members, trying to persuade them to leave terrorism behind, when he was killed in a drone strike that also killed the Al Qaeda members who must have been the target of the strike. Farea Al-Muslimi, who testified before the Senate committee, had been educated in the United States and was a sort of "goodwill ambassador" to Yemen, seeking to convince Yemenis to work together with the United States to root out Al Qaeda from their country. One week before his testimony his village was struck by a drone missile. He told the senators, who listened intently, that support for Al Qaeda has grown since this attack and their recruiting efforts have been more successful than ever before.

One of our 2013 Human Rights Defenders Forum participants, Mossarat Qadeem of Pakistan, works with mothers of radicalized youths, with the goal of helping the youths leave Al Qaeda and the

Taliban. By appealing to their religious beliefs and a positive inter-pretation of the Koran, she has helped ninety-two young men return to productive lives. After the drone strikes, however, her job became much more difficult. Many of their relatives regard these radicals as patriotic heroes fighting against an America that is insensitive to their personal needs and national sovereignty.

It is difficult to envision how our country can regain its commitment to human rights if we remain entangled in permanent global warfare, even if it is supposed to be in the shadows. In retaliation for drone strikes in Pakistan, leading politicians there have exposed the identity of our top CIA officials in Islamabad, resulting in their replacement and heightened tensions between our two governments. There is no way to maintain secrecy with the explosion of communications tech-nology and the eagerness of people to speak out about what they con-sider to be injustice.

International bombing raids and missile attacks on cities engender casualties involving many women, children, and elderly, and in civil wars too it is impossible to concentrate destruction just on soldiers serving in military forces. In addition, there has always been ancillary abuse, especially of women, when the inherent brutality of war tends to remove normal inhibitions that restrain potential rapists and others who assault the weak and vulnerable. This was demonstrated vividly by Japanese soldiers in Korea and China during the 1930s and 1940s and is a source of major concern at this time in eastern Congo and in other areas of combat by militia groups. Even within civilian populations, the acceptance of violence as a normal course of action is a special cause of additional abuse of women and girls.

7 | OBSERVATIONS AS A TRAVELER

My mother was serving in the Peace Corps in India at the age of seventy, contributing her services as a registered nurse. She was stationed in the small village of Vikhroli, near Bombay (now Mumbai), that was owned by the very wealthy and fairly benevolent Godrej family. About twelve thousand people lived there and worked in the various Godrej factories. Most of them had the social status of *dalits*, or untouchables, and Mama fit into this category because of her work among them, her contact with human feces and other bodily excretions, and her habit of mopping floors and doing other menial work in her own living quarters. She earned a small stipend and was prohibited by Peace Corps rules from receiving money from her family back home.

The gardener for the owner's family was quite friendly to Mama and surreptitiously gave her vegetables and sometimes flowers. He told her that he had a son and a daughter, but his income permitted only the boy to be in school. Having no other way to repay him, she offered to teach the young girl how to read and write. She sent us a photograph of the child sitting with her on a big rock during one of the lessons. My sister Gloria Carter Spann collected the letters that my mother wrote from India, and they were later published in a book, *Away from Home: Letters to My Family*, that was quite popular after I became president. Later the publisher used the photograph on the rock as the cover of the paperback edition.

In 2006 Rosalynn and I led a group of Habitat for Humanity volunteers to build a hundred homes near Mumbai. We went a day early so we could visit Vikhroli, as guests of the Godrej family. They were very proud that we were visiting and had arranged for some of the people who had known Mama to meet us, including the doctor in whose clinic she worked and others who had been mentioned prominently in her letters. Almost a hundred people were assembled in a large room where Godrej consumer products were displayed, and we were all excited to meet each other. Toward the end of our scheduled time together, I noticed several copies of Mama's book lying around and I asked what had happened to the young girl in the photograph on the cover. Mr. Godrej responded that she was present and motioned for her to stand. She told us that she was president of the local university. Having spent my life in a society where there is little distinction between male and female students in educational opportunity, I still become emotional when I recount this vivid example of the advantages of education in the life of often excluded girls in the developing world.

Although I teach Bible lessons regularly, there are some parts of the New Testament and Hebrew text that I avoid, especially those that can be interpreted as promoting unnecessary violence or violating the basic standards of justice. There was a period in my life when I spent a lot of time studying the details of the Koran and how certain passages were interpreted by different believers. When I was president and American hostages were being held by Shiite Muslims in Iran, and during the war that followed between the Iranian Shiites and the Sunni Muslims in Iraq, I wanted to understand how I might use their religious beliefs to secure the release of the American diplomats and help bring peace to the region. I read through an English translation of their holy book, and the State Department and CIA provided some Islamic experts who conducted a series of sessions in the Oval Office to give me more detailed explanations. I came to understand more clearly how, in all major faiths, there is the essence of justice, peace, and compassion but that biased interpreters can twist their meaning.

As in Christian communities, the societal status of women varies widely within the Islamic world, and we in the West quite often fail to understand the high degree of political freedom and equality many of them enjoy. The Carter Center has monitored elections in Jordan, Egypt, Lebanon, Libya, Tunisia, Indonesia, Palestine, and Sudan, and we have assisted in preparation for elections in Bangladesh. In all these countries, as well as in Algeria, Iraq, Oman, Kuwait, Morocco, Syria, Mauritania, and Yemen and a number of others where Sharia law has a major influence, women and men have equal voting rights. There is no religious impediment to equal political rights for women ordained in the Koran.

This is a moment of truth, and people of faith working for human rights must be honest and acknowledge the role our own leadership plays for good or ill. We must speak out about the power of Islam to affect positive change in the lives of women, girls, and all people. We must take responsibility to spread this message. We should not wait for leaders to tell us, we should begin in childhood, at the grassroots, to educate our young about human rights, peace-building, and coexistence. By raising the voices of the voiceless, here we become a chorus and in sharing our ideas we support each other's efforts to advance the course of human rights around the world.

ALHAJI KHUZAIMA, EXECUTIVE SECRETARY,
ISLAMIC PEACE AND SECURITY COUNCIL IN GHANA

Saudi Arabia is a special case when dealing with the issue of gender equality. Saudi women have never been granted voting rights but may be permitted to vote in 2015, at least in municipal elections. There is a 150-member Consultative Assembly, or Shura, whose limited authority includes proposing laws for the king to consider, and it is encouraging to note that in 2013 he appointed thirty women as members. There is no doubt that Saudi Arabia plays the leadership role in the Islamic world, with its enormous wealth and its sovereign being the Custodian of the Two Holy Mosques. As president, I learned how valuable their assistance could be during some of my most challenging days. When Iran and Iraq went to war and their oil was removed from the world's supply, the Saudi king sent word to me that his kingdom would greatly increase production to help stabilize prices. There was an outpouring of condemnation from Arab leaders when I announced plans to go to Camp David with Israel and Egypt to negotiate a peace agreement, but I received quiet assurance from Saudi Arabia of their backing, and the king was the first to call me with congratulations when I left Egypt after announcing that a peace agreement was concluded.

These expressions of support were not made public because the Saudis strive to maintain harmony among the twenty-two members of the Arab League, and they deviate from majority opinion only with reluctance. Later, in 2002, Crown Prince (now King) Abdullah proposed an offer of peace with Israel based on recognition of the pre-1967 border between Israel and Palestine, which was supported by all Arab leaders and subsequently by the fifty-six Islamic nations (including Iran). When we launched the Carter Center program to eradicate Guinea worm in Asia and Africa, I went to Saudi Arabia to request a contribution from the king. One of my key points of persuasion was that this was a terrible affliction in Yemen and Pakistan and in African countries where many Muslims lived. He smiled and responded, "We will contribute $9 million, but want it to be used equally among people of all faiths."

On one of the visits that Rosalynn and I made to Riyadh, there had been an extraordinary rainfall of several inches just before our arrival, and pumps and tanker trucks were all over the city attempting to remove the standing water from low places. We were informed that King Fahd and his entourage were about 250 miles away in the desert, where he was meeting with tribal chieftains who had come to consult with him. The next day we boarded a helicopter for a flight to the encampment, and we were amazed at how the desert had blossomed with flowers, almost overnight. From the air we saw dozens of large tents arranged in a circle; connected to each one was a mobile home with attached electric generators and satellite antennae. A few miles over the sand dunes we could see a similar but smaller campsite that our pilot told us was for women.

Rosalynn was whisked away by Land Rover to join the women when we landed, while I joined the men. We lounged against large pillows on beautiful carpets spread on the leveled sand, and I spent a few hours discussing official business with the king. Then he granted my wish to observe the proceedings as a series of tribal chieftains came in to pay their respects, make their requests, and discuss matters of common interest. I spent two nights with them and enjoyed wonderful meals and entertainment. A number of sheep were roasted over charcoal flames, and we had a special treat of desert truffles that had been found after the rain. There were long and relaxed conversations around the campfires, with many vivid accounts of warfare and ribald stories about bedroom conquests and how the men choose the four wives permitted by their faith. Late each night we went into the luxurious air-conditioned mobile homes.

We knew about the strict dress codes for women, we had never seen women alone on the city streets, and we knew they were not permitted to drive an automobile or ride a bicycle. Each woman had an assigned male guardian, and only men could vote or hold public office. I was feeling somewhat sorry for Rosalynn, who I thought was stuck with a group of women whose faces were concealed and who were constrained by being treated as second-class citizens. Instead she had one of the most exciting and enjoyable visits of her life. The women bubbled over with pleasure as they extolled their enhanced status in Saudi society, with its special protection, plus freedom and privilege. They described their family vacations in more permissive Arab countries and special excursions to the French Riviera or the Swiss Alps. Her companions were, of course, mostly members of the royal family and wives and daughters of sheikhs and desert leaders, but we later learned that other women in the kingdom relish some customs that Westerners consider deprivations.

Changes are taking place. A majority of Saudi working women have a college education (compared to 16 percent of working men), and almost 60 percent of university students are women. However, about 78 percent of female university graduates are unemployed because of religious and cultural opposition. One manager of a grocery chain is challenging this policy and recently said, "We are promoting recruitment of Saudi women because they have a low level of attrition, a better attention to detail, a willingness to perform and productivity about twice that of Saudi men." Despite his best efforts, however, fewer than 5 percent of his employees are Saudi women. A Gallup poll in December 2007 indicated that the majority of women and men support women's rights to work and to drive. In October 2013 dozens of Saudi women in several cities protested the ban by openly driving; unlike in previous demonstrations, they were neither arrested nor punished.

The issue of polygamy comes up often in discussions with Muslims, and the key verse in the English translation of the Koran is 4:3: "If ye fear that ye shall not be able to deal justly with the orphans, marry women of your choice, two or three or four; but if ye fear that ye shall not be able to deal justly (with them), then only one, or that which your right hands possess, that will be more suitable, to prevent you from doing injustice." This scripture is interpreted in various ways in the Islamic world. As when the Bible was written many centuries earlier, husbands were all-powerful, and the desires and interests of women were considered to be relatively insignificant. I have discussed this issue with desert chiefs and other influential men in Arab countries, and most feel that the Koran permits them to have as many as four wives at a time. They usually emphasize that the intention of the Prophet was to enhance the status of women and orphans and that in modern days the willingness of the potential brides and the approval of existing wives are factors in determining the expansion of a family with additional marriages.

The Saudi ambassador in Washington, Prince Bandar, was especially helpful to me when I was president, and I invited him down to Georgia to observe our remarkable pointer and setter dogs in a quail hunt. We were on a large plantation in southwest Georgia, and after spending all day on horseback we enjoyed a typical southern supper and then gathered around an outdoor campfire with some friends of mine. They were quite interested in learning about hunting with falcons and plied the ambassador with many questions about his nation. One early query was, "How many wives do you have?" He replied, "I have only one, like many of my younger countrymen, but the Koran permits as many as four—at a time." He explained that a wife could be divorced just by the husband saying "I divorce thee" three times. Under further questioning, he commented that one of the senior princes had had fifty-six wives but had always retained his first wife as head of his household and never had more than four at a time. Each of those who were divorced was given a nice home and a stipend for life.

Islamic women at The Carter Center Human Rights Defenders Forum in 2013 insisted that the consequences for many women in multiple marriages could be devastating. They sometimes have little choice about who and when they marry, and because husbands have the religious and political authority to make all the decisions, wives suffer uncertainty about the future for themselves and their children.

The place of religion in our societies and in many states today, particularly in the Middle East, is the determining issue for our future. The issue of women's rights is the main battleground for determining the identity of a nation. If we protect women's rights, we get everything right. If we do not protect women's rights, everything will disintegrate. We have to settle the place of religion in our societies, and discuss it without fear of intimidation. When a society has not invested in protecting women against violence, religious leaders must stand up and demand that the state do so, with measures like street lights, police training, and prosecution of violators. The United Nations Human Rights Council has called upon all governments to prioritize such actions.

MONA RISHMAWI, OFFICE OF THE UNITED NATIONS
HIGH COMMISSIONER FOR HUMAN RIGHTS

The first extended overseas trip I made after leaving the White House was to China, to accept a long-standing invitation from Vice Premier Deng Xiaoping. In addition to visiting some of the most notable tourist sites with my family and a few friends, we also went to a number of rural areas where the first small and cautious experiments in free enterprise were becoming visible. Deng especially wanted me to witness one experiment, which was limited at that time just to farm families who did not live in a village or town. They were granted the right to grow their own private crops on as much as 15 percent of the land on communal farms and could have one small private commercial venture and retain the earnings. For instance, a family could repair bicycles, make horseshoes, produce iron nails, mold clay pots, or have as many as five chickens, pigs, goats, mink, or sheep, but only one of these enterprises at a time, and they could retain the income. The most impressive thing we observed was how proud and enthusiastic the chosen families were, and the apparent equality of treatment of women in managing the choice projects. This was something we had rarely seen in the developing world, before we began our later projects in Africa.

Rosalynn and I have visited China regularly since I left public office and have seen the improvements in the status of women. Statistics show that in education and employment they have equal opportunity, and their numbers in these areas are increasing rapidly. Marriage laws have removed sexual discrimination, and of the 2,987 members of the National People's Congress, 699 (23.4 percent) are women. There are now fourteen female cabinet officers, although women have never been represented among the top officials in the Central Committee. *Forbes* lists several Chinese women billionaires, and the Grant Thornton "International Business Report" states that half of senior management jobs in China are held by women, far above only 20 percent in the United States and a global average of 24 percent.

Nicholas Kristof, who lived for many years in China, writes in *Half the Sky* that "no country has made as much progress in improving the status of women as China has. Over the past one hundred years, it has become—at least in the cities—one of the best places to grow up female." This notable improvement is related directly to the role that women played in the Chinese Communist Party's long military struggle for power. A treatise entitled "Women in the Chinese Revolution (1921–1950)" states, "The battle for women's emancipation was closely tied up with the battle for social revolution in which they fought side by side with men." In 1950 the Marriage Law declared, "The arbitrary and compulsory feudal marriage system, which is based on the superiority of men over women, and which ignores the interests of children is abolished. The 'New Democratic Marriage System,' based on free choice of partners, on monogamy, on equal rights for both sexes and on protection of the lawful interests of women and children, shall be put into effect." It did not recognize a head of household and accorded equal status in the family to husband and wife.

There are exemplary guarantees of equal treatment in the laws of China and the ratification of the key international agreements, but the ancient traditions of gender discrimination are persistent, especially in remote rural areas. Officials explain that many women who held the higher-paying jobs in rural areas resigned and moved to the cities, leaving others behind, and claim that they are struggling to correct this disparity.

With a commitment to human rights as the foundation for our foreign policy when I was president, our nation abandoned its historic alliance with the dictatorships of Latin America. We observed with interest—but without involvement—the revolution in Nicaragua that was successful in overthrowing the regime of Anastasio Somoza Debayle in 1979. The revolutionary forces were headed by the Sandinistas but included a wide coalition of academics, business and professional leaders, and especially women. Women composed at least 30 percent of combatants in the revolutionary army, and their influence in shaping the new legal structure was unprecedented in the Western Hemisphere's independence struggles, with gender equality being a primary goal of the new government. One of the revolutionary leaders who came to visit me in the White House, along with the Sandinistas and others, was Violeta Chamorro, who was to be elected president of the nation in the first free and fair election, in 1990. Although she was timid in promoting women's issues during her time in office, the revolutionary commitment to women's rights has prevailed over the years. Nicaragua has by far the largest portion of women in Parliament in the Americas, at 40 percent. There have recently been some disturbing restrictions on the fairness and transparency of the electoral process and women's access to reproductive health services, but Nicaragua still stands out among all other countries in this hemisphere as foremost in gender equality, as measured by the World Economic Forum. In fact, only nine nations ranked higher than Nicaragua in this regard. Most European countries ranked lower, and the United States ranked only twenty-third.

It is not easy to determine or predict what historical events can help to equalize the status of women, but their enhanced status in China and Nicaragua indicates that military service contributes to this increased influence. Most Western nations admit women to serve on active duty in some capacity other than in the medical corps, and the United States has recently begun to assign women to combat roles, as do Canada, Denmark, Finland, Germany, Israel, Italy, New Zealand, Norway, Serbia, Sweden, Switzerland, and Taiwan. Their performance has been exemplary, and they have overcome the misgivings of many skeptics, including me. I have learned that my former doubts about the service of women were unjustified. Being "equal" in the military service helps to ensure that women will be more likely to demand and achieve the same status as men in political and economic matters.

8 | WOMEN AND THE CARTER CENTER

The Carter Center has confronted the issue of sexual discrimination and abuse of women through our work with families in remote communities in more than seventy developing nations, and we have seen how religious beliefs and violence have impacted their lives in patriarchal societies. Of even greater significance is what we have learned about the vital role that liberated women can play in correcting the most serious problems that plague their relatives and neighbors. Almost everywhere, we find that women are relegated to secondary positions of influence and authority within a community but almost always do most of the work and prove to be the key participants in any successful project. Whenever men are plagued with poverty, disease, or persecution, the women are suffering more. When there is a shortage of food or limited access to education, the men and boys have first priority. When there are few opportunities for jobs or desirable positions in any facet of life, they are rarely filled by women. When a civil conflict erupts, women are the primary victims of bombs and missiles, the displaced adults in charge of children, and the victims of rape. Beyond all this are the special biases that come from the distortion of religious beliefs and the imposition of discriminatory tribal customs that lead to honor killings, genital cutting, or child marriage.

Waging peace, fighting disease, and building hope are the major themes of The Carter Center, and one of our basic principles is not to duplicate what others are doing or to compete with them. If the U.S. government, World Health Organization, World Bank, or any university or nongovernmental organization is adequately addressing a problem, we don't get involved. We try to fill vacuums in the world, both in the projects we undertake and the regions in which we serve. Over the years we have mediated peace agreements, increased production of food grains in Africa, enhanced freedom and democracy by monitoring troubled elections, and defended human rights.

Somewhat to our surprise, we have been asked increasingly to concentrate our financial and personal resources in reducing the ravages of neglected tropical diseases, concentrating on trachoma, lymphatic filariasis (elephantiasis), onchocerciasis (river blindness), schistosomiasis, and dracunculiasis (Guinea worm). Under the direction of Dr. Don Hopkins, director of all our health programs, we also target malaria, since the same mosquito is the vector for filariasis. Although no longer found in developed countries, these diseases still afflict hundreds of millions of people in Africa and some regions in Latin America and Asia.

Early on we received criticism from well-meaning liberal friends that by saving lives in Africa we were contributing to the population explosion in the region and would be better engaged in improving education and agricultural production. I brought these suggestions to our health director at the time, Dr. William Foege, who was the former director of the Centers for Disease Control and had played the key role in eradicating smallpox. He produced official data to show me that the best way to reduce a high birthrate is for parents to be convinced that their children will live. There is a direct relation between reducing the infant mortality rate and a subsequent decrease in population growth. The logical explanation is that parents in poor regions depend on a certain number of surviving offspring to provide support in their older years; when child survival is doubtful, they produce the maximum number of children. It is also clear that a family's health is dependent on the knowledge of the mother about the advantages of good sanitation, proper diet, and other factors that can prevent or control prevalent diseases. Our primary health programs have been built on these premises for more than three decades.

Carter Center personnel or domestic trainees go into the most remote villages in the jungle or desert to teach people about their disease and what they can do to prevent it or ease the suffering. In doing this work, we have to become intimately involved in the daily lives of the people. If medicines, filter cloths, pesticides, or protective nets are required, we work with national health ministers, but we still retain control of the delivery system and let the local people do the work themselves. We give them full credit for success. Our focus on the most worthy projects is helped by the International Task Force for Disease Eradication (ITFDE), which is located at our Center and is the only organization of its kind. With participants from leading health organizations, the ITFDE regularly assesses all human illnesses to determine which might be targeted for elimination in a particular region or for global eradication.

Our most highly publicized struggle has been with dracunculiasis, or Guinea worm, and we are approaching our goal of having this be the second disease in history that is totally eradicated. This has been a massive effort lasting more than twenty-five years and involving direct intervention by our staff or trainees in more than 26,000 isolated villages in twenty countries. This long struggle has given us an unprecedented insight into the special role of women in some of the most destitute families on earth.

Guinea worm disease is caused by drinking contaminated water from a pond that fills during the rainy season and then becomes stagnant and slowly dries up during the rest of the year. Microscopic Guinea worm larvae in the water are consumed by tiny water fleas, which then are swallowed by people drinking the water. Inside a human's abdomen, the parasite larvae mate. Over about a year, the female matures and grows into a worm two to three feet long and begins emerging through the skin. The exit point is usually through the feet or legs but can be at any other part of the body.

A large sore develops around the emerging worm and is very painful, sometimes destroying muscle tissue so the aftereffect in a joint is similar to polio. There is almost unbearable pain for about thirty days, and the victim is incapacitated, unable to go to school or work in the field. There is no medical cure available, and the cause of the disease is usually unknown to villagers; many believe it must be a divine curse, derived from drinking goat's blood, the confluence of stars, or some other source. The only treatment for thousands of years has been performed by local religious leaders (or witch doctors), who wrap the emerging worm around a stick or other object about the size of a pencil and exert enough pressure to expedite the process by a few days. Care must be taken to pull out the entire worm, as any part remaining in the body will rot and become infected.

I first saw Guinea worm in a small village in Ghana, where about 350 of the 500 residents had worms coming out of their bodies. The villagers were assembled in an open space under large trees, except for about two dozen whose affliction was too great for them to walk or leave their hut. I noticed a lovely young woman on the edge of the crowd, holding a baby in her right arm, and after the ceremonies I went over to ask her the name of her child. But there was no baby; instead she was holding her right breast, which was almost a foot long and had a worm emerging from the nipple. Later I learned that a total of twelve worms emerged from different places in her body.

We had a wealthy man with us, and he paid for a well to be dug and a pump installed, so within a few weeks the pond was abandoned as a water source for the people. They have never had another case of Guinea worm in their village.

Like most other diseases in developing nations, Guinea worm especially affects the female members of a family. The first person expected to assist a sufferer is the mother or a girl child who must then be kept out of school. If people have learned the source of the disease, they naturally blame the women, who are almost invariably the ones who bring the water from the pond, often carrying five-gallon containers on their heads. To retrieve the water they walk into the pond, and if worms are emerging from their bodies thousands of eggs may be released to perpetuate the cycle. Fortunately it is also the women who assume responsibility for protecting their family and their village. For instance, more than 95 percent of our last remaining cases have been in South Sudan, where we are now concentrating our efforts. These final cases are very difficult to detect early and to control, and we have to expend an extraordinary effort to isolate people who contract the disease but also to monitor closely all the hundreds of villages where another case might reappear. Although in South Sudan there were 520 cases in 2012 and only 113 in 2013, we have retained about 120 people on our full-time payroll to perform these duties, most of them native to the area. They are assisted by more than ten thousand unpaid volunteers, all of them trained women who are trusted by other villagers.

Since the beginning of this effort in 1990, 131 women have served as our technical advisors, most of them holding a master's degree in public health. They have served in Sudan, South Sudan, Togo, Benin, Uganda, Ghana, Chad, Niger, Ethiopia, Nigeria, and other endemic countries. At our Carter Center headquarters in Atlanta, women have led our effort to gain publicity for the program and to secure funding to cover its costs. All these women have interacted with each other and gained a special insight into the massive challenges and how to overcome them. Among the six thousand women who conducted the extensive survey to detect new cases in Ghana, one leader expressed the feeling of many of her fellow workers, most of them previously excluded from leading such efforts: "It's about time they involved us. We're the only ones who know how things work anyway."

The final stages of eliminating Guinea worm disease from Nigeria were headed by the country's former president General Yakubu Gowon. When excluded from a decision about how to treat a village pond in Nigeria, a group of women with newfound self-confidence confronted him and stopped the process because approval had been obtained only from the male village leaders. Gowon quickly corrected his mistake.

In the beginning one of our biggest obstacles was to educate people in all the small and isolated communities about this ancient blight and how to eliminate it. Without television or radio service and when communities five miles apart speak different languages and only a few men are just partially literate, we had to devise a completely new form of communication. We finally resorted to cartoons: simple drawings of women dipping water from a pond and drinking it. Those who were shown using a filter were all right, but the others had worms coming out of their body. Women wrote original plays and songs to explain the process and printed the colored cartoons onto cloth, which was used to make dresses and shirts for other members of their family. I was proud when they gave me one of the shirts on a visit with them.

Some of the people had never seen a picture or photograph before, and this would occasionally cause problems. One group of Peace Corps volunteers in a remote area of Niger made some of the drawings, showing the women standing in the knee-deep pond. When the villagers first saw the cartoon, a chorus of voices cried, "I'd rather have Guinea worm than no feet!"

Of all the "neglected" diseases on which The Carter Center has focused its efforts to control or eradicate, blinding trachoma is the only one twice as common in women as in men. It also is the only one of these diseases that I knew when I was a child. We depended on horses and mules to pull our plows and vehicles and raised cattle, sheep, hogs, goats, geese, ducks, and chickens to provide food for our family and surplus meat, eggs, and milk to sell for additional income. Our barn lot was usually ankle deep in manure and rainwater, and most of what my sisters and I swept from our yard with brush brooms was droppings from the free-roaming fowl. We were always surrounded by swarms of houseflies, even inside our home, despite screens on our doors and windows, and they were especially attracted to children's eyes as they sought moisture and sustenance. Flies carry filth that causes infection, and I was almost constantly afflicted with sore eyes that my mother would treat to prevent development into the more serious trachoma. Some of our neighbors were not so fortunate. The advanced stage causes the upper eyelids to turn inward, slashing the cornea with every blink and causing blindness. I was reminded of this in more recent years when we visited the villages and homes of Dinka and Masai families in Kenya, Sudan, and other African countries. From a distance the children appear to be wearing eyeglasses; nearby, it is seen to be a ring of flies encircling their eyeballs, searching for moisture.

Except for cataracts, trachoma is the most prevalent cause of blindness, still afflicting tens of millions of the world's poorest people. The Carter Center combats trachoma in almost a dozen countries in Africa, having begun this effort in Ghana in 1998. There is a comprehensive treatment program recommended by the World Health Organization that uses the acronym SAFE: surgery, antibiotics, face washing, and environment. We have eliminated blinding trachoma in several countries, and our major challenge is now in Ethiopia, where we have concentrated our efforts for many years. In 2000 the Pfizer pharmaceutical company agreed to my request for a free supply of azithromycin (Zithromax), which is the best antibiotic for treating trachoma. In November 2013 we administered our one-hundred-millionth dose. We have taught several thousand health workers, mostly women, to perform eyelid surgeries, a simple process with adequate training, and provided them with the necessary sterile instruments. They now perform about 40 percent of these operations in the world. We also marshaled schoolteachers and parents in the endemic areas to encourage children to wash their face, which they had never thought of doing before.

In correcting the problem in a community, women are the agents for change in health education, responsible for cleanliness in the home, taking care of laundry, and educating their children in hygienic behavior. In treating trachoma and other diseases on a broad scale, the Ministry of Health in Ethiopia has learned that women enjoy a greater level of trust from heads of households and better access to neighbors' homes than men. We have been able to train 6,500 health extension workers in the Amhara region, and all are women. They lead teams that now distribute up to 20 million doses of Zithromax each year to treat infected eyes. In recent months the ministry has implemented a new all-volunteer corps of female health workers, called the 1 to 5 Health Development Army because they select one-fifth of the families and train them to minister to four others. Early in 2013 we mobilized over twenty thousand of these volunteers and saw the population coverage with Zithromax increase to almost 93 percent. Our health experts attribute this success to the Health Development Army having a personal and close relationship with their neighbors and therefore noticing if specific individuals are missing treatments.

Our specialists in trachoma observed that one new volunteer to become an "eye surgeon" had a scar on her eyelids. She explained that her advanced trachoma infection had been corrected by surgery performed by one of her trained neighbors. Her life was changed; instead of having a disabling condition leading to misery, poverty, and total blindness, she became an active health promoter for her community. She was proud yet tearful when she told her full story.

Having dealt with surgery, antibiotics, and face washing, (S-A-F), this left the problem of the environment (E): the ubiquitous flies that breed and feed on a constant supply of human and animal excrement and carry infection from one person to another. Surprisingly, it was a "women's liberation movement" that gave us a major breakthrough in solving this problem. I remembered that we had had an outdoor privy behind our house (the only one on the farm) and that we had covered our home site with strong doses of powdered or liquid DDT, a poison that controlled flies, mosquitoes, and other insects. This was a key factor in ridding ourselves of both trachoma and malaria. (It was later learned that DDT was also eliminating butterflies and many birds, especially those species like hawks and other raptors that consumed bodies within which the long-lasting pesticide had accumulated, so the outdoor use of DDT is now prohibited throughout the world.) We knew that in Ethiopia and other regions in Africa many men simply step behind a bush to defecate and are often seen urinating alongside roads and highways, but we learned that it was absolutely taboo for a woman to be seen relieving herself. The most convenient recourse for themselves and their daughters was to find a concealed place in or around the family home. Working with local people, we taught them how to build latrines as a means to improve the environment by reducing the population of flies. It is a very simple design that consists of a hole in the ground, some way to prevent the hole from caving in while a person stands or squats over it, and an enclosure of brush or cloth for privacy. If the family provides the labor, the financial cost is only about a dollar. We were hoping for a few thousand latrines to be built during the first year, but the word spread from village to village as Ethiopian housewives adopted this as a practical move toward liberation, and the total number of latrines built that year was 86,500! By the end of 2012 we had seen 2.9 million latrines built as more wives and mothers demanded this beneficial addition to their freedom and health. I am proud of my growing reputation as the world's most preeminent sponsor of latrines.

This somewhat humorous account illustrates that despite their inferior social status, these women were strong and even dominant, deeply involved in all aspects of improving health care, and extremely effective in solving their own problems, with associated benefits to their entire community.

In fact, though formerly excluded from positions of leadership or responsibility, dedicated and competent women have been the key to our success in every health project. We responded to a request from the prime minister of Ethiopia in 1992 to train health workers for the general population of about 82 million. He stipulated that they would not be permitted to leave Ethiopia in the process, as he was concerned that they would not return after graduation. We developed a curriculum for each of the diseases and health problems they faced (about seventy) and used local university campuses for classes. The final result after ten years was 7,000 graduates who have the capability of a physician's assistant or registered nurse, plus 27,000 with training equivalent to a licensed practical nurse. This was enough to provide a female health worker for every 2,400 citizens, deployed as evenly as possible throughout the country.

A significant revelation of these programs has been that people who live with poverty and disease, with little self-respect or hope for a better future, can have their lives and attitudes transformed by tangible success brought about by their own efforts. They have demonstrated vividly that, despite their devastating poverty, they are just as intelligent, just as ambitious, just as hardworking as people with much greater economic and educational resources. Like people everywhere, they seek to secure physical, emotional, and spiritual health for their families and their communities. And it is most often the women who lead in these initiatives.

In 1986 we launched a program in Africa to increase the production of basic food grains, mostly maize (corn), wheat, rice, sorghum, and millet. Our partners were a Japanese philanthropist, Ryoichi Sasakawa, and Dr. Norman Borlaug, who had been awarded the Nobel Prize for Peace in 1970 for inaugurating the "green revolution" in India and Pakistan. We named the program Global 2000 and worked only with subsistence farmers who usually had no more than a hectare (about two acres) of land on which the entire family depended for food and, in good years, some surplus to sell for cash income. Utilizing my own experience as a full-time farmer for seventeen years and especially the scientific and practical advice from Dr. Borlaug, we were able to double or triple production for those who used good seed, planted in rows, controlled the weeds, harvested at the right time, and had storage facilities that minimized damage from moisture, insects, and rodents. Eventually 8 million families in fifteen nations completed our program, and we gave awards to the most outstanding farmers in each nation.

One memorable event occurred when Rosalynn and I went to Zimbabwe to present this award to a farmer who lived about 125 miles from Harare, the capital. When we arrived in the village we found the entire population of the area assembled in the town square, a bare spot surrounded by homes and a few trees. Local officials were assembled under a large tree, and we noticed one man standing with them, erect and nervous, wearing a dusty black suit and a flowery tie. He was introduced to us as the Global 2000 Outstanding Farmer, and we gave him a plaque and a financial award.

We had made prior arrangements to eat lunch in his home, where he was quite loquacious and kept us amused with anecdotes about his parents, his early life, and some of his adult exploits. After we finished our meal, carefully served by his very quiet wife, I suggested that we visit his crops. He objected strenuously—about the path being rough, getting our clothes dirty, and the heat. I insisted, pointing out that we lived in South Georgia and had spent many years on the farm. Furthermore I had worn my khaki trousers and work boots, so I didn't mind getting dirty. He finally yielded, and we walked down the hill to a beautiful stand of maize. I was impressed and asked him a series of questions involving the variety he planted, spacing in the row, growing season, fertilizer used, and expected harvest date. He did not know how to respond to any of the questions, and in every case he turned to his wife for the answer. Very shyly, she explained the entire process she had followed in actually becoming the most Outstanding Farmer in Zimbabwe. We learned that her husband just cared for the cattle and collected the money when his wife's good crops were sold.

Although our Center is not involved directly in microloans, we have observed women's groups initiate their own programs. Often for the first time, these loans gave the recipients some financial independence from their husbands for purchasing personal items for themselves and their children. Using profits from producing or processing grain or making soap or handmade products, women started local banks that made small loans to others, and the custom spread widely. Since women are the primary farmers in many areas of Africa, it became increasingly common to see them directly managing the harvest, storage, and even marketing of grain. Rosalynn and I visited one of our agricultural sites in Togo as the maize crop was being brought in to a central marketplace, and all the weighing, accounting, assignment to storage bins, and disbursements were being conducted by women. It was like a combined farmers' market and bank. They had devised a computer system using a row of nails, all of the same height, and had stacks of coins with perforated centers; exactly ten coins would fit on a nail, so the decimal system was automatically utilized as tabulation proceeded. The women were also grinding corn into meal and selling it along with handicraft items, including exquisite pottery. We still have some of the pots on our back porch.

If the [developing] world was a molecule put under a powerful microscope, we would see a complex web of barriers that keep women from fully realizing their inherent human rights and living in dignity. Strands of this web include barriers to securing property rights; pursuing an education and earning a decent living at fair wages; making decisions about love, sex, and marriage; controlling one's reproduction; and obtaining health care. We would also see the invisible DNA that keeps this web intact: a sense of powerlessness, enforced by social coercion, rigid gender roles, homophobia, violence, and rape. Finally, we also would see that only the women

who face these barriers can push them aside, change their
own lives, and transform the societies in which they live. It is
our obligation to support them.

RUTH MESSINGER, PRESIDENT,

AMERICAN JEWISH WORLD SERVICE

In 1978 I was the first American president to visit Sub-Saharan Africa, and it was not incidental that one of my destinations was Liberia. That nation's government had been founded in the early nineteenth century by freed American slaves, freeborn blacks from the United States, and others who were liberated from European ships that were taking them to the New World to be sold. I had known Liberia's president, William Tolbert, when he was the leader of the Baptist World Alliance. Two years after my visit, President Tolbert and all his cabinet were assassinated and the country was afflicted with civil strife, until a peace agreement was finally reached in 1995. During that time Rosalynn and I and other representatives of The Carter Center made many visits to the capital, Monrovia, and to the 95 percent of the country that was under the control of various warlords. We monitored the process when an election could be orchestrated, and the strongest warlord, Charles Taylor, was elected in 1997, primarily because many voters feared that civil war would again erupt if he was defeated. He was a despotic and oppressive ruler who promoted warfare in neighboring countries. After he was overthrown and forced into exile by opposition headed by a phalanx of women, in 2005 we monitored another free and fair election that was won by Ellen Johnson Sirleaf, the first woman to be elected president in Africa. (Taylor was convicted of war crimes by the Special Court for Sierra Leone and sentenced to fifty years of imprisonment.)

The vast region of Liberia formerly controlled by warlords had become isolated from the central government and was basically lawless. The new president asked us to help her minister of justice evolve a legal system in the rural areas that would protect human rights, be understandable to the populace, and make the citizens and their local political leaders feel that they shared the responsibility of maintaining the laws. As our programs evolved, it became increasingly apparent that their most powerful impact was on women, who had little protection under previous laws and tribal customs.

We worked to inform the people, for the first time, that rape was a crime and that perpetrators could be punished, that women could own property, that a wife could inherit her deceased husband's estate, that both parents had claims on their children, that there was a minimum legal age of marriage, that female genital cutting was not mandatory, and that a dowry was a gift and did not have to be returned if a marriage broke up. Most of this was new to them, of course, and there was opposition in a society where women had never demanded nor been granted these rights.

Using the carefully chosen slogan "Empower Men and Women Together," we began to frame issues of gender equality and violence with community dramas, training of traditional leaders, and use of radio broadcasts. For the first time women were encouraged to participate equally in the performances, discussions on the radio, and face-to-face debates. The most intriguing, and sometimes disturbing, subject for the traditional chiefs was the relationship between customary and statutory laws. With support from the minister of justice and the local leaders, we worked with the Catholic Justice and Peace Commission to establish forty-seven community justice advisors (CJAs), of which seventeen are women. They now operate in the five largest counties and have opened almost seven thousand cases, 71 percent of which have been resolved. About 40 percent of the cases involved domestic disputes, 33 percent related to financial and property claims, and 15 percent were criminal cases. The largest group that uses the CJAs are young women, and the largest single case category is child abandonment. Through March 2013 cases had been initiated by 2,694 men and 2,773 women. An independent study by Oxford University of four hundred representative cases reported an improvement in legal knowledge, a reduction in bribery, and an increase in community acceptance of the law, producing "large socioeconomic benefits . . . not by bringing the rural poor into the formal domain of magistrates' courts, government offices, and police stations, but by bringing the formal law into the organizational forms of the custom, through low-cost third-party mediation and advocacy."

Even more significant was a statement by Ella Musu Coleman, a leader of the National Traditional Council of Liberia: "The Carter Center doesn't tell us what to do. They help us understand what the law is, and why some of our traditions are not correct. We decide amongst ourselves if we want to get rid of certain practices." Both she and Chief Zanzan Karwar, the chairman of Liberia's National Traditional Council, attended the 2013 Human Rights Defenders Forum at The Carter Center and expressed strong support for the seminal improvements that have been made in the lives of their people.

Deliberately we did not set out to address the issue of female genital cutting (FGC), which is deeply entrenched and a subject not normally discussed publicly. Liberia is one of the African countries where no laws have been adopted to curtail the practice. However, it has been debated among women leaders and in the government and international NGOs, who have faced opposition to its abolition from local men and women. A partner of The Carter Center, Mama Tumah, the head female *zoe* (traditional leader), has been open to new ideas, and in her own village she has removed the sacred grove involved in FGC ceremonies. Most recently she convened a group of women *zoes* from all of Liberia's fifteen counties to discuss the issue among themselves. The closing ceremony was attended by four female government ministers.

It is clear that more equal female involvement in community affairs is beneficial to *all* citizens but is best achieved by letting the local people—both men and women—make their own decisions. The experiences of The Carter Center and our African coworkers show that there are ways to encourage these changes in social norms, but this work will require a lot of patience and a tremendous amount of humility and mutual respect.

An issue that The Carter Center has addressed on a global basis for fifteen years is access to information. Headed by legal expert Laura Neuman, this program seeks to encourage all nations to provide citizens with the ability to know what their governments are doing by passing laws that reveal how decisions are made, how public funds are spent, the terms of contracts for mining and timber harvesting, and the accurate and timely promulgation of voter lists and the results of elections. Access to such information is one of our fundamental human rights, enshrined in Article 19 of the Universal Declaration of Human Rights, which states, "Everyone has the right to . . . seek, receive and impart information." This same language is repeated in the International Covenant on Civil and Political Rights, the American Convention on Human Rights, and the European Convention on Human Rights. I have attended regional conferences on this subject in Ghana, Peru, Jamaica, Costa Rica, and China and an international forum in Atlanta. Having this right to information increases citizens' confidence in their leaders, makes public administration more efficient and effective, guarantees that natural resources will be better utilized, and increases confidence of potential investors. It also promotes the desire of citizens to become involved in elections and other public affairs.

Even in countries that have legal guarantees of these rights, one tragic finding is that the marginalized, poverty-stricken, least educated people are mostly excluded from access to fundamental information. This is especially true for women. As explained in the UN Millennium Development Goals report of 2011, women perform 66 percent of all the work but continue to form the largest bloc of the world's poor, an estimated 70 percent of the 1.3 billion people living in poverty. Girls are less likely than boys to attend primary school, and more of them have to leave school because of poverty or a need to work. This trend accelerates for secondary education. The *Global Education Digest* of 2012 concludes that this has led to approximately 66 percent of illiterate persons being women. Their relative poverty, illiteracy, lack of mobility, and much smaller proportion of membership in parliaments make clear that women suffer most from lack of information—and from corruption. A study conducted by the United Nations Development Program and UN Women found that " 'petty' or 'retail' corruption" (when basic public services are sold) affects poor women in particular and that "women and girls are often asked to pay bribes in the form of sexual favors." In a vicious circle, lack of access to public officials leaves women vulnerable to corruption, but their low income diminishes their ability to pay bribes, further restricting their access to basic services. In addition, their need to take care of their family often prevents women from having time to seek protection from corruption.

We have come to the conclusion that many of the other abuses of women and girls (slavery, genital cutting, child marriage, rape) can be reduced only if women have more access to information about the international, national, and local agencies that are responsible for publicizing and ending these abuses. It is difficult for women and their defenders to demand their legitimate rights if they don't know what they deserve under their own nation's laws. We are conducting studies in Liberia and Guatemala to ascertain how well international standards are being met. Liberia is making good progress under the leadership of President Johnson Sirleaf, but Guatemala is greatly lacking in transparency.

Top Guatemalan officials have agreed to cooperate with our program, since official reports of rape and sexual assault increased by 34 percent from 2008 to 2011, and an estimated 50 percent of women have suffered from domestic violence. During the first six months of 2013 more women were murdered in Guatemala than in any other complete year, and only one in ten cases of violence against women results in punishment of the offender. In our assessments so far, 75 percent of interviewees claim that women receive less public information than men; this is due to their timidity about asking for information, fear of retribution, lack of awareness about availability of information, and lack of mobility. For instance, 90 percent of those entering the birth registry department and 80 percent entering the business registry office during our observation period in early 2013 were men, and men received interviews and help from public officials much faster than women, who were largely ignored.

These are some of the basic questions we are asking in our studies in Liberia and Guatemala:

> *Education:* Are women able to access information on educational policies, school budgets, curricula, nutritional programs, and scholarships?
>
> *Land ownership:* Are women able to access information on land policy, their rights to own or inherit land, and do they have access to land titles?
>
> *Starting a business:* Do women have access to information about obtaining a business license, procedures for starting and sustaining a small business, access to loans, laws regarding taxation, imports, or marketing?
>
> *Farming:* Do women have access to information about prices for land rent, seed, fertilizer, irrigation water, or about market prices at harvest time?

When these surveys are complete, we will convene meetings of international and regional groups to consider how best to improve access to information for women as a way to reduce existing impediments to their equal treatment as citizens.

9 | LEARNING FROM HUMAN RIGHTS HEROES

Our continuing experiences in different countries and with other organizations have been correlated with efforts to promote human rights more specifically. We have had Human Rights Defenders Forums at The Carter Center for many years with participants from the United Nations and about a dozen of the most prominent human rights organizations to discuss urgent issues. Our custom has been to invite about forty of the most notable human rights heroes from nations with oppressive regimes and then to use our best efforts to obtain permission for them to join us. My personal intercessions are sometimes inadequate, but just focusing our attention on them provides some protection even if they are not permitted to leave their country. Those who are able to attend these conferences of human rights defenders can learn from each other about tactics, and they derive encouragement from being together for frank and unrestrained discussions of the challenges they face. We have been successful each year in arranging a roundtable interview on CNN in Atlanta and for some of the key participants to go to Washington for meetings with representatives from the U.S. Congress and leaders from the executive branch.

Over the years human rights activists have increasingly emphasized that the example set by the United States was having enormous influence on whether their own governments, often with less commitment and experience with the rule of law and protection of human rights, would follow in America's footsteps. For example, America's "war on terror" gave governments from countries like Kenya, Pakistan, Egypt, and Nigeria more latitude to violate prohibitions against torture and indefinite detention without due process in a vague and open-ended pursuit of national security. We decided to convene a session in 2003 titled "Reinforcing the Frontlines of Freedom: Protecting Human Rights in the Context of the War on Terror." News of the establishment of the Guantánamo Bay detention facility for the purpose of detaining indefinitely people suspected of terrorism, along with what the majority of the world considered an illegal aggressive war against Iraq, led many to believe it was necessary to launch a movement for renewed commitment to the provisions of international law and the Universal Declaration of Human Rights.

The forum issued the "Atlanta Declaration," which called on all governments to align national security policies with human rights principles such as the absolute prohibition of torture, access to due process of law, fair trials for any person deprived of liberty, and adherence to the Geneva Conventions and other international humanitarian laws. I wrote a book, *Our Endangered Values*, about this set of challenges and delivered a speech at the Democratic National Convention in 2004 that focused on the urgent task of restoring America's position as a champion of human rights and democratic ideals. In our forums we included women activists, as the Center considers women's rights issues a key component of all our programs rather than a separate concern. Women suffer most during and after war and have a central role to play in advancing peace and preventing the radicalization of young people during times of conflict.

During the 2003 forum, one of Afghanistan's greatest leaders, Dr. Sima Samar, the nation's first female doctor and government minister, expressed her view that by waging war "in the name of democracy and human and women's rights," the international coalition might embolden the extremists. She insisted that progress was possible only through supporting credible and legitimate Afghan democratic forces and initiatives and that an excessive military approach would undermine these objectives. Over the next several years, Dr. Samar expressed growing alarm at the increase in civilian deaths, intrusive and deadly night raids, assassination by drones, and indefinite detention of Afghans in facilities that mirrored conditions at Bagram prison or Guantánamo Bay. Sadly many of the same issues we discussed in 2003 persist. Later I wrote an op-ed for the *New York Times* in which I described in detail how the United States was currently violating at least ten of the thirty articles of the Universal Declaration of Human Rights.

In 2007 we convened our Human Rights Defenders Forum on the theme of "Faith and Freedom," in which we explored how religious leaders and communities can become stronger in their advocacy of human rights. We found reluctance among some secular human rights organizations to examine intersections with religion. The history of oppression on religious grounds is well known and is a matter of sensitivity among advocates who rely on global agreements that are seen as transcending religion, such as the Universal Declaration of Human Rights. We also encountered resistance among some religious persons and leaders because of their perception that the human rights concept focuses on the individual instead of collective well-being. We also were quietly informed that many religious people and institutions automatically associate the human rights framework with the promotion of homosexual and abortion rights, so they were reluctant to become too closely associated with the movement.

Despite these impediments, the conference was very successful, and we began exploring ways that religion can be a powerful force for equality and universal human dignity. This exploration led us to the conclusion that there is no greater challenge than the full embrace of women's equal rights by religious leaders, institutions, and believers alike. We found also that we could hardly address the deprivations of women's rights without also confronting an even larger challenge posed by a growing acceptance of violence. These two forums, held ten years apart, brought us to the same conclusion: that a new commitment to universal human rights and to end unnecessary violence is desperately needed if humanity is to escape the cycle of war, poverty, and oppression.

During this series of forums and our other work at The Carter Center, we became increasingly aware that one of the most crucial issues is the pervasive violation of the rights of women and girls, and in 2011 this was the subject of our assembly. Many of the participants were from Islamic countries, and they recommended that we move one of our subsequent venues to a predominantly Muslim community.

I wanted to understand more fully the attitude of internationally admired and prominent men toward women in an Islamic society, and that led me to the Egyptian Naguib Mahfouz, the 1988 Nobel Laureate in literature. I remembered that when Anwar Sadat was widely condemned throughout the Islamic world after signing the peace treaty with Israel in 1979, Mahfouz was a prominent defender of Sadat's decision. Like Sadat, Mahfouz was attacked by an assassin and severely wounded in 1994; he died twelve years later. I obtained his book *Life's Wisdom from the Works of the Nobel Laureate*, which was described by the editor as a "distilled collection of quotations from this great author's works." I found that they provided a fascinating if disturbing array of comments from the perspective of a man I knew as a progressive and thoughtful Islamic intellectual:

> Girls today no longer have the ability to get along with people. Where are the ladies of yesteryear?
> Only men can ruin women, and not every man is capable of being a guardian for them.
> Marriage is the ultimate surrender in life's losing battle.
> The virtue of marriage is that it takes care of one's lust and so purifies the body.
> Marriage is just a big deception. After a few months as tasty as olive oil, your bride turns into a dose of castor oil.

Women's lack of ideology or philosophy proves that ideology and philosophy hinder real, vital activity. A woman
is only concerned with creation and all things connected,
she is a beautiful creator, and creation is the center of her
life. All other activities are of man's making and are necessary for domination, not creation!

Just as one can find a deviant housewife, there's an honorable
working woman.

The love of a woman is like political theater: there is no doubt
about the loftiness of its goal, but you wonder about the
integrity of it.

A woman without children is like wine without the power to
intoxicate, like a rose without scent, or like worship without strong faith behind it.

I was relieved to read this lonely quotation toward the end of this
presentation of his work:

Women's liberation is not limited to equal rights and duties:
it also implies their full participation in the political and
economic as well as social and cultural spheres.

These comments by a world-renowned Islamic scholar indicate that
even within a modern and ostensibly secular society there is a tendency
to ridicule and derogate women and their role in the family and the
general society.

Equality between women and men in the Quran is clear. But
I have a suggestion for men: they need to support women in
the issue of equality by sometimes just being silent.

SHEIKH OMAR AHMED TIJANI NIASS,
SPIRITUAL LEADER OF THE TIJANI SUFI ORDER OF ISLAM

We monitored very closely the overthrow of President Hosni Mubarak of Egypt in 2011 in a popular uprising, and our Center closely witnessed the subsequent elections for a parliament, a president, and the formulation of a new constitution. I had first met Dr. Mohamed Morsi in 2011 when he was head of the engineering department at Zagazig University near Cairo. Neither of us had any idea that he would be the first democratically elected president. During the subsequent months he assured me that the terms of the Egypt-Israel peace treaty would be honored and that any modifications desired by the Egyptians would be negotiated peacefully with Israel. Another issue on which we reached agreement was the rights of women. Dr. Morsi told me that he was working with a panel established by the grand imam of Al-Azhar on a statement that would spell out policies on the status of women and girls in an Islamic society. The grand imam was president of Al-Azhar University, which had 120,000 students, and was the spiritual leader of Sunni Muslims.

I met with Grand Imam Ahmed el-Tayeb on my subsequent visits to Egypt and found him to be quite moderate concerning the basic freedoms of society and dedicated to formulating a public statement concerning the gender issue. After our private discussions he always invited about a dozen leaders of the various Christian denominations in Cairo for more broad-ranging topics. The Christian leaders were not involved in drafting the Al-Azhar statement on the rights of women but likely would be guided by the stated policies of Muslims, who comprise 90 percent of the nation's population. Because of the sensitivity of women's rights in many Islamic countries and because of promised support by President Morsi, the grand imam, and the pope of the Coptic Church, we made plans to hold our annual Human Rights Defenders Forum in Egypt in June 2013 and were assured by government authorities of their approval and support.

The Egyptian military establishment seemed to grant authority to the new government, but they had ruled Egypt for almost sixty years and all the members of the Supreme Court had been appointed by

former president Mubarak. These justices declared the carefully monitored and successful election of parliamentary members to be invalid,
and the police force was strangely ineffective in maintaining order on
the streets. Very little foreign aid flowed into Egypt except for military
purposes. Under these circumstances, President Morsi proved an ineffective leader and turned increasingly to his own Muslim Brotherhood
associates for support and guidance. After massive popular demonstrations by opposition forces Morsi was overthrown and imprisoned
by military coup in July 2013, with total authority reverting to the
military.

Meanwhile, the threat of street demonstrations had required us
to change the location of our Human Rights Defenders Forum from
Cairo to The Carter Center. We contacted everyone on our guest list
and invited them to come to Atlanta, and almost all of them were
able to do so. The subject was "Mobilizing Faith for Women," and the
world's major religions and geographical regions were represented. The
participants included religious leaders who were Protestant, Catholic,
and Coptic Christians, Sunni, Shia, and Sufi Muslims, conservative
and progressive Jews, Baha'i, tribal traditionalists, and other activists
who focused the work of their organizations on rape, slavery, child
marriage, genital cutting, economic and social deprivation, and other
sexual abuses.

Before our session I read *Half the Sky*, a remarkable book by Nicholas Kristof and his wife, Sheryl WuDunn, its title derived from a statement by Chairman Mao Zedong: "Women hold up half the sky." The
authors interviewed hundreds of courageous women and girls who were
suffering from persecution because of their gender and who were willing to describe their plight. Often they were struggling, at the risk of
death, for their human rights. Nick has traveled with us at times to
observe our Center's efforts to promote peace and freedom and to control the many diseases that take their heaviest toll among women and
children. He and Sheryl have done as much to promote women's rights
as anyone I know.

We learned at our conference that it is easier for Christians to deviate from certain Bible scriptures with which they disagree or consider not applicable to modern society than for Muslims to disregard similar passages in the Koran. However, in both Christian and Islamic societies, secular customs vary widely in the treatment of women.

From the participants in our conference we derived as much information as possible about different religions and geographical areas concerning the status of women and girls. The delegates from Egypt represented the grand imam, the Coptic pope, the Library of Alexandria, and women activists. Although the final version of the Al-Azhar Declaration on Women's Rights was not issued because of the political turmoil, we were given a working draft that was quite encouraging. A quote from the preamble sets the tone:

> The Islamic point of view regarding the position of women,
> their rights and duties towards themselves, their families
> and their societies, stems from the values which represent
> legal principles and general rules out of which rulings and
> arrangements directed to both men and women are born.
> These represent an equal and comprehensive view of man-
> kind of both genders, with the aim of achieving happiness
> and stability to the individual, the family and society.
> . . . Contemporary women's positions need to be safe-
> guarded, hence the need for this document. For proper posi-
> tioning represents the most important element of reforming
> society and purifying it from wrong practices as well as
> recent social customs that are not based on clear textual evi-
> dence or proper jurisprudence, and which bring injustice and
> pain to men and women, though their toll falls more heavily
> on women.

After a reminder that "the Council of Senior Religious Scholars launches this document free of any outside pressures or transient political leanings," there is this statement:

It comes from a perspective that respects Islamic heritage. Both its principles and branches work to maintain and renovate this heritage according to its own values and logic, while reminding all that these values and rulings represent a leap in the liberation of women in classical Islamic times, on a world scale, when Arab traditions in this field were backward and religious thinking in the medieval European period questioned whether a woman was human or something else! These values and practical principles were implemented in the golden age of Islamic civilization; thus the Muslim woman enjoyed financial independence a thousand years before her peers in the West, and her right to inheritance, suitable employment and unlimited education. In fact, many Imams studied with renowned women scholars themselves. Similarly a woman enjoyed the right to choose a husband, look after the affairs of her family, demand *khul* (annulment of marriage) or separation in the event of damage or need. This is the reason why Muslim societies did not witness familial struggles or women's social revolutions that other societies suffered from.

I have found the grand imam to be remarkably immune to "transient political leanings" and have high expectations for a reasonable and spiritually inspired text when the final document is published. Its balanced position on the rights of Muslim men and women will have a beneficial effect on those spiritual and secular leaders who are seeking to apply the teachings of the Koran in modern times. However, although the grand imam is the spiritual leader of more than 80 percent of all Muslims, political leaders in predominantly Islamic nations are not bound by his statements or declarations on societal relationships.

While Egyptian women are ready to seek change in society, the culture is still not ready to view them as equals. We must

change this by challenging students and religious leaders
to re-think and re-read the Koran for gender justice. As a
Muslim, I believe that Islam came with a feminist revolution
in Arabia. But what we have right now is a very patriarchal,
traditional understanding of Islam, and this understanding
is widespread. Religious leaders must support women's rights
and gender justice in Egypt by leading their followers back
to the true essence of religion: the equality and democratic
nature at the heart of Islam. Despite these restraints, women
are active in the streets of Egypt, in Upper Egypt in the rural
areas. They are defending their voices to be heard, and they
reject marginalization.

DR. RIHAM BAHI, SCHOLAR OF ISLAMIC AND
SECULAR FEMINISM AND ASSOCIATE PROFESSOR AT
THE AMERICAN UNIVERSITY OF CAIRO

When Rosalynn and I founded The Carter Center in 1982 we had
an office on the campus of Emory University. I was teaching
and giving lectures regularly, planning and raising funds for a presidential library, and receiving some visitors who sought appointments with
me to discuss issues left over from my White House years. One of these
requests came from a Coptic priest in America, and I was surprised
when about two dozen priests crowded into my office, all in their sober
black robes and hoods. They explained that their pope, Shenouda III,
was under house arrest in a desert monastery in Egypt and that the
worldwide functions of their faith were severely handicapped because
all official actions were legitimate only if the directives were from their
cathedral, which he was forbidden to visit.

I promised to help and soon learned that the detention order was
supported by President Mubarak. I had known him well as the hand-
picked vice president and personal emissary of President Sadat. I called
Mubarak and told him that I was speaking for the Copts as a fellow
Christian. The pope was released from captivity in January 1985. I became interested in their ancient beliefs and customs, and on subsequent

visits to the Middle East I have attempted to meet with their leaders and to understand their special problems as a minority group in an overwhelmingly Islamic region.

Two of the Coptic participants in our Defenders conference were women, one a psychiatrist and the other a university professor. They gave me a doctrinal booklet entitled *Women*. It summarized the premise that women are equal to men in all religious and secular affairs—*except* when it comes to leadership roles in the Church. This has helped me understand the policies of Roman Catholic and other, more orthodox Christians that prohibit a woman from being ordained as a priest or deacon. I do not agree with this distinction, but I include key excerpts here because so many of my fellow Christians hold this belief and because the text includes some intriguing comments.

Overwhelmingly the treatise disagrees with sexual discrimination derived from the Bible. It explains biblical teachings of sexual equality and also outlines economic history to show the waxing and waning of a woman's role in family life. It begins by stating:

> Man is created twice: The first creation: "God created man in His own image, in the image of God He created him; male and female He created them." (Genesis 1:27) The second creation described by Jesus: "Truly, truly, I say to you, unless one is born of water and the Spirit, he cannot enter the kingdom of God. That which is born of the flesh is flesh, and that which is born of the Spirit is spirit." (John 3:5, 6) The first creation is physical and there is a clear distinction between the male and female sexes, but with no partiality, for both express the image of God. The second creation has no distinction between male and female, for it is a purely spiritual creation. "There is neither male nor female; for you are all one in Christ Jesus." (Galatians 3:28)

The Coptic authors proceed to explain that over time men assumed dominion in the home because they were better suited to hunting, carrying heavy loads, and physically protecting the weaker women and children. When machines were introduced, women found them to be "fearful and dangerous." Men thus used the power of machines to establish their own strength and authority, though in fact the power of the machine was replacing that of man, for the responsibility of running a machine does not depend on physical strength. At this point women woke up and discovered the rights they had lost through their own passivity, revealing the truth of the original statement that God's blessing was granted at the creation to men and women equally and that authority was given to them equally, on condition that they work together in harmony and unity toward a single aim. Equality was proven when women began to be involved in the struggle for a living, learning, and employment and attained the levels of achievement that had for long ages been reserved by men: "The success women attained in every field returned to them all the rights they had surrendered in the false belief that they were created inferior to men."

In the explanation of Paul's letter to the Galatians quoted above, the treatise says, "He deliberately uses the words 'male' and 'female' rather than 'man' and 'woman' to eliminate all aspects of differentiation or discrimination. . . . When a woman is united with Christ she is exactly like a man who is united to Christ, and if a man is united to a woman in Christ, they become in Christ one perfect human being. . . . The Holy Spirit, moreover, does not eliminate the beauty of the first creation, but removes its pitfalls and restores it to its original perfection."

In many places the New Testament describes how Jesus ignored the lowly place of women among Jewish leaders, such as the pious Pharisee who "gave thanks to God every day in his morning prayers that he was not born 'a woman or a leper or an unclean gentile.'" Christ forgave the woman sentenced to death for her adultery, treated as an equal the Samaritan woman who was an outcast among her own despised people by drinking from her cup and sending her into the village as one of the first known evangelists, and appreciated the loyal support of a group of women who "followed him wherever he went and served him in every way they could." Referring to Jesus' followers, the religious pamphlet adds, "The appearance of the women and their going about openly among the crowds, leaving their homes, was a significant event in Israel since it represented an overthrow of the Jewish traditions concerning women and formed part of the official complaint lodged against Christ, which led to his crucifixion: 'We found this man perverting our nation.' " (Luke 23:2)

When the followers of Christ were suffused with the Holy Spirit at the time of Pentecost, the Bible says, "All these with one accord devoted themselves to prayer, together with the women and Mary the mother of Jesus, and with his brothers." (Acts 1:14) The treatise declares:

> The coming of the Holy Spirit upon the women in the same way as He came upon the men, and his filling the women in the same way as He filled the men, is the first permanently effective indication that women had entered into grace and were to be granted equal rights with men in the Kingdom of God. . . . God was aware of how degraded, isolated and abused women had become throughout the ages of the natural law, when man was living by simple skills and was of limited understanding. He Himself took the initiative in order to strike off the fetters that human society had placed on women's hands as on the hands of slaves.

In the Coptic booklet the apostle Paul's declarations that women should keep their heads covered, not cut their hair or wear jewelry, and refrain from speaking out during public worship or assuming a position of leadership are explained as admonitions to address local disturbances by rude and unruly women at services in some particular early church. Paul is also quoted in his letter to the Romans, where he lists heroines of the early Church. It is the same phrase, *fellow-worker*, that Paul uses to describe his associates in the apostolic mission, including Timothy, Titus, and Epaphroditus. In another letter Paul mentions Euodia and Syntyche and adds, "I ask you also, true yokefellow, help these women, for they have labored side by side with me in the Gospel together with

Clement and the rest of my fellow workers whose names are in the book of life." (Philippians 4:2, 3) The Coptic treatise adds, "It is noteworthy that the names of Euodia and Syntyche come before the name of Clement, who became pope of Rome."

This interesting document concludes its analysis of the status of women by rationalizing the policy of the Orthodox Church about excluding women as priests: "So just as the Apostles' wives went with them, having a mission complementary to that of the Apostles in serving the women, just as prophetesses arose in the church alongside the men prophets according to the Gift of the Holy Spirit, though to serve the women, and just as the older women served the church in the same way as older men, and all these with no special ordination rite, so we find alongside the deacons, deaconesses to teach the women also with no special rite of ordination. That is to say, for every service carried out by men there is a service allotted to women." To me, this argument ignores the fact that women prominent in the New Testament ministered to both men and women and leads to the impractical conclusion that there should be separate churches for male and female worshipers, with women apostles, priests, deacons, and bishops leading the worship services attended by women and girls. There are good arguments to be made on both sides of the question of women being equal in serving God, but there can be no justification in extrapolating this to discriminate against and abuse women in our secular society.

I am sure this theological debate will continue about the proper treatment of women, within the Coptic Church and throughout Christendom, and I am equally certain that the words and actions of Jesus Christ will eventually prevail.

We call on all religious leaders throughout the world to take a firm stand and collectively commit to promoting the basic rights of girls and women. This will constitute one of the most important movements in religious history, leading to peace and well-being in our societies. It is a responsibility of any sincere religious leader who seeks to make this world a better place to live. The Carter Center can help bring leaders and people of conscience together for this purpose in a way that will sustain these difficult but necessary efforts to advance equality, justice, dialogue, and peace—across cultures, nations, and continents to assure that our efforts are universal.

SHEIKH MUHAMED CHÉRIF DIOUP,

ISLAMIC RIGHTS SPECIALIST AND

CHILD PROTECTION OFFICER, TOSTAN, SENEGAL

We had several Jewish participants in our Human Rights Defenders Forum, and they described some of the same historical trends and sharp debates among Jewish religious scholars who interpret Holy Scriptures in different ways. The status of the ultra-Orthodox, or Haredim, has changed dramatically since I first visited Israel as governor, primarily because of their high birthrate. They now comprise about 10 percent of the total population and, if current rates continue, are expected to increase to 30 percent in the next three decades. Although some originally refused to become involved in politics, they later formed a number of parties with increasing influence, and in Israel's special form of parliamentary government it has been necessary to include these relatively small groups to give the governing leaders a majority in the Knesset (parliament). This became a matter of sharp debate in the election of January 2013, when the party led by a newcomer to politics, Yair Lapid, won a surprising second place. One of his most popular campaign promises was to eliminate some of the special privileges of the Haredim. To some degree, this issue had been called to public attention by the Haredim's policy of restraining the freedom of women.

The ultra-Orthodox in Israel have always been given tacit permission to control their own neighborhoods, and when they lived in relatively small and clearly defined areas there were few problems. But as their ranks have swelled and different Jewish religious groups have become more integrated within communities, the Haredim's enforcement of strict dress codes, even among passersby on the streets and students entering and leaving schools, has resulted in verbal and physical attacks on women and girls who dress conservatively but in ways that the more strict sects of Haredim consider indecent. Large posters warn women to dress "modestly," and on some bus lines non-Orthodox women are forced to sit in the rear seats or are sometimes forbidden to ride at all. Visual images of women or girls are not permitted, and some ultra-Orthodox men consider it improper to have a nonrelated woman near them or to hear a woman sing or speak in public. This has caused some highly publicized confrontations, especially among the few who are serving in the military. Some women's insistence on worshiping at the Wailing Wall has caused additional personal conflict and resulted in cases now being decided in the judicial system.

These encounters among Israelis of different religious groups have grown increasingly serious, and many are now being resolved through the courts, with some early decisions seeming to be in favor of women's rights. The basic issues are still in doubt and can be resolved only by seminal laws that are being considered by the Knesset concerning the special status of ultra-Orthodox believers and how they are permitted to practice their faith among neighbors who have different beliefs. More women candidates have sought and won seats in the Knesset and now make up 23 percent of its members. There are no women included in the lists of the ultra-Orthodox parties and little indication that wives or daughters in these families are demanding more political or personal rights. It is interesting that 60 percent of these women are in the workforce, while only 45 percent of the men have jobs. There are special government grants to help these devout families support themselves.

As with Christians and Muslims, Jews have come to realize that the basic rights of women are strongly affected by how men choose to interpret and apply the meaning of Holy Scripture. When our mothers, wives, sisters, and daughters are considered both different and inferior in the eyes of the God we worship, this belief tends to permeate society and everyone suffers.

It is difficult for me, as an American Christian, to understand how deprivation of women's rights in Muslim countries can best be confronted and alleviated. At our Human Rights Defenders Forums we listen attentively to participants from different religions and geographical areas, but we refrain from any involvement in their affairs unless requested. One of the most competent and courageous contributors has been Zainah Anwar, who is a defender of human rights for women in Malaysia. She has concentrated on the actual teachings of the Koran and emphasizes that the sacred text of Islam is her most powerful asset. "I am outraged that my religion is distorted and used to justify patriarchy and the discrimination and oppression of women. This totally contradicts what I believe in a just God and a just Islam," she says.

The problem of using a distorted interpretation of Holy Scripture to repress women has been addressed only recently in Western nations, but it began in the 1970s in Malaysia, where women were beginning to receive higher education and become economically independent, and some religious leaders saw this as a threat to their authority. That is when Anwar became active. In 1988 she organized a group called Sisters in Islam (SIS), which petitions the government to reform sexist laws, organizes major conferences, trains women on existing laws and how some contradict their religion, and publicizes their beliefs and activities. They revisit the original teachings of the Koran to prove there is no basis in Islam for viewing women as inferior to men. Anwar explains, "A bunch of us decided that it was really important to find out whether our religion is oppressive toward women, because that's not how we've been brought up to understand Islam."

These women decided not to depend on human rights techniques that were used in the West but to concentrate on the original teachings of the Koran and its message of equality. SIS members point out, "In Islam, everyone is treated equally, and no one comes before the other, and certainly nobody comes from anybody's broken rib. Creation is always spoken of in the Koran in terms of pairs—both are created equal and both are created at the same time, and one is not the derivative of the other." It is not surprising that SIS has earned trust and gratitude in other Islamic countries, as pointed out by Rakhee Goyal, executive director of the Women's Learning Partnership, a nongovernmental organization that works with Muslim women in many regions: "They are at the forefront of study not just in Malaysia but also within Muslim majority societies in looking at how we define the role of women vis-à-vis Islam."

When appropriate, SIS supplements its emphasis on religious law with arguments based on international human rights covenants, national laws, and local social issues. Anwar and her SIS associates are working actively in northwest Africa, Indonesia, the Philippines, and Singapore and have played an important role in the work of The Carter Center. She says, "There is a whole variety of opinions, different interpretations, a multiplicity of laws—this splendid diversity that is part of the Muslim heritage provides us with an incredibly rich source of information, scholarship, and opinion that we can work with to promote our belief in an Islam that upholds the principles of justice and equality, of freedom and dignity."

The work of SIS has aroused opposition in Malaysia, where recent Islamic laws have tended to restrict women's property rights, make polygamy and divorce easier for men, and subvert efforts to thwart domestic violence legislation. This presents Malaysian women with a dilemma, says Anwar. "The choice before us is: Do we accept what these kinds of mullahs are saying, or if we want to be a feminist, do we then reject our religion? For us, rejecting our religion in order to become a feminist is just not a choice. We want to be feminists, and we want to be Muslim as well."

She emphasizes that it is counterproductive for SIS to be too closely associated with Western ideals or organizations:

That [kind of support] doesn't help because those who are not familiar with our work see us as the kind of group that the West wants to develop in Muslim countries. We are not a product of the West; we are a product of our own society and the challenges that we face within our own society. One way for the West to play a productive role is to encourage comprehensive scholarly inquiry into the Islamic canon by developing stronger transnational links between universities. Some of the best work by Muslim scholars is occurring at colleges in the United States and Europe, and these researchers need to be given a platform to speak in places where moderate Islam is under threat. The scholarship that is emerging in the West now is extremely important, and to expose that scholarship, that new thinking, to Muslims in Muslim countries is important.

Upon returning to Ghana after participating in the Carter Center human rights conference, "Mobilizing Faith for Women," we were asked: "Are you on a genuine mission to empower women and make them more productive to support their husbands and families while in marriage? Or are you being paid by your white masters to advance the course of women who develop to become unmanageable, uncontrollable and independent from men?" This is very worrisome because it illustrates the fundamental reasons why we decided to struggle for the rights of the disadvantaged in our communities. The solution is advocacy and training at the top level of Islamic leadership in developing countries. Assisting Imams, Islamic scholars, Muslim chiefs, and opinion leaders as well as youth leaders in this way will advance understanding of the struggle for the empowerment of women and all of us who believe in human rights for all.

ALHAJI KHUZAIMA, EXECUTIVE SECRETARY,
ISLAMIC PEACE AND SECURITY COUNCIL IN GHANA

I was pleased when Pope John Paul II accepted my invitation to visit me during his tour of America in 1979. I remembered that when John Kennedy was campaigning to be the first Catholic president, his critics had predicted that the pope would be a guest in the White House, and in my welcoming speech I remarked that this dire prediction had finally come true. During his stay the pope and I had a long and quite relaxed and informal conversation, as he had requested. We talked about political issues with which I was dealing at the time, a possible visit by him to Jerusalem and the West Bank, religious developments in China in which we both were involved, and our mutual hope that growing competition between Roman Catholics and evangelical Protestants in Latin America would be without rancor.

When I brought up the subjects of the use of condoms to combat sexual diseases or the status of women in the Church, I found him surprisingly conservative concerning any possible changes in Church practice. I asked him if the Catholic Church had gotten stronger or weaker in the previous five years or so, and he replied that it dipped following Vatican II because of the dramatic changes made in Church liturgy and the opinion of many believers that the Church had become too liberal, but he thought it was regaining influence and strength, at least in some parts of the world, as more traditional values were reemphasized. I was aware of the plea of some American nuns to the pope of "the possibility of women . . . being included in all ministries of the church" but didn't pursue this matter further.

Made up of about 80 percent of Catholic nuns in the United States, the Leadership Conference of Women Religious (LCWR) was formed in 1956 with approval from the Vatican "to assist its members [to] carry out public services of leadership to further the mission of the Gospel of Jesus Christ in today's world." Its other avowed goals are to foster dialogue and collaboration within the Church and in the larger community and to strengthen relationships with groups concerned with the needs of society, thereby enhancing the potential for effecting change. This relatively progressive commitment was reinforced by the results of Vatican II (1962–65), which was convened under Pope John XXIII, when some of the more stringent controls of the Vatican were loosened and there was an implication that the Church would accommodate more influence from sisters. In 1979, during the visit of Pope John Paul II to the United States, the president of LCWR made a formal plea for more involvement of women. Since then, most Church leaders have continued to emphasize "bedroom" issues, including abortion, birth control, and homosexuality, and have also affirmed a rigid adherence to the traditional role of women that excludes their admission to the priesthood or other positions of authority. It is estimated that there are now only about a third the number of nuns in America as during the time of Vatican II, but they remain active and have made some specific requests for consideration.

Despite being told by the Vatican to stop talking about their ordination as deacons or priests, some nuns have continued to demand more gender equality in the Catholic Church. In February 2009 the Vatican under Pope Benedict XVI announced that a "doctrinal assessment" of the LCWR would be conducted because of the tenor of their official statements and the content of certain speeches at the organization's annual assemblies. After the assessment was completed, an archbishop from Seattle was appointed to oversee changes in the LCWR to correct what were considered to be positions that differed from Church teachings on sexuality and "certain radical feminist themes incompatible with the Catholic faith."

The sisters pushed back. They have denied any radical feminist tendencies, misbehavior, or deviation from the Church's position on any issue, and explained their reasoning behind previous positions. Some of them expressed a belief that the present pontiff, Pope Francis, was not adequately informed about the history of the dispute between themselves and the Vatican, and in May 2013 the pope made a statement

JIMMY CARTER | 110

intended to correct what he considered to be a mistake and demanded obedience to the Church and its doctrines, citing this as inseparable from the divinity of Jesus Christ. This dispute within the Church is still unresolved, but some nuns, if not the LCWR officially, seem resolute, especially in their request for women to be included in all ministries of the Church. A group called the Women's Ordination Conference works solely for the ordination of women as priests, deacons, and bishops.

Dr. Phyllis Zagano of Hofstra University sent me the following statement on the subject, which seems to be correct but is perhaps optimistic:

> The Catholic Church requires that individuals with real authority be clerics, that is, ordained persons. The ordinary means of entering the clerical state is by ordination to the diaconate. Despite the Church's objections to ordaining women as priests, discussion about restoring women to the ordained diaconate—an ancient Christian tradition—continues to grow internationally, especially after Pope Francis gave a fairly unqualified "yes" to the concept on his plane ride back from the 2013 World Youth day in Rio de Janeiro. More recently, in August, the pope said, directly, "It is necessary to widen the space for more incisive feminine presence in the church." Catholic deacons are charged with ministry of the Word, the Liturgy, and Charity. They cannot celebrate Eucharist (say Mass) or hear confessions, but can baptize and witness marriages, proclaim the Gospel during Mass, and can hold certain Church offices. More importantly, ordained persons—in this case deacons, who serve *in persona Christi servi* (in the person of Christ, servant)—represent the Risen Christ. For the Catholic Church to ordain a woman and have that woman proclaim the Gospel in St. Peter's would send the strongest possible message to the world that women are made in the image and likeness of God, that women can and do represent Christ.

Nuns are not the only Catholics convinced that women should be permitted to serve as deacons and priests. A public opinion poll by CBS News and the *New York Times* in 2013 reported that 70 percent of U.S. Catholics believe that Pope Francis should authorize women to become priests. There are also a number of long-serving and dedicated priests who have expressed this belief. One of the most noteworthy is Father Roy Bourgeois, who was ordained in 1972 and assigned to work in a slum near La Paz in Bolivia. He was arrested and deported when he criticized the Bolivian dictator, Hugo Banzer, for abuse of poor people, and he then turned his attention to an example of oppression in El Salvador. When Archbishop Oscar Romero was assassinated and four nuns were raped and murdered by Salvadoran military troops who had been trained at Fort Benning, Georgia, Father Bourgeois demonstrated against American involvement in strengthening dictatorships throughout Latin America. He was arrested, convicted, and sentenced to serve eighteen months in prison. The military training program continued and the *Washington Post* reported that techniques of torture were added to the curriculum in 1982. In 1989 U.S.-trained graduates led troops into Jesuit University in San Salvador and killed six priests, plus their servants.

In 1995 Father Bourgeois wrote a letter to Pope John Paul II, urging that priests be permitted to marry and that women be treated as equals. Two years later he participated in a conference in Rome and repeated this proposal during a public radio broadcast. There was no response from the Vatican, but after he took part in the ordination as a priest of Janice Sevre-Duszynska in Lexington, Kentucky, in 2008, he was notified that he had brought "grave scandal" to the Church and would be excommunicated if he did not recant. He replied that he could not betray his conscience, and continued his role as priest and public supporter of equal rights for women. Three years later he received a similar notice from his immediate superior, with a fifteen-day deadline for compliance. He responded that he had been a Catholic priest for thirty-nine years and added, "In my ministry over the years I have met many devout women in our Church who believe God is calling them to be priests. Why wouldn't they be called? God created men and women of equal dignity and, as we all know, the call to be a priest comes from God." He joined an international delegation that went to the Vatican to deliver a petition from fifteen thousand supporters of women's ordination as priests, and in November 2012 he received a final official notice that he was "dispensed of his sacred bonds" as a priest. Father Bourgeois stated that he regretted the decision but was filled with hope that women will one day be treated as equal to men.

The Vatican's position can best be described by an edict issued in May 2010, "Normae de gravioribus delictis," that the attempted sacred ordination of a woman is one of the gravest substantive canonical crimes in the Church, on a par with sexually abusing a child. (Very few priests have been excommunicated who were found guilty of child abuse.) Although there is no current sign, even from newly chosen Pope Francis, that rigid Church doctrine is likely to change, there are some practical trends that may force reconsideration in the future. One is the obvious and almost universal practice of Catholic families of ignoring the mandate against the use of contraceptives to limit family size; another is the knowledge that the prohibition against the use of condoms contributes to the spread of AIDS. Bishops and priests look the other way when contraception is practiced in Africa and other regions and do not confront the issue when their own parishes are involved. A troubling trend within the Church organization is the growing shortage of celibate men who come forward to be priests and the possible effect this sexual restraint has had on the worldwide scandal of priests found guilty of child abuse. There are now more than fifty thousand parishes in the world that do not have an assigned priest, and the need for more parish leaders is even greater in the United States, where the number of priests has steadily dropped, from 58,909 in 1975 to fewer than 39,600 in 2013.

It is known that the first pope, Saint Peter, was married, because Jesus healed his mother-in-law. Because of these kinds of biblical premises and other pressures to emulate the ministry of Christ among parishioners, there may come a time when Catholic priests are permitted to marry and qualified women are called to serve God on an equal basis. Until that time, the enormous influence of the Church could be used forcefully to condemn sexual assaults, genital cutting, child marriage, inadequate pay for women, honor killings, and deprivation of equal rights for women in economic and political affairs. I have written a letter to Pope Francis outlining these opportunities to improve the status of women without addressing the sensitive issue of women as priests. In the Vatican's response, His Holiness thanked me for my concern and reiterated his insistence on "the need to create still broader opportunities for a more incisive female presence in the Church." He also believes that "demands that the legitimate rights of women be respected, based on the firm conviction that men and women are equal in dignity, present the Church with profound and challenging questions which cannot be evaded."

I am pleased that many other Christian denominations are modifying outmoded traditions and responding to pressure from individual worshipers by treating women as equal to men in all aspects of religious life. As is the custom in some Baptist churches, members of our congregation meet in conference to make all significant decisions, including the democratic election of pastors, deacons, and committee members. As I mentioned earlier, we have a male and a female pastor, and half of our deacons are women (including my wife). Our church is affiliated with the Cooperative Baptist Fellowship, and the recently elected leader of this denomination is also a woman. It has long been customary to have women as pastors among African American churches, and in November 2013 the governing body of the Anglican Church voted to move forward a proposal to allow the appointment of women bishops; a final vote will likely take place in 2014. This is part of a general and inexorable trend among Methodists, Presbyterians, Episcopalians, Lutherans, and other major Protestant denominations in all nations to adopt this same enlightened policy. There have been extended and sometimes heated debates in their annual conferences, but ultimately the collective will has prevailed. It seems that those who are resisting change are losing both numbers and influence among their members in crucial societal matters.

10 | THE GENOCIDE OF GIRLS

During our 1981 visit to rural China, we found local officials very proud of their strictly enforced family planning program. The nation's population then was just exceeding a billion, and the common slogan throughout China was "One is best, two at most." We were already familiar with attempts to control the population in another large country, when my mother served as a Peace Corps volunteer in India. Prime Minister Indira Gandhi requested that as a registered nurse she teach sex education to poor families and assist the local doctor in performing mandatory vasectomies on fathers after their first child. Mama objected but had to comply.

In China we saw a number of billboards and posters depicting two happy parents walking through a public park or other nice place and proudly holding the hands of their only child. In every case the child was a boy. At the time, we presumed that this was just the choice of the photographer, but over the years I have come to realize that parents' special pride in a male child would have serious consequences.

Historically, on a global basis, slightly more males than females have been born, a natural disparity that anthropologists and demographers cannot explain. In a few nations, however, there has been a significant deviation from this ratio, indicating the result of a preference for boys. World Health Organization data show that in India the ratio of girls to boys is 100 to 112. When sex ratio studies began in China in 1960, they found 100 females to 106 males, near the upper border of the normal range. In 1990 the discrepancy had increased to 100 females to 112 males, and by 2010 the ratio was 100 to 118. The *PBS News Hour* reports that in some areas of India there are only 650 girl babies living for every 1,000 boys, a ratio of 100 to 154! Infanticide, either at the time of birth or later, seems to be the cause. With the availability of sonogram examinations, a new option was presented to parents, who can ascertain the sex of a developing fetus as early as twelve weeks after conception. Inexpensive sonograms can now be hooked up to laptop computers and are widely available even in remote rural areas. In some places the abortion of female fetuses is relatively easy and legal and has even been encouraged.

When these percentages are multiplied by the total number of children born in some of the world's largest nations, the number of girls that have been eliminated by abortion, neglect, or murder is horrendous. The Indian Nobel Laureate Amartya Sen estimated in 1990 that there were 50 million females "missing" in China, and more than 105 million worldwide. Almost all of the decisions to terminate the existence of these girls were made privately, within families, and not ordained by governments. Shadowline Films produced a documentary entitled *It's a Girl* that had its Hong Kong premiere in November 2013. One episode presents a mother in India who states calmly that she has strangled eight of her newborn daughters. This selective murder of girls is called *female gendercide* or *femicide*.

In India sexual discrimination also occurs among children who survive birth. A UN Children's Fund report issued in October 2013 reveals that India accounts for 20 percent of child mortality worldwide. Although there has been some improvement in recent years, India's under-five child mortality rate in 2012 was 56 deaths per 1,000. By comparison, the rate in equally poor Bangladesh was 41; in Brazil, 14; and in the United States, 7. A special tragedy is that 131 little girls died in India compared to each 100 boys of the same age.

Efforts in India, China, and South Korea to outlaw gendercide or the use of sonograms for the same purpose have been predictably unsuccessful. Mara Hvistendahl is a contributing editor to *Science* magazine, and in 2012 she wrote *Unnatural Selection: Choosing Boys over Girls, and the Consequences of a World Full of Men*. In this carefully researched book, she estimates that there are now at least 160 million missing females. This is equivalent to an entire generation of girls being wiped from the face of the earth. To put this into perspective, it is estimated that 500,000 Tutsis were killed in the Rwanda genocide of 1994, and that 6 million Jews were victims of the Nazi Holocaust.

Most of these lethal decisions are still concentrated in the Asian countries mentioned above, but the option of femicide is also exercised in smaller nations and in the more advanced Western world. It appears that more than twice as many girls have been killed by their parents during my lifetime as the total number of combatants and civilians lost in World War II.

One unanticipated result has been a disturbing shortage of brides and a demand for prostitutes to assuage the desires of men without partners. News reports from South Korea indicate that imported brides from less affluent Asian nations are selling for a high price. The latest data show that 12 percent of all marriages of South Korean men are with foreign women from Vietnam, Cambodia, the Philippines, and Japan. There is a thriving market, with the price of a bride ranging from US\$88 to US\$660. The girls' parents receive from US\$11 to US\$22. The organization Human Rights in China reports that it is usually cheaper to buy a bride from traffickers for about US\$320 to US\$640 than to pay the normal bride price, which is often two to five times higher. Chinese police report that an average of 17,500 women who were sold into marriage or slavery against their will are rescued each year. Between 1991 and 1996, 143,000 human traffickers were arrested and prosecuted.

This pervasive elimination of girls, both before and after birth, is obvious and well known, but it continues. Preventive laws have been ineffective, and the only apparent solution is to convince parents that a daughter can, in all respects, be an asset to the family. This can be accomplished only by ensuring that girls are educated and given equal opportunities to develop their talents, to earn an income, and to serve their family and community.

11 | RAPE

According to the U.S. Justice Department, there were 191,610 cases of rape or sexual assault in the United States in 2006, and 91 percent of the victims were female. That's more than 475 women assaulted every day. The estimate is that only 16 percent of these cases are reported to the police; the rate drops to fewer than 5 percent on college campuses. Girls and women of all ages and all backgrounds suffer from the same or worse sexual violence throughout the world, and some traditional practices constitute, extol, and perpetuate sexual violence against women and girls.

Radha Kumar is an author and expert on ethnic conflicts and has been a director at the Nelson Mandela Centre for Peace and Conflict Resolution in New Delhi. She describes rape in India as one of the nation's most common crimes against women, and the UN's High Commissioner for Human Rights asserts that it is a "national problem." India's National Crime Records Bureau reports that rape cases have doubled between 1990 and 2008. There were 24,206 cases registered in India in 2011 (one every twenty-two minutes), and many attacks go unreported. The gang rape in Delhi of a twenty-three-year-old student on a bus in December 2012 is one of the most horrible examples: she was raped by several men, who then used an iron rod to penetrate her genitals so deeply that her intestines had to be surgically removed. She died thirteen days later.

There was a tremendous public outcry in India and abroad, and in September 2013 the rapists were sentenced to be hanged. Many have supported the sentence, but human rights activists are raising the alarm that executing these men might actually harm the cause of women's rights. Divya Iyer, a senior researcher at Amnesty International, makes a compelling case: "The death penalty does not offer a transformative idea in a social context where violence against women often involves notions of honor. It does not change patriarchal attitude and feudal mindset that trivialize and condone violence against women—be it from the man on the bus or a senior politician. . . . The debate around the death penalty deflects attention from the harder procedural and institutional reform that the government must bring about to tackle violence against women more effectively." This gets to the heart of the matter. Effective law enforcement is crucial, but financial and human resources are not expended on those government functions that actually will prevent sexual violence.

It seems remarkable that such violence is occurring in a Hindu society in which there are many female deities and in which the Sanskrit saying "Mata, Pita, Guru, Deva" (Mother, Father, Teacher, God) emphasizes how prominent are mothers in the life of a Hindu family. In August 2013 the *New York Times* ran an intriguing article by Vinita Bharadwaj, an Indian journalist now based in Dubai who described her life in India as being subject to "stares, glares, whistles, hoots, shout-outs, songs, 'accidental' brushing-past, intentional grabbing, groping and pinching" by men. In addition to enforcement of the existing laws by police and the courts, she writes, "what India desperately needs is a women's revolution, led by men—fathers, sons, grandfathers, brothers, uncles, nephews, boyfriends, husbands, and lovers who are comfortable with the rise of their women. It's a change that must begin in our homes."

In 1994 the world witnessed the terrible slaughter by extremist Hutus in Rwanda of an estimated 500,000 ethnic Tutsis and thousands of Hutus who opposed the killing campaign. Retribution came quickly as Tutsi-led rebel forces routed the Hutu government forces causing an evacuation of the country by Hutus fearing further retribution. A million Hutus fled across the border into eastern Zaire, many to a massive refugee camp in the city of Goma. Large numbers also fled east to Tanzania. All the nations of the Great Lakes region (Uganda, Tanzania, Kenya, Zaire, Rwanda, and Burundi) suffered greatly from the upheaval and violence. Former Hutu soldiers in the refugee camps rearmed and began raiding across the Zaire-Rwanda border.

When United Nations efforts to bring about a regional peace conference collapsed in 1995, the leaders of the Great Lakes region reached out to me and The Carter Center. We explored what needed to be done. Rosalynn and I visited the enormous refugee camp in Goma, where large numbers of people moved in and out, and the small staff made it clear that very little order could be maintained. Rape and abuse of women were rampant. The Carter Center launched a major effort to bring peace. We brought together all the presidents of the region in Cairo in November 1995 and in Tunis in March 1996. Agreements were reached that should have moved the region forward. However, international support was not forthcoming and the agreements were not implemented.

The ramifications included a terrible civil war in Zaire. The victor, Laurent-Désiré Kabila, named himself president and changed the name of the country back to the Democratic Republic of the Congo (DRC). Kabila was assassinated in 2001 and was succeeded by his son Joseph.

The Carter Center has continued its interest in the DRC, and we have monitored two nationwide elections since then. The 2006 election was well run and relatively free and fair, but the election five years later was marred by misconduct and resulted in a crisis of legitimacy for the reelected President Kabila. Throughout this time the Rwandan government has supported militia forces in eastern Congo in order to promote its interests there, including the transfer of Congo's bountiful precious minerals to overseas markets.

The terrible aftermath of these military and political events has been one of the worst epidemics of rape in history, as Tutsi, Hutu, and Congolese militiamen surge back and forth in control of disputed territory and systematically and brazenly abuse women in the areas they control. In addition to sexual gratification, the soldiers use bottles, sticks, and even bayonets to torture the women and to declare their masculine supremacy. They treat this practice as a prerogative of warfare. In November 2012 Congolese troops trained by the U.S. government perpetrated a mass rape of 135 women and girls in the eastern town of Minova, which received little response from the international community. The Congo has become known as the "world capital of rape." Despite this terrible sexual carnage, neither the secretary-general nor the UN Security Council has chosen to make these crimes a top priority.

There is a remarkable incidence of rape in the region of southern Africa, as recorded by the South African Medical Research Council in 2009 and by the *Lancet Global Health* journal in 2013. Interviews of thousands of men revealed that more than 20 percent in Tanzania, 26 percent in South Africa, and 34 percent in eastern Congo had "forced a woman not [their] wife or girlfriend to have sex." In most other developing nations, only 2 to 4 percent of men gave this response, and the level was lower in the industrialized world. The basic causes for this sexual abuse against women and girls were determined to be the combination of a strongly patriarchal society, tribal divisions, minimal law enforcement, and extreme poverty. Official condemnation by the UN Security Council and enforcement of the International Violence Against Women Act (IVAWA) and other laws are the only potential remedies for this plague of violence. As will be seen, there is encouraging progress in this area being made by a British diplomat and a Hollywood actress.

The blame for sexual abuse is often placed on the victim. We have 776 citizens living in Plains, and there are usually between seventy-five and a hundred Hispanics; almost all have legal work permits and jobs in local companies, but only a few are American citizens. Our small church has a regular ministry among the most deprived families of all races, using funds from the sale of audio and video tapes of my Bible lessons. Rosalynn participates in the monthly visits to about thirty homes at a time. The Hispanic workers are especially dedicated to their jobs and are extremely careful not to violate any laws because they do not wish to be deported. Under Georgia's oppressive legislation, they are not permitted to obtain a driver's license and therefore have to walk or ride a bicycle to their job or to do their shopping. They send as much of their income as possible back to their families in Latin America, and occasionally some will make a bus trip to visit their home country.

Recently one of our church friends returned to Mexico, leaving his wife and children in Plains. A man broke into their home, threatened the children, and raped their mother. She called our pastor, who reported the crime to the local police and also to her husband. The rapist evaded the authorities, and the husband blamed his wife for the rape and refused to return. The wife and children feared for their safety and moved to another town about thirty miles away to live with an aunt. Blaming the victim, even among my neighbors, is all too common.

Myanmar (formerly Burma) suffered under a despotic military dictatorship for more than fifty years, but the election of 2011 resulted in legitimately chosen leaders, almost all former high military officers who initiated a remarkable transformation toward freedom and democracy. As the country moves toward its next election in 2015,

The Carter Center will maintain a permanent presence to observe the electoral process and to assist as requested in overcoming the many challenges still facing the different ethnic and religious groups that are learning to live together in a more liberated society. One of the most formidable problems is the conflict that has erupted as the overwhelming Buddhist majority dominates the minority Muslims in Rakhine State near Bangladesh and Christians who are concentrated mostly in Kachin State on the border with China.

A related challenge is to formulate cease-fire agreements between the central government and more than a dozen regional ethnic groups and then to write a permanent constitution that will guarantee political, economic, and social equity among them.

I have visited Myanmar twice while writing this book and have learned from multiple sources how women and girls are bearing the brunt of the existing conflict and discrimination. I met with leaders of religious groups who are Roman Catholic, Protestant, Muslim, Hindu, and Buddhist and found them compatible with each other. When I asked them about the status of women, almost all responded that within their religious group "women are treated as equals—but considered to be either separate or different." This reminded me of my childhood days, when black people were legally considered "separate but equal." They were kept largely separate and certainly not treated as equals.

Still existing in Myanmar are camps for internally displaced persons who have been forced from their homes by strife or prejudice. I was given the results of a scholarly study conducted in Kachin State of the special problems of women and girls among this group. It is particularly interesting because it is the only study I have found that describes the situation that likely prevails in most camps for displaced persons and refugees in the world. With very few separate facilities for toilets, sleeping, or bathing, all sexual encounters are fraught with violence and danger, and the consumption of alcohol and drugs aggravates the situation. There are no doors to separate living areas, but only flaps of canvas and cloth. Children of all ages are in danger when left alone by their parents, and spousal abuse is common when wives object to a lack of privacy during sex or are fearful of pregnancy because no birth control is available. Women claim that it is fruitless to report sexual abuse because the administrators are usually men and frequently among the worst culprits, and their response to the women is most often laughter or a wave of dismissal. Any remaining restraints are ignored when a cease-fire is broken and armed troops of another tribe or religion invade the area. These abused and fearful women and girls can only pray for a time of peace and law enforcement.

The military is still dominant in Myanmar, with their half-century accumulation of wealth, property, and influence, and also with the right of the top commanding officer to appoint (and peremptorily remove) 25 percent of the members of the Parliament. When I met with him on two visits he extolled the performance of his troops in maintaining order and assisting (but not interfering with) the local police. He said that the only role for women in the military is to serve in the medical corps and that he had never appointed any women to parliamentary seats, but he promised to consider this option in the future. (In January 2014, I was informed that two female officers have been chosen as legislators.)

In areas of conflict between armed combatants or where displaced persons have no homes and are crowded into camps, the prevailing atmosphere of violence is combined with the loss of normal family privacy and mutual protection. Women, children, and other defenseless people become especially vulnerable to abuse. All too often, this tragic situation is condoned by local officials and ignored by the international community.

12 | SLAVERY AND PROSTITUTION

The world experienced a gigantic political, economic, and military struggle during the nineteenth century to end the blight of trafficking in human beings, primarily from Africa to the New World in ships owned by Europeans. During the three and a half centuries of the transatlantic slave trade, it is estimated that 12.5 million slaves were taken from Africa to the Americas. This was a terrible and unforgivable example of abuse of people.

My great-great-grandfather, Wiley Carter, owned several dozen slaves when he died during the last year of the War Between the States. Family records show that when they were freed soon thereafter, his estate lost two-thirds of its monetary value. As I write, we are commemorating the 150th anniversary of the decisive Battle of Gettysburg, where my great-grandfather and his two brothers fought under General Robert E. Lee. The Civil War was the most deadly single event in our nation's history, and there was, at least eventually, a sigh of relief from both sides that the time of slavery was over.

Although there is no longer any legal slavery in the world, the Global Slavery Index report released in October 2013 estimates that 29.8 million people remain enslaved today. Using a broader definition of slavery, this includes those living in bondage as forced laborers, those in marriages against their will, and prostitutes engaged involuntarily in the sexual trade. The UN International Labor Organization reports that there are now approximately 20.9 million people engaged in forced labor. *Foreign Affairs* magazine observes, "Slavery and the global slave trade continue to thrive to this day; in fact, it is likely that more people are being trafficked across borders against their will now than at any point in the past."

Modern slavery generates approximately $32 billion in profits each year, about half of which goes to rich industrialized nations such as our own. The Global Slavery Index listed the United States as currently having almost sixty thousand people in bondage, while Mauritania ranks highest in the percentage of its citizens who are slaves (about 4 percent). When I first visited its capital, Nouakchott, in 1994 and raised the subject, the president and other top officials claimed that they had passed laws to prohibit the crime but admitted that the practice was so ingrained in the culture of some regions that it was impossible to control. More than 1.1 percent of India's citizens are living in bondage, a total of 13,956,010, by far the highest of any nation, with China second at 2,949,243.

Many books have been written about the modern slave trade. The author of one of the most definitive and thoroughly researched is Siddharth Kara, who was born in Tennessee but spent much of his youth in India. He is a former investment banker, business executive, lawyer, and director of Free the Slaves, an organization devoted to exposing and abolishing slavery. He has spent several years of his life traveling to the nations most deeply involved in the procurement, movement, and exploitation of slaves and has conducted thousands of interviews with people living in slavery. Kara has used his business training to estimate the illicit profits derived from these criminal activities within individual regions and countries. Using the same definition as the Slavery Index, he agrees that there are about 30 million people in the world who are living unwillingly under the domination of their masters.

Kara estimates that those who own and operate brothels can acquire a slave prostitute for less than $1,000 in Asia and from $2,000 to $8,000 in Western Europe and North America, with a worldwide average price of $1,900. The annual net profit to the slave's owner is about $29,000. Even in comparison with crime cartels engaged in the drug trade this is an attractive business; whereas cocaine or opium can be consumed only once, the sexual services of a woman can be sold thousands of times each year. Police and other local officials who condone or even participate in prostitution are at much less risk than those assigned to deal with the trade in illicit drugs, and by claiming that the prostitutes are selling their favors freely they can rationalize their complicity in the women's brutal duress. Kara concludes that the best way to combat the sex trade in young women and girls who have been seduced or abducted into forced prostitution is to concentrate on the male customers, who provide the enormous financial profits that keep the slave masters and brothel owners in business.

The U.S. State Department estimates that about 800,000 people are traded across international borders each year, and 80 percent of these victims are women and girls. More than three-fourths of them are sold into the sex trade. During our recent Human Rights Defenders Forum at The Carter Center, it was reported that between two hundred and three hundred children are sold in Atlanta alone each month! Our city is considered to be one of the preeminent human trafficking centers in the United States, perhaps because we have the busiest airport in the world and because, until recently, the penalty for someone convicted of selling another human being was only a $50 fine. A much heavier penalty of up to twenty years' imprisonment can be imposed by the federal government, but only if there is proof that the trafficking took place across state lines.

An analysis by Atlanta social workers found that 42 percent of the sexual exchanges they investigated were in brothels and hotel rooms in the most affluent areas of the city, while only 9 percent were in the poorer neighborhoods in the vicinity of the airport. Like Kara, they too conclude that the primary culprits are the men who buy sexual favors and the male pimps and brothel owners who control the women and garner most of the financial gains. Lax law enforcement, from top political officials to police on the street, is always a crucial element in the sex trade.

Modern social media have resulted in an interesting and tragic development in the field of prostitution in America: housewives and others who sell themselves for sexual purposes through the Internet. Although there are some apparent advantages to the women in eliminating the control of pimps and brothel owners and retaining their entire fee, there can be tragic consequences to operating in an environment that is not familiar to them and without having anyone to provide a modicum of protection. Since their activities are illegal and embarrassing if revealed, they are also unlikely to report brutality or sexual abuse to law enforcement officials.

In July 2013 the *New York Times* ran a feature story entitled "The New Prostitutes" that described the experiences of ten of these women, all of whom had advertised their services on Craigslist, Backpage, TheEroticReview, or one of the hundreds of other available websites. The women met their temporary partners in their own home or in a rented apartment or hotel room. Their rates ranged from $250 to $400 per hour, and they often made as much as $2,000 on a busy night. The bodies of all ten women were found buried in sand dunes or alongside highways on Long Island. Economist Scott Cunningham, at Baylor University, surveyed the sex market in New York City in 2009 and found that an average of 1,690 sex-worker ads were posted online every day.

It is known that teenage girls are sold by pimps and placed in brothels in all large American cities, almost invariably with the local police being complicit or waiting for "more important" things to command their attention. There was no comprehensive law to prosecute domestic or international traffickers in the United States prior to October 2000, when the Trafficking Victims Protection Act (TVPA) was enacted. President George W. Bush announced that the TVPA was designed to (1) prevent human trafficking at home and overseas, (2) protect victims and support them in rebuilding their lives in the United States, and (3) prosecute the traffickers. The law also allows victims of international trafficking to become temporary U.S. residents and avoid immediate deportation. It was strengthened three years later, when $200 million was authorized to combat human trafficking.

It is hard to know how many women and girls are trafficked in India, but the U.S. State Department, the United Nations, and India's Human Rights Commission have identified that country as a major hub in the international sex trade. Poverty is a major factor. Many desperate parents are enticed by promises of training and employment of their daughters, and sell them to traffickers who promise that a portion of the girls' earnings will be returned to them. Rapid urbanization and the migration of large numbers of men into India's growing cities create a market for commercial sex, as does the gender imbalance resulting from sex-selective abortion practices that has created a generation of young men who have little hope of finding a female partner. The relative affluence in some communities is also a factor, luring foreign women into the sex trade. The caste system compounds the problem; many victims of sex trafficking come disproportionately from disadvantaged segments of India's society.

The trafficking of girls from Nepal into India has been the focus of much international attention. UNICEF reported that as many as seven thousand women and girls are trafficked out of Nepal to India every year, and around 200,000 are now working in Indian brothels. They are induced to leave their home communities by promises of lucrative jobs in Kathmandu or across the border in India, marriages to attractive husbands, free education, training to be beauty technicians, teachers, or nurses or to sell popular consumer products. Some girls have been forcefully abducted from the streets. Once in the hands of their traffickers, they are transported to their destination, raped, beaten, or drugged into submission, and then delivered to a brothel to service numerous men each day or to an "owner" who can use them as slaves. Escape is discouraged by warnings of worse physical punishment, incarceration under vigilant supervision, or threats to the girls' families back home.

Top Nepalese law enforcement officials inform me that they know of the many thousands of Nepalese women enslaved in sexual or other servitude every year, but that it is quite easy for the traffickers to obtain false high-quality passports and visas to transport them to rich communities in a foreign country. There are orders from some Arab nations for women who will serve as second or later brides, mostly for the work they will be forced to do within their husband's household. The books I have read about the lucrative global system of slavery always cite Nepal as one of the worst examples. Neither the former monarchy nor the new democracy (still struggling to form a government and draft a constitution) provides protection for poor and vulnerable families, in which parents often bemoan the birth of a daughter and celebrate with the community when the newborn baby is a boy. Every effort is made to educate boys, but fewer than 5 percent of women are literate in some of the poorer communities.

We have visited Nepal several times, to climb in the Himalayas and more recently to help monitor their elections and help them form a government. While there to prepare for the election held in November 2013, Rosalynn and I had an opportunity to meet with a group of young women who had escaped sexual slavery. The organization that was helping with the rescue and providing protection was known as Stop Girl Trafficking (SGT) and was financed largely by a longtime friend of ours, Richard Blum. He and Sir Edmund Hillary, who was the first to climb Mount Everest, are the founders of the American Himalayan Foundation, which has many other benevolent projects in the region. Richard explained to us on the way to Kathmandu that SGT had been working closely with the Rural Health and Education Service Trust (RHEST) for fifteen years. The primary tool that RHEST has found to be effective in sustaining the freedom of the rescued women is to provide them with an education. This restores their self-respect and assures that literacy and marketable skills can sustain them and their families in the future.

The young women who met with us were relaxed and unrestrained as they recounted their experiences and their plans for productive lives in the future. There were outbursts of laughter as they described circumstances or events in their past, which helped to prevent any embarrassment as they discussed some of the intimate details. None had been enrolled in school at the time they were taken into captivity, and they all agreed that their current classrooms were the best places to prepare for the future. Some had not been reconciled with their family after their parents learned of their forced sexual activities, but they were either resigned to the familial estrangement or expressed the hope that their future would improve the relationship. Many of them had been helped to escape from bondage by friends who were familiar with SGT, and they told us that they looked for opportunities to help those who were still enslaved.

The SGT and RHEST leaders expected to have ten thousand women and girls in their program during the year 2013. This will include a large number who had been indentured servants, "rented" by wealthier families from among those people in Nepal who are *dalits* (untouchables). The rich family pays an agent about $50, of which the girl's family gets about $14. Each year a new transaction is concluded. Some are treated well; others are beaten, denied any educational opportunities, and often attacked sexually by the men or boys in the house.

After we thanked the women for their testimonies and had a round of photographs, we heard from administrators of SGT about their efforts to address the root causes of slavery by working for more effective legislation, improving protection for girls in the poorest families, creating public education programs about this cancer in their midst, and offering educational opportunities to the younger girls in the most vulnerable families. There was special concern about the common practice of forced child marriage in Nepal. The interim constitution of 2006 set the legal marriage age of women at twenty, but the penalty for violation is only annulment of the marriage and a fine of $8. The consequence for the child bride is that she is disgraced and unfit for a more appropriate husband. The willing, usually poverty-stricken parents of the girls accede to opportunities to receive a small payment or to reduce the number of mouths they have to feed. A young bride is often not expected to serve as a wife and mother but as just another servant in her new home. When I asked some we met if they would rather be sold into slavery or sold as a child bride, all said that a forced marriage would be the worse of the two terrible choices.

It is important to note that forced prostitution is most prevalent in societies where "nice" girls are strictly protected until marriage. Young men and others turn to prostitutes for sexual gratification and are often able and willing to pay more for younger girls. There is a large bonus for the rare virgin.

Violence against women remains one of the greatest ills of our time. It is shameful that for many women and girls walking in the streets, relaxing in parks, going to work, or even staying at home can become a brutal experience. When women and girls feel unsafe, half of humanity is unsafe. Violence against women and girls is perpetuated by centuries of male dominance and gender-based discrimination. But the roles that have traditionally been assigned to men and women in society are a human construct—there is nothing divine about them. Religious leaders have a responsibil-

ity to address these historic injustices. Respect for human
dignity should not be dependent on whether one is a male
or a female.

MONA RISHMAWI, OFFICE OF THE UNITED NATIONS
HIGH COMMISSIONER FOR HUMAN RIGHTS

To address the worldwide problem of millions of people being enslaved, the U.S. State Department is required to file a Trafficking
in Persons Report annually to indicate how other nations are combat-
ing slavery and to encourage them to be more aggressive in their efforts.
The latest report, in 2013, included 188 countries and measured them in
three categories, or tiers, according to how well they met eleven bench-
marks. Tier 1 includes thirty countries that have met the minimum
standards to combat slavery but acknowledge that they can make more
progress; tier 2 comprises ninety-two countries that have made some
tangible effort but do not meet the minimum standards; and there are
twenty-one countries in tier 3 that have taken no affirmative steps to
fight human trafficking. These are the eleven criteria:

1. Prohibit trafficking and punish acts of trafficking.
2. Prescribe punishment commensurate with that for other serious
   crimes.
3. Make serious and sustained efforts to eliminate trafficking.
4. Vigorously investigate and prosecute acts of trafficking.
5. Protect victims of trafficking; encourage victims' assistance in
   investigation and prosecution.
6. Provide victims with legal alternatives to their removal to punitive countries and ensure that trafficked victims are not inap-
   propriately penalized.
7. Adopt measures, such as public education, to prevent trafficking.
8. Cooperate with other governments in investigating and prosecuting trafficking.
9. Extradite persons charged with trafficking as with other serious
   crimes.

10. Monitor immigration and emigration patterns for evidence of trafficking, and assure that law enforcement agencies respond to such evidence.

11. Investigate and prosecute public officials who participate, facilitate, or condone trafficking.

U.S. government officials acknowledge that, although our country meets the minimum tier 1 standards, there are many challenges still to be met. In addition to the mostly female sexual slaves that are sold freely in America, there are those in our country who are held as prisoners and forced to work under duress because they have immigrated illegally. Often they owe a large sum of money to the person who transported them that is beyond their means to repay. There is continuing partisan debate in Congress about whether stronger legal protection should apply to Native Americans, undocumented immigrants, and transsexuals forced into prostitution or include counseling or contraceptives to victims of sexual abuse. Some conservative women's organizations and the U.S. Conference of Catholic Bishops oppose the legislation on these grounds.

On a few occasions abused people have taken legal action to protect themselves. For almost twenty years The Carter Center has been attempting to assist the tomato harvesters in Immokalee, Florida, to achieve justice in their working conditions, and we have observed with pride the additional efforts of the Coalition of Immokalee Workers (CIW) to expose wealthy landowners who were holding their farmworkers in involuntary servitude. The CIW helped fight this crime by uncovering and assisting in the federal prosecution of slavery rings preying on hundreds of laborers. In such situations, captive workers were held against their will by their employers for many years through threats and beatings, shootings, and pistol-whippings. In 2010 the CIW followed up these exposés and convictions by developing a mobile Slavery Museum that they brought to Atlanta for us to see and then took it on a tour of the southeastern United States to demonstrate what was happening to poor and defenseless workers.

There needs to be much more vigorous investigation and prosecution of those who are engaged in modern-day slavery. Although seldom utilized, a stringent law exists, as stated in Title 18 of the U.S. Code, Sec. 1589 ("Forced Labor"):

> Whoever knowingly provides or obtains the labor or services of a person
>
> (1) by threats of serious harm to, or physical restraint against, that person or another person;
>
> (2) by means of any scheme, plan, or pattern intended to cause the person to believe that, if the person did not perform such labor or services, that person or another person would suffer serious harm or physical restraint; or
>
> (3) by means of the abuse or threatened abuse of law or the legal process,
>
> shall be fined under this title or imprisoned not more than 20 years, or both. If death results from the violation of this section, or if the violation includes kidnapping or an attempt to kidnap, aggravated sexual abuse or the attempt to commit aggravated sexual abuse, or an attempt to kill, the defendant shall be fined under this title or imprisoned for any term of years or life, or both.

This sounds good, but the law is essentially ignored. Although the U.S. Department of State has estimated that there are at least sixty thousand people being held against their will in the United States, only 138 traffickers were convicted in this country in 2012.

❧

> There is something powerful the U.S. government could do, right now, to stop gender-based violence globally. The International Violence Against Women Act (IVAWA), which has awaited action in the U.S. Congress for six years, lies

dormant because not enough voices have yet risen to demand its passage. IVAWA would make America a leader in ending violence against women and girls. It would be a new beacon of light for millions of women and children who cower under the hand of an abuser, who dare not attend school because they will be shot, and who remain in a corner of darkness because there is no one to receive them in the light. Let us help receive them. Let us pass IVAWA now.

RITU SHARMA, COFOUNDER AND PRESIDENT,

WOMEN THRIVE WORLDWIDE

It is crucial for political leaders and all of us to understand the interrelationship among politics, the sex trade, and the general welfare. This can best be demonstrated in Africa, where the AIDS virus originated and where preventative and curative medicines have been introduced in tardy and inadequate ways. Containing only 15 percent of the world's population, 70 percent of those who are HIV-infected and die with AIDS are Africans. Much of the infection, especially in South Africa, has been spread by truck drivers, miners, and other men who work away from home, patronize brothels, and then transmit the disease to their wives and families. I learned about this tragedy on a visit to the continent in 2002.

Bill Gates Sr. was in charge of the enormous foundation established by his son, and he was planning his first visit to Africa in 2002 to meet some of the top leaders and get acquainted with the region and issues in which they planned to invest. He asked Rosalynn and me to accompany him and his wife, Mimi, on a trip around the periphery of the continent so he could learn as much as possible about the devastating AIDS epidemic. At the time, there were two key features of an effective anti-AIDS program: antiretroviral medicines for those who were known to be infected and a public awareness campaign that emphasized the gravity of the epidemic.

We met Bill and Mimi in Johannesburg, South Africa, where about

25 percent of the citizens were suffering from HIV/AIDS, greatly exacerbated by the claim of President Thabo Mbeki that the value of antiretroviral treatments was unproven and they were likely to be toxic and were being foisted on innocent black people by white leaders from Western nations. He had condemned the use of any of these drugs, including the well-proven nevirapine, which can protect babies of HIV mothers from the infection. Our expert on the trip was Dr. Helene Gayle, who had recently left the Centers for Disease Control to head the Gates Foundation's global crusade against HIV/AIDS. She emphasized that nevirapine given to prospective mothers would reduce by half the sixty thousand annual infant AIDS deaths.

We were informed that there would be a meeting in Soweto to publicize the issue, and I decided to invite former president Nelson Mandela to join us. Bill told me that Mandela had expressed doubts about "Western" drugs at a meeting with the Gates Foundation officials in Seattle, Washington, when he was president of South Africa, so I was pleasantly surprised when he accepted my invitation.

The meeting was in a large tent. Bill, Mandela, and I were asked to sit on the stage and make brief comments. Conveners of the session had asked us not to defy or criticize President Mbeki's policies but simply to express our hope that the raging epidemic might be controlled. The event was well publicized. Television stations broadcast our remarks and newspapers carried a photograph of the three of us holding babies and their mothers, who had AIDS, sitting in the front row. Bill was feeding his crying baby with a bottle.

That night and the next morning the publicity was enormous in South Africa, because it was the first time Mandela had expressed approval for the treatment of AIDS with Western medicines; Mbeki had not even acknowledged the need for an aggressive response to the devastating impact of AIDS in their country, where the rate of infection had grown in the previous twelve years from less than 1 percent to more than 20 percent of all adults, with an estimated 1,800 new people being infected each day. There were predictions that 7 million already infected people would die in the next eight years. Some leaders of minor political groups had been attacking the African National Congress leaders for their refusal to confront the problem.

Bill and I met with groups of sex workers in brothels who volunteered to discuss how they became prostitutes, their special problems, family affairs when not "on duty," and awareness of their possible role in the spreading of AIDS to transient workers and others who would carry the infection to their wives and families back home. The women said there were about five thousand sex workers in the community but they were acquainted with only a small number of them. Even those who had been introduced to the trade involuntarily by being sold by their parents or others let us know that they now continued their work on their own volition. We found small groups of women who told us that they insisted on their customers using condoms, but this restraint commanded lower fees and was not appreciated by the brothel's supervisors. All of them denied having any symptoms of AIDS and seemed to have a fatalistic attitude toward their chances in the future. It was obvious that their customers were aware of the threat of AIDS and often expressed a preference for younger girls, who they believed were more likely to be free of the infection. Unlike in most other African countries, Rosalynn and I never saw an anti-AIDS poster or billboard in South Africa.

We flew to Capetown to meet with President Mbeki and found him waiting for us with his minister of health, Manto Tshabalala-Msimang. As Bill and I began to explain the purpose of our visit, the president interrupted and insisted that there was no scientific connection between HIV infection and AIDS and that the antiretroviral medicines we were promoting were toxic. The discussion became heated, and he and I rose from our chairs and faced each other in an angry confrontation. Mbeki accused us of attempting to introduce Western medicines into Africa to interfere with the progress being made by black people in eliminating the last vestiges of colonialism, and he claimed that President Robert Mugabe of Zimbabwe was also aware of our plot. We left South Africa without reconciling our differences, but since then I have worked harmoniously with President Mbeki in trying to bring peace to the people of Sudan.

We next visited Namibia (with a 23 percent infection rate), Angola (8 percent), and Nigeria (5.8 percent). President Olusegun Obasanjo brought representatives from all thirty-two Nigerian states to Abuja, where we had a discussion about the incidence of AIDS in different regions. When Bill and I visited with commercial sex workers, one group in the ghetto area of Mabushi, who were especially young and beautiful, told us they demanded that their clients use condoms. Some reported being offered five times their standard rate for "naked sex." Few of the other five thousand sex workers took any precautions against AIDS.

On Saturday afternoon President Obasanjo informed me that the next day there would be a Baptist religious service in the presidential chapel and that I was scheduled to deliver a sermon—about AIDS! I gave a lot of thought to the subject that night and decided that the best approach was to make it easy and acceptable for both men and women to report their infection by minimizing the stigma involved. I tried to explain to the large and emotional congregation how Jesus would address the problem of illicit sex, contagion, and suffering. I quoted texts about his attitude toward Mary Magdalene (who was cured of seven sins), the Samaritan woman at the well (with five lovers), and the woman caught in adultery and sentenced to be stoned to death. I said that all these actions showed his love and forgiveness and that Matthew 25's "unto the least of these" put the responsibility on all of us to reach out to the afflicted with forgiveness and love. President Obasanjo complimented me on my choice of biblical references and said that the congregation responded well.

We made a last-minute decision to stop in Bangui, Central African Republic, one of the most isolated and poverty-stricken countries in the world. We visited their only AIDS clinic, and it was a heartrending experience. There was a line of 267 people with AIDS, mostly mothers holding emaciated babies, but there was no medicine available. They were waiting for the daily allowance of a morsel of food. When the women were no longer able to walk, they were moved to the nearby hospital to die. Ninety percent of the hospital beds were filled with these patients. There was a young Japanese woman running the clinic, whose dedication reminded us of Mother Teresa, and Bill promised the Gates Foundation would provide special help to her and her patients.

In Kenya, President Daniel arap Moi was deeply involved in the AIDS issue and able to report a recent decrease in the national infection rate to 13 percent, although 20 percent of the citizens of Nairobi were infected. He joined us in a large public discussion on HIV/AIDS, where we heard vivid testimony from AIDS victims, commercial sex workers, AIDS orphans, students, workers, employers, and officials in the nation's AIDS programs.

We knew at that time that 35 percent of the citizens of Botswana were HIV-positive, and later the Gates Foundation joined with Merck & Co., a major producer of antiretroviral medicines, to concentrate on Botswana, with an emphasis on both prevention and treatment, to set an example for the rest of Africa.

With increased financial assistance from the President's Emergency Plan For AIDS Relief (PEPFAR), the U.S. government program promoted by President George W. Bush, improved education programs, and support from President Mbeki's successors and other political leaders, there has been dramatic progress in Africa. Eight times as many people are now receiving antiretroviral treatment, deaths from AIDS have been reduced by one-third, and new HIV infections are 25 percent lower than in 2002.

One of the setbacks in Africa has been in Uganda, which had a superb anti-AIDS program when we were on this trip. By using the standard "ABC" program (abstinence, be faithful, and condoms) the HIV/AIDS rate had dropped from more than 15 percent to 6 percent and was continuing its decline. In addition to teaching the ABC approach in schools, the Ugandan government conducted an aggressive media campaign using print, billboards, radio, and television. However, shortly after our trip, the president's wife was convinced by conservative Christian leaders in America to restrict the use of condoms, and the government shifted to promoting abstinence as the sole means of controlling the spread of AIDS. The result has been a lack of further progress in reducing the rates of death and new cases. Human Rights Watch has commented that the change in policy "leave[s] Uganda's children at risk of HIV," which is disputed, of course, by some of the faith-based groups. A report by the Joint United Nations Program on HIV/AIDS on Uganda in 2012 stated, "The number of newly infected people per year has increased by over 50 percent, from 99,000 in 2001 to 150,000 in 2011."

Most transmission of AIDS in Africa is through heterosexual activity. Women are less able to protect themselves from unwanted sex, and are most willing to implement the restraints of abstinence and the use of condoms. Except for professional sex workers, women are also less likely than men to transmit HIV/AIDS into a previously healthy home. Pregnant women are also eager, if infected, to protect their babies with antiretroviral medication. Protection of women from rape and providing them with preventive instruction and treatment should be priorities in the war against AIDS.

13 | SPOUSE ABUSE

A very difficult Christian text for battered women is Matthew 5:39, "If anyone slaps you on the right cheek, turn to them the other cheek also." This text is invoked to convince battered women it is "Christian" to just take abuse, and it is a very difficult text for them. But theologian Walter Wink, in his book *Engaging the Powers*, shows us the real meaning of that text in Jesus' time was nonviolent resistance. Jesus rejected the two common ways of responding to being treated violently, either violent resistance or passive acceptance. Instead, Jesus advocated a third way, that is, an assertive but nonviolent response when understood in the context of how Romans treated Jews in ancient Israel. A woman who is being beaten can choose the third way of active, but nonviolent resistance, by going to a battered women's shelter. That was the real meaning of Jesus' teaching.

REV. DR. SUSAN BROOKS THISTLETHWAITE,
PROFESSOR OF THEOLOGY AND FORMER PRESIDENT,
CHICAGO THEOLOGICAL SEMINARY

The World Health Organization reported in 2013 that more than a third of all women are victims of physical or sexual violence and that the vast majority are attacked or abused by their husbands or boyfriends. To some degree, this situation is perpetuated by local custom or helpless acquiescence by the abused women. About a third of countries do not have any laws against domestic violence, and many wives consider it mandatory and proper to submit themselves to their husbands for punishment. A recent UNICEF survey among women ages fifteen to forty-nine revealed that 90 percent of wives in Afghanistan and Jordan, 87 percent in Mali, 86 percent in Guinea and Timor-Leste, 81 percent in Laos, and 80 percent in Central African Republic believe that a husband is justified in hitting or beating his wife under certain circumstances.

At some time in their lives, one-fourth of all American women are victims of domestic violence. The Federal Bureau of Investigation reports that while 3,200 servicemen were killed in battle between 2000 and 2006, there were 10,600 domestic homicides in the United States; 85 percent of these victims were women. Since reports of such crimes by local police are discretionary, these data are an underestimation. The usual way of preventing these crimes has been to send battered women to protective shelters, but this has been only partially effective and imposes punishment on the victim instead of the attacker, especially when women have to leave children behind or take them into extended hiding.

A New Yorker magazine article by Rachel Louise Snyder in July 2013 describes a new approach that was initiated in Massachusetts in 2005, designed to prevent domestic homicide by using existing legal means to anticipate when it might happen. The most persistent predictor of these crimes was a prior incident of physical abuse: half of the female murder victims had earlier sought protection from the police. Although poverty of the family did not indicate likely violence, chronic unemployment of the husband was significant. Legal restraining orders on the abuser's movements had often been violated, but the combination of a "dangerousness" assessment and a court-ordered GPS locator on the abuser proved to be remarkably effective. Since the new program was put into effect there has not been a homicide in the test area and none of the offenders monitored by GPS has committed an act of domestic violence. In the most recent report, only 5 percent have had to go into a shelter for protection, while 90 percent would have done so before the new system was established. Thirty-three states have introduced or already passed laws to permit the use of the GPS restraint in domestic violence cases, and more than five thousand people from thirty states have been trained to implement this surprisingly inexpensive system.

Another rapidly expanding approach to reducing extreme cases of spouse abuse was described in *Bloomberg Businessweek* in September 2013: letting women in the developing world obtain a divorce from an abusive husband. The divorce rate has almost tripled since 1980 in Mexico, and there has been more than a fivefold increase in China, Iran, Thailand, and South Korea. Analysts attribute this increased freedom of women to make decisions with the implementation of the UN's Convention on the Elimination of All Forms of Discrimination Against Women. Simply put, many abused wives have been able to obtain a legal right to leave a troubled marriage permanently. Major challenges still remain, as rape within marriage is not a crime in 127 countries.

Ending violence against women requires advocacy to blossom into engaged global support by both leaders and community members. Each of us will be held accountable by God to take a stand against all forms of injustice in both private and public spheres. Preventive domestic violence education and training of religious leaders and communities must be institutionalized through sermons, premarital counseling, marital seminars, awareness campaigns, signed declarations, resource development, research, and survivor programs and services. We human beings all want the same thing—love and peace. Collectively we can create a world where we put into practice the universal principle of wanting for others what we want for ourselves—to best sustain peaceful families, communities, and nations.

IMAM MOHAMED MAGID, PRESIDENT,

ISLAMIC SOCIETY OF NORTH AMERICA, AND

MAHA B. ALKHATEEB, CODIRECTOR OF PR AND

RESEARCH, PEACEFUL FAMILIES PROJECT

We have all heard about the extreme derogation of women and girls in Afghanistan in regions controlled by the Taliban, and I have been involved personally in one perhaps illustrative case. Even when a girl is able to obtain a good education and escape a forced marriage at an early age, she is still not free to shape the rest of her life in a culture that supports male domination.

One of my best friends is Mashuq Askerzada, a former Muslim army officer from Afghanistan, who came to nearby Fort Benning, Georgia, for advanced military training after an earlier education at the Royal Military Academy Sandhurst in England. When Soviet troops invaded Afghanistan in December 1979, Mashuq decided to remain in America, married and had a family, and became a high school teacher. He attended my Bible class in Plains and became a Christian, and his family moved to our town to live. They are members of our church, and Mashuq teaches when I'm not there. (Some regular church members have been heard to say that they're glad when I'm away.)

Mashuq retained close contact with his relatives in Afghanistan and was especially proud of a young relative named Khatera. She had completed high school and two years of college and was preparing to become a teacher in one of the few institutes girls were permitted to attend. The family was relatively affluent and influential, and were greatly embarrassed and distressed early in 2007 when her father was arrested and falsely charged by the local judge with involvement in the misdeeds of his former business partners.

Two months later Khatera answered the telephone one day in their home and was surprised when the caller identified himself as the judge, who informed her that he had total power over her father and then violated sensitive cultural norms by saying he had heard that she was very beautiful and also well educated. She expressed her dismay and said she would hand the telephone to her mother, who had received an earlier demand from the judge for a payment of $10,000 for her husband's freedom and had already paid him $4,000. The judge told Khatera that if she informed her mother of his call, her father would never be released and it was very likely that her seventeen-year-old brother would be killed. He added that he would guarantee the family's safety and the father's freedom if Khatera would marry him. He told her he was a young bachelor and would provide her with a good life.

Her mother found her weeping in her room, but she decided not to tell anyone about the threats and promises. Later that week two trucks loaded with armed militia came to the house and surrounded it. The judge's sister entered and repeated her brother's offer to Khatera's mother, who was shocked and angry. In the meantime, in order to protect her family, the young woman had decided to accept the offer of marriage.

Three days later the judge arrived, accompanied by a mullah who read the proper religious words in the presence of the mother. Then the judge was permitted to approach Khatera, who was completely veiled. She saw that he was at least twenty-five years older than he had led her to expect. On the wedding night the husband brandished a large knife and said he would cut her into bits if she was not found to be a virgin.

Khatera bled as expected and was informed the next day that her father had been released from prison. That was when she met the judge's two other wives, one of whom was put in charge of her. When Khatera's mother learned of his former marriages, she berated the judge, after which he beat her daughter severely and repeatedly, warning her never again to share any information with her family. She was put on starvation rations and was soon notified by the other wives that their husband was searching for a fourth. Although Khatera did not complain, her mother was aware of her plight and told her that the judge had put her father back in prison. Khatera learned that she was up for sale when she was forced to unveil herself and greet two strange men, whom the judge identified as his "friends." A daughter of the judge later told her that she had heard them bargaining about the price to be paid. A few weeks later Khatera's mother induced the judge to permit her daughter to attend a wedding for another member of their family. Khatera was accompanied by members of the judge's militia and was taken back to her husband's home after the ceremony. Her mother appealed to the local governor and other officials, but they all sided with the judge, who accused the mother of trying to kidnap her daughter.

This was when Mashuq informed me about his family's problems. Some of his acquaintances in Afghanistan appealed to a high official who was from the same community. There was a temporary stalemate, and Khatera was escorted to a United Nations office in Kundu. When the judge went there with ten of his militia and threatened to burn down the office, the terrified staff members called a distant relative of the Askerzadas who was living nearby and who took Khatera to a UN office in the capital city, Kabul. I first interceded by telephone to outline the history of the case to the U.S. ambassador and offered to call the White House and the UN secretary-general. Khatera was transferred to a women's shelter in a secret location, which she later described as a prison.

I knew Burhanuddin Rabbani, who had served as president of Afghanistan for a brief time late in 2001, and he and I were able to obtain some influential help in Jalalabad, the judge's hometown. I wanted Khatera to come to America, but she was still officially married and there was no way we could overcome the multiple legal impediments. Although he and Khatera never saw each other again, her husband was induced to make a public declaration in the presence of officials that he was divorcing her and pledge never again to harm her or her family. He was suspended from his duties and later was shot in a Taliban attack and lost both legs. (President Rabbani was killed in 2011 in a suicide bombing.)

Khatera's journey to a normal life began when she resumed teaching in a girls' school in Afghanistan for two years and served as principal for a year. But then her school was bombed in a Taliban attack. Threatened that she would be cut to pieces if she returned to work, Khatera moved with her mother and youngest brother to Tajikistan. At that point Mashuq's son, William, realized that the only way to cut through most of the bureaucracy was to marry Khatera. He went to Tajikistan to meet her and, to his surprise, they fell deeply in love. William returned to America to file a petition for his fiancée to join him. I helped expedite the visa process, and after a few months Khatera was reunited with William and joined her relatives in Plains. Khatera and William were married and now have a handsome young son named for his father.

The significance of this story is that the drama of a beautiful and intelligent young woman would have had an entirely different ending if her family had not been able to depend on a former president of the United States and a former president of Afghanistan—and her cousin—for help. Few other women have such resources.

The need to secure women's rights, as a notion that is both Islamic and Afghan, is imperative in order for Afghanistan to be able to safeguard women's rights in the long term, particularly as security is transferred to domestic forces. In this traditional society where Islam shapes culture, traditions, and customs, there is no better way to raise the sensitive topic of women's rights than through community-level religious leaders themselves. Although we can help to facilitate these conversations, it is the Imams who share the message of women's rights according to Islam in a direct but non-threatening manner to a wider population—something that needs to happen more often.

PALWASHA KAKAR, DIRECTOR OF WOMEN'S
EMPOWERMENT AND DEVELOPMENT PROGRAMS,
THE ASIA FOUNDATION

14 | "HONOR" KILLINGS

Although widely condemned in the modern world, the terrible custom of "honor" killings is either legal or not prosecuted in some countries. It has a justification in the ancient Holy Scriptures of Jews and Christians. I remember when, during my first year in the White House, a Saudi couple who were living together were executed publicly; their desire to be married was rejected by her father. A British journalist researched the story and developed it into a film entitled *Death of a Princess*. Saudi government officials complained strenuously when the dramatized documentary was shown in Great Britain and were unable to prevent its showing by the Public Broadcasting System in the United States despite pressure from an oil company that was a major PBS sponsor.

This was the first time I became aware of the special laws and customs relating to the extreme consequences of a woman having sex outside of an approved marriage, but I was aware of a passage in the Holy Bible that espoused this ultimate punishment. In Deuteronomy 22:13–14, 20–21 we read, "If a man takes a wife and after lying with her dislikes her, and slanders her and gives her a bad name, saying, 'I married this woman, but when I approached her I did not find proof of her virginity,' . . . if the charge is true and no proof of the girl's virginity can be found, she shall be brought to the door of her father's house and there the men of her town shall stone her to death. . . . You must purge the evil from among you."

It is hard to believe that there is still a prevailing custom in many communities to murder a woman who has been raped, refuses to accept an assigned husband, has an extramarital affair, or even wears inappropriate clothing. This is done in order to salvage the honor of the besmirched family. It is difficult to obtain accurate data on how widespread this practice may be, because many of the killings are reported as suicides. They occur most frequently in the Middle East and South Asia, but also in other regions of the world. In 2010 the police reported 2,823 honor attacks in the United Kingdom. A BBC report estimates that globally more than twenty thousand women are victims of honor killings each year. There was a highly publicized case in Pakistan in 1999 of a mentally retarded girl whose rapist was identified and arrested. She was killed by a group of her tribesmen who claimed she had brought shame to the tribe. She was sixteen years old. Such murders are usually carried out by the girl's father, uncle, or younger brother.

The right to life of women in Pakistan is conditional on their obeying social norms and traditions.

HINA JILANI, PAKISTANI HUMAN RIGHTS
ACTIVIST AND AN ELDER

Human Rights Watch defines honor killings as "acts of vengeance, usually death, committed by male family members against female family members, who are held to have brought dishonor upon the family. A woman can be targeted by individuals within her family for a variety of reasons, including: refusing to enter into an arranged marriage, being the victim of a sexual assault, seeking a divorce—even from an abusive husband—or for allegedly committing adultery. The mere perception that a woman has behaved in a way that 'dishonors' her family is sufficient to trigger an attack on her life."

This definition does not include the killing of girls because their dowry is inadequate, but it applies to those who object to marriage because they believe they are too young or prefer a different husband than the one chosen by their parents. It is a custom, all too widely accepted, that derives from the belief that girls and women are the property of the males in their family.

There are some pressures from the global community to end the custom of honor killing, but these are having mixed results. King Abdullah II of Jordan and his wife, Rania, have attempted to end the legal practice, but their best efforts have been thwarted by strong community beliefs. The previous law stated, "He who discovers his wife or one of his female relatives committing adultery and kills, wounds or injures one or both of them, is exempt from any penalty." Stricter legislation concerning murder has been passed, but courts can commute or reduce sentences in honor killings, particularly if the victim's family (who are usually the culprits) asks for leniency. In many cases, the custom is to let the crime be committed by a brother who is less than eighteen years old, that is, a juvenile, so that any punishment will be quite minor.

Just an allegation is often adequate to condemn the girl, without any proof of improper conduct. The director of Jordan's National Institute of Forensic Medicine has found the hymens intact in a number of postmortem examinations of victims of honor killings. A recent study by researchers from Cambridge University stated, "While stricter legislation has been introduced—despite conservative fears—cultural support for violence against women who are seen as breaking norms has remained widespread." The university's Institute of Criminology found that almost 50 percent of boys and 20 percent of girls interviewed in the capital, Amman, believe that killing a daughter, sister, or wife who has "dishonored" or shamed the family is justified.

Tragically the practice is still all too prevalent in the Islamic world. Egypt's interior minister reported in 2000 that 16 percent of homicides were family killings to "wipe out shame." Between 2002 and 2003 the Egyptian Association of Legal Aid for Women reported that perpetrators of violence were husbands, fathers, brothers, and uncles in 75 percent of the cases; women represented the other 25 percent. It is almost impossible for a rape victim to prove her innocence, because she must have four adult male Muslim eyewitnesses testify on her behalf. Such killings have also been committed in Hindu and Sikh communities in India, and by Christians within highly patriarchal cultures.

15 | GENITAL CUTTING

One of the most serious and least understood examples of abuse of girls is the removal of all or part of their genitalia. Known as female genital cutting or female circumcision, the operation is usually performed without anesthesia, with a knife or razor blade by women who are known as "cutters." Some cutters use sutures to close the wound, leaving a small hole for the girl to pass urine and menstrual blood. At the time of marriage or childbirth, the hole is enlarged enough to accommodate the husband's penis or the infant.

FGC can result in lifelong health consequences, including chronic infection; severe pain during urination, menstruation, sexual intercourse, and childbirth; and psychological trauma. Some girls die from the cutting, usually as a result of bleeding or infection.

The World Health Organization estimates that about 125 million women and girls have undergone FGC, ostensibly to "purify" them by reducing their enjoyment of or desire for sex. Some practitioners claim that female genitalia are dirty and should be made flat, rigid, and dry. In many communities the operation is considered to be the passage of girls into womanhood, although it is most often performed at a very young age. Some believe that it helps to enhance men's enjoyment of the sex act. There are no Holy Scriptures that mandate the practice, but some Christians, Jews, Muslims, animists, and nature worshipers have adopted FGC as part of their local religious teaching.

The subject of female genital cutting was discussed at the World Conference on Human Rights in Vienna in 1993 and declared to be a serious abuse of small girls. Since then almost all countries have passed laws that forbid or restrict the practice, and in December 2012 the United Nations General Assembly unanimously passed a resolution banning the practice. However, these international and national resolutions and laws have had practically no effect in restricting the abuse, and legal punishment is almost nonexistent.

The resistance to outside interference and the need for local people to make their own decisions have been most vividly demonstrated in Senegal by the work of Tostan, founded by Molly Melching, who was a student at the University of Dakar in 1974 and later an exchange student and a U.S. Peace Corps Volunteer. She settled in a village of three hundred people in the eastern region of the country and became assimilated into the local society. She used her good education to teach the women how to read and write, about the outside world, and how to care for themselves and their family's health. Perhaps more important, she taught women that they had basic human rights, of which they had previously been unaware. Molly recognized that the Senegalese women, and not outsiders, had to be the ones to make decisions about their own lives, and she developed a system of community empowerment that later adopted the name Tostan, or "empowerment." Molly emphasizes that 99 percent of the Tostan staff are Senegalese.

The practice of female genital cutting was accepted without question in many Senegalese villages, along with the assumption that the status of women was inherently inferior to that of men. In 1997 one group of women decided to abandon the practice in their community, based on the new understanding that it was harmful to their health and a violation of their human rights. They also learned from the words of respected Muslim leaders that it had no basis in the teachings of the Koran. Village by village, this awareness has spread throughout many Senegalese regions where the practice is traditional, and as of 2013 women in more than 6,400 villages, primarily in Senegal but also in Guinea, The Gambia, Mauritania, Djibouti, and Somalia, have decided to abandon the practice of genital cutting and also the forced marriage of children. Molly states that the key factor in this achievement by African women was informing them about the universal agreements concerning the rights of women and then letting them make the decision for themselves.

A report issued by UNICEF in July 2013 showed a very gradual reduction in genital cutting but emphasized that it was still overwhelmingly prevalent in some countries, especially those in Africa where the Islamic faith prevails. UNICEF estimates that 91 percent of women in Egypt, 98 percent in Somalia, 96 percent in Guinea, 93 percent in Djibouti, 89 percent in Eritrea, 89 percent in Mali, 88 percent in Sierra Leone, and 88 percent in Sudan have undergone some form of genital cutting, and more than 50 percent of the women in Burkina Faso, Chad, Ethiopia, The Gambia, Guinea-Bissau, and Kenya have also been cut.

There have been surprising reductions in Kenya and Central African Republic. It is not clear why this is so, but it seems obvious that outside pressure has had little effect except in encouraging the education of young women. For instance a 2008 report in Egypt showed that although 81 percent of fifteen- to nineteen-year-old women had been cut, 96 percent of women in their late forties had been subjected to the procedure—evidence of a slight but significant reduction among the younger generation. A public opinion poll that same year revealed that only a third of the younger women wanted to see the practice continue, while two-thirds of the older women supported its continuation. Because the decision to perform FGC is made almost exclusively by mothers, without consulting their husbands, these numbers give hope that the next generation of daughters might be spared. Another hopeful trend observed in several countries was that the more severe forms of genital cutting were less prevalent among younger women.

Although UNICEF found little evidence of progress in Senegal, the researchers explained that their survey did not include the area where Tostan has been most active; in addition, they surveyed women age fifteen to nineteen, while in Senegal 75 percent of girls are cut between birth and age four. In fact, UNICEF was confident that the Tostan effect would prevail in the future.

This is an extremely sensitive subject, especially when criticism of the practice comes from "outsiders" who are suspected of wanting to change the cultural, religious, and sometimes political heritage of the local people. Nevertheless, this abuse of girls is too serious and too important to be ignored or accepted by national governments where it exists or by the UN and other international organizations. Local efforts like Tostan should be supported and replicated to ensure sustained eradication of such harmful practices.

16 | CHILD MARRIAGE AND DOWRY DEATHS

Another serious and pervasive example of gender abuse is the marriage of young girls, often without their consent and contrary to their best interests. There are an estimated 14 million girls married every year before they reach the age of eighteen, and 1 in 9 of these are younger than fifteen. This includes 48 percent of young brides in South Asia; 42 percent in Sub-Saharan Africa; 29 percent in Latin America and the Caribbean; and 18 percent in the Middle East and North Africa. Girls from poor families are nearly twice as likely to be married at an early age as girls from wealthier families. This is a traditional practice in many societies, primarily because girls are not considered equal in value to boys and are often believed to be a burden to their family. When poverty is a factor, marrying off a daughter is a convenient way to eliminate the need to feed her. Another financial incentive is the "bride price" paid to the girl's family.

A traditional practice that has become subject to serious abuse is the payment of a dowry by the bride's family. Especially in India and Pakistan and their neighbors it has become more prevalent in recent years, and the amount paid has also increased. Recognizing this burden, especially on poor families, India and other countries have outlawed the practice, but the law is widely ignored, even among the more affluent families. Since girls are considered to be a burden on the family and unmarried ones an embarrassment, many families are willing to go bankrupt to get them married. As a result, thousands of young women suffer. In January 2012, the *Times of India* reported an increase in the killing of brides by greedy husbands and in-laws when they don't receive enough money and jewelry from the bride's parents, or in lieu of returning unsatisfactory brides (along with the dowry) to their parents. This terrible crime is called "dowry death," and women's organizations in India have increased pressure for more stringent laws against it. In 1986 a law was passed against murder resulting from harassment for dowry, with a section added later to define more specifically the crimes of harassment and cruelty by the husbands and their families. However, these stricter laws have had little effect: when cases are actually brought to trial, conviction rates have dropped. In 2000, 6,995 dowry deaths were reported under these new laws; in 2010, 94,000 cases were reported, with a conviction rate of just 19 percent; in 2012 the number of cases fell to 8,233. There is no data yet available for the conviction rate.

There are proven disadvantages for child brides concerning their health, education, safety, and loss of the basic human right of making decisions about their own lives. Young brides under fifteen are five times more likely to die in childbirth than women in their twenties, and when a woman is under eighteen her baby is 60 percent more likely to die in its first year of life than a baby born to a woman just two years older. Few child brides are permitted to remain in school, which deprives them of the ability to support themselves or a family. In addition, they are more likely to suffer domestic violence and sexual abuse. All these statistics are derived from publications of United Nations agencies. This mistreatment contravenes both the Convention on the Rights of the Child and the Convention on the Elimination of All Forms of Discrimination Against Women.

If the abuses of child marriage continue at the present rate, then about 15 million girls will be added each year to the list of victims. This terrible situation has been ignored by most of the international community, largely because the young girls are inarticulate, their families have a selfish financial interest, and political leaders consider the prohibition of forced child marriage a taboo issue since it is supported by traditional and religious culture.

I am a member of The Elders, a group of former political leaders, peace activists, and human rights advocates who were brought together by Nelson Mandela in 2007. The goal Mandela set for us was to use our "almost 1,000 years of collective experience" to work on solutions for problems involving peace, human rights, climate change, and disease. One of the criteria we adopted is to be free of political pressures by not holding public office, but all of us have had experience in high positions.*

The Elders have been active in attempts to promote peace and human rights in the Middle East, Sudan and South Sudan, North and South Korea, Zimbabwe, Cyprus, Kenya, Egypt, and Myanmar and in addressing the impending disaster of global warming. But one of our most challenging and exciting commitments has been to promote equality for women and girls.

We had an extensive debate when I presented my concerns about the adverse impact of religious beliefs on women's rights to this group of fellow leaders and advisors in 2008, because they represent practicing Protestants, Catholics, Jews, Muslims, and Hindus, and their faiths

---

*The Elders are Martti Ahtisaari, president of Finland, Nobel Peace laureate; Kofi Annan, secretary-general of the United Nations, Nobel Peace laureate; Ela Bhatt, founder of the Self-Employed Women's Association of India; Lakhdar Brahimi, foreign minister of Algeria and United Nations envoy; Gro Harlem Brundtland, prime minister of Norway and director-general of the World Health Organization; Fernando Henrique Cardoso, president of Brazil; Jimmy Carter, president of the United States, Nobel Peace laureate; Hina Jilani, Pakistani lawyer and UN special representative on human rights defenders; Graça Machel, education minister of Mozambique and widow of Nelson Mandela; Mary Robinson, president of Ireland and United Nations high commissioner for human rights; and Ernesto Zedillo, president of Mexico.

have different policies about the status of women. We finally decided to draw particular attention to the role of religious and traditional leaders in obstructing the campaign for equality and human rights and promulgated the following statement: "The justification of discrimination against women and girls on grounds of religion or tradition, as if it were prescribed by a Higher Authority, is unacceptable. Having served as local, state, national, and world leaders, we understand why many public officials can be reluctant to question ancient religious and traditional premises—an arena of great power and sensitivity. We are calling on all those with influence to challenge and change the harmful teachings and practices—in religious and secular life—that justify discrimination against women, and to acknowledge and emphasize the positive messages of equality and human dignity."

After The Elders agreed to adopt the eradication of gender abuse as a priority project in 2008, it soon became obvious that the greatest opportunity for our group to make a direct and immediate contribution was by concentrating on child marriage. The Elders formed a global partnership with about three hundred nongovernmental organizations from more than fifty countries that share the commitment to end child marriage. We named this coalition Girls Not Brides, and it grew to such an extent that it was separated into an independent organization in 2013, with The Elders still fully supportive of its goals. All the NGO partners are continuing work in their own areas, and substantial progress is being made in raising international concern about the issue. Plans have been announced to raise the subject with the UN Human Rights Council, with the hope of reaching a General Assembly resolution condemning the practice.

In the meantime other action is being taken. In 2013 Human Rights Watch released a ninety-five-page report on South Sudan that documents the near total lack of protection for girls and women who try to resist marriage or leave abusive marriages and the obstacles they face in achieving any relief from their plight. The U.S. Congress has passed a law that requires the inclusion of child marriage in its annual Human

Rights Report and mandates that the secretary of state develop a strategy to prevent child marriage, including diplomatic and program initiatives. Both the United Nations and the World Bank have announced commitments to publicize the problem and to induce nations to end the practice.

There are many encouraging developments; one is a special effort to assess the links between child marriage and slavery and to sharpen national and local laws so they are more specific and punitive when girls are forced to act against their will. Despite the persistence of the practice in many communities, these efforts have had some tangible benefits. In ninety-two countries surveyed in 2005, 48 percent of women forty-five to forty-nine years old were married as children, but the proportion is only 35 percent for women who are now twenty to twenty-four. The trend is good news, but the number is still far too high!

17 | POLITICS, PAY, AND MATERNAL HEALTH

On a global basis, women are habitually denied full and equal participation in political affairs, despite provision for it in the UN's Universal Declaration of Human Rights. The United States has struggled with the issue. The Fifteenth Amendment to the U.S. Constitution granted black men the right to vote in 1870, ninety-four years after the declaration "All men are created equal." It was fifty years later that American women won the same constitutional status (though, with few exceptions, only white women could enjoy this right in practice), and slow progress was realized after that time. Franklin D. Roosevelt was the first president to select a woman to occupy a cabinet post, and other presidents and I have chosen women for major roles in our cabinets and White House staff. I was able to appoint women to key cabinet posts, and a growing number of women are now serving as governors, in the House and Senate, and as chief executive officers of major corporations. In nations as diverse as India, Pakistan, Indonesia, Israel, Great Britain, the Philippines, Liberia, and Nicaragua women have served as presidents and prime ministers. These nations represent citizens who are predominantly Hindu, Muslim, Jewish, and Christian and include two of the three largest democracies on earth.

As University Distinguished Professor at Emory University, I lecture in all the divisions: arts and sciences, law, theology, medicine, nursing, public health, and business. I usually speak for about thirty minutes and then answer questions from the students (and sometimes the professors). One of the subjects that I cover frequently is human rights, often involving gender discrimination, and a "trick" question I ask is "When did women gain the right to vote in the United States?" Hands shoot up and someone always offers the standard reply: "With the passage of the Nineteenth Amendment to the U.S. Constitution in 1920." I point out that this amendment applied only to white women, and that it was with the Voting Rights Act of 1965 under President Lyndon Johnson that all black women gained this privilege. This makes the point that racial, religious, and gender discrimination are often interrelated.

Globally, women first won the right to vote early in the twentieth century, beginning with New Zealand, Australia, and the Scandinavian countries. The Arab nations were the last to grant this privilege, and Saudi Arabian women are still not permitted to vote. (There is a promise that this opportunity will come in 2015, but similar commitments in 2009 and 2011 were rescinded.) Only recently have women begun to make real progress in holding major office in the political world. At this time there are fourteen female heads of state, the best known being Angela Merkel of Germany, Dilma Rousseff of Brazil, Cristina Kirchner of Argentina, Ellen Johnson Sirleaf of Liberia, Park Geun-hye of South Korea, and Joyce Banda of Malawi. There are about 46,500 parliamentarians in the world, and women occupy 21 percent of the seats. Rwanda ranks first, with 64 percent; Cuba has 49 percent; the five Scandinavian countries average 42 percent; the parliaments in the Western Hemisphere have 25 percent, Europe 23 percent, Sub-Saharan Africa 25 percent (but Nigeria only 7 percent), Asia 19 percent, and the combined Arab states 16 percent. This is inadequate progress.

When I was elected president in 1976 there were only eighteen women in the U.S. Congress (about 3 percent), but the number has increased steadily to 102 elected in 2012. This amounts to only 18 percent of the total, far below the world average and leaving our nation ranked 78th in women's participation in government. In state and local government in America, seventy-three women now hold elected statewide positions, or 23 percent of the total, after a steady decrease from 28 percent, the high point, in 1993. In Los Angeles, a community of almost 10 million people, there is only one woman in the entire government, a position in the city council. She recently commented, "When I was in elementary school, there were five women on the city council."

As with racial discrimination, it is very difficult to change historical societal patterns even when there is a desire to do so. I experienced this problem as president in overcoming the exclusion of women from service in the federal district courts and the more senior appellate courts. When there is a vacancy, White House staff members usually consult with the U.S. senators from the state involved, then give the president a list of potential appointees; then the president's nomination for judge is submitted to the Senate for confirmation. Prior to my election, only eight women had been appointed to the federal bench, and I was determined to correct this inequity. By the end of my term, I had a chance to fill about 45 percent of the seats in the federal courts.

At that time the primary obstacle in nominating qualified women was the relatively few female graduates of law schools, and not many of those had acquired enough seniority to become leaders in law firms or deans in university law schools. Another persistent problem was that many senators had close friendships and political obligations to men who occupied those positions. There was even an argument between my White House staff members and the attorney general I appointed, who claimed that there were very few qualified women and minority candidates. There was also some blatant prejudice against women serving as judges, and a few senators were able, through "senatorial courtesy," to block my choices.

Despite these obstacles, I was successful in having the Senate confirm five times as many women as all my predecessors combined, and in addition was able greatly to increase the number of judges from minority groups. I was fortunate also to have 88 percent of my judicial nominees approved by the Senate. There has been an encouraging increase in the number of women judges chosen by my successors, and the total in the United States is now at about 25 percent, compared to a worldwide average of 27 percent. It is obvious that, even under the best of circumstances, women have not been able to reach their potential of equal participation in executive, legislative, or judicial affairs.

One of my most interesting and ultimately gratifying experiences with female candidates began in 1994 with the visit to our home of an Indonesian official who was seeking a site to build small airplanes he had designed that could be modified very quickly from hauling cargo to carrying passengers. B. J. Habibie was a superbly trained aeronautical engineer from Indonesia who had earned his advanced degrees in Germany and became famous as a designer of innovative machines. He was serving as minister of research and engineering in the government of Indonesia's president Suharto.

I extolled the advantages of Georgia as the best location for a factory, and we had a long and enjoyable conversation about his interesting career and his new life in the world of government. I described some of the work of The Carter Center, including our having initiated the process of monitoring elections under often difficult circumstances. He and I communicated with each other a few times afterward, and he eventually informed me that plans for the manufacturing plant had been abandoned. Later I read with some surprise that President Suharto had been placed under house arrest, accused of corruption; he had chosen the nonpolitical engineer to be his vice president. When Suharto was forced to resign, Habibie became president of the largest Islamic nation in the world, which had been governed by dictators for forty-one years.

A few weeks later I had a call from President Habibie asking if The Carter Center would consider leading a team to observe their first democratic election, and I agreed to do so. We had a crash course in the history and culture of Indonesia and soon learned that there were almost fifty political parties with candidates seeking five hundred seats in the Parliament and that two hundred more members would be added from the military, women, youth, and other groups. After being assembled as a body, the seven hundred parliamentarians would then choose a president, presumably from the party that had prevailed in the election.

Rosalynn and I went first to Bali, a beautiful vacation site and home of the leading woman candidate, Dyah Permata Megawati Setiawati Sukarnoputri, who was known as Megawati and was the daughter of Indonesia's first president, Sukarno. It was the custom to demonstrate support for a candidate by flying a small party banner from the top of a tall bamboo pole, and we noticed the overwhelming prevalence of Megawati's following, especially in the small villages and rural areas. Indonesia comprises about nineteen thousand islands spread over a broad area of the western Pacific Ocean, and our one hundred observers covered as many of the key voting areas as possible.

Although there were heated debates among the many candidates, the people were thrilled to have the chance to choose their own political leaders and were especially careful to comply with the law and election rules. Ninety percent of registered voters cast their ballots, there was an honest counting procedure, and Megawati's party prevailed with 36 percent of the vote. This was followed by Suharto and Habibie's ruling party, with 23 percent. Three others received about 10 percent each, and the rest of the votes were scattered among minor parties.

Most of our observers returned home after the votes were counted, but we left a small group to observe the convening of the Parliament and choosing of a president. Habibie withdrew from contention, and it was widely assumed that Megawati would be elected, but there was intense opposition from some of the more militant Islamists to a woman having the highest office, and the Parliament voted instead for Abdurrahman Wahid, known as Gus Dur, a religious leader who had been aligned earlier with Megawati in reformist efforts. Since Wahid's party had received only 10 percent of the popular vote and elective legislative seats, this decision was hotly condemned, and the Parliament compromised by electing Megawati as vice president. Over the months Wahid proved to be an inept administrator and was forced to resign in 2001. Megawati became the first female president of Indonesia and the fourth chief executive of a Muslim nation, after Pakistan, Turkey, and Bangladesh elected women leaders. Megawati and other party leaders invited The Carter Center back to observe the next election, in 2004, after the constitution was changed to permit direct election of the president, and the incumbent was defeated in a runoff.

It is interesting to note that an overwhelming majority of citizens in the world's three largest democracies have different religions: India (81 percent Hindu), the United States (76 percent Christian), and Indonesia (87 percent Muslim). Two of them have elected women as leaders of their government.

One of the most widespread and punitive examples of sexual discrimination is in compensation for work. As women have achieved higher education levels, slow but steady progress has been realized since I was president thirty years ago, when the disparity in pay between American men and women was 39 percent. Although women compose almost half the U.S. workforce and now earn more college and graduate degrees than men, government statistics show that full-time female workers still earn about 23 percent less than men. Over the past decade there has been little improvement: the U.S. Census Bureau reports that women's full-time annual earnings were 76 percent of men's in 2001 and 76.5 percent in 2012.

There is also a wide variation in pay equality among nations. The Organization for Economic Co-operation and Development, which includes thirty-one countries that are committed to democracy and an economic system of free enterprise, reports that the pay disparity against women varies from 4 percent in New Zealand to 37 percent in South Korea, with a global average of 18 percent. Even in the most advanced countries women are paid less than men for the same work.

The difference at the executive level is even greater. Recent statistics show that among Fortune 500 companies only twenty-one CEOs are women, and at this top executive level women received, on average, 42 percent less compensation than men. Interestingly, Catalyst, a nonprofit organization, found a 26 percent better return on investment among American corporations whose board membership was more than one-fifth female than among those with no women serving. Perhaps the presence of women injects a wider range of perspectives, enriching the decision-making process; or it may be that those corporations with a more flexible and innovative approach—factors in success—were the ones inclined to involve women at the top level of governance.

There is every indication that it is beneficial for a business to have women directly involved in its management, but this change is slow in coming. In its annual analysis of 235 large European companies, McKinsey & Company has found that, despite concerted efforts in some countries to increase the number of women at senior levels, progress has been very slow, with only a 6 percent increase during the past ten years. They concluded in 2012 that even "if improvement continues at the present rate, ten years from now women will have less than 20 percent of the seats on boards or executive committees." Among the companies they surveyed only 2 percent of the chief executive officers were women, only 9 percent were on executive committees, while 37 percent were among total employees at all levels.

When my fellow Elder, Gro Brundtland, was prime minister of Norway (1990–96), she led her Labor Party to adopt a rule requiring at least 40 percent of each sex represented on political committees and elected groups. She told me that at times there was a problem finding enough qualified men to reach the 40 percent mark. Later, in 2003, a law was passed in Norway that required all publicly traded companies to appoint women to at least 40 percent of their board membership or the company would be removed from the Oslo Stock Exchange. After ten years there are mixed opinions about its impact. A relatively small group of women now occupy many different board positions and have come to be known as "golden skirts." One of them is quoted in the *New York Times* as saying that "it hasn't had a ripple effect" in bringing more female success in positions of importance in business. The prevailing sentiment, however, is that the law has been helpful in boosting women toward equal standing in the overall society, and the director of the Institute for Social Research in Norway states that having more female directors has had "a slightly positive effect" on economic performance.

When I was a student at Plains High School, there were only two male classroom teachers, plus one who concentrated exclusively on educating boys like me as future farmers. I remember how different it was when I became a freshman in 1941 at Georgia Southwestern College, where most of our professors were men. A 2011 report from the American Association of University Professors (AAUP) states that even in 1974–75, thirty years after I was a college student, only 22 percent of the full-time professors were women; the rate increased during the next thirty-six years, but only to an average of 42 percent.

Even in the field of higher education, where female enrollment is quite high, the economic disparity for women still prevails. According to the AAUP report, the number of women exceeded 57 percent of both undergraduate and graduate students in American universities. However, they held just 28 percent of full professorships. Among current presidents of colleges and universities, 23 percent are women, the number having doubled during the past twenty-five years, but the overall pay gap was about the same as in general employment, with women's pay in full-time faculty positions about 80 percent of men's.

A 2013 study at Yale University showed that established professionals in science, technology, engineering, and mathematics (the STEM subjects) are much more willing to give a job to a young male scientist than a woman with the same qualifications. If they did hire the woman, her average annual salary was nearly $4,000 lower than the man's. It was striking to note that interviewed female scientists were at least as biased against hiring and paying women as their male counterparts.

On the other hand, it is encouraging that over the past forty years the proportion of women PhD recipients has increased in engineering from 0.2 to 22.5 percent, in the geosciences from 3 to 36.6 percent, and in the physical sciences from 3.7 to 27.9 percent. However, women still hold far fewer full professorships than do men. Although women held 62 percent of the PhDs in psychology in a recent year, they held only 19 percent of tenured positions.

In terms of geography and college major, there are substantial differences between male and female students in U.S. universities, with a wide variation among different regions. For instance, in 2005 there were 40 percent more women than men students in the Southeast, and 10 percent fewer in Utah. The following shows the percentage of women enrolled in different disciplines in that same year: arts and humanities, 53 percent; biology, 53 percent; business, 43 percent; education, 69 percent; engineering, 15 percent; physical sciences, 43 percent; social sciences, 66 percent; technical, 27 percent; and computer sciences, 22 percent. These disparities in choice of major study are the result of many factors, including family influence, personal choice, preference for particular professors, and bias in hiring, but academic discrimination in enrollment is not significant.

I remember from my childhood during the Great Depression the very real threat that a woman might die during or shortly after giving birth. At that time, the death rate due to complications from childbirth for all American women was more than 600 per 100,000 births, and black women died at a much higher rate. My mother worked with the African American midwives in our Archery community to improve their skills. It was not the custom for prospective mothers to go to a hospital unless they were known to have an abnormal pregnancy, but the more affluent families could afford to have a trained obstetrician come to supervise home deliveries. Mama was the operating room nurse at Wise Sanitarium in Plains, and the chief surgeon, Dr. Sam Wise, was eager to reduce the amount of time away from her duties. It happened that there was an empty room available; Mama occupied it, and I turned out to be the first American president born in a hospital.

With the advent of antibiotics and more sterile techniques during childbirth, the maternal death rate for all American women decreased dramatically, reaching its lowest point in 1987 at 7.2 deaths per 100,000 live births. But since then it has been creeping upward. Because of poverty and other causes, black women are three to four times more likely than white women to die during pregnancy and childbirth. When the Centers for Disease Control and Prevention began assessing the causes of maternal deaths in 1987, hemorrhage was blamed for more than one in four deaths. Now the causes have shifted to stroke and other diseases of the heart and blood vessels, with obesity an increasing cause of concern.

Women's bodies can be particularly vulnerable because of our responsibilities and our duties around pregnancy, birth, and childcare. So for me, knowing the needs of women and ensuring the rights of women to fair and equal access to healthcare is core to the work of bioethics. The free market argument, while it has worked out for some, clearly has failed to deliver a world of peace and justice. The voice of religion says there has to be areas of human life that are not subject to the justice of the market. Most of those areas are ones about love, one's family, the human body, where those aspects of human life can't be sold and can't be commoditized in ways that are fair, because they live outside the language of the exchange. And here we need language about hospitality, generosity, abundance, and love.

DR. LAURIE ZOLOTH, BIOETHICIST AND PRESIDENT
OF THE AMERICAN ACADEMY OF RELIGION

On a global basis, one of the most notable examples of discrimination against women is their comparative lack of access to adequate health care. According to the World Health Organization, the fourth leading cause of death for women worldwide is poor conditions at childbirth, exceeded only by HIV/AIDS, malaria, and tuberculosis. Some significant progress is being made in most areas, as overall health care improves. In 1980, my last year in office, there were 526,300 deaths of women worldwide while pregnant or during childbirth, and 287,000 in 2010, which was a 45 percent reduction. The United Nations Millennium Development Goals had called for a 75 percent reduction by 2015, a target that obviously will not be reached. In Sub-Saharan Africa the maternal death rate is actually increasing. Globally 99 percent of maternal deaths occur in poor developing countries. This dramatic difference in maternal care between rich and poor countries is demonstrated clearly by the maternal mortality rate (MMR), the number of mothers' deaths for each 100,000 births.

According to the most recent data published by the World Health Organization and UNICEF, the MMR world average is 210, ranging from 2 in Estonia to more than 1,000 in Chad and Somalia, and the MMR average for all of Sub-Saharan Africa is 500. The average rate in Scandinavian countries and Western Europe is less than 10, and in the United States is 21. This places America at the bottom among industrialized nations, despite spending more per average patient than any other. The highest total number of deaths occurred in India (56,000), with a rate of 200, and Nigeria (40,000), with a rate of 630. Not surprisingly, the risk of maternal mortality is highest for adolescent girls under fifteen. Aside from the death itself, the tragic consequences for surviving children are tremendous.

One nation that is making good progress in correcting this problem is Ethiopia, among the poorest countries on earth, which we began visiting in 1988, when the oppressive communist dictator Mengistu Haile Mariam was still in power. It is said that he had gained his authority over the populous nation by personally smothering Emperor Haile Selassie in his bed, and all Western nations had broken diplomatic relations with his regime. While observing one of our agriculture projects in Tanzania in 1989, I received an urgent request from the International Red Cross and UN High Commissioner for Refugees to go to Addis Ababa to negotiate some arrangement by which supplies could be delivered to the two large refugee camps in Ethiopia that sheltered people escaping the ravages of wars in neighboring Somalia and Sudan. After an argument between these agencies and Mengistu, he had forbidden their access to the camps, and Rosalynn and I made an appointment to meet with him. Almost immediately he accepted my proposal to let the two agencies deliver food, water, and medicine to the camps, provided his troops could supervise the process. I became interested in the country, and later became a friend of Meles Zinawe, a revolutionary from Tigray, who eventually overthrew Mengistu, forcing him into permanent exile in Zimbabwe.

Meles became prime minister after a series of elections and launched a number of projects to improve the lot of his people, especially in the rural areas. On one of my visits, he asked if The Carter Center might be willing to train health workers, and, as described in a previous chapter, we met this request with an emphasis on providing women throughout Ethiopia with skills in midwifery, because maternal deaths were extremely high there. These workers also help with other projects of our Center in Ethiopia, including the treatment and elimination of malaria, trachoma, Guinea worm, and river blindness. Still at a very low level of income per person, Ethiopia has benefited greatly from an enlightened prime minister, dedicated cabinet officers, and citizens who are determined to improve their own lives. We are now planning similar training programs for public health workers in Sudan and Nigeria.

In 2008 the International Monetary Fund described the speed of Ethiopia's progress as "fastest for a non–oil exporting country in Sub-Saharan Africa." Ethiopia was also ranked as the second most attractive African country for investors. Meles was given the Africa Political Leadership Award and donated the $200,000 to a foundation called Fre-Addis Ethiopia Women Fund, which was dedicated "to empower girls through providing educational opportunities" by giving support to needy and orphan rural girls to pursue their education.

Intensive work is in progress to establish the post-2015 Millennium Development Goals. When they are adopted by the UN there is little doubt that maternal health will remain one of the top priorities, still unreached. It is hoped that publicity about sexual discrimination in politics, economics, work, and education plus stronger and more persistent demands from women's organizations will help to minimize these abuses.

18 | THE ROAD TO PROGRESS

There is no religion that despises women. Hatred cannot
come from the heart of God. If there is hatred, its source
is not the Creator. Only humans have the capacity to see
and treat others as less than they truly are. It is our minds
and hearts that must change to release women, girls, men,
and boys from the bondage of gender-based limitations or
violence. That change is happening, right now in this very
moment, in thousands of homes, schools, synagogues, cha-
pels, mosques, and centers of power around the world. That
change is coming. Have faith. It will be here soon.

RITU SHARMA, COFOUNDER AND PRESIDENT,

WOMEN THRIVE WORLDWIDE

It is interesting and helpful to have a way to assess how different countries compare in achieving equal status between men and women and
to ascertain if they are making progress. The World Economic Forum

has performed this service with its Global Gender Gap Report for the past seven years. It "assesses countries on how well they are dividing their resources and opportunities among their male and female populations, regardless of the overall levels of these resources and opportunities." The four primary criteria used in these assessments are (1) economic participation and opportunity (salary level and skilled employment); (2) educational attainment (access to basic and higher education); (3) political empowerment (involvement in decision making); and (4) health and survival (life expectancy and sex ratio of surviving children).

A score of 1.000 would indicate that women and men are treated with absolute equality. Iceland has the highest score, .8731, and other Scandinavian countries plus Switzerland, Ireland, New Zealand, the Philippines, and Nicaragua are in the top ten, all with scores above .7700. Other rankings and scores of interest are for Cuba (which ranks nineteenth, with a score of .7540), the United States (twenty-third, with .7382), Israel (fifty-third, with .7032), and Bangladesh (the highest ranked Islamic country at seventy-fifth, with .6848). The entire report can be found on the Internet. The individual factors indicate that the United States lags behind in wage equality at sixty-seventh and in numbers of women in political office at sixtieth.

The reports cover the status of gender equality in 136 countries, and since women comprise approximately half a nation's talent base, there is usually a direct relation between their treatment and their homeland's economic status. As expected, most of the Arab nations and those in Sub-Saharan Africa rank quite low. The general conclusion is that during the seven years of assessment the majority of countries have made very slow progress on closing the gender gap. For instance, the United States improved from .7042 in 2006, an increase of about 5 percent in seven years, but during the past year dropped from twenty-second to twenty-third in the global ranks.

One tremendous untapped resource in the global move to enhance women's rights is the private but formidable influence of first ladies and other prominent women who don't hold elective office. Let me give a few examples with which I am familiar. In the United States the most vivid illustration of this point has been Eleanor Roosevelt, who was a courageous spokesperson for black people while her husband was president, long before there was a detectable civil rights movement. I remember that she was despised by many in the Southland, even while FDR was winning repeated campaigns with overwhelming support from this region, which was overwhelmingly Democratic at the time. When World War II ended and nations began striving to conclude agreements to end war and protect human rights, Eleanor Roosevelt played a key role in representing our nation in the formulation of the Universal Declaration of Human Rights. This remarkable document, which could not be formulated and approved in our much more polarized world, has remained the solid foundation and inspiration for generations of individuals and organizations that strive to protect women and girls from abuse.

President Lyndon Johnson used his exceptional influence in the U.S. Congress to orchestrate the passage of civil rights legislation in the mid-1960s, and his wife, Lady Bird, helped in this effort, also exerting her charm and status as first lady to originate the concept of using native shrubs and flowers to beautify highways and cities throughout America. She broke precedent and worked directly with Congress to help pass the Highway Beautification Act and later, in retirement, continued to manage the family's large media conglomerate that she founded before her husband became prominent in politics. Rosalynn and I visited her and her family often during those days.

We first knew Betty Ford when, as first lady, she visited us in the Georgia governor's mansion. In addition to being a stalwart supporter of her husband, President Gerald Ford, she was a pioneer in espousing women's rights. She became famous for her unprecedented support for the Equal Rights Amendment to the U.S. Constitution and for being remarkably outspoken regarding her breast cancer and addiction to drugs when she underwent a mastectomy and later became addicted to painkillers and alcohol. Later she and Rosalynn would go to Washington to lobby for their special projects, approaching both Democratic and Republican legislators to promote legislation to support the treatment of alcoholism, drug addiction, and mental illness.

Not only did my wife play a vital and unprecedented role in my campaigns for governor and president, but she was active in promoting her own projects. She inspired and directed the work of blue-ribbon commissions to promote mental health at the state and federal level and has become a world leader in pursuing this goal since we left the White House. She worked tirelessly, but unsuccessfully, to secure passage of the Equal Rights Amendment, calling hundreds of state legislators to induce them to vote for it. With the exception of state secrets that involved security, I discussed all my major challenges with Rosalynn and sought her advice when I had difficult decisions to make. I did not always accept her recommendations, but my personal staff and cabinet officers knew that their best access to me was through Rosalynn, and she and I shared this knowledge as a personal joke.

Rosalynn has been a full partner with me in founding and operating The Carter Center and, aided by a worldwide group of queens and first ladies, has become the foremost champion of mental health. The Rosalynn Carter Institute for Caregiving does exploratory work on the potential and needs of those who are caring for loved ones suffering from Alzheimer's or other debilitating ailments; tens of thousands of these dedicated volunteers are being trained by a cyber university that telecasts lessons from South Korea. She urged me to write this book and will join me in striving to reach its expressed goals. I hope that all first ladies and other women who occupy positions of influence will adopt this project and pursue it with determination.

The international community has made significant strides in assessing the problems and prescribing cures in the arena of sex discrimination, and official statements, declarations, and covenants have had a beneficial impact. A major international conference on women was held in Copenhagen, Denmark, when I was president. Just its convening in July 1980 was controversial. Our country had been struggling with the failed adoption of the Equal Rights Amendment to the U.S. Constitution, and many countries had reacted adversely to the innovative recommendations issued by the first women's conference five years earlier, in Mexico City. The delegates had set minimum targets for the UN and every nation to meet by 1980, focusing on equal access for women to education, employment, political participation, health services, housing, nutrition, and family planning. Some religious leaders of all faiths openly opposed the idea of sexual equality, as did entrenched politicians who didn't want female challengers and employers who wanted to continue paying less to clothing workers and other female employees. Several of my closest political allies warned me that my endorsement of the meeting would be damaging during the coming presidential election, following my bitter primary battle with Senator Ted Kennedy.

Despite these concerns, there was a consensus that significant progress was being made on women's rights as representatives of 145 nations met in Copenhagen, because the UN General Assembly had recently adopted the Convention on the Elimination of All Forms of Discrimination Against Women (CEDAW), one of the most powerful instruments for women's equality. The Convention, which has been termed "the bill of rights for women," obligates signatory states to report within one year of ratification, and then every four years, on the steps they are taking to comply. It was at this conference that I directed my representative, Sarah Weddington, to sign CEDAW on behalf of the United States.

For Muslims, the Revelation was made by God to protect
the rights of all people, especially those most vulnerable,
and to promote the human dignity of all people. Because of

this, no religious leader can remain silent or refuse to become engaged given the serious discrimination and abuse of many women and young girls in the world today. Any attempt to provide religious justification for refusing girls their right to education or for condoning practices such as female genital cutting, child marriage, exploitation, or enslavement [is] a betrayal of the very principles that religious leaders have the role to defend.

SHEIKH MUHAMED CHÉRIF DIOUP,
ISLAMIC RIGHTS SPECIALIST AND
CHILD PROTECTION OFFICER, TOSTAN, SENEGAL

There was concentrated opposition to the planned participation at the Copenhagen conference of Jehan Sadat, wife of the Egyptian leader who had signed a peace treaty with Israel and was condemned by almost all other members of the Arab League. Unlike other wives of Islamic political leaders, she openly espoused justice for women and had played a key role in promoting a series of legislative reforms in Egypt, known as "Jehan's laws," that greatly enhanced gender equality, such as the right to alimony and custody of children in case of divorce. She is the founder of the Arab-African Women's League and has led unprecedented efforts to promote children's welfare and to endorse peace efforts as an alternative to war in Africa and on other continents. She became world famous as she participated in conferences in many countries, and her condemnation by Arab political and religious leaders has only enhanced her reputation as a spokesperson for women and for peace. Her status as first lady of Egypt changed the global image of Arab women.

I was concerned when many Arab governments ordered their representatives to boycott any speech made by Jehan, because it would be difficult for women from Saudi Arabia, Oman, or the United Arab Emirates to disobey such directives. When her scheduled address approached, those women obeyed their orders to leave the assembly hall, though all of them shook hands with or embraced Jehan on the way out.

The conference closed with a call for all people to:

> Involve more men in improving women's roles in society.
>
> Let women exert more political will.
>
> Recognize crucial contributions women were already making to society.
>
> Permit women to participate in planning for the future in all aspects of life.
>
> Assess societal damage caused by a shortage of women in decision-making positions.
>
> Publicize the benefits of women's leadership in cooperatives, day care centers, and credit facilities.
>
> Acknowledge the value of making even small financial resources available to women.
>
> Give women more access to information about their government and untapped opportunities available to them.

The participants also reemphasized the beneficial contributions women could make in promoting peace, enhancing economic progress, ending colonialism and racism, and improving education and health care.

The Convention on the Elimination of All Forms of Discrimination Against Women has now been ratified by all nations except Iran, Palau, Somalia, Sudan, Tonga, and the United States. Its key provision is to prevent "any distinction, exclusion or restriction made on the basis of sex which has the effect or purpose of impairing or nullifying the recognition, enjoyment or exercise by women, irrespective of their marital status, on a basis of equality of men and women, of human rights and fundamental freedoms in the political, economic, social, cultural, civil or any other field." Subsequently two other resolutions of the UN Security Council were adopted, without objection by the United States, and are therefore binding on our country. Resolution 1325 is an international law that requires UN member states to engage women on all levels of decision making on peace and security issues. Resolution 1820 officially links sexual violence as a tactic of war with the maintenance of international peace and security. It also requires that the UN secretary-general make an official report on its implementation and how additional steps can be taken to end sexual violence. Although the scope of CEDAW is much broader than the others, it is obvious that all three international mandates need to be implemented together, as they share a common acknowledgment of the benefits to all people of giving equal status to women and the commitment to strive for this goal.

The issue of abortion is the major impediment to American approval of CEDAW and similar international agreements that protect women's rights. If there is any possibility of encouraging sex education that might lead to the use of contraception or abortion, then Christian fundamentalists, the U.S. Conference of Catholic Bishops, and fervent pro-life activists often join forces and can prevent the passage of otherwise acceptable legislation. There is a consensus within our Christian churches, liberal and conservative, that a developing fetus should be protected whenever possible. This is a difficult issue for me. In many ways, every abortion is an unplanned tragedy, brought about by a combination of human errors, and my Christian faith convinces me that a prospective parent should not make this decision unless the life of the mother is threatened or the pregnancy is caused by rape or incest. I accepted my obligation as president to enforce the Supreme Court ruling in *Roe v. Wade* that authorized some abortions, but I attempted to minimize their number through sex education, making contraceptives more available, special economic assistance for women and infant children, and the promotion of foster parenthood.

Many fervent pro-life activists do not extend their concern to the baby after it is born, ignoring the fact that two-thirds of women who interrupt their pregnancy assert that their primary reason is inability to pay the costs of raising the child. It has long been known that there are fewer abortions in nations where women have access to contraceptives, the assurance that they and their babies will have good health care, and at least enough income to meet their basic needs. And it has been proven that strict prohibitive laws have no significant effect on the number of abortions. The *Lancet* medical journal reported in 2012 that the rate of abortions per 1,000 pregnancies varies from 12 in Western Europe to 23 in the United States and 43 in Eastern Europe. The number exceeds 50 in some nations where there is abject poverty and the use of contraceptives (and abortion) is prohibited.

Good education for women is a positive factor in any society. One of the well-meaning but counterproductive approaches to prevent abortion is to refrain from teaching young Americans how to avoid pregnancy, instruction that is given in many other nations. There is now adequate government funding for sex education, but unfortunately it is quite often tied to a legal prohibition against any mention of contraception, despite the fact that a strong majority of American teenagers report having sex before they are eighteen years old. The Associated Press reported in December 2010 that young people in Western Europe had equal levels of sexual activity, are about equally promiscuous, but, deprived of proper sex education, American girls are much more likely to become pregnant than girls in Western Europe. There were 33 births per 1,000 teenage girls in the United States in 2011, while in Italy the rate was 8, France 7, Germany 5, and in Switzerland 2.

Regardless of how one feels about abortion, there is an inescapable fact in American politics: in order to secure U.S. congressional approval of CEDAW and other international agreements that guarantee women's rights, a provision to preclude promotion or financing of abortions must be accepted. This does not include the prohibition of sex education or the use of contraceptives.

I made one of the major speeches at the historic World Conference on Human Rights in Vienna in 1993, where sexual abuse was discussed at length, and was gratified when, a year later, the Violence Against Women Act (VAWA) was adopted with bipartisan support in the U.S. Congress. The new law recognized that this was a basic premise of the Universal Declaration of Human Rights and would encourage further economic and social progress by bringing more capable women into the mainstream of society. Unfortunately, although VAWA was reauthorized several times, it was allowed to expire in 2012 because of conservative opposition to amendments designed to extend protection to same-sex couples and undocumented immigrants.

Phyllis Schlafly and other women leaders and a number of devout Catholics and Mormons who had opposed the Equal Rights Amendment to the U.S. Constitution were in the forefront of opposition to VAWA, denouncing the legislation as "creating an ideology that all men are guilty and all women are victims" and claiming it was "designed to promote divorce, breakup of marriage and hatred of men." The U.S. Conference of Catholic Bishops opposed the act because it addressed sexual orientation and gender identity. However, with aroused support from other women's organizations and human rights organizations, an expanded bill finally passed both houses of Congress by a 2:1 majority and was signed into law in March 2013.

The language of the new law provides only a partial victory. The international version of this legislation includes required action by nations and international organizations that will put additional economic and political pressure on countries known to be especially abusive to women, but this provision has not yet been adopted by the United States. The much more incisive international version of the bill has been introduced in the U.S. House of Representatives by a bipartisan group of members of Congress, and there are indications of similar support from both parties in the Senate. Its primary sponsor, Representative Jan Schakowsky, Democrat of Illinois, says:

> Violence against women is a humanitarian tragedy, a vicious crime, a global health catastrophe, a roadblock to social and

economic development and a threat to national security. . . .
Sexual violence has been systematically used to destroy communities and to instill a sense of despair and hopelessness
within a population. IVAWA would make ending violence
against women a U.S. foreign policy priority, promote health
programs and survivor services, civil and criminal legal pro-
tections, educational opportunities and economic opportunities for women and girls. Passage of IVAWA would give
us critical tools in the fight against gender-based violence
around the world.

This is an impasse that needs to be resolved, which could make the
United States the preeminent driving force in reducing sexual violence
of all kinds.

For many centuries there has been a debate about the best way to
reduce the extent of prostitution and the forced female slavery and
spread of sexually transmitted diseases it precipitates. During the past
few years I have spoken with the ministers of health in two European
countries that have taken opposite approaches. One of these approaches
seems to be having a beneficial effect.

The Dutch government decided in 2000 that the best way to control prostitution, reduce the rate of sexually transmitted diseases, and
protect women and girls from abuse was to legalize prostitution and the
operation of brothels while regulating the trade. I remember how surprised I was to walk down the street on my first visit to Amsterdam and
pass windows in which attractive women were displaying themselves.
The intent of the law was to give the prostitutes some protection by is-
suing work permits and mandatory health inspections. A sex tourism
boom resulted, and in 2008 there were 142 licensed brothels in Amsterdam and about five hundred window displays. However, a former
mayor of the city has stated that the enormous business of more than

$100 million annually has been largely taken over by Eastern European crime syndicates that are trafficking women and illegal drugs. So, although prostitution remains legal, there is now a government move to rescue these women and help them find other trades.

Sweden tried for a hundred years to pass legislation making illegal the purchase of sex by men, and when new legislation was drafted and debated in 1999 this was the key issue. There was a strong sentiment that the women themselves should not be punished, since it was believed that many were improperly enticed or actually forced into prostitution. Although Sweden has the highest proportion of women parliamentarians in Europe, they were divided on the key issues. The final legislation made it illegal to buy sexual services, to act as a pimp, or to operate a brothel, but the prostitutes were not considered to be acting illegally. The number of sex workers in Sweden dropped more than 40 percent during the next five years, and their prices have also fallen.

Other European countries watched these two experiments closely, and both Norway and Iceland passed laws similar to Sweden's. Nick Kristof reports, "Customers can easily find an underage Eastern European girl working as a prostitute in Amsterdam, but not in Stockholm." Germany adopted the Dutch model in dealing with prostitution and found that the trade increased by 70 percent in its larger cities. As I write this, in December 2013, the most intense public debate in France is whether to adopt a law similar to that in Sweden. The legislation has passed the Assembly and is expected to be approved by the Senate in June 2014. At the same time, the Supreme Court of Canada voted unanimously to strike down the country's three basic laws governing the sex trade: prohibiting the operation of a brothel, banning pimping and preventing prostitutes from hiring security guards, and making soliciting or communicating to clients illegal. The Parliament was given a year to devise alternative legislation.

The key to the relative success of Sweden's approach is to prescribe punishment for those who own and operate the brothels and control the women, as well as the male customers who provide the profit motive.

This was the strong recommendation of participants in our Human Rights Defenders Forum who are trying to control the trafficking of women in Atlanta and other places where sexual slavery is rampant. There is little doubt that public exposure in a trial and the imposition of a heavy fine or jail time for prominent male citizens or police officers who patronize or profit from the sex trade would be extremely effective. The opposite policy still exists in the United States, where there are fifty times as many female prostitutes arrested as their male customers and handlers.

There was one encouraging case in Atlanta in September 2013, when a pimp was sentenced to life imprisonment for abusing a fifteen-year-old girl. He was found guilty by a jury on charges including human trafficking, pimping, aggravated sodomy, child molestation, statutory rape, and false imprisonment. The convicted man had contacted the teenager online before meeting her in person the previous November, imprisoned her in his home, raped her, and then set up appointments for male customers in various hotels and took all the money she collected. This teenager was one of the more fortunate: she was able to obtain a cell phone from one of her customers and called her parents; they notified the police, and she was rescued after a relatively short period in captivity.

Pastor Paul Palmer is the founder of the Atlanta Dream Center, whose mission is to serve and rescue minors held in sexual slavery in that city, and during our conference he was asked what religious leaders could do to address this terrible crime. He responded with some emotion, "Buyers do not wake up and think that they want to go out and buy children. They start with something else, pornography or perhaps they were abused as young boys, and tend to struggle with abusive expressions of masculinity. We have not taught men that we need to honor these women as our sisters. . . . We have failed in religious leadership because we have assumed that this is just what young men are going to go through. We must take a stand and say 'No more!' "

Morocco has provided a sterling example of what can be done to enhance women's rights in a political environment where Islamic law is a powerful factor. The first time we visited the country, more than thirty years ago, Rosalynn and I traveled to Fez, Marrakech, and other cities before returning to Rabat to meet with King Hassan II. He had become a good friend of my mother; he told me they engaged in surprisingly personal banter. As his guest on an earlier visit to Morocco, she had declined a gift of several bottles of expensive perfume, claiming that she had no room in her luggage. He promised to deliver the gift in person, and when he and his two sons came to the White House on a state visit, the king asked that Mama attend the official ceremonies. That first night he knocked on her door and with a broad smile presented her with an enormous bottle of Chanel #5 perfume. She exclaimed, "You're just like every other man off on a trip without his wife!" I doubt that anyone had ever spoken to His Majesty in this way.

We laughed about my mother's comment when we had supper later as the king's guests in the palace and had a delightful conversation about family affairs. He commented that he was trying to find a wife for his oldest son, Mohammed, and explained that it was the custom in Morocco for a prince to marry the daughter of a nonrelated desert chieftain, who was believed to have strains of independence and vigor in her genes. Prospective brides would be presented at the palace and "tried before selection" by the prince. His Majesty complained that Mohammed had decided to do his own choosing. In the end the Crown Prince married Salma Bennani, who is the daughter of a schoolteacher and has a degree in engineering. As Princess Lalla Salma, she is the first wife of a Moroccan king to receive a royal title; others had been known simply as "mother of the king's children" or something equivalent.

King Mohammed VI now rules the kingdom, and, over substantial opposition, including massive public demonstrations, he proposed improvements in the status of Moroccan women. In 2004 the Parliament finally accepted his proposals. The new laws raised the minimum age of marriage to eighteen unless exceptions are made by a judge, prescribed husband and wife equal and with joint responsibility for their family, granted women more rights in setting the terms of marriage contracts, and did away with mandatory male guardians when a girl comes of age. Women can no longer be married against their will, nor are they subservient to their husband in child-rearing decisions, and any marriage disputes must be settled within a month. Whichever parent cares for the children owns the house. Both daughters and sons have the right to inherit property, and children born out of wedlock can acknowledge their own paternity. King Hassan II had two wives, but the new law permits a second marriage only if a judge determines that there are exceptional reasons for it, if the first wife gives her approval, and if the husband proves that he can support two families. A divorce can be granted only in a secular court, with no religious involvement, and attempts at reconciliation must first be exhausted. If spouses have independent incomes, they can negotiate a contract separate from the marriage vows concerning the management and ownership of assets.

Other Islamic kingdoms, and all Western nations, should implement these reforms.

A partnership between a political leader and an actress provides another example of rapid progress in resolving a serious problem. The abuse of women in the Bosnian war was the subject of a dramatic motion picture, *In the Land of Blood and Honey*, produced and directed by Angelina Jolie. British foreign secretary William Hague was encouraged by one of his assistants to watch an advance screening of the film, and it convinced him to launch a major diplomatic effort to publicize the problem of rape in war zones and marshal as much international support as possible for corrective actions by governments. In May 2012 he announced an alliance with Jolie, who was special envoy to the UN High Commissioner for Refugees, pledging to establish a seventy-member team from the United Kingdom that would be deployed to war zones to gather evidence and testimony for use in the prosecution of those involved in sexual violence in conflict zones, to encourage individual nations to adopt more effective laws, and to utilize doctors, lawyers, police, and others to protect and care for rape victims. Secretary Hague and Ms. Jolie declared that more than twenty thousand women were raped in Bosnia and Herzegovina, more than fifty thousand in Sierra Leone, and at least 250,000 were raped during the one hundred days of genocide in Rwanda in 1994. Only a few men have ever been brought to justice for these crimes. Similar reports are now emerging from the civil conflict in Syria.

Hague and Jolie recently visited eastern Congo and Rwanda to meet survivors of sexual abuse and with regional political leaders who claim to have some authority over the militia groups who are known to be the brutal rapists. The foreign secretary pointed out that rape is used as a weapon of war in conflict zones and that, more often than not, the international community ignores these brutal crimes and so the perpetrators repeat the cycle of abuse. It was reported that 74 percent of survivors of rape treated in a hospital in Goma, in eastern Congo, were children, and eleven baby girls between the ages of six and twelve months had been raped! Jolie said, "For too long these innocent victims of war, responsible for none of the harm, have been bearing the worst of the pain."

Three weeks later Hague presided over a meeting of foreign ministers from Canada, France, Germany, Italy, Japan, Russia, and the United States, who all approved a new international agreement declaring that rape and sexual violence are grave violations of the Geneva Conventions and that universal jurisdiction can apply; it also provided for documentation and investigation of these crimes to be used in the prosecution of the guilty. In hopes of preventing such crimes altogether, a primary thrust of the agreement is that perpetrators of sexual violence will not be granted immunity in peace treaties. When the United Kingdom acted as president of the UN Security Council in June 2013, Foreign Secretary Hague used this opportunity to open the debate on sexual violence in conflicts. The result was a unanimous vote for a Security Council resolution on the subject, with forty-five nations as cosponsors. When I visited Secretary Hague in July 2013, he told me that he intended to convene a global gathering on the same subject during the UN General Assembly in September 2013, and he met this commitment. This recent effort by a diplomat and a movie star to force the long-ignored issue of rape during wartime onto the international agenda has been a notable achievement.

One of my personal heroes is Ela Bhatt, also an Elder, from India. Her parents were Brahmins, and she received a superb education leading to a law degree. In 1955 she joined the legal department of the Textile Labor Association (TLA), founded by Mahatma Gandhi, and soon became the leader of its women's wing. In 1972, when the textile mills of Ahmedabad, India's fifth largest city, were failing and workers were laid off, Ela visited their neighborhood and found that the women were supporting their family through vending and home-based work like sewing and cigarette rolling. This work was low-paying and exploitative. She became increasingly concerned when she realized that there were state laws protecting industrial workers but not the thousands of self-employed women who worked to provide their family with an income. She organized them into the Self-Employed Women's Association (SEWA), with herself as the general secretary. She followed the example of Gandhi, who believed that an organization of workers should cover all aspects of their lives as a holistic defense against oppressive laws or state policies. SEWA was soon seen as more militant than the TLA, and the interests of the self-employed women were sometimes at odds with those working in large factories.

There were riots in 1981, when high-caste Indians protested the reservation of jobs and opportunities for untouchables. Since a large portion of SEWA members were from the untouchable caste, Ela and SEWA defended the downtrodden group. They were expelled from the TLA for their outspokenness, but the result was that SEWA expanded rapidly in membership and influence. Today SEWA is the largest primary union in India, with 1.7 million women members. Ela has formed more than a hundred cooperatives among women who were extremely poor; nearly three-fourths lived on less than 20 cents a day and had no prospect of income after their working days were over. Now there are more than 100,000 women enrolled in SEWA's health and life insurance program and 350,000 depositors in its bank. Most loans are in the neighborhood of $100, and even with a fairly high interest rate of about 15 percent to cover administrative costs, the bank reports that the repayment rate exceeds 97 percent.

In accepting the Indira Gandhi Prize for Peace, Disarmament and Development in February 2013, Ela Bhatt described the character and contribution of working women with these beautiful words:

> I have faith in women. . . . In my experience, as I have seen within India and in other countries, women are the key to rebuilding a community. Why? Focus on women and you will find an ally who wants a stable community. She wants roots for her family. You get a worker, a provider, a caretaker, an educator, a networker, a forger of bonds. I consider thousands of poor working women's participation and representation an integral part of the peace and development process. Women bring constructive, creative and sustainable solutions to the table. . . . A woman who tends a small plot of land, grows vegetables, weaves cloth, and provides for the family and the market, while caring for the financial, social, educational and emotional needs of her family is a multifunctional worker and the builder of a stable society.

During deliberations of The Elders, Ela usually listens to our debates without interrupting; then she raises her hand and everyone gets quiet to listen. On almost any issue she can point out how it affects the well-being of poor female workers, and she invariably describes how their proper treatment and incorporation into the larger society can be of benefit to everyone. She defines women's poverty as "violence with social consent."

> Violence against women is the most prevalent and the most hidden injustice in our world today. As I lay out in my book *On God's Side*, what has been missing from this narrative is the condemnation of these behaviors from other men, especially men in positions of power, authority, and influence—like those in our pulpits. In a section of that book, I say "we need to establish a firm principle: the abuse of women by men will no longer be tolerated by other men." The voices of more men need to join the chorus to make that perfectly clear.
>
> JIM WALLIS, AUTHOR, FOUNDER AND EDITOR OF *Sojourners* MAGAZINE

After years of concerted effort by The Carter Center to alleviate the mistreatment of women and girls, one of the most important lessons we have learned is that outside organizations like ours, even when working with women who are fighting their own abuse, cannot bring about an end to child marriage, genital cutting, or exclusion of women from equal treatment without the support of the entire community, especially including traditional chiefs and other male leaders. Molly Melching, the head of Tostan, said that when men were asked to join their discussion groups the women began calling their goal "human rights" instead of "women's rights." Including men had a positive effect, because Tostan began making real progress in ending genital cutting and child marriage only when the men gave their quiet approval or began speaking out in favor of the reforms. One of the most effective inducements for local chiefs and other men to oppose child marriage, for instance, is to show them how families can become more prosperous if the girls can go to school and be gainfully employed rather than sold at an early age to become a servant in their husband's home.

After attending one of our local human rights sessions in the Democratic Republic of Congo, a traditional chief attended our Human Rights Defenders Forum in Atlanta and then returned home to discover that a local soldier had raped a fourteen-year-old girl. The chief personally found the soldier, tied him to a chair, and waited for the police to arrive and arrest him. He then used his influence to prevent anyone from condemning or ostracizing the girl. The benefits from this kind of bold action have been proven in Malawi, Senegal, Liberia, Ghana, and other African countries. When some of these leaders have recognized the societal advantages of making changes, they have become effective spokesmen among their own people and in nationwide councils.

Another good example comes from the *Atlantic* magazine, which in June 2013 told the story of an English teacher named Kwataine in central Malawi. As a young man he had seen a woman struggling in labor; unable to reach the local health clinic in time to stop her bleeding, she died. When Kwataine became chief, he decided that all women should have a "secret mother" to advise her during pregnancy and then should be attended by a qualified person at the time of birth. He imposed fines of a goat or a chicken if the family permitted a woman to go into labor in her home without care. His strict policies have resulted in no maternal deaths during the past three years, whereas there were forty in his district in 2007. Kwataine is now recruiting young girls as skilled midwives and has set a goal of having two thousand midwives by 2015. The president of Malawi, Joyce Banda, has recognized his good work and is offering Kwataine as an example for the other twenty thousand chiefs in the country.

What prevents us from following the example of Kwataine and the Congo chief and taking action to secure basic human rights for women? Some of us are paralyzed by the extent and complexity of the problems. Some of us have become desensitized by societal violence and no longer recognize it when it occurs. Some have misinterpreted Holy Scripture and believe God has ordained a lower status for women. Some men are afraid of losing their advantages in a paternalistic society. But these two simple success stories illustrate how the suffering of women and girls can be alleviated by an individual's forceful action and how the benefits of such actions stretch out into the larger society. Political and religious leaders share a special responsibility, but the fact is that all of us can act within our own spheres of influence to meet the challenges.

My hope is that this book and the publicity that will result from its promotion will be of help. The Elders will continue to devote significant effort to fighting discrimination and abuse of women and girls, and all of us at The Carter Center are eager to contribute whatever resources we have to join others in this effort. For example, The Center's initiative Mobilizing Faith for Women is preparing to offer an online resource for those who wish to be involved, either by being inspired to take action or by reporting on what they are doing. The following are actions that we will monitor and support, and we encourage readers to visit our website, www.cartercenter.org, and participate with us in this effort.

1. Encourage women and girls, including those not abused, to speak out more forcefully. It is imperative that those who do speak out are protected from retaliation.
2. Remind political and religious leaders of the abuses and what they can do to alleviate them.
3. Encourage these same leaders to become supporters of the United Nations High Commissioner for Human Rights and other UN agencies that advance human rights and peace.
4. Encourage religious and political leaders to relegate warfare and violence to a last resort as a solution to terrorism and national security challenges.
5. Abandon the death penalty and seek to rehabilitate criminals instead of relying on excessive incarceration, especially for non-violent offenders.

6. Marshal the efforts of women officeholders and first ladies, and encourage involvement of prominent civilian women in correcting abuses.

7. Induce individual nations to elevate the end of human trafficking to a top priority, as they did to end slavery in the nineteenth century.

8. Help remove commanding officers from control over cases of sexual abuse in the military so that professional prosecutors can take action.

9. Apply Title IX protection for women students and evolve laws and procedures in all nations to reduce the plague of sexual abuse on university campuses.

10. Include women's rights specifically in new UN Millennium Development Goals.

11. Expose and condemn infanticide of baby girls and selective abortion of female fetuses.

12. Explore alternatives to battered women's shelters, such as installing GPS locators on male abusers, and make police reports of spousal abuse mandatory.

13. Strengthen UN and other legal impediments to ending genital mutilation, child marriage, trafficking, and other abuses of girls and women.

14. Increase training of midwives and other health workers to provide care at birth.

15. Help scholars working to clarify religious beliefs on protecting women's rights and nonviolence, and give activists and practitioners access to such training resources.

16. Insist that the U.S. Senate ratify the Convention on the Elimination of All Forms of Discrimination Against Women.

17. Insist that the United States adopt the International Violence Against Women Act.

18. Encourage more qualified women to seek public office, and support them.

19. Recruit influential men to assist in gaining equal rights for women.

20. Adopt the Swedish model by prosecuting pimps, brothel owners, and male customers, not the prostitutes.

21. Publicize and implement UN Security Resolution 1325, which encourages the participation of women in peace efforts.

22. Publicize and implement UN Security Resolution 1820, which condemns the use of sexual violence as a tool of war.

23. Condemn and outlaw honor killings.

ACKNOWLEDGMENTS

I want to express special thanks to Karin Ryan and my other partners at The Carter Center who made it possible for me to write this book. As our leading specialist on human rights, Karin has orchestrated our annual assembly of human rights heroes from around the world, which we call Human Rights Defenders Forums. Over the years, she has emphasized the increasing importance of discrimination against women as an issue for us to address, and has assembled the foremost protectors of women's rights to share their information and advice with us. The incisive comments of some of the key participants in our 2013 session were especially useful to me.

This is the eleventh time that I have enjoyed the benefit of having Alice Mayhew as editor, and she and the other editors and designers at Simon & Schuster have been of great help. Their generous stream of questions, suggestions, and corrections have made the entire process both challenging and gratifying.

Since 1981, Dr. Steve Hochman has monitored my university lectures, my speeches, and the texts of all my books, and his emphasis on clarity and accuracy continues to increase my own desire to reach his high standards.

INDEX

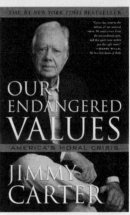

Kill My Darling

The brand-new Bill Slider mystery

When Melanie Hunter goes missing, the men in her life come under suspicion. And there's plenty to suspect: lies, half-truths, deceptions. When you pull one thread, the whole fabric of family life can come apart. There are secrets in Melanie's past, and pain she tried to hide from the world. Slider and his team need to answer two questions: who loved Melanie, and who loved her too much...

*Recent Titles by Cynthia Harrod-Eagles
from Severn House Large Print*

THE COLONEL'S DAUGHTER
A CORNISH AFFAIR
DANGEROUS LOVE
DIVIDED LOVE
EVEN CHANCE
HARTE'S DESIRE
THE HORSEMASTERS
JULIA
LAST RUN
THE LONGEST DANCE
NOBODY'S FOOL

The Bill Slider Mysteries

GAME OVER
FELL PURPOSE
BODY LINE
KILL MY DARLING

Kill My Darling

A Bill Slider Mystery

Cynthia Harrod-Eagles

Severn House Large Print
London & New York

This first large print edition published 2012
in Great Britain and the USA by
SEVERN HOUSE PUBLISHERS LTD of
9-15 High Street, Sutton, Surrey, SM1 1DF.
First world regular print edition published 2011 by
Severn House Publishers Ltd., London and New York.

British Library Cataloguing in Publication Data

Harrod-Eagles, Cynthia.
  Kill my darling. -- (The Bill Slider mysteries)
  1. Slider, Bill (Fictitious character)--Fiction.
  2. Police--England--London--Fiction. 3. Missing
  persons--Investigation--Fiction. 4. Family secrets--
  Fiction. 5. Detective and mystery stories. 6. Large type
  books.
  I. Title II. Series
  823.9'2-dc23

ISBN-13: 978-0-7278-9842-5

Severn House Publishers support The Forest Stewardship Council
[FSC], the leading international forest certification organisation. All
our titles that are printed on Greenpeace-approved FSC-certified paper
carry the FSC logo.

MIX
Paper from
responsible sources
FSC
www.fsc.org
FSC® C018575

Printed and bound in Great Britain by the
MPG Books Group, Bodmin, Cornwall.

One

Failure to Lunch

At first Connolly thought he was crying; but after a few minutes she realized he just had a left eye that watered. The gesture of taking out a handkerchief and drying it was too automatic not to be habitual.

He was spare, rangy – one of those old men who are all bones and sinews, with blue-veined, knuckly hands and the deeply-lined face of a smoker. She supposed his age to be about seventy but she was aware she was not much good at judging ages and he could have been fifty-five for all she knew. She was also wary of old people in general: they were unpredictable, and frequently had no boundaries. Back home in Dublin you were always being seized by the arm by some owl one you barely knew, and subjected to an embarrassing catechism. It was one of the reasons she had come to London in the first place. Your man here had a very sharp and knowing eye. He looked as if he might say anything.

She was also wary of basements: she had entered his flat gingerly, but although it was gloomy and bare, it was tidy and, thank you

5

Baby Jesus and the orphans, clean, with no worse smell than a faint whiff of stale tobacco. Actually, it wasn't entirely a basement. Because the big old house on Cathnor Road was built into a slope, it was a basement at the back and the ground floor at the front; for the same reason, the flat upstairs was ground floor at the back and first floor at the front, with steps up to an imposing door with a portico over it. Above that the house had been divided into two more flats, one to each level, which had their entrance at the side.

Outside, despite being April, it was bitterly cold – the country still in the iron grip of a north wind coming directly down from the Arctic, so sharp you could have filleted sole with it. It wasn't any too warm inside here, either. Your man was obviously the Spartan type. She kept her coat on, but she unbuttoned it and loosened her scarf – otherwise, as her mammy said, she wouldn't feel the benefit when she went out again.

'So, it's about your neighbour upstairs, is it?' she asked, having refused an offer of tea that sounded too perfunctory to be accepted. She took out her notebook and rested it on her knee. The flat was one long room, lit by a window at each end, the rear one subterranean, looking out on to a well. Both were barred – did Victorian servants have to be kept from escaping? A small kitchen at the rear end was divided off by a kitchen counter, at which a solitary stool indicated where the eating was done. On the counter was a twelve-inch TV, so ancient the instruction manual was probably in Latin.

The front end of the room contained a bed against the wall under the window, a single armchair in front of the gas fire, a Utility sideboard and a tall, narrow wardrobe. Through a partly-open door she could see the small, windowless bathroom. And that was it.

There seemed to be no possessions, papers, photos – nothing on display. Whatever – she checked her note – Mr Fitton owned, it was tidily stowed away. The bed, on which he sat, for want of anywhere else, was neatly made with a grey blanket and a single pillow, and he himself was clean and shaved, his hair neatly cut. There was something about this almost monastic spareness and order that was familiar. The solitary man, the ingrained tidiness – had he been a soldier? She had family back in Ireland who'd been in the army. Or, wait, a sailor – neatness enforced by the confined space on shipboard? Whatever. She recognized it from somewhere. It'd come to her, eventually.

'What's her name?' Connolly asked, pencil poised.

'Melanie. Melanie Hunter.' He watched her write it down.

'And when did you last see her?'

'To speak to, not for a few days. But I heard her go out last night. She parks her car just outside my window. She went out about half seven. And I heard her come home later.'

'What time would that be?'

'Round about ha'pass ten. I was watching the ten o'clock news and they'd got on to the weather forecast.'

'Did you see her?'

'No, but I heard the car. And there it is,' he concluded, with a jerk of his head. Through the bars you could see the green Polo parked on the paving where the front garden had once been.

'Did you hear her go out again?'

'No, but I might not hear her if she went out on foot. Probably would if she took the car.'

'So what makes you think she's missing? She could have gone out again this morning.'

He shrugged. 'I wouldn't have thought anything about it if I hadn't heard Marty up there.'

'Marty? Is that her boyfriend?'

'The dog,' he said shortly, as if she should have known. She had noticed it, of course, when she came in – she liked dogs. It was a big mongrel, black with ginger linings, the colour of a Dobermann, but more like an Alsatian in its squareness and sturdiness and the density of its coat and tail. It had stood up politely when she entered but had not approached her, and now was lying on the floor at the end of the bed, chin on paws, looking rather depressed. Its ginger eyebrows twitched as the brown eyes moved from face to face, following the conversation, and when Mr Fitton spoke its name, the tail beat the ground twice, but it did not otherwise move.

'Oh. I thought it was yours,' she said. 'Marty.' She wrote it down.

'First I heard him bark. That was unusual enough. Normally he's quiet as a mouse. A good dog, that.' He looked down, and the tail beat again. 'But he gave a sort of wuff or two about

8

eightish this morning. Then for the next couple of hours he was barking on and off. Then this afternoon he starts howling as well.' Fitton shook his head. 'I knew something must be wrong. I started wondering if she'd had an accident. Slipped in the shower or something, and he was trying to call for help. So I went up and knocked. There was no answer, but Marty started barking like mad, so I let myself in.'

'You have a key?' Connolly asked, trying not to sound interested.

But he gave her a canny look that said *wanna make something of it?* 'Yeah, I got a key. *She* gave it me, years ago. I've waited in for workmen for her, taken in parcels, that sort of thing. Why not? She's at work all day and I'm – not.'

There was the faintest hesitation before the last word, and Connolly wondered if he had been going to say 'retired' – which was what she expected – and why he had changed it.

'Fine. So you went in?'

'I called out, but there was no answer. Poor old Marty was frantic. He led me straight to the kitchen. Both his bowls were empty, and he'd done a pee on the floor. That was what was upsetting him most, I reckon. It worried me, because she was devoted to that dog. I looked into the other rooms, but I guessed she wasn't there, or Marty would've led me straight to her. So I cleaned up the pee, took his bowls and his bag of biscuit and brought him down here with me. I couldn't leave him alone. I took him out for a quick walk, just round the block. But she's still not turned up. So I rang you lot.' He met her

9

eyes with a steady look she couldn't quite interpret. 'I didn't want to get involved,' he said. 'But I knew something must've happened to her.'

Connolly found the look unsettling. She lapsed into automatic. 'I understand you're concerned about her, sir, but I think it's a bit early to be talking about her being missing. I mean, it's only Saturday afternoon, and you don't know when she went out – it could be just a few hours, and she could be anywhere.'

That was as far as she got. 'You're not listening to me,' he said. 'A dog will hold its bladder all day rather than foul the house, so he must have been left alone longer than he could hold on. I reckon she must have gone straight back out last night. Meant to come back but was prevented. She'd never put Marty through that deliberately. If she was held up somewhere she'd've rung me. She knows I've got the key and I never mind seeing to him.'

'Do you often look after him?'

'No, not often, but now and then. If she was just going to be away just the one night she might ask me to take him out and feed him. If she was going away a long time – like, on holiday – she'd take him round her mum's. They live out Ealing way.'

'Have you spoken to them? They might know where she is.'

'I haven't got the number. But if I had, I would not go blurting it out to them that something's wrong. I keep telling you, she wouldn't've left the dog like that. Something's happened to her.'

10

'It's nice that she has you to worry about her,' Connolly said placatingly.

'She's a nice girl,' he said. 'Smart, too. She's a palaeontologist. Works down the Nat His Mu.'

'The what now?'

'Natural History Museum. Down Kensington. Always called it the Nat His Mu when I was a kid. Yeah, she's smart, Mel. Got a degree. Not that that always means anything, but she's smart all right. But she never looks down on you. Always polite and friendly. Not like her boyfriend.'

'You don't like him?'

'It's not me has to like him, is it?' He paused a beat, then added, as if it were justification, 'He's an estate agent.'

Connolly almost smiled, but realized he meant it. 'That's bad, is it?'

'I reckon there's something shady about him.' He made the 'money' gesture with his forefinger and thumb. 'On the make. He came down here once, trying to persuade me to sell this flat. Said he had a buyer interested. I know what his game was. Wanted to buy it himself, knock it back through with Mel's, turn it into a maisonette.'

He gestured towards the oddest feature of the room, the staircase that went up behind the kitchen wall and ended at the ceiling. When the house was a house, it would have been the servants' access to 'upstairs'. Now it was being used to store the only personal items in view – a small collection of books. It hadn't occurred to her before, but stairs made a good bookcase. She could see some of the titles from here. Dickens,

Shakespeare, Graham Greene, Hemingway. Hold me back! And what was that big fat one, looked like a textbook? Con-something. Constitutional history? Ah, yes, *Your 100 Best Acts of Parliament*. Janey Mack! That lot was so dry you could use 'em to mop up oil spills.

'Be worth a fortune, a maisonette,' he went on, 'price of houses round here. But *he* tries to make out that mine's not worth anything. "Needs too much doing to it," he says, like he'd be doing me a favour, taking it off my hands.' He made a sardonic sound. 'I know what it's worth, thank you very much, Mister Smarmy. The parking spaces alone are worth a mint.' He jerked a thumb towards the front window. 'I bought all three when I had the chance, years ago. And that was *before* residents' parking. I rent 'em out. Seventy quid a week, each.'

Connolly wasn't sure this was getting them anywhere. She tapped her pad with her pencil. 'This boyfriend – have you got his name and address?'

'Name's Scott. Scott Hibbert.'

'Address?'

'He lives upstairs. They live together.'

'Oh, I didn't realize.'

'Been here two years. Don't know what she sees in him. He's not *that* good-looking. I suppose he's got money in his pocket. Maybe she just likes to have someone to take her out, buy her meals. Women are funny: go for real creeps rather'n be on their own. What's wrong with your own company?'

He seemed actually to be asking her, and she

reflected that it was the opposite to what she was usually asked – which was, from the aunties and neighbours back home, when are you getting married, why haven't you got a boyfriend? But the first rule of interviewing was don't get sidetracked into responding. *Ve vill ask ze qvestions.*

'Where was the boyfriend last night, so?'

'I don't know. Mel told me he was going away for the weekend, when I saw her Thursday morning. I was outside having a smoke when she was leaving for work. I said, "Never mind, nearly the weekend," and she said, "Yeah, I'm looking forward to it. Scott's going away and I've got it all to myself." Something like that. Said she was going to lie on the sofa and watch soppy films all weekend.'

'She didn't say where he was going?'

'No.'

'Only, she might have gone to join him,' Connolly said, thinking aloud.

He drew an audible breath. 'I've told you,' he said with suppressed energy, 'she would *never have left the dog.*'

'Right,' said Connolly. She was finding being with him in this confined space unsettling. She wanted to be out of here. 'I don't suppose you have his mobile number? No. Well,' she concluded, standing up, 'I'll make a report about it, but unless it's a minor, there's not much we can do at this early stage.'

She didn't add that it also needed a more involved person than the downstairs neighbour to report someone missing. Mr Fitton plainly felt himself to be Melanie's gateway guardian, but that was not how the law saw it; but she didn't want to rile him any more with the suggestion. There was a sort of gleam deep in his eyes that made her nervous. Old geezer or not, he had a sort of wiry strength about him that required cautious handling.

Nobody liked missing persons cases. Most of them were just a waste of time: the subject turned up in due course with a perfectly reasonable excuse, or a perfectly excusable reason – or, on the odd and more entertaining occasion, with the guilty look of a dog with feathers round its mouth. Then they cursed the reporting party for making them 'look a fool'. Such was human nature, the police often got it in the neck for 'interfering', and came in for a helping of bile. There's always so much to go around.

The exceptions, when the missing person really was missing, were even less likeable: time-consuming hard work, often unresolved; and when there *was* a resolution, it was hardly ever a pleasant one.

It was the quiet time of a non-match Saturday afternoon when she got back to the station, and she found her boss, Detective Inspector Slider, propping up the doorway of the charge room talking to *his* boss, Detective Superintendent Fred 'The Syrup' Porson. Connolly, a latecomer to Shepherd's Bush nick, had assumed that the sobriquet was ironic, since Porson was noticeably, almost startlingly, bald. It had had to be explained to her that when his dear wife had died, he had abandoned the rug: a hairpiece so unconvincing – so said Slider's bagman and friend, Detective Sergeant Atherton – it was not so much an imitation as an elaborate postiche. Connolly had had to have that one explained to her as well. She had not been impressed. Atherton, she opined, might be a bit of a ride, but he'd want to ease up on the gags. He was so smart you'd want to slap him.

It was not Porson's weekend on, but as he was not a golfer, he didn't have much to do outside the Job since his wife died. His only daughter was married and lived in Swindon so he didn't see much of her, and he often found himself turning up, faintly surprised, at the shop when he should be elsewhere, like a cat returning to its former home. Slider was leaning comfortably, arms crossed, but Porson, who never stood still, was fidgeting about in front of him like a partnerless man dancing the schottische.

They both looked relieved at the interruption of Connolly's arrival.

'Hullo,' Slider said cordially. 'How was it?'

'What's this? Been out on a case?' Porson enquired eagerly.

Connolly explained and Porson deflated gently like a balloon on the day after the party. 'Nothing in that. Ten to one she turns up before long.'

'Yes, sir. But he was very insistent she wouldn't have left the dog. Said she was pure dotey about it.'

'Not much of a dog lover if she keeps a big dog in an upstairs flat,' Porson complained.

'It's actually the garden flat, sir,' Connolly said, uncertain if she should be correcting the

15

Big Cheese.

'Still leaves it alone all day when she's at work,' Porson pointed out triumphantly.

'Maybe she'd asked someone to take care of it, and they forgot,' said Slider, making peace. But Connolly could see he had taken the point. There was a slight thoughtful frown between his brows.

Porson's had drawn together like sheep huddling from the rain. 'Waste of bloody time. The dog that barked in the night? Or didn't bark, or whatever it was.'

But Connolly, encouraged by the fact that Slider evidently trusted her instincts, made bold to say, 'I just got the feeling there was something in it, sir. This Mr Fitton – there was something about him. I'm not sure what it was, but...'

'Wait a minute,' Porson said, suddenly interested. 'Fitton, you say? Not *Ronnie* Fitton?'

Connolly glanced at her pad. 'Fitton, Ronald. That's right, sir.'

'Come with me,' said Porson.

When the record was brought up on the computer screen, Connolly recognized the face of her interviewee, despite the accretion of years. In fact, he'd had all the same lines when the mugshot was taken, they'd just got deeper; and his hair, though longer and bushier then, had been grey already. The intense eyes were the same. He'd been quite a looker, in the lean, craggy, Harrison Ford sort of mould.

'Fitton, Ronald Dean,' Porson said. 'Recognize him now?'

'I think it's the same man, sir,' said Connolly. But Porson was talking to Slider.

'I don't know that I do,' he said.

'Maybe it was before your time. He was quite a cause celeb at the time. Got sacks o' love letters from daft women.' Porson shook his head in wonder. 'One bit o' fame and they're all over you like a certifiable disease, never mind what you've done.'

'What *did* he do, sir?' Connolly asked.

'Murdered his wife,' Porson said. He looked at her, as if to judge her reaction. Connolly got the idea he was enjoying himself, and remained sturdily unmoved. 'Caught her in bed doing the horizontal tango with the bloke next door and whacked her on the head. She died in hospital a couple of hours later. Funny thing, he never touched the bloke. Just threw his clothes out the window and told him to hop it. Bloke ran out in the road starkers and nearly got run over; white van swerved to avoid him and went into a lamp post.'

'I remember the case now,' Slider said. 'It was before my time, but I remember reading about it.'

'Couldn't miss it, with details like that.' He rubbed his hands with relish. 'White van man turned out to have a load of stolen plant in the back, so they got him at the same time. Then Fitton's ripped the leg off a chair to hit her with. You wouldn't've thought it to look at him – stringy sort of bloke. The tabloids were burbling about madmen having the strength of ten.'

'But he went down, didn't he?'

'Oh yes. Funny, though, he could've got off with a lighter sentence – he was respectable, got no previous, never been in trouble, he only hit her the once, and there was provocation. And like I said he never touched the bloke. Only, he wouldn't express any remorse. Said she had it coming and he'd do it again in the same circs. Said adulterous women deserved to die. That didn't go down well with the women jurors. And prosecuting counsel was Georgie Higgins – remember him?'

'Wrath of God Higgins? Yes, he was quite a character.'

'Anyway, he thundered on about taking justice into your own hands and judgement is mine sez the lord and let him who is without doo-dah stow the first throne and so on. That all went down a treat with the beak, who happened to be old Freeling, who was so High Church God called him sir. Freeling gives Fitton one last chance to say he's sorry, and Fitton not only refuses but comes out with he's an atheist, so Freeling goes purple and jugs him as hard as he can. You could see he was itching to slip on the black cap, if only they hadn't gone and abolished hanging.'

'So he got life?'

'Yes, and then he buggered up his parole by getting into a fight with another prisoner and putting him in the san.' He stroked his nose reflectively.

Now Connolly had placed that monk-like spareness and tidiness: not a soldier or sailor but a long-sentence con. 'Nice class of a character

18

you had me visiting,' she muttered.

'Well, apart from that he was a model prisoner. And there was provocation,' Porson said. 'The other con had it in for him, apparently, and he had form for starting barneys. So,' he reflected, 'Fitton's back on our ground, is he? And a young lady he's interested in's gone missing.'

Oh, right, Connolly thought. *Now* she's a missing person. That's what happened when bosses came in on their days off. What Mr Porson needed was a hobby. She glanced at Slider and saw the same thought in his face.

'Too early to say that, sir,' Slider said mildly.

'It's the early bird that gathers the moss,' Porson retorted. 'If it goes bad, the press'll be all over us for not jumping to it right away. You know what they're like. They love a damson in distress.'

Slider barely blinked. He was used to Porson's hit-or-miss use of language, and the old boy was sharp as a tack and a good boss. A bit of Bush in the boss was worth bearing for the sake of the strand in hand.

'But we've got no reason to think she *is* missing,' he said. He anticipated Porson's next words: 'And Ronnie Fitton would hardly call us in and draw attention to himself if he *had* done something to her.'

'Hmph,' Porson said.

'It's not even twenty-four hours yet. And nobody close to her has reported her missing.'

'As you say,' Porson said, and took himself off as if tiring of the subject; but he turned at the end of the corridor to say, 'I just hope it doesn't

19

come back and bite you in the arse.'

Connolly caught Slider's momentary stricken look, and when Porson had gone said indignantly, 'The meaner! That was below the belt, guv.'

But Slider did not let his firm criticize senior officers – not in front of him, anyway. 'Haven't you got a report to write up? And if you're short of something to do, I've got some photocopying.'

Slider was not on the following day. He was celebrating a Sunday off by sitting on the sofa, nominally reading the papers and watching little George while Joanna practised in the kitchen, but in reality conducting frequent essential checks on the inside of his eyelids, when the telephone rang.

It was Atherton, obscenely breezy. 'Your supposed missing person just got missinger.'

'That's not even a word,' Slider rebuked him with dignity. 'And what are you telling me for?'

'I thought you'd like to know. The boyfriend just reported she's gone walkabout. We haven't told him Fitton already reported it, just in case.'

'In case what?'

'Well, Mr Porson thinks Fitton did it.'

'That doesn't mean he didn't.'

'What a *volte face*! Yesterday you wouldn't admit there was an it for him to have done. Connolly said you had to bite your cheeks at the suggestion.'

'In any case, the boyfriend must know by now that Fitton spoke to us, because Fitton has the dog and he'd have had to go to him to get it back.'

'That's a point. He didn't mention the dog. All right, you go back to sleep. I'll handle everything. And if I need help, I can always pop upstairs and ask Mr Porson.'

Slider sat up. 'Bloody Nora, what's he doing there?'

'There's no way to answer that without laying myself open to disciplinary action.'

'And what do you mean, he didn't mention the dog?'

'Do you want me to read you the interview transcript?' Atherton enquired sweetly.

'No, no. You win. I'll come in,' Slider said, sighing like a whale with relationship problems. 'Connolly felt there was something to it. That girl's developing good instincts.'

'But you did the right thing,' said Atherton. 'Couldn't go on Fitton's say-so. And we still don't know she's missing, for the matter of that – only that she's not at home. She may just have done a runner, and from the look of the boyfriend, who would blame her?'

'If you're trying to comfort me you must think things are bad.'

'Not *yet*, they're not,' Atherton said significantly.

Joanna was used to such interruptions but she was human. She only said, 'It's a pity I've already put the beef in,' but combined with the scent of it on the air, it was enough to break a man's heart.

'You and Dad will enjoy it, anyway,' he said.

His father shared the house with them, a very nice arrangement for babysitting, and for relieving him of anxiety about the old man living alone. 'I probably won't be gone very long.'

'Why have you got to go in, anyway? Just for a missing person?'

'There's an ex-murderer involved.'

'Ex, or axe?'

'Ex as in former.'

'Can you *be* a former murderer? Surely what's done is done.'

'You quibble like Atherton. Anyway, Mr Porson's gone all unnecessary over it, so I want to make sure everything's in place, just in case it turns out to be anything.'

'You'd sooner do it yourself than inherit someone else's mess,' she summarized.

'Wouldn't you?'

She kissed him. 'Go, with my blessing. Cold roast beef's almost better than hot, anyway.'

He kissed her back. 'You're a very wonderful woman,' he said.

'I said "almost",' she reminded him.

Slider was not a tall man, and Scott Hibbert was, and since he didn't like being loomed over, he freely admitted that he started off with a prejudice against the man. Hibbert was both tall and big, but going a little bit to softness around the jaw and middle. He was not bad looking, in an obvious, fleshy sort of way, except that his mouth was too small, which Slider thought made him look weak and a bit petulant. He was wearing jeans and an expensive leather jacket, and

22

shoes, not trainers (one plus point), which were well polished (two plus points); but the jeans had been ironed with a crease (minus a point). His carefully-cut hair was dressed with a little fan of spikes at the front like Keanu Reeves, and his chin was designer-stubbled (minus too many points to count).

Having privately indulged his prejudices for a satisfying few seconds, Slider dismissed them firmly, and prepared to interview Hibbert with a completely receptive mind.

'So, Mr Hibbert, tell me when you last saw Miss Hunter.'

'I already told the other guy everything,' he complained.

Guy. Another minus – no, no, no. Concentrate. 'I'm sorry, but I really would like you to tell me again, in your own words,' said Slider.

Hibbert looked uneasy, and kept crossing and recrossing his legs, and though he was not sweating, his skin looked damp. He licked his lips. 'Look, shouldn't you be *doing* something?' he asked querulously. 'Like, I mean, *looking* for her or something?'

'I assure you the other officer will already have put things in train for a general alert. I need to hear your story so that we can refine the search. You last saw her when?'

'Like I said, Friday morning, before we went off to work,' he said, frowning. 'We usually walk to the tube together, but I was taking my car in because I was going down to the West Country later, so I offered to drop her off at the station. But she said no, she'd rather walk.' His

23

left leg was jiggling all on its own, and he sniffed and wiped the end of his nose on the back of his hand. Slider found these unstudied gestures reassuring. Stillness and composure in witnesses were what worried him. 'She was a bit pissed off with me, if you want the truth,' Hibbert added in a blurty sort of way. 'I was going away for the weekend and she was narked about it.'

'Because?'

'I was going to this wedding in the West Country – my mate Dave – we were at school together – and she didn't want me to go.'

'Why not? Wasn't she invited?'

'Oh, she was invited and everything. Of course she was. Except there was this stag thing on the Friday night that was men only. She didn't want to go to the hen night because she didn't really know Julie, that Dave's marrying, and anyway she'd already got this thing arranged for Friday night with some of her girl friends. I said, so come down on Saturday, then, but she wouldn't. She said she hates weddings anyway, and she never really liked Dave. Well, she can't stand him if you want to know the truth. I mean, they've only met a couple of times and it ended in a stand-up row both times, and she said she never wanted to see him again. I suppose he's a bit blokeish for her, but he's a laugh, and he's my best mate. There's some of her friends I don't like. Well, that's all right – she has her friends and I have mine, why not? We don't have to do everything together. And I couldn't let old Dave down, not on his wedding day, could I?'

Slider guessed he was hearing the essence of

the row that had been. Hibbert was justifying himself to him. He nodded neutrally.

'When I first told her about it, she said it was all right, I should go on my own and she didn't mind,' he went on. 'But Friday morning she was really narky about it, kept saying things about me and Dave getting drunk together. Well, what's a stag night for? And everybody gets drunk at weddings. I said *you* won't have to see us, so what's the problem? And she said wild horses wouldn't drag her there. We had a bit of a barney and she storms off to the bathroom. So then I cool down a bit and when she comes out I say d'you wanna lift to the station, babes, and she gives me a look and says no, she'll walk. And she did.'

'She works at the Natural History Museum? And where do you work?'

'Hatter and Ruck – you know, the estate agents? – in Knightsbridge.'

Posh, Slider thought. 'So you could have dropped her off at work, instead of just offering a lift to the station? You'd go right past it.'

He looked uneasy, and shifted to another buttock. 'I wasn't going in to the office first thing, I was going to look at a house in Hendon. I don't normally take the car in when I'm just in the office because parking's a nightmare up there.'

'And that was the last time you saw her?'

He nodded, looked stricken at the reminder, and found yet another buttock to shift to. How many did he have in there?

'Or spoke to her?'

'No, I rang her Friday evening, while she was

25

out with her mates. I rang her up to make peace, if you want to know, but she was all right again by then. She'd got over and it and just said have a good time and everything and I'll see you Sunday. She's like that – she never stays mad for long.'

'And that was the last time you spoke to her?'

He nodded.

'Did you go home after work on Friday?'

'No, I went straight down to the West Country.'

He kept saying the West Country. Slider thought that odd. 'Where, exactly?'

'Salisbury,' he said. 'Dave lives in Salisbury.'

'And what time did you eventually get home?'

'I was supposed to come back Sunday night – there was a lot of us from the same school and we were going to get together Sunday lunchtime – but I was missing Mel, so I called it off. Well, we'd been talking and drinking all Saturday afternoon and evening, so I reckoned we'd said everything anyway. I didn't sleep very well Saturday night so I got up really early Sunday morning and left. I was back home, what, about ten? She wasn't there, and I knew right away something was up.'

'How?' Slider asked.

Hibbert stared in perplexity at the question.

'How did you know something was wrong?'

'I don't know,' he said. Now he was still, thinking about it: buttocks at rest at last; even the lone break-dancing knee had stopped and held its breath. He scowled with the effort of analysis, and Slider got the impression he was

26

not very bright; and yet, of course, it is easy enough to fake being dumber than you are. It's the opposite that's impossible.

'I dunno,' he said at last. 'It just felt wrong, as if no one had been there.' He thought some more. 'Oh, for one thing, the answer-machine wasn't on. If she'd gone out, she'd have put it on. And she'd have left me a note to say where she was going. She always leaves a note.'

'Even if she was still mad at you?'

'But she wasn't any more. When I spoke to her Friday night she was all right again.'

'Anything else?' Slider prompted. Hibbert looked puzzled by the question, having apparently gone off on another train of thought. 'Anything else you noticed that made you think something was wrong?' He was going after the dog, absence of, but what he got was quite unexpected.

Hibbert's face cleared. He looked as though he'd just got the last answer in the jackpot pub quiz. 'Her handbag was there.'

'Her handbag?' Slider said, trying not to sound like Edith Evans.

'Yeah, her handbag,' he said excitedly. 'With her purse and phone and everything in it. But not her door keys.'

'Excuse me,' Slider said. 'I have to make a phone call.'

27

Two

Deep-Pan, Crisp and Even

Joanna was resigned. 'I'm not surprised,' she said. 'I know once they get hold of you, they won't let you go. That place is a black hole.'

Even over the phone, he thought he could smell the roast beef and Yorkshire. 'It's not that,' he said. 'The case just turned into a case. The girl's handbag is in the flat.'

'Her *handbag*, singular? Tell me any woman of that age who only has one.'

'The handbag she was using, I mean. With her gubbins in it. So it's looking more like foul play, I'm afraid.'

'Oh dear. Well, keep the chin up. There may be an explanation you haven't thought of, and she'll come wandering in looking surprised.'

'I'll settle for that. See you later.'

Atherton drew up just short of the house and craned his head to look. 'No press. Thank God. Amazing no one's spilled the beans yet. Now, where's that key?' He felt in his pocket for the key ring Slider had received from Scott Hibbert.

He was hampered by the seat belt and Connolly only watched him struggle for a millisecond before saying, 'Undo the belt, you looper. And don't bother, because I have me own.' She dangled it before his eyes. 'I got it off Mr Fitton before I left.'

'How did you manage that?'

'He volunteered. Gave it me and said, "I won't be needing this any more."'

'Did he, indeed?'

'Ah, cool the head, it doesn't mean anything. Sure, he'd know we'd check on him as soon as I got back, and find his record, and then we'd want the key offa him anyhow.'

'Yes, but saying he wouldn't need the key any more suggests he knows she's dead.'

'Well *I* know it, so why not?'

'You don't know any such thing. It's still odds-on she'll walk back in any minute. They usually do. And don't forget she took her keys with her. Why would she do that if she wasn't coming back?'

'Don't *you* forget she left her mobile. She'd grab that before her keys, every time.'

Atherton yawned ostentatiously. 'Well, if there is anything in it, we've got the prime suspect under wraps back at the factory, so relax.'

'Scott Hibbert? He didn't do it. He's just a big gom.'

'I take it "gom" is not an expression of approval.'

'Why do you *talk* like that?' Connolly cried in frustration.

Atherton smiled, satisfied now he had goaded her. 'Why don't you like him?'

'What's to like? He's like a big transport-caff

29

fry-up. Everything right there on the plate, and none of it very appetizing. I like a bit of subtlety.'

Atherton slapped his chest. 'Right there,' he addressed the invisible audience. 'She stepped right into my heart, folks. Subtlety, *c'est moi.*'

Connolly gave him a look so cold it could have hosted the Ice Capades. 'What are we looking for up there?'

He became sensible. 'Firstly, anything that suggests she was doing a runner – empty spaces in the wardrobe and so on. Secondly, signs of a struggle, anything that might have been used as a weapon, signs of blood. Also signs of hasty cleaning up. Someone who's just killed someone is usually in too much of a panic to clean properly, which is lucky for us. And always, of course, anything that strikes you as anomalous.'

'As a what now?'

'Odd. Out of place. Wrong. Peculiar.'

'Why didn't you say so in the first place?'

Atherton, having done this so often in Slider's company, used his nose first, as Slider would have, and noticed that the flat had a cold smell about it, as if no one had been there for a while. It occupied a big area in square-footage, but the conversion was an old one, and clumsily done, so the space was not well used. On either side of a large, wasted entrance hall there was a sitting room and a bedroom, both with bay windows on to the front, with a slice cut off at the back to make a bathroom and kitchen, side by side. It all needed modernizing; and a cleverer architect (or

30

indeed, given when it was done, any architect at all) could have made a much nicer flat out of it. If recombined with the basement (as Fitton had said Hibbert had been plotting) it would make a very glamorous maisonette, with a big kitchen/breakfast-room downstairs, and living room, two beds and modern bathroom upstairs. With the big rooms, high ceilings, mouldings and so on, it would fetch a stone fortune in up-and-coming Shepherd's Bush; so it wouldn't be wonderful if Hibbert, who was in the business after all, had spotted the potential.

Leaving aside the property-developing crying-shame it represented, Atherton noted that the furniture was modern but cheap, and that the place was ordinarily tidy. In the bedroom, the bed had been made, in that the duvet had been pulled up, but it hadn't been straightened or smoothed. There was a built-in wardrobe with sliding doors and a free-standing one so stuffed with clothes the doors wouldn't close at all. An exercise bike in the corner had clothes heaped over its saddle, and there were more clothes dumped on a wicker armchair – it would be fun trying to work out what she had been wearing, should the need arise. But there were no used plates or mugs or dirty clothes strewn around, and the floor was clear and the carpet clean. The sitting room was tidier, with only a newspaper, a novel (Laurie Graham, *At Sea*, face down and opened at page 64) and an emery board lying around to show occupation. And the handbag, large and tan leather, which was on the sofa, at the end nearest the door.

Connolly gestured to the remote, lying on the coffee table next to the emery board. 'She coulda been sitting here, doing her nails and watching the TV. See, the TV's not been turned off at the switch – it's on standby.'

'Ninety per cent of people habitually turn off the TV with the remote,' he said. 'Doesn't mean she was interrupted.'

In the bathroom he observed that the inside of the shower and the bath were dry, as were both bath towels, stretched out on a double towel-rail, and the bath mat, hanging over the side of the bath. But there were drops of water still in the basin, and the hand towel was crumpled and damp inside the creases.

'Which accords with no one having showered in here since Friday,' he said. 'Sonny Boy says he came home at ten this morning. So he didn't shower, but did at least wash his hands. Probably after he went to the loo. There are droplets round the loo bowl as well.'

'To much information,' Connolly said, making a face.

'Water droplets, from the flush. Don't be sensitive. Got that torch?' he asked.

The bathroom was fully tiled, and there was tile-patterned acrylic flooring, but both were old, chipped here and there, the grouting discoloured and breaking. Atherton went over everything with the torch, looking sidelong to catch any smearing or marks, shone the torch down the plug holes and under the rim of the toilet ('Rather you than me,' Connolly said) and then did the same in the kitchen – equally old and shabby, but clean and tidy, with the last lot of washing-up (cereal bowls and mugs and a small plate – Friday's breakfast?) clean and very dry in the dish rack.

'A big fat nothing,' Connolly concluded, sounding slightly disappointed.

'If she was abducted, she went without a struggle,' Atherton said, 'and if she was killed here, it was very quick and clean. Or Hibbert's a better housekeeper than he looks. Or –' he gave Connolly a look – 'she walked out of her own accord and will shortly come prancing back through the door demanding to know what we're doing here.'

Connolly studied him. 'You don't think that any more. You're starting to think there's something in it.'

'Not really. Except for the mobile. You've got me worried about the mobile.'

'Hah!'

'Only a bit,' he equivocated. 'If she was just popping down the offy for a packet of fags she might not grab it along with her keys.'

'But then she'd have taken her purse.'

'Not if she took a tenner out of it.'

'But then she'd have come back.'

He shrugged. 'I just think, on balance, given her age and sex, she'd have been more likely to have taken her mobile, and that that constitutes an anomaly. Unfortunately, the only one. If we'd found signs of a struggle or clean-up we could have got a forensic team in, but as it stands there's no evidence to justify it. But we'd better take the handbag back with us. Might be all sorts

33

of goodies in it, besides the phone. Run and get an evidence bag, will you?'

On her way back from the car, when she got to the foot of the steps, Fitton appeared suddenly round the side of the house, where his own front door was, and stood looking at her.

'You came back, then,' he said. 'Decided there was something in it after all.'

'Well,' she said, wondering what it was right to say to him.

He examined her expression in a way that made her shiver. He was too noticing. 'You know about me,' he said flatly, his mouth making a downturn that was more sad than sour.

'How——?'

'I can tell from the way you're looking at me. Like I'm a mad dog that might bite.'

'No,' she protested. 'It's not like——'

'Didn't take long,' he said. 'Knew it wouldn't.' He poked his forehead with a finger and thumb. 'Branded for life.'

'It's just standard procedure,' she said helplessly, not understanding why she wanted to protect his feelings. 'Our Super recognized your name. But it doesn't mean——'

'Just remember I called it in,' he said. 'Benefit of the doubt. All right?'

'It's all in writing,' she said. The dog, Marty, padded round from the side of the house – Fitton must have left the door open – and came up behind him, shoving its head up peremptorily under his hand. He caressed it automatically, and the tail swung.

'You've still got her dog, so,' Connolly said,

34

and cursed herself for the stupid remark.

He jerked his head towards the upstairs flat. *'He* never asked about him. Dipstick probably doesn't even remember he exists. I'll keep him till somebody takes him away.' He started to turn away, the dog sticking close to his side, then looked back to say, 'Benefit of the doubt. Remember.'

'I'll remember the dog likes you,' she said to his retreating back. What an eejitty thing to say. God, she was a thick! She scurried up the steps before she did anything else to embarrass herself.

Swilley was going to see the parents. She had often drawn the short straw in these cases because (a) she was a woman and (b) she was regarded as unflappable. It was better for bad news to be delivered by someone with an air of calm. But since having a child of her own she had liked this task less and less.

Joining the Job at a time when women had to prove themselves not just as good as men, but the same as men, she had early grown a shell against taunts, insults, slights, come-ons and filthy jokes. She had been helped by being tall, blonde, athletic, and beautiful in a sort of wide-mouthed, small-nosed, *Baywatch* way, which rendered most of her tormentors tongue-tied if she actually faced them one-to-one. She was also blessed with an iron head and concrete stomach, which meant she could match them pint for pint and curry for curry; and she was deceptively strong, was a blue-belt in judo, had

35

twenty-twenty vision, and was a crack shot.

Joining Slider's firm had been wonderful for her, because he thought she was a good detective and treated her as one, and at least had the decency to *appear* not to notice her gender. After one early, disastrous mistake she had made it an iron rule not to go out or get involved with any of her colleagues. After a time they had stopped trying and written her off as frigid and probably a lesbian, which she had borne patiently; and eventually had accepted her as one of them, an honorary bloke. Her nickname, Norma, was a tribute to her machismo, and she had worn it with pride. It had been hard won.

So for years she had maintained an icy virginity at work and a wonderfully patient, amazingly understanding secret boyfriend at home; but eventually Tony had grown restless. He disapproved of her refusal to go for promotion. Well, the money would have been nice, but she did not want to have to go through that whole process of training a new lot of resentful males to accept her for herself. The very prospect exhausted her. Also, patient though he was, Tony was still all man, and he didn't like the fact that she kept him secret, as if she was ashamed of him. Not ashamed of him, she told him, but of *them*. But in the end she had to give him *something*, and the price of being allowed to go on being her was first marriage, and then the baby.

She was very happy being married, and Tony had reverted to being patient, adaptable, and helpful to a saintly degree when her job prevented her doing wifely and motherly things; and she adored little Ashley and wondered how they had ever lived without her. But she paid with whole new layers of sensitivity towards lovers, married people, parents, the bereaved; and new layers of fear that the things she saw happening daily to the anonymous victims of crime might happen to her own small family. She had become vulnerable; she had lost her ice. She hoped she had not also lost her edge.

But she approached the present task with resignation. There were lots of things in the Job you didn't necessarily relish – smelly houses, vomiting drunks, decomposing corpses, road accidents – but you did them just the same.

Melanie Hunter's parents weren't called Hunter – she had them down as Wiseman, Ian and Rachel, so either the mum had remarried, or Melanie had changed her name for some reason. They lived in a nice part of Ealing, typical suburbia, Edwardian semis on a street edged with those trees that went into pink blossom like screwed up tissue paper in spring. Of course, they were bare now, the freezing weather having held everything back. Most of the houses had turned their gardens into hardstanding for cars, but where they still had front gardens, they were neatly kept, with clipped privet hedges, and hard-pruned sticks that would be roses later, and oblongs and squares of bare, weeded earth that would be flower beds, showing only the blunt green noses of bulbs.

The faint, watery sun had broken through, and even though it did nothing to mitigate the biting cold, it gave an air of festivity to the street. As it was Sunday, there were cars parked before most of the houses, kids were trundling about on bikes and scooters, and one brave or barmy man was washing his motor with a hose with a foaming sponge attachment. All very Mrs Norman Normal – as were all lives until the meteor of chance hit them, the hurtling rock from the sky crashed at random through their roof.

In the front garden of the Wisemans' house, there was a girl of about eleven or twelve, in a cropped top and skinny jeans that exposed her belly button (why the hell wasn't she freezing? Kids these days! Swilley thought), picking the sugar-pink varnish from her nails with all the destructive boredom of Sunday afternoon. She eyed Swilley with intense interest, scanning her from her pull-on woolly hat down through her camel wool wrap-around coat to her long boots.

'Hello,' Swilley said. 'Are your mum and dad Mr and Mrs Wiseman?'

She nodded.

'Are they in?'

'Mum is,' the girl said, and then, in a burst of confidence: 'She won't buy anything. She never buys anything at the door.'

'That's all right, cos I'm not selling. Can I have a word with her? It's important.'

The girl twisted her head over her shoulder without removing her eyes from Swilley's face and yelled through the half-open front door, '*Mu-u-um*! There's a lady wants you.'

Oh, ever so much a lady, Swilley thought.

'Are you a social worker?' the girl asked

38

abruptly. 'She's not my real mum, she's my stepmum. I like your colour lipstick. What's it called? Do you like vodka?'

A woman appeared behind her, saving Swilley from answering. She was middle aged and ordinary, dressed in slacks, a cotton jumper and an unattractive big, thick, chunky cardigan. She had her glasses in one hand and a biro in the other, and a look between wariness and embryo annoyance on a face that held the remains of prettiness behind the soft plumpness of middle-aged marriage. 'Yes?' she said.

'Mrs Wiseman? I wonder if I could come in and have a word with you,' Swilley said, and showed her warrant card. The woman looked immediately put out and flustered, but the child's eyes opened so wide Swilley was afraid she'd see her brain.

'You're the cops,' she breathed. 'Are you going to arrest Mum?'

'Bethany!' the woman rebuked automatically, but her worried eyes were searching Swilley's face. 'Is it Ian? Is it an accident?'

'No, nothing like that. It may be nothing at all. Can I come in?' Swilley said. The man two doors down had ceased wiping his car's roof and was staring with his mouth ajar and the hose soaking his feet, ha ha.

'Oh, yes. Yes, come on through.'

Bethany slipped in before Mrs Wiseman shut the door firmly behind Swilley. 'Come in the lounge,' she said. Swilley followed her, and as she turned with a question in her face, made a quick sideways gesture of the eyes towards the

39

child, which fortunately the woman was *compos mentis* enough to catch and interpret. 'Bethany, go out in the back garden and play,' she said, sharply enough to be obeyed.

'Play?' the girl complained. 'What am I, a kid? I don't *play.*'

'And shut the back door after you. Don't let all the heat out.'

The girl extracted herself by unwilling inches, leaving Swilley alone with her mother in a knocked-through lounge decorated and furnished in exactly the sort of middle-income, suburban taste Swilley would have expected.

'Would you like to sit down?' Mrs Wiseman said automatically.

Swilley saw she had been doing some sort of paperwork on the coffee table in front of the sofa, and took an armchair.

Mrs Wiseman sat in the chair opposite, looked enquiringly at Swilley, and then suddenly something seemed to come over her. She swayed, gripped the arm of the chair, and said almost in a whisper, 'Oh my God, it's Melanie, isn't it? Something's happened to Melanie!'

She stared at Swilley, white with some awful foreknowledge, and Swilley thought perhaps it was there, latent, in every mother's mind, an instinct born at the moment of conception: the fear that one day some stranger would come and tell you your child had been taken from you. She felt horribly impressed, and a little queasy.

'It's probably nothing to worry about,' Swilley said, though Mrs Wiseman's certainty had communicated itself to her, now. 'It's just that

40

Melanie's not at home, and her boyfriend does not know where she is. Have you heard from her lately?'

'I spoke to her – Friday,' Mrs Wiseman said. 'She rang me from work. She rings me two or three times a week, just for a chat.'

'You're close, then?' said Swilley.

'Always have been,' she said, but with some reservation in her voice Swilley didn't understand.

'Did she tell you anything about her plans for the weekend?'

'She said she was going out for a drink with friends on Friday evening. It was her best friend Kiera's birthday, and they were meeting some others at the Princess Vic.'

'And what about the rest of the weekend?'

'She said she hadn't any plans. Scott – her boyfriend?'

Swilley nodded.

'He was going away for the weekend, so she said she was just going to relax. I asked her to come for Sunday lunch but she said she had some work to catch up on. She's a palaeontologist, you know,' she added with a huge pride that carried the touch of bewilderment of any parent whose child surpasses them by such a length. 'She works at the Natural History Museum. They think the world of her there. I don't know where she gets her brains from,' she added with a little affected laugh. 'It can't be me. I was never even in the sixth form.'

'From her father, perhaps?' Swilley suggested, wanting to keep her talking.

A shadow passed over Mrs Wiseman's face: it looked to Swilley almost like wariness. 'Her father's dead,' she said abruptly.

'Oh, I'm sorry.'

'He was killed in the Greenford rail crash,' she said, as though that ended the topic for good and all. That had been – Swilley counted – eleven years ago: it had been in all the papers, of course. Rail crashes were so thankfully rare, they were all remembered, catalogued in the public mind for ever by their location: Potters Bar, Hatfield, Southall ... Greenford had had an unusually high number of fatalities. 'Ian's my second husband,' Mrs Wiseman concluded.

'Of course,' Swilley said. 'That accounts for why Melanie has a different surname. And Bethany is...?'

'She's Ian's, from his first wife. He was a widower too.'

'So has Melanie any brothers or sisters?'

'No, I just had the one. Why do you ask?'

'I'm wondering if there was anyone she might have gone to visit, that's all. Any aunts, cousins?'

'Not that she'd go and visit. I've got a sister, but we're not close, and Melanie never cared that much for her cousins.'

'What about your husband's family?'

'You mean Ian's? Oh, she would never go to *them*,' she said firmly.

'Does she not get on with her stepfather?'

'They're all right, they get on OK, but they're not what I'd call close. She doesn't think of him as her stepfather, anyway, just my husband. No reason why she should. She was practically grown up by the time I married, and I told her from the beginning, I'm not marrying him for you, I'm marrying him for me.'

Some history there, Swilley thought, making a mental note. Smoothly she went on, 'What about her boyfriend, Scott? Is everything all right between them?'

'Oh yes,' she said with enthusiasm. 'He's a lovely boy – just the sort of man I always wanted for her. Steady, nice manners, a good job. Very polite to me and Ian. And they're mad about each other, no doubt about that.'

'But he went away for the weekend without her,' Swilley suggested. 'Did she mind that?'

'Oh no,' she said quickly. 'You mustn't think that. You see, Scott's got this friend from school, they go way back, but he's not Melanie's sort at all. Loud, and – well, what I'd call vulgar. Tells dirty jokes; and the way he is with women...! Always leering, and making coarse remarks, *you* know. Melanie can't stand him, but of course Scott's fond of him, knowing him all his life – in and out of each other's houses when they were kids. Well, Dave, this friend, was getting married so of course Scott had to go, but there was no need for Melanie to put herself through that. Scott understands. It was all quite amicable. She told me on Friday she was quite happy to stay home, and Scott would enjoy himself more if he went on his own. But...' She faltered, remembering what she had happily forgotten for a few moments. 'You're saying he doesn't know where she is?'

43

'She wasn't there when he got home this morning, and she hadn't left him a note, so he was worried.' She didn't mention the dog or the handbag: no point in upsetting the woman yet. 'I just thought, if they'd had a row, she might have walked out on him – to teach him a lesson, sort of thing...'

'Well, she was all right with him when I spoke to her on Friday,' Mrs Wiseman said, frowning, 'but of course they might have quarrelled since then. I wouldn't know. But if they'd quarrelled that bad, why wouldn't she ring me, and come over here?'

'Could be many reasons,' Swilley said inventively. 'If she knows how much you like him, she might not want to admit to you they'd had a row. So, can you think of anyone else she'd go to? This friend Kiera, for instance – can you give me a contact number or address for her?'

'Yes, I've got that somewhere. She might go to Kiera – they're very close. And she's got lots of other friends. I don't know who they are, really, but Kiera could tell you. There's one she works with, Simone, at the museum – she talks about her sometimes. She gets things from me for her – for Simone. Cosmetics and perfume. I sell cosmetics from home,' she added, casting a glance at the paperwork. 'I've always been in Product Demonstration, you see, ever since I left school. Started off at the Ideal Home. I've done all the big shows. I used to sell Tupperware, when I was married the first time, but cosmetics and fashion jewellery pay better – and you meet a nicer class of person.' She looked at Swilley with professional interest. 'I see you take care of your skin. I could let you have some nice things, if you're interested. It's a good discount. And they're all quality products, top names.'

It was odd, Swilley thought, given the dread she had exhibited at first, how difficult she seemed to find it to keep that at the front of her mind. Perhaps it was a defence mechanism – think about anything except that something might have happened to Melanie. Or perhaps there was something even worse she was trying to keep at bay – something she didn't want Swilley to discover.

She let her yatter on about her products for a bit while she thought about it, and then went about taking her leave. She got the address and phone number of Kiera, and of Scott's parents in Salisbury because she really seemed to want to give them; and she asked for and received a very good photograph of Melanie, taken the year before, which she had been looking at, sand-wiched between heavy glass with a silver foot on a chiffonier across the room. It was quite a formal picture, of a very pretty young woman sitting on a stool with her hands in her lap, smiling at the camera. She had thick tawny-blonde hair, artfully highlighted, hanging in a bob to her shoulders, regular features and very nice teeth. Swilley could see the resemblance to her mother, but she had better cheekbones and a more interesting nose.

'It was a studio portrait,' Mrs Wiseman said proudly. 'She had a whole session last year – Scott paid. It was her birthday present. He's got a friend who's a photographer so he got a discount. He says when they get married they'll get a really good deal.'

'Are they going to get married?' Swilley asked.

'Well, eventually, of course, but they haven't any plans just at present. But I hope it will be soon. She doesn't want to leave it too long to have children. And Scott will make a lovely father. It was him insisted she give this picture to me – he knew I'd like it. Always so thoughtful – such a nice boy. I think *he*'d get married tomorrow but Melanie's hesitating – you know what girls are like these days. Don't want to give up their freedom. But Scott was hinting about next year the last time I saw him. He doesn't want them to have kids without being married, which is just the way it should be.'

She was smiling now, and Swilley mentally shook her head at this degree of self-hypnosis. Far be it from her to shatter the protective bubble. Maybe Melanie would turn up before she need look her fears in the face.

At the door she asked, 'By the way, what does your husband do?'

'Ian? He's a teacher at Elthorne Manor – PE and sports. He's out at the moment – Sunday League down the Rec.'

But the new subject had done it. The smileyness drained from her face and the dread was back in the eyes.

'You'll find her, won't you?' she asked in a husk of a voice. 'She'll be all right? Only, it's not like her just to go out like that, and not say

46

anything.'

'I'm sure there's a logical explanation,' Swilley said hearteningly, and made her escape. She was sure there was a logical explanation, but that didn't necessarily mean it would be good news.

As she was getting into her car, a silver Ford Galaxy pulled up on to the Wiseman hardstanding and a man in a tracksuit got out, pulling a sports bag after him. He was of medium height, well built about the shoulders, with very dark hair and a tanned, hard face that missed being handsome by some small, inexplicable degree. He stood for a moment staring at Swilley, scowling, his head up as if ready to take affront. She wondered if he had seen her coming out of his house as he drove up. She hastened to get into her car, not wanting to talk to him, especially as he did not seem in a good mood. Let Mrs W explain all – she had had enough for one day.

When a young woman is murdered, there is always one photograph the press latches on to. It is splashed over every paper and news bulletin all through the investigation, at the arrest, during the trial, and on sentencing. It defines the case, and sometimes even the age, so that forever after that person, who would have lived out her life in obscurity, is as instantly, iconically recognized by millions as Marilyn Monroe with her skirt blowing up, or Princess Di looking up from under her fringe. It was as if, Slider thought, their fate had been decided at the instant the photographer's finger had pressed the button. From that moment, they moved as inevitably towards their doom as a package on a conveyor belt.

Slider had always found old photographs unsettling, and he'd had a bad feeling from the moment Swilley returned with the studio portrait of Melanie Hunter. He knew they would use it, because it was clearer than the snapshot Hibbert had given them from his wallet; and he knew the media would love it, because she looked pretty and smiley and good, a nice girl with a good school record and a fine career ahead of her. How much more saleable of newspapers than a grim-looking, shaven-headed kid with a string of ASBOs.

He was afraid that from now on that studio portrait, taken with pleasure in mind, would go together with the words 'The Melanie Hunter Murder' like gammon and spinach – or, nowadays, like hamburger and fries. He felt horribly, guiltily, as though they had sealed her fate by taking over that photograph. He had no hope now that she would wander back home or they would find her alive, and he felt ashamed of his defeatism.

An urgent phone call to Swilley from Atherton had diverted her on her way back from Ealing and she had arrived with a stack of pizza boxes, so they had all had lunch after all – rather belated but better than nothing. Connolly had made Slider a proper cup of tea to go with his, but he had eaten absently, looking at Melanie Hunter's picture in between reading the reports from Connolly, Atherton and Swilley and trying not to fear the worst.

48

They had done all they could by way of circulating the picture and description to police and hospitals and the usual agencies, and ringing anyone she might have visited or telephoned, while outside the thin sun had dipped out of contention through a red sky, and the icy cold had returned like a marauder, as if it had been hanging around in the shadows all day just waiting for its chance.

There was no news of Melanie Hunter, either good or bad, by the time Slider called it a day and went home to a cold beef supper, which he could not taste through the dust and ashes of his certainty that she was a goner. And too many people now knew she was missing for it not to get to the press, and there would be all the parade and palaver that the media so loved, the questions and appeals and endlessly repeated factlets about her last known movements, all presided over by the photo – the photo – the photo; until eventually the sad, crumpled, discarded body would be found, and they'd have a murder investigation on their hands. Sometimes he hated his job.

Three

Babe in the Woods

Probably it was the pizza, but he had a restless night, not falling asleep properly until half past five; and then the telephone roused him at seven from such a depth it was almost an agony to open his eyes. But his brain clicked back into position an instant later, and he knew as he reached for the bedside phone what it would be.

It was Atherton. 'Found her.'

'Where?'

'By Ruislip Lido. In the woods.'

'Oh God.'

'My sentiments exactly.'

'I'll see you there.'

Slider had lived a large part of his first marriage, to Irene, in Ruislip, so he knew it well. He had taken the kids to the Lido on sunny Sundays. It was the poor man's seaside – in his case, time-poor as much as anything. The north part of Ruislip ran up into the foothills of the Chilterns, so it was both hilly and much wooded – surprisingly country-like, considering it was still part of London. The Lido itself had started life as a man-made reservoir intended as a feeder for the

Grand Union Canal, before becoming a swimming-and-boating day resort in the thirties. It had declined since its heyday, but still had a sandy beach, children's playground, pub/restaurant and miniature railway. The woods came down to it for three quarters of its circumference. They were popular with ramblers, dog walkers and horse riders, so they were not exactly unfrequented, but they covered several hundred acres, so could still be reckoned a good place to abandon a body if you got off the main paths. Slider anticipated a long trek from the car park. Still, it had been freezing cold for so long – he'd lost count now how long, but weeks, anyway – the ground at least would not be muddy.

There had been a frost in the night, such a stiff one it was lying along the branches like snow, half an inch deep; roofs were white with it, and in the fields every stem of grass was outlined and rigid like the blade of a Zulu spear. The woods looked beautiful as the sun reluctantly rose for its low-slung hibernal trajectory across the sky, sparkling and tinged with pink.

The hard winter had taken its toll on the road surfaces, and in Reservoir Road, the approach to the Lido, there were potholes you could find lost tribes in. Slider bumped and manoeuvred his way carefully down to the car park. Despite the early hour, there was quite a crowd there already. Some, all, or more of the people they had spoken to yesterday must have contacted the press, because they were out in force; and the residents of surrounding streets had followed the flashing blue lights for a good morning gawp. It

51

was only lucky it was Monday and a school day, or there'd have been no getting through them.

Barriers were in place and the car park was being kept clear for the police and associated vehicles. Two local bobbies were manning the access, and Slider had to tell them who he was. Ruislip fell within Hillingdon, a different part of the Met altogether.

But Porson was there – good grief, did the man never sleep? – gaunt as the first Duke of Lancaster, swathed in his Douglas Hurd-style greenish greatcoat, the folds of which were so voluminous a Bedouin could have kept his entire family in there, and several of his favourite horses as well. He was talking to his Hillingdon counterpart, Det Sup Fox, known down the ranks as Duggie. Slider had thought for a long time his name must be Douglas, but in fact it was Clifford. But Fox was a very large man in all respects and had, apparently, noteworthy man-breasts.

He also had the coldest eyes Slider had ever encountered. Slider could feel the frost creeping across his skin as the chilly grey orbs took him in, analysed him and filed him, probably under No Action Required. The Syrup swung round to see who was being freeze-dried, and his eyebrows went up in a greeting that was effusive by comparison.

'Ah, there you are. I've just been telling Mr Fox that you know this area like the back of your onions.'

Fox looked pained. Not everyone could cope with Porson on an empty stomach.

'He's very kindly going to hand the case over to us.'

'Very kind, sir,' Slider said with an irony so deep Beebe couldn't have reached it.

'We've got more than enough on our hands as it is,' Fox said – though, given that Heathrow Airport was in his ground, that was probably no more than the truth. And then, perhaps feeling he had been ungracious, he said, 'After all, you've done the preliminary work, and the investigation will mostly fall in your ground – tracing the last movements and so on. Makes sense for you to handle it. We'll hand over as soon as you've got enough men here. Of course, Fred,' he added to Porson, 'we'll give you any help we can. Can't promise you any warm bodies, I'm sorry to say.' He looked about as sorry as a lottery winner. 'But smoothing the path, local knowledge and suchlike. Just ask. But as you say, your man here knows the ground...'

'We'll manage. Thanks, Cliff. Appreciate your corroporation,' Porson said with dignity.

Slider left the mighty to confer at their exalted level, and went to find someone lowly to talk to. He spotted one of his own, DC McLaren, on the far side, nearest the woods, conferring with a Hillingdon detective, Pete Remington. He headed that way. There was something odd about McLaren that he couldn't put his finger on. Also he would have wondered how McLaren had got here first, given that he didn't live out this way, but he had other things on his mind.

In response to his terse question, McLaren filled him in. 'She's in there, guv.' He nodded

53

towards the woods behind him. 'Not far in, but off the path. Fully dressed, shoes and all.' Shoes often went missing when a body was moved. 'Looks like she was whacked on the head and strangled.'

'Who found her?'

'Local man, sir,' Remington answered. 'Name of William McGuire. Walking his dog early this morning – dog led him to her.' It was funny – or perhaps not – how often this was the case. Without dog walkers, Slider wondered, how many bodies would remain undiscovered? 'He lives in Lakeside Close,' Remington went on. This was one of the little cul-de-sacs off Reservoir Road. 'He was very shaken up. As it was close by, we sent him home with one of our uniforms – Patsy Raymond. No sense keeping him standing here in the cold.'

'Quite right,' Slider said. 'I'll talk to him later. I'd like to see the body first.'

'We had the photo you sent out,' Remington said, 'and there's no doubt it is her. That's why we got right on to you.' He cleared his throat. 'Sorry it turned out this way,' he offered. 'It's always a bugger when a young woman goes missing, but you always hope ... Well, anyway.'

Slider nodded to the unexpected sympathy, saw Remington look at something over his shoulder, and turned to see the firm's wheels, Freddie Cameron's Jaguar, and Atherton's car bumping into the car park in careful convoy. And a short way behind them, even more welcomely, the tea waggon. Someone early on the site must have sent out the 'teapot one' call sign

54

as a first priority. Slider had left breakfastless, and last night's supper had not had much staying power: the sight gave him the first comfort of that cold morning. And it made him realize what it was that had been odd about the look of McLaren: for perhaps the first time in his life, he wasn't engaged in eating anything.

She was lying on her back in the litter of dead leaves and other natural debris, half under a bush a short distance from the path. It looked as if some attempt had been made to hide the body, but not much of one. As soon as anyone strayed this way – as they well might if their dog suddenly dashed off excitedly – they would have seen it: it wasn't covered in any way. Was the murderer scared off, or had he sickened of the whole business by then? He could have gone a lot further from the car park and done a lot more concealing. For the matter of that, there were other woods in the general area that were more dense and less frequented – though on the other hand, they didn't all have easily accessed car-parks. If you were shifting a body by car, that was a consideration. Of course, she may have walked into the woods on her own two feet and been killed here. Probably that was more likely. If you were intending to hide a body, you would surely go a bit further from civilization.

She was dressed in a black skirt-suit over a sapphire blue jumper, and a thick grey wool reefer jacket; flat black shoes and opaque black tights. Because her clothes were all present and correct, it was unlikely she had been sexually

55

assaulted: as the forensic pathologist, Freddie Cameron said, it would be a particularly obsessive and bonkers killer who would put his victim's clothes carefully back on after death. It was difficult, too – as with trying to get your tights back on in a swimming pool changing room. 'So I'm told,' he added hastily as Slider's eyebrow went up.

The strangling had been done with a silk scarf, presumably her own – it was Indian-patterned in shades of blue, purple and bottle-green – and the scarf was still in place round the neck, but there was no sign of the swelling or reddening that usually accompanied strangulation.

'A pretty half-hearted effort,' Freddie said, easing the silk away from the neck to look underneath. 'In fact, I'd say it was for show only. It's hardly marked the skin. It was the whack on the head that did for her, pound to a penny.'

Slider was grateful for any small mercies. When you've seen enough of them you can be objective about dead bodies, but you never stop *minding*. He was glad of a seemly corpse, quietly composed: her eyes were closed, her mouth just a little open, her head naturally over to one side; no signs of struggle or convulsion. One hand was resting on her chest, the other was down by her side; there were dead leaves in her hair, which was thick and heavy, and fell back from her face on to the moss beneath her head. He recognized the face from the photograph Swilley had brought back, but of course this was not Melanie Hunter, just the fleshly envelope that had once housed her. She had departed, permanently; how, was what he had to find out.

Freddie was demonstrating to him now the wound to the skull, slipping his hand under the neck to turn the head with professional skill but still, somehow, a gentleness. 'See, here – the parietal bone is completely fractured, just above the junction with the occipital. I'd say just one blow, but a pretty hard one. Death would have been almost instantaneous.'

'So there wouldn't necessarily be much blood?' Slider said.

'Maybe, maybe not. Scalp wounds can bleed a lot in a short time. But there's nothing here, under the head, just a smear or two. Of course, the body must have been moved – she wouldn't have fallen on her back like this from a blow to the back of the skull – so there may well be some more blood somewhere else, either in the immediate area, if she was killed here, or wherever she was killed.'

'Or in the car that was used to move her,' Slider finished.

'Well, quite.'

'Time of death?'

Freddie pursed his lips. 'It's hard to say, in this cold weather. The cold tends to slow down the processes. There's still some rigor in the limbs, so perhaps less than three days. Between two and three days. You've got her disappearing when?'

'So far, the last she was seen was on Friday night.'

'Well, that would work. Friday night or early

57

Saturday morning. But you know, old dear, that anything over eight hours and it's just guesswork.'

Slider nodded, and stared away through the trees, getting the lie of the place, the impression of light and shade, the undergrowth and open spaces. The forensic boys would do a fingertip search of the immediate area, in case something had been dropped or there were footmarks or fabric threads or anything that might identify the murderer. Why here? he was wondering. Why not further in? Perhaps she was too heavy to carry. She was not a tall girl, and was lightly built, but the dead weigh more than the living. Hard to tell in this sort of woodland if she was dragged. The ground was too hard to take impressions. It was horribly cold here, out of the little warmth the sun could give; numbingly cold. Slider could see his breath rising before him, and his fingers and the tip of his nose were aching.

Breaking his reverie, Atherton, beside him, said, 'It looks as if there's been some digging – just there.'

'Probably the finder's dog,' said Bob Bailey, the Crime Scene Manager.

'It's an animal, all right,' Freddie said. 'But I think it's more likely a fox. There's some damage to the fingers of this hand.' He raised the hand that was lying among the leaves by her side. 'A bit of gnawing's gone on. I suppose it was too cold and hard actually to remove them. And the left ear's been bitten, too, the one that was nearer the ground – though those teeth are smaller. Too small for a dog or fox. Stoat, maybe.'

Slider heard their voices as if at a distance, echoing a little in the empty woodland air. Further off he could hear a murmur of talk from the people gathered in and around the car park; far away, in the country quiet, a crow was yarking monotonously. And the dogs shall eat her in the portion of Jezreel, he thought. An undeserved fate – but wasn't it always? Otherwise it wouldn't be murder.

'Well?' said Atherton as they made their way back over the safe-route boards. 'What do you make of it?'

'Nothing, yet,' Slider said. 'Just the usual questions. Why her? Why here?'

'There is one thing that leaps to mind.'

Slider frowned at him. 'You couldn't make it leap a bit higher, I suppose?'

'One blow to the head – the same way Ronnie Fitton killed his wife.'

Slider sighed. 'Well, I suppose he's got to look like a tasty suspect. Certainly the press will see it that way as soon as they find out who he is. But what reason would he have to kill her? The only person he's ever killed is his wife.'

'Sexual jealousy,' Atherton said. 'The strongest motive of all. He could have been brooding about her for years, while she's been going out with Hibbert, who is not worthy of her.'

Slider shook his head. 'Then he'd kill Hibbert, surely.'

'No, no. He'd make sure of his Precious – put

her beyond the greasy Hibbertian fingers for ever.'

'You're not serious.'

'On sheer propinquity alone,' Atherton said.

'Hibbert propinks just as well.'

'If not more so,' Atherton admitted. 'What now?'

'We go and talk to the bod who found her. By the way,' he added, as they crossed the car park and the tea van reminded him, 'what's wrong with McLaren? When I got here this morning, he wasn't eating anything.'

'I noticed that,' Atherton said. 'He has been off his nosebag, lately. And there are no food stains down his front – in fact, I think that's a new tie.'

'It's unsettling,' Slider said.

'You're right. I'll do a bit of detective work when I've got a minute.'

'We've more important things to do. Don't waste any time on it,' Slider cautioned.

'No, no,' Atherton reassured him. 'I'll take the short cut. I'll ask him.'

William McGuire lived in Lakeside Close, the fancifully-named cul-de-sac that led off Reservoir Road on the side further from the Lido, and was therefore not on the lakeside, even had the Lido been a lake. The house was a tiny little Victorian railway worker's terraced cottage, a typical two-up, two-down yellow-brick, slate-roofed doll's house that only a greedy developer could have thought worth splitting, and then only in a serious housing shortage. McGuire had the downstairs remnant, for which 'maisonette'

60

was an overgenerous description. It was a bed-sitting room opening straight off the street, with a kitchen at the back and a bathroom crammed between the two. The only advantage it boasted was the garden, twelve feet wide and fifteen feet long, but as McGuire was plainly no gardener, and it ended in a British Leyland hedge that had been allowed to grow to twelve feet high, it had nothing but underprivileged grass in it, and had no view but the tops of the trees in the woods behind.

It was the policewoman, Raymond, who opened the door to them, with a look of hope that quickly faded to disappointment. 'I hoped you were my replacement,' she said. 'I think they've forgotten all about me, sir.'

Slider thought it likely. Most of the Hillingdon contingent had gone by now. 'I'll get one of my own people in as soon as I've done here,' Slider reassured her.

'Thanks,' she said. 'He's in the kitchen. He hasn't been talking at all. I think he's really upset about it.'

The tiny cramped rooms were depressingly decorated in woodchip paper covered in histori-cal layers of beige paint so they resembled con-gealed porridge, or a skin disease. There was cheap beige carpet on the floor, with stains that would have been of interest to an archaeologist, and the cheapest, nastiest furniture, the sort that shows the chipboard underneath when the veneer gets knocked off. The curtain over the front window was hanging by the last few hooks from a broken curtain rail, and the place smelled

of dog, alcohol and feet in about equal propor-
tions. It was, however, tidy, and the bathroom, as
they passed it, looked clean, though shabby.

Slider had heard the dog barking ever since
Raymond opened the door, and when he reached
the kitchen door, it came bustling importantly
towards him, stood its ground a foot away and
barked officiously, woofing so hard it lifted its
small body slightly off the ground at each explosion. It was a stout, short-legged Jack Russell
type, mostly white, but with a few black patches,
including one over one eye that gave it an
unreliably jolly look.

The kitchen had cheap units painted yellow, a
melamine table with two plastic chairs, lino on
the floor, and a half-glazed door on to the
garden. There were two empty mugs on the
table, and McGuire was sitting in front of one of
them, his elbow on the table and his head prop-
ped in his hand in an attitude almost of despair.
The smell of booze was stronger still in here,
easily beating feet and dog into second and third
places: it was coming from McGuire, reeking
from his pores so you could almost see it. He
had evidently tied one on last night.

'Mr McGuire?' Slider said politely, when he
was sure the dog was not going to do more than
mouth off. 'I'm Detective Inspector Slider and
this is Detective Sergeant Atherton.'

The man finally looked up, tilting red and
doleful eyes that wouldn't have been out of
place on a basset hound in his direction. His
nose and cheeks were rife with the broken veins
of the boozer, and he looked haggard with

emotion at the moment, but otherwise it was not an unhealthy face. He was brown with the settled tan of someone who works out of doors; his hair was thick and light brown, going grey; his body was sturdy and his hands looked strong, though seamed with manual work. The most surprising thing about him was the beard. There were not so many men these days who wore beards; and this was not one of those little dabs here and there such as young men sometimes affected, but the full Captain Haddock, thick and bushy and a darker shade of brown than his hair. While trying not to be pognophobic, Slider instinctively distrusted beards, on the basis that a man could change his appearance so completely by growing one or shaving it off, he might become unrecognizable. In his business, you needed to know who you were dealing with.

'I'd just like to ask you a few questions, if that's all right,' he went on, when it seemed that McGuire was not going to volunteer anything. 'About what happened this morning.'

At once, large tears formed in the basset brown eyes and rolled over, but McGuire roused himself enough to wipe at them almost angrily with the back of his hand, and to say sharply, 'Toby, *shut up!*'

An astonishing silence fell. The little dog looked at him, and then almost with a shrug turned and pottered away, hopping through the dog door into the garden with a familiar flip-flap sound.

McGuire got out a large handkerchief, blew his nose and wiped his eyes. There was something about the weariness of the action that suggested he had been blowing and wiping for some time. 'Would you like another cup of tea?' Slider suggested in sympathy.

'Yeah – thanks,' he said. He made no move to get up, though, and Slider looked at Raymond and jerked his head towards the kettle.

'I'll make it,' she said obediently. 'What about you, sir?'

'Yes, thanks, No sugar.'

Atherton declined. Slider took the other seat at the table, so Atherton lounged gracefully in the doorway, trying not to look threatening – there simply wasn't any other place he could be. As it was, Raymond had to ooze past him to get to the kettle. The dog came flip-flapping back in, stared at them all a moment in case there was any more barking that needed doing, then went to his basket in the corner, turned round three times and flopped down, chin on paws.

When Raymond put the mugs on the table, McGuire roused himself to say, 'Thanks,' and felt in his jacket pocket and brought out a pill bottle. 'Aspirin,' he said, seeing Slider's look. 'Got a rotten headache.' He unscrewed the bottle one-handed and slid two into his palm, tossed them into his mouth, re-lidded the bottle and holstered it like a fancy gunslinger displaying his dexterity. Again, seeing Slider watching, he said, 'Had a bit to drink last night.' He shrugged. 'I suppose you guessed that.' Slider nodded, and it seemed to touch some pride in him. He straightened a little in the chair and said, 'I only drink at the weekends. That's my prerogative, right? I don't let it interfere with work.' And almost immediately the expression of despair returned to his face and he slumped again by the inches he had pulled back.

'What job do you do?' Slider asked him.

'I work for the council. Parks and Gardens department. Mowing, cutting, pruning, planting – you name it. You can ask them – I've got a good employment record. Two years with never a day off.'

'I'm sure you have,' Slider said. 'You look well on it.' He could imagine the lonely-man regime, working off by physical exertion through the week the booze taken on board at weekends. Though if he didn't let it interfere with work, how come he was boozing on a Sunday night? Friday and Saturday ought to be his drinking nights.

'I keep all right,' McGuire admitted.

'And I expect Toby gives you plenty of exercise,' Slider suggested pleasantly, edging him back closer to the point. 'I expect you try to give him a walk every morning before work?'

'He comes to work with me,' McGuire said. 'That's one of the good things about the job. But it isn't the same as a walk. A dog needs a couple of good walks a day, never mind what else he's doing.'

'Well, you're living in the right place for it,' Slider said. 'Lots of good walks round here. Tell me about this morning. Was it your usual routine?'

The brown eyes moved away and he frowned, remembering. 'Yeah. I was up at six, same as

65

usual. Got ready for work.' He was dressed in a battered tweed jacket, tough-looking cords and work boots scarred and stained with ancient mud – his work clothes, presumably. 'Took Toby out. Went through the car park into the woods.'

'Do you always go the same way?'

'Nah, different every day. Just as the fancy takes us.'

'And that would be – what time?'

'About half past, give or take. Time I'd washed and had a cup of tea and a bit of toast.'

'Go on.'

He shrugged. 'Not much to tell. Just walking through the woods when suddenly Toby goes stiff all over, like he's seen something. I thought it was a squirrel – he likes to chase 'em. Then he goes off to one side, growling, his whiskers sticking out and his hair all on end. It wasn't like him, usually, so I followed. And there—' He swallowed. 'There she was.' The tears welled up again effortlessly. 'That poor girl,' he said in broken tones. 'Who would do such a thing? That poor—' His face was quivering. He dragged out the handkerchief, blew and wiped and regained control. 'Have you found out who she is?' he asked from behind it.

'Yes, we know who she is,' Slider said.

'Her parents – they must be going mad, wondering. If she was my kid ... Have you told them?'

'Someone will be with them now,' Slider said. It was usual to send a uniform round with the news – more official and reassuring than plain clothes, so was the thinking.

66

McGuire shook his head. 'I'll never get over seeing her there like that. I'm just – I can't get my head round it.'

'I know,' Slider said. 'Just tell me what you did. Did you touch her or move her in any way?'

'No, of course not,' he said quite sharply. 'I know better than that.'

'Not even to check if she was dead?'

'Didn't need to. I could see she was. I just grabbed Toby and came back here to phone the police.'

'Did Toby touch the body?'

'No, he wouldn't go near it, just stood growling and whining. He was upset. See him now, sleeping – that's not like him, this time of day. Normally he'd be raring to go. I suppose dogs can feel shock, same as us.'

'So you didn't recognize the girl?' Slider pursued.

'Course not. Why should I?' he said sharply.

'No reason. I just thought you might have seen her walking round here before. A lot of people come here for walks, don't they?'

He seemed disconcerted by the question. 'She wasn't dressed for walking,' he said in the end.

'So you've never seen her before?'

'I said so, didn't I?'

'And have you seen or heard anything suspicious, the last two or three nights? Cars coming down here late at night, for instance, or anyone acting strangely.'

'There's people coming down here all the time,' he said. 'I wouldn't notice anyone, particularly.'

'But movement or noises in the middle of the night?'

He shook his head.

'Were you at home Friday and Saturday nights, and last night?'

'I was out Friday night,' he said. 'I went down the pub.'

'Which pub?'

'The Bells.'

That was the Six Bells on Duck's Hill Road, the nearest – in fact, only just round the corner.

'And Saturday night and last night?'

'I stayed in,' he said, and added, as if as an afterthought: 'It's cheaper.'

Atherton made a restless movement behind him, and Slider agreed – there was nothing for them here. Most people didn't notice cars going past, whatever the hour, and would probably only notice someone shifting a dead body if they attempted to bring it into their own front room. He drank off his tea, and stood up. 'Well, thank you, Mr McGuire. If you do remember anything that might help us, anything at all, please give us a ring.'

McGuire stood up too, looking at Slider with a desperate sort of appeal in his eyes, as if begging not to be left alone with his memories. 'She – that girl—?' Slider paused receptively, but all he said was, 'Do you think she suffered?'

Of course she suffered – she was murdered, Slider's brain shouted impatiently. *What do you think?* But outwardly he showed nothing, and seeing the man's haunted eyes, he did the best he could for him. 'We believe death was almost instantaneous,' he said. Between the 'almost' and the 'instantaneous' lay the cavern full of horror, but there was nothing he could do about that. And perhaps McGuire, hung-over as he was, wouldn't notice.

At the street door, Atherton said, 'Well, that was fun.'

'You have to go through the motions. But the chances of him knowing anything, given that she'd probably been there two days, were slim.'

'It amazes me that no one found her before. Unless she was hidden somewhere else and then moved last night.'

'Thanks, we don't need any more intriguing possibilities.'

'So – what now?'

'Back to the factory, start tracing her last movements,' Slider said. 'Until and unless Freddie comes up with anything different, we'll assume she was killed on Friday night and taken straight to the woods. You have to start somewhere.'

Raymond had followed them to the door and, blinking in the sunlight, said, 'What about me, sir?'

'As far as I'm concerned, you can leave him now. I don't think he has anything more to tell us. Why don't you radio in and ask your skipper?'

'Right, sir, thanks.' She glanced over her shoulder. 'Maybe I should check if he's got someone he can call to come over. He's really upset.'

69

'That's a kind thought,' Slider said, and left her to it with a faint and guilty feeling of relief that it was someone else's problem. McGuire didn't strike him as the sort of person who had either friends or relations. 'But he's got Toby,' he said aloud as they headed back towards the car park. 'Man's best friend.'

Four

I Only Have Pies For You

Kiera Williams, the Best Friend – these days the title tended to come with capitals – was a tall, eager-looking young woman with thick, curly brown hair and a wide mouth made for smiles. She reminded Slider – and he meant nothing insulting by it – of a nice, big dog. She was at the moment, however, more bewildered than smiling. He had noticed before that in the early period after learning about a death, people often did not know what they ought to be feeling, and were puzzled by their apparent failure to conform to any predigested norm.

'I just can't take it in,' she confessed. 'It doesn't seem real.'

Slider nodded. 'The realization comes later.'

'Does it? I suppose you'd know. You must have gone through this so many times. But I've never known anyone who got murdered before. And Melanie, of all people! I mean, who would want to hurt her?'

'That's what we hope to find out,' he said.

She frowned and recrossed her legs. She was wearing a very smart dark-green calf-length skirt over long boots, and a chunky dark-brown

71

crew-neck sweater. Her creamy, lightly-freckled face was carefully made up, but she still did not manage to look entirely like a grown-up. It was the wideness of her eyes and the unstudied expressions of her face, he decided, that made her seem younger than her years. She had not adopted that unlovely cynicism and world-weariness that was currently fashionable.

She had come direct from work, having set off that morning before the news broke generally: now it was on the rolling TV news and all over the Internet. Who needed newspapers any more? He had had her brought up to his office – no need to subject her to the horrors of the interview rooms – and provided her with good coffee from Atherton's filter machine next door. Despite the situation, she had been looking around with noticing interest ever since she arrived, and he liked her for it. Improving the shining hour was something he was always urging on his children.

'So, tell me about Melanie,' he said. 'You've known her a long time?'

'We grew up together, in Northwood – practically next-door neighbours. We lived in Chester Road and they lived round the corner in Hallowell Road, so we were in and out of each other's houses. And we went to the same school,' she said. 'St Helen's. We were scholarship girls.' She made an equivocal face – an automatic apology for being bright. 'We both did maths and sciences, so we were outcasts anyway – I suppose that's what kept us close. We were the Geeks, and that was before there

72

was any Geek Chic, like now – when it was still an insult.' He smiled, and she responded with a glimmer of her own that hinted at what she could do if she really gave it everything. 'Then we both went to London University, though not to the same college. She went to Imperial and I went to UCL. But we shared a flat, with some other girls at first and then just the two of us, until we graduated. Then she went to the Natural History Museum and I started working for Shell – I'm in data analysis. They're on the South Bank, so it wasn't really convenient any more to share. But we've always stayed friends. We talk to each other every week on the phone, and meet up whenever we can, and—' She stopped, thrown off balance by the present tense.

'It takes time to come to terms with it,' he said, answering the appeal in her eyes.

'I'll never see her again,' she said. 'I can't believe it.'

'Don't try. It'll come in its own time. Did you have any brothers or sisters of your own?'

She took the question like medicine, knowing it was good for her. Talking stopped her thinking. 'No, I was an only child as well. I suppose that was another reason we were close.'

'You must have been a great comfort to her, when her father died.'

'Oh, God, that was terrible. We were just fourteen, fifteen, when the train crash happened. That's a hard time anyway, for a girl. And then, you couldn't get away from it. It was everywhere, the same pictures over and over again, in the papers, on the television, as if they were

73

trying to make it worse, as if they were gloating. I hated them then – the media. But Mel was wonderful. I'd have been totally trashed, but somehow she held it together. I think she, like, pushed a lot of it down inside, bottled it up. You see, her mum was no use to her – she just went to pieces, and Mel had to comfort *her*, instead of the other way round. And she'd always loved her dad so much, in spite of everything.' She paused, looking carefully at Slider.

'Go on,' he said.

'Well, the thing is – I don't want to speak ill of the dead – but her dad was never a very satis-factory person. He never had a steady job, and he was always having these mad ideas that were going to make a fortune, but they never did, they just left them broke again. Like the time he went in for ostriches: ostrich meat was going to be the next big thing, but of course it all fell through – after he'd put all their savings into it. And then another time he invested everything in this camel farm. This man convinced him there was going to be a market for camel's milk and yoghurt and stuff. They were going to call it the Dromedairy.'

Slider saw it was all right to smile, and she smiled too, ruefully, and shook her head.

'He was always looking for the easy way out, the money for nothing, and of course what they always ended up with was the nothing. Mel never had any nice clothes – everything was second-hand. Mrs Hunter had to work, and they lived most of the time on what she could earn, which wasn't much. She used to do those

Tupperware parties for extra cash. Mel always felt ashamed about that. I told her it was silly, that there was nothing wrong with it, but she couldn't help it. But through all that, she still loved him. He was one of those charming losers, you know?'

Slider nodded.

'I was mad about him too, when I was a kid. He used to take Mel and me out for these Saturday outings – our Adventure Days, he used to call them. The Round Pond, the Kensington Museums, art galleries, Trafalgar Square, the Lido in summer, or the Serpentine – anything that didn't cost anything. Sometimes it was just a ride on the top of a bus – we'd sit in the front seat and pretend to be the driver, and he'd tell us stories and we'd sing songs together. Whatever it was, it was always fun. He was always smiling and jolly, and telling jokes, and he could do conjuring tricks – you know, finding a coin behind your ear, that sort of thing? – so he didn't really seem like a grown-up at all, not like my dad, who was really boring. But then when I got older I could see the difference between my dad, who went to work every day without complaining and kept us properly, and Mr Hunter, who was lovely but always letting people down. Mel saw it too, but she couldn't help loving him. Well, he was her dad,' she concluded simply.

'So it must have been devastating when he died,' Slider said, to keep her going.

'Yes. He was on his way down to Devon or Somerset or somewhere to "see a man" about some new scheme that was going to make him

75

rich. No surprises there. He was always going to "see a man" and it was always going make a fortune. But then the train crashed and all those people were killed, and one of them was Melanie's dad. It was awful.' She looked down at her hands, frowning at the memory. 'Then a year later, her mum married Ian. I suppose she just couldn't cope on her own. He was a widower – his wife had died suddenly, and he had a baby daughter, so it made sense for him. He was very different, though – a teacher. You couldn't get any more respectable and steady than that, could you?'

'You didn't like him?' Slider hazarded.

'Oh, he was all right, just a bit strict and churchy and – you know, by the book. Not like Mel's dad. Not that I had much to do with him – just about then, for some reason or other, I didn't see so much of Mel. I don't know if he was stopping her going out or something, but I never seemed to see her outside of school, and in school she was sort of quiet and – moody maybe. I suppose it was a bit of an adjustment for her, a new stepdad and everything. But she settled down in the end. After a few months she was back to normal – not like before her dad died, exactly, but normal for like she's been ever since. Well, we were just about to go to university, so that made it easy. We got into a flat share and Mel left home, and Ian and Mel's mum moved to Ealing, to be nearer his school. So he and Mel never had to live together after that, which probably made it easier. Mel's mum always said he wasn't meant to be a father to

76

Mel, just her husband. She told Mel no one expected her to call him "Dad", and she never did.'

'And then there was Scott,' Slider suggested.

She made a face, and then put her hand over her mouth apologetically. 'Oh, I shouldn't say anything. He's all right, really. And Melanie's mad about him.'

'Is he mad about her?'

'Well, they're all over each other. Very lovey-dovey. They're living together now, and he's talking about marriage and everything.'

'What don't you like about him?'

She seemed alarmed. 'I didn't say I didn't like him. He's perfectly all right. My goodness, some of my friends go out with real horrors! I just don't think he's good enough for her – but she's my Best Friend since forever, so I don't expect I'd think anyone was good enough for her.' She smiled disarmingly. 'I think he's a bit dull, that's all. But if it's what she wants – after all, she had a bellyful of a lovely, fun man who was no good as a husband when she was a kid. I expect she wants reliability now, above anything.' She stopped herself again, and looked dismayed. 'I forgot again. How could I forget?' She looked at him appealingly. 'How long does this go on? It's not *real*!'

'Give yourself a chance,' he said kindly. 'It's all very new to you. Tell me about Friday.'

She pulled herself together visibly. 'It was my birthday drinks. We always do that on each other's birthdays. I was twenty-seven on Friday.' She shook her head in wonder at the thought. 'Melanie's six months younger than me, she's still only twenty-six. She always rags me about that, calls me old lady and gran and so on. Anyway, she arranged for half a dozen of us to meet at the Princess Victoria for drinks and a meal.'

'Isn't that a bit far from home for you? I'd have thought you'd meet half way.'

'Sometimes we did, but my mum's not been well so I said I'd go and spend the weekend with her afterwards. She still lives in Northwood. And two of the other girls come from out that way, and one of them, Rebecca, doesn't drink, so she said she'd drive us back straight from the pub. It was a bit of a waste, really, with Scott being away – Melanie and I could have had a nice long time together – but we've got some other things planned so it didn't matter too much. I mean, we *had*,' she finished dolefully.

'How was she that evening? Was she in normal spirits?'

'Oh, yes, she was in great form. We had a laugh.'

'She didn't have anything on her mind at all? Wasn't worried about anything?'

'Not that she mentioned.'

'Everything all right with Scott?'

Her eyebrows went up. 'Oh, I see what you're after. She said she was feeling a bit guilty because she'd been crabby with him earlier. Did you know about that?'

'Yes, I heard it from Scott. About the wedding.'

'Right. He's got these very thick friends he

78

likes to hang out with. But it was nothing. She'd sort of snapped at him, and then she was sorry. It happens.' She shrugged. 'Anyway, he called her during the evening, and they were all lovey-dovey again, so that was all right. She and Scott were fine, really. You weren't thinking...?' She looked alarmed.

'I'm not thinking anything yet. Just trying to assemble a picture for myself. So were you all together at the pub the whole evening?'

'Yes. We met up between half past seven and eight, had some food and some bottles of wine, and we stayed until about ten.'

'That seems early. It wasn't as if it was a work night.' Slider put a question mark at the end, and she nodded.

'I suppose it was, but Mel – well.' She looked awkward, and lowered her voice. 'She'd got the curse and she wasn't feeling all that brilliant. That's probably why she snapped at Scott earlier. Anyway, about ten-ish she said she was all in and apologized and said she wanted to go, so that broke up the party really.'

'You wouldn't go on without her?'

She smiled faintly. 'That's the sort of person she is. If she leaves, it all goes flat. She's just – I don't know. If I say "the heart and soul of the party" it makes it sound as if she's loud, but she isn't a bit. She's just nice, and kind, and good, and everybody loves her, and everybody wants to be with her, and – well, if you were having a party, you'd find out what date she could make first, before you asked anyone else.'

'I understand. So she didn't talk about any-

79

thing in particular that evening? Any concerns she had, or plans? Anything different in her life, any changes ahead?'

'Nothing at all. It was just the usual chat.'

'Did she say what she was doing the rest of the weekend?'

'She was going to veg out on Saturday – you know, get up late, do the laundry, get a takeaway and watch a movie. That was all she felt like. And Sunday she said she had some work she had to catch up on. Stuff for the museum. She wanted to get it done before Scott got back Sunday evening, while it was quiet.'

'And did anyone else ring her during the evening?'

She frowned. 'I don't know. Everybody's on the phone all the time these days, I probably wouldn't notice. I only know about Scott because I was sitting next to her and talking to her when he rang, so he interrupted me. And of course I heard her side of it, so I knew they'd made up and everything.'

'Weren't you sitting next to her the whole time?'

'No, we moved about and changed seats a bit. So she might have had other calls, I just wouldn't notice.' She looked at him. 'So you've no idea who did this? None at all?'

The usual thing was to say 'we're following up various lines of investigation', but meeting the clear gaze in the young, freckled face, he couldn't prevaricate. 'Not yet.'

'But she wasn't attacked on the way home? Didn't it say on the news she went home from the Vic all right, and then disappeared?'

'So it seems.'

'But I don't understand – why didn't Scott know she was missing? They were always talking to each other on the phone. They were like two little lovebirds. If she didn't answer the phone, he'd surely think something was wrong.'

It was a good question, Slider thought when she was gone. There was definitely something about Mr Hibbert that invited investigation; but everything in its time.

Fred 'The Syrup' Porson might have had the looks and charm of a bunion, but he had still managed to beguile Duggie Fox into lending him enough uniforms to do the immediate house-to-house canvass. Of course, this only involved the lightly-housed Reservoir Road and the three small culs-de-sac that led off it, so it wasn't in the order of a lifetime commitment; but Slider gave his boss all credit for extracting anything at all from a man whose attitude towards beneficence resembled that of the proverbial duck's rectum to pond water.

It meant that most of Slider's firm had drifted home by the time he held the first meeting: Mackay and Fathom were still at the house. McLaren and Connolly had done a forage stop on the way back, at the stall on the corner of the market, where they not only did sausage sandwiches and bacon sandwiches, but also a home-made meat pie specifically designed to be eaten on the move without spilling anything down the front – a masterpiece of pastry engineering, very popular with lorry drivers. Connolly had brought a sandwich for Slider – 'Sausage, guv. Wasn't it rashers last time? And I remembered the tomato sauce!' – and he scoffed it in huge bites before going out into the squad room. It was all very well for him to wave a benevolent hand and say, 'Carry on eating,' to the troops, but he had his dignity to maintain.

At the last minute, Porson oozed in, carrying a cup of tea with the saucer on top as a lid, on which reposed two custard creams. He raised an eyebrow at the general noshing that was going on – and his eyebrows were so large and bushy, it was not a negligible gesture, something akin to the raising of Tower Bridge – but he only said, 'Late lunch? Keep it off the papers, that's all!'

Slider gave him a distracted look, having to tear his attention from the fact that McLaren – the man who *knew* the answer to the question 'who ate all the pies?' – had empty hands and an empty mouth, and was gazing off into space with a sappy look of contentment on his face.

Porson perched on a desk off to the side, gently eased his cup on to its saucer, nudging the biscuits along to make room, and barked, 'Right!'

Slider snapped back to attention as DS Hollis, the beanpole Mancunian who was always office manager in these cases, began. 'The murder of Melanie Hunter, age twenty-six. She was found around six thirty this morning in the woods by Ruislip Lido. We are assuming, for lack of any evidence to the contrary, that she was killed some time on Friday night, after ten thirty when she's last known to have come home from a night out.'

'But it's possible, isn't it, that she was abducted first, and held somewhere, and killed later – say on Saturday night?' said Atherton.

'Possible,' Slider said, 'though there were no visible marks of violence or restraint on the body. It's hard to hold someone against their will without marking them.'

'Doesn't that suggest she left the flat of her own free will – whatever time it was?' Swilley asked.

'You can be abducted,' Atherton returned, 'by wiles and beguilement. I was only meaning to point out that we don't know she was killed on Friday night.'

'And I was only meaning it was likely someone she knew,' said Swilley. 'It usually is.'

There was always a bit of tension between those two, but sometimes it could be productive, so usually Slider left them to get on with it. He nodded to Hollis to carry on.

'Death was apparently caused by a blow to the back of the head, but there wasn't a lot o' blood at the site, so she may have been killed elsewhere and the body taken to the woods to hide it.' He looked up. 'Might've been killed at the flat, maybe?'

'There was no sign of disturbance when we went in,' Atherton said. 'So unless the murderer was very thorough at cleaning up...?'

'We've got a forensic team in there now,' Slider said. 'If there's any blood, they'll find it. It's not easy to carry a body downstairs and get it into a car without making a noise, and without anyone seeing anything. But that's the next thing on the list – canvass the other residents of the house, and the immediate neighbours.'

'If she was killed at the flat, you're thinking it was the boyfriend that did it?' Swilley said.

'He wasn't even in London,' Atherton objected.

'So he *says*.'

'He was at a wedding. Hundreds of witnesses. You can't fake that.'

'That is something we'll have to check on,' Slider said.

Hollis made a note. 'Hibbert alibi.'

'Add "Hibbert motive" while you're at it,' said Atherton.

'It's not just him,' Connolly put in. 'So far everybody loved her. She was so nice she'd get on your nerves.'

'It needn't be Hibbert, even if she was killed at the flat,' Atherton said. 'Could be someone she invited in. Or someone who followed her home.'

'McLaren's been looking into her route home,' Slider said.

Connolly jabbed an elbow into McLaren, who returned to earth with a bump. 'Yeah,' he said, 'there's a street camera right opposite the Princess Vic that's got her coming out eight minutes past ten. You can see it's her clear enough. Then she turns down Becklow Road, where she's parked the car. You can see her get in and drive off, towards Askew Road, the way she was facing.'

'But if she didn't get home until nearly half

ten,' Connolly said, 'that's too much time. Sure, it's only five minutes – ten at most – in the car.'

'She must have stopped somewhere,' Swilley said.

McLaren was nodding. 'I was gonna say, there's a camera at the Seven Stars, and that's the way she'd come, if she was going straight home. She'd go down Becklow, left into Askew, left at the Seven Stars on to Goldhawk, left into Cathnor, bosh. But she never appears out of Askew Road. I went all the way up to midnight.'

'So either she went all through the back streets to get home, which is daft,' said Hollis.

'Or she doubled back and went home the Uxbridge Road way,' said Swilley.

'But why would she?' said McLaren.

'Maybe she thought of something she wanted on the way home from the shops on Uxbridge Road,' Swilley said. 'There's a couple of late-nighters along there.'

'Like what?' McLaren demanded.

'Tampax,' Swilley suggested, to embarrass him, but it was Hollis who blushed.

'Or maybe she went somewhere else completely,' said McLaren.

'She couldn't have gone anywhere much if she was back home by half past.'

'She could have picked someone up and taken them home with her,' said Atherton. 'Fitton didn't see her go in, only heard the car, so she could have had someone with her.'

'And then later she could have offered to drive them home,' McLaren said excitedly, seeing a possibility.

'She left her handbag behind, you plank,' said Connolly.

'If it wasn't far, she might just've grabbed her keys,' he defended himself. 'If she wasn't gonna be long.'

'And the murderer returned her car afterwards and put the car keys back in her handbag?' Atherton said witheringly.

But Swilley repeated his words in an entirely different voice. 'And the murderer returned her *car*, and put the *keys* back in her *handbag*! That solves all the problems!'

'Except that the dog didn't bark when the murderer let himself in at some unearthly hour, with her blood on his hands?' Atherton countered.

'I'm about sick of that dog not barking,' Porson said, making them all jump, because they'd forgotten he was there. 'This is not a bloody Shylock Holmes story. You're all forgetting one thing: we've only got Ronnie Fitton's word for it that she got home by ten thirty. Or at all.'

It gave them pause. Slider had had that possibility in the back of his mind all along, but he had been hoping not to have to look at it, because if Fitton had no alibi, there was no reason he should have, which was the worst of cases to prove. He knew the victim and had the key to her house, and he knew the dog. But he'd had two days to cover his tracks, if tracks there were, so how would they ever catch him out?

'If the victim's car was used, that meant it left the space in front of Fitton's window and return-ed there without him hearing anything,' he said.

'Or he's lying about not hearing anything,' Porson concluded.

Slider caught Connolly's eye, and a sympathy flashed between them. He could see she didn't want it to be Fitton either, though presumably for different reasons. 'Why would Fitton kill her?' she said. 'He liked her.'

'Maybe he liked her too much,' said Atherton.

'Well, there's got to be a car in it somewhere,' said Slider. 'She didn't walk to Ruislip. We'll take hers in, check it for traces. We'll have to canvass the immediate area, Cathnor Road and Goldhawk to either side of the turning, see if anyone saw anything. Interview the people upstairs – they may know something, or have heard something. Any cars in the area behaving suspiciously – check any possible route from Cathnor Road to the Lido for that. And Mc-Laren, you carry on checking her route home – all the cameras there are, bus cameras, shops, private houses, the lot. And we'll have to get after the motive. We'll have to talk to her friends and family, find out who else was in her life recently, what she's been up to, who she knew.'

'There's one other thing no one's mentioned,' Porson said. They all looked at him. 'Stamford House.'

'What's that?' Connolly asked. She was fairly new to the area.

'It's a secure home for violent young offenders,' Slider said. 'Right next door to Cathnor Road.'

'Just over the wall from their back gardens, in fact,' Atherton expanded. 'They had a lot of

87

trouble there a couple of years ago. Drugs, fights, breakouts. I thought they'd got it all under control again, though. I haven't heard of anyone getting out recently.'

'Doesn't mean somebody didn't get over the wall and back in before anyone noticed,' Hollis said.

Slider said, 'I'm reluctant to jump immediately into suspecting the obvious suspect—'

'Obvious is as obvious does,' Porson said obscurely.

'—but in any case, it doesn't fit in with the whole body-in-the-woods scenario. A violent random attacker would just leave the body where it was. And none of those kids would have a car.'

'Always steal one,' McLaren said with a shrug.

'Better look into it,' Porson said. 'Find out if any motors went missing from the area that night. And whether any of the YOs went AWOL. Best to leave no stone unthrown. You never know.'

Slider sighed. A tea urn had nothing on him. That was the trouble, he thought. Sometimes you never did.

By the next day the press had got hold of Ronnie Fitton's past history, and it was splashed all over everywhere, all the details of the murder of his wife, the court case and the sentence, with photographs from the time. By the time Slider got in to work, there had been telephone calls of complaint from the upstairs neighbours that the house was besieged by press and they couldn't get out. Uniforms had been dispatched to clear the access, but there was no way in law to stop reporters shouting questions at the residents as they hurried to their cars, or taking photos of them through the car windows as they backed out.

When Slider reached his room, the phone was ringing. It was Freddie Cameron. 'You'll get the full report in writing, of course, but I thought you'd like to know—'

'You've done the post-mortem?' Slider interrupted. He wasn't at his best until the first cup of tea hit his bloodstream.

'No, I've been using my magical powers to peer into the past,' Freddie said with patient irony.

'Sorry,' said Slider.

'Granted. I thought you'd like to know that death *was* caused by the blow to the head. A single blow of considerable force with a rigid object, probably metal, at least eight inches long, probably with squared edges.'

'Something like a large spanner?'

'That's possible. Unconsciousness would have been immediate and death probably followed within a very short time, a minute or two at the most. So there will be blood somewhere, but possibly not much of it.'

'And you've nothing more to say about the time of death?'

'Sorry, can't help you. But the hypostasis suggests that she was probably placed where you found her straight away. As you know, the livor mortis starts much sooner after death than the rigor – in as little as twenty minutes – and the staining is permanent. So we'd know if she'd been moved into a different position.'

'Right,' said Slider. 'But she could have been abducted first, and killed later than Friday night?'

'Except that there were no signs of her having been restrained or tied up, no marks of rough handling, and, as we guessed from the fact she was fully dressed, no sexual violence.'

'What about consensual sex?'

'Not recent,' Cameron said, and became extra dry. 'The subject was menstruating, old bean. That vacancy had been filled.'

That fitted with what Kiera had said. 'What about the ligature?' he asked.

'Ah yes, there was some bruising of the neck, but manually inflicted, and very superficial. I had to look hard for it. Someone might have gripped her and shaken her in a fit of pique, but without any intention to cause serious harm, or even as a joke, perhaps. The ligature was placed post-mortem.'

'Why on earth—?'

'That's your job, old thing, not mine,' said Cameron. 'Human nature's a mystery to me. It's the reason I became a pathologist – nice, quiet dead patients, no lawsuits.'

Slider was thinking. 'Perhaps the stomach contents can give us an idea of when she died?'

'I've secured them and sent them for analysis. And I've sent the blood for a tox screen, but there's no pathology to suggest drugs of any sort. And I've sent off the clothes. Apropos of which, they were pretty neat and tidy – again, no sign that she had been held anywhere, tied up in a dusty attic or crammed in a car boot. And she must have been carried, not dragged, after death.'

'Well, that all adds up to a mystery,' Slider said.

'It's the way you like 'em,' Cameron said cheerfully.

'I don't like 'em at all,' he said, 'but I still get 'em.'

His tea arrived, with Connolly on the other end of it.

'I've had Mr Fitton on the phone, guv, complaining that we ratted him out to the press,' she said. 'He says they're all round the house. I told him it wasn't us – it wasn't, was it?'

'Not officially. And I'm very down on leaks. But there must be a hundred people here and in Hillingdon who know about him being her neighbour. Any one of them could have spilled the beans, and there's no way to find out who.' He eyed her curiously. 'Are you feeling sorry for him?'

'Not him,' she denied hastily. 'The dog. He says to me, how can he take the dog out for its walks with them surrounding him every step, and he daren't shove 'em aside for fear they'll put a charge on him.'

'So he still has the dog?'

'Yeah, boss – he says your man Hibbert's never asked about it. Too heartbroken, maybe.'

She hesitated.

'Yes? Out with it?'

'Well, guv, apparently the parents used to look after the dog when she went on holiday. So I thought, maybe if one of us was to go over to fetch it and take it to them...?'

'You're not a dog warden.'

'But it'd be a chance to have another go at Mr Fitton.'

'If I want to talk to Fitton I can have him brought in.'

'At least that'd give him a bit of peace and quiet,' Connolly grumbled. 'But, guv, if I did the dog thing first, it'd look friendly, not so official, and he might tell me things he wouldn't say in an interview room.'

Slider considered. 'I think you may be under-estimating Fitton. Someone who's done fifteen years inside knows how to guard his tongue.'

'Then you'd never scare anything out of him, either,' she said reasonably. 'Might as well let me try charming it out, guv. What harm?'

Slider considered. 'D'you want to take some-one with you?'

'Sure God, he'd never open up to me if I'd a minder with me. And he'd have to be a mentaller to take a crack at me with all them peelers and the world's press outside.'

'Well, you can have a go,' Slider said, 'but don't get your hopes up too much.'

'OK, guv. At least it'll be a kindness for Marty.'

'Marty?'

'The dog.'

'Oh, yes.' Probably not for Fitton, though. As things stood, the dog was likely the only friend he had in the world. 'It'll be a good opportunity for talking to the parents, as well,' he said. 'I'd like to see them for myself. Pick me up when you've got the dog and we can go together.'

'Yes, guv,' she said, leaving Slider to wonder why she looked so pleased about it.

Five

All Mad Cons

When Ronnie Fitton let her into his flat, Connolly appreciated what Slider meant about him giving nothing away: there was no sign in his face or manner that the murder of the girl upstairs or his hounding by the pack outside had affected him at all. He did not look haggard or sleep deprived or worried or indignant. The only thing about him that was not blankness was that same glint of fire in his eyes that had made her nervous before. But he had let her in readily, and she did not believe he meant her harm.

She had telephoned ahead and explained the plan, and he had agreed, and he opened the door just enough for her to sidle in as soon as she knocked, while behind her the shutters shut and the questions snapped like mosquitoes, trying to get in before the door closed.

'Sorry about all that,' she said, gesturing over her shoulder. 'Mad bunch a gougers! It wasn't us, I swear.'

He shrugged. 'Bound to happen. Cup o' tea?'

It wasn't offered with any more enthusiasm than before, but this time she accepted, the better to get chatting to him. 'Ah, thanks. Me mouth's rough as a badger's arse.'

He went to put the kettle on. 'You're right about Marty though. It's no life for him here.'

The dog was lying on the floor between the bed and the bathroom door, where she had seen him last time, though now he had a folded blanket under him for comfort. 'He looks down in the mouth,' she said. He was chin-on-paws again, but this time did not look at her. He was staring at nothing, and when she crouched beside him and stroked his head, he did not even move his tail in token acknowledgement. 'Poor owl feller. Aren't you the heart-scald?'

'I think he knows she's gone,' Fitton said – surprising her, because it was a bit of a girl thing to say, really, for a man who'd survived fifteen years in the Scrubs. 'It'll be better for him out of here, at her mum's.'

'You'll miss him, though.'

He shrugged. 'Never had him more than a night at a time. He's not my dog.'

'I wonder you don't get one of your own, you like 'em so much,' Connolly said.

'Haven't got the time for one.' The kettle clicked and he poured water into mugs. 'Milk? Sugar?'

'Milk, no sugar. Thanks.'

He brought her the cup and sat down on the bed, looking at her. She had a feeling he knew exactly why she was here.

'Thanks,' she said again, gesturing with the cup.

'All mod cons,' he said. 'Don't know how long they'll last, if I can't get out to the shops. An-

95

other reason old Marty ought to go.'

'What about your job? Are they all right with you not coming in?'

He shrugged.

'What was it you did, again?'

'I don't have a job,' he said. Again he made the finger-and-thumb gesture, like a beak pecking at his forehead. The vulture of retribution. 'I'm branded, remember? Criminal record. Nobody would take me on.'

'That's terrible,' she said.

He gave a cynical smile. 'Well, would you? Mad wife-murderer, me – or didn't they tell you?'

She refused to be baited. 'Have you never had a job, so, since you came out?'

'Not what you'd call a job.'

'And that's – what? – ten years? How'd you pass the time? Doesn't it have you driven mad with boredom?'

He shook his head a little, wonderingly, as if asking himself what she would say next. 'I know all about boredom,' he said. 'Expert on it.'

'Sorry. What was I thinking? Pay no mind to me – me tongue runs like a roller towel, so me mammy says.'

He sipped his tea and said, 'Why don't you ask me what you want to ask me? You've come here full of questions, and you're not going to sucker me by pretending to be a thick Mick, which I know you're not, or pretending to be interested in my welfare, which I know you're not either. I knew you lot'd come after me sooner or later. I'm just glad they sent you instead of some sweaty plod with big feet.'

'They didn't send me. It was me own idea to come.'

'And they let you? Visit a woman-murderer alone in his flat? Don't they like you?'

He was playing a game with her, and she wasn't going to blink first. 'Ah, sure God, you wouldn't harm me, with all them people outside. They'd break the door down the minute I screamed.'

'Maybe. But it'd be too late for you by then, wouldn't it? You'd be dead. And prison doesn't scare me any more.'

'But you wouldn't want to go back,' she said shrewdly.

Something changed in his eyes. He wasn't baiting her now. 'Ask your questions,' he said, and she had to stop herself shivering.

She searched around for the best way in. She was sure she wouldn't get to ask many questions, so she needed to ask the right ones. 'What did you think of Melanie and Scott Hibbert?'

She had surprised him – it wasn't the question he expected. That was good.

'She was mad about him. But she knew he wasn't good enough for her. She was talking herself into it.'

'Why would she do that?'

'There's a lot you don't know about her. She wasn't a happy person. She had things in her past.'

'D'you mean her father getting killed?' she asked when it was clear he wasn't going to say any more.

97

He neither assented nor dissented.

'Wasn't that a long time ago, though? I mean, what, ten years or more? Surely she'd got over it?'

Still nothing.

'You must have known her well to know how she felt about her dad's death.'

'We talked sometimes,' he said.

'Here? Or in her flat?'

'Just in passing. Tuesday mornings, putting out the bins. She told me more than she thought she did. She hadn't got anyone to talk to, that was her trouble.'

'I thought she had loads of friends. And her mum, and Scott...'

'You ever see someone, always the life and soul of the party, and everybody's feeding off 'em? It's like they've got to perform, put on the show, and everybody goes away satisfied except them. They have to act. Nobody cares what they want, what they really feel. And everyone says what a great person they are, but inside they're just—'

He stopped, as if hearing that he had said too much. But Connolly thought, this is a controlled man, who knows just what he's saying. He *wants* me to think he's just blurted something out. But what?

'Boy, you really did know her well,' she said in an awed murmur. 'I'd no idea.'

'I know people, that's all,' he said. 'Plenty of time to observe 'em.'

'So, d'you know who killed her?' She hadn't known she was going to ask that, but she was glad she had, though for a moment she went cold and thought, *what if he says he did? What in the name a God do I do then?*

But he said, 'No. But your bosses will think I did, and I don't blame them. I'd probably think it was me if I was you. I'm on the spot. And I've got no alibi.'

Connolly thought of the secure home over the back. 'Were you here all the time on Friday?'

'Why?'

'I was wondering if you saw anyone hanging around.'

'I was out all afternoon.'

'Where?'

'My business.'

'Was someone with you?'

'My business. I was here to see Mel come home at half past ten. That's all you need to know.'

'You didn't hear anything else that night? Anyone else arriving? Melanie going out?'

'I slept soundly. Always do. I got a clear conscience.'

She knew that wasn't an answer. 'But you'd have heard if she – or anyone else – drove her car away later that night?'

'Maybe. But I didn't.'

'Or if there was any kind of a row upstairs? A fight, furniture turned over, a body hitting the floor?'

'I didn't hear anything.'

She shook her head in frustration. 'Where d'you keep your car?' she tried. 'I mean, you rent out these spaces—'

99

'Haven't got one,' he said. 'I can't drive.' His eyes gleamed as though he was enjoying watching her flounder.

'Really? That surprises me. I mean, most men—'

'Never saw the need. Lived in London all my life.' He put his mug down and leaned forward, resting his elbows on his knees, to look at her more closely. 'You're just a kid,' he said. 'Look, I didn't kill her, and you'll never prove I did, but you'll waste a lot of time trying because I am who I am. Tell your boss that.'

'Mr Slider?'

'Yeah. I know a bit about him. Tell him to leave me alone.'

'Is that a threat?' she said doubtfully.

His expression changed. He stood up, and she got quickly to her feet, not liking having him tower over her. 'And that's enough questions,' he said coldly. 'You take Marty to her mum and dad's. I hope they're not too out of it to look after him. But anywhere's better than here.'

He went to the kitchen, found two plastic carriers and put the dog's bowls into one and the opened pack of dog biscuit into the other. Then he got the lead and went over, knelt down by the dog and stroked it for a long time, and the dog looked up at him and wagged its tail, and after a bit rolled over on its side like a good dog. Finally Fitton snapped on the lead and, without turning, held it out behind him to Connolly. 'Go on, then,' he said. He wiped his eyes with his handkerchief, and she wondered whether he was crying, or if it was just the old leakiness.

When he turned, his face was set again. 'I hope you can get out all right.' He urged the dog to its feet and Connolly led it over to the door. Fitton put his hand to the latch. 'Ready? You'll have to be quick.'

'I'm ready,' she said, though, loaded with bags and the reluctant dog, she didn't think she'd be able to manoeuvre too nimbly.

Fitton looked at her as though he wanted to say something, and she paused, raising her eyebrows receptively. But all he said was, 'There's things you don't know about Mel. Things no one knew.'

'Not even you?' she asked.

'Me least of all,' he said, and opened the door.

In the top floor flat lived Andy and Sharon Bolton. Mr Bolton was at work, and Mrs Bolton was heavily pregnant, bored, and ready to take full advantage of any thrill that was going to wile away the time.

'It's my first,' she told Swilley, making instant coffee in the tiny slope-roofed kitchen. 'Of course, it's not suitable, having a baby up here – all those stairs for one thing, and only one bedroom – but rents round here are terrible and we can't afford anything bigger. We've been on the list for a council flat for years and I thought we'd get moved up with the baby coming, but my mum says all the flats go to unmarried mothers and asylum seekers. My dad says Andy and me shouldn't ought to've got married, then we'd be set up, but he's only kidding. They both love Andy – well, everybody does. He's a gas fitter –

it's a really good job, he's got City and Guilds and he's Corgi registered and everything – but in the evening he's an Elvis impersonator. You should see him – he's wonderful! He really looks like Elvis. He's got the hair and he can do that thing with his mouth going up one side. And he's got a lovely singing voice. He does weddings and parties and bar mitzvahs and everything – ever so much in demand. Makes a lot of money at it.' The glow faded a little and she sighed. 'But it's still not enough, with the baby coming and me giving up work.' She brought the coffee over to the table and sat down. 'And now with this awful stuff happening downstairs, we've *got* to move. We're going to have to go further out, but all Andy's work's round here and it'll mean driving a lot more. But my mum says if we go out somewhere like Greenford or Hayes we can get a bigger place for the same money, only it'll mean coming off the council flat list. But Andy says they're never going to give us a flat anyway. We're better off going private. I forgot, do you want sugar?'

'Yes, please,' said Swilley.

She heaved herself to her feet again and went for the tin and a spoon. 'I've stopped having it,' she said. 'I was putting on too much weight. It's surprising how you don't miss it, after a bit. I tried to get Andy off it, but he burns it off, he's on the go so much. We're saving for a place of our own with his Elvis money, but you've got to have such a big deposit these days. But we've *got* to move now. It gives me the willies, thinking about that poor Melanie – such a nice girl she was. Of course, I only knew her just to say hello to, but she was always friendly and nice – not like that lot underneath, the Beales, always complaining if we so much as scrape a chair, and making a fuss about Andy practising. And is that right, him in the basement turns out to be a murderer? I read in the paper he killed his wife. Why haven't you arrested him?'

'There's no evidence to suggest he had anything to do with it,' Swilley said, trying to be patient.

'Well, it must have been him. Stands to reason. If he's killed once, he's bound to kill again. None of us are safe as long as he's around. There was this woman on a phone-in this morning when I was getting Andy his breakfast, who said it was a disgrace he was on the loose, any of us could be killed in our beds for all anyone cared. I always thought he had funny eyes – not that I've ever spoken to him, he keeps himself to himself, but they always do, don't they? My mum says—'

'So you didn't know Melanie very well?' Swilley broke in before the flood could carry her away again.

'No, like I said, just to say hello to. But Andy's friends with Scott. They go drinking together sometimes, when Melanie works late or she's out with her friends. I don't go, I don't like pubs. But Andy brings him back here for coffee and a chat. And Scott goes to Andy's gigs sometimes, helps out with the sound equipment, that sort of thing. He wants to be an impersonator himself, Scott does, but he hasn't got the voice. I mean, you can't just wiggle about for half an hour – people expect the songs as well. Andy does "Heartbreak Hotel" so's you couldn't tell it *wasn't* Elvis, he's that good,' she said proudly.

'Do you like Scott?' Swilley got in while she took a breath.

'Oh yes, he's lovely. Oh –' her face changed to tragedy-mode – 'he must be heartbroken about Melanie. He was mad about her. They were such a lovely couple. Besotted. He must be kicking himself that he went away for the weekend. If he'd been here, it wouldn't have happened.'

'Do you know where he was?'

'Oh yes, he told Andy. It was a friend's wedding, and he was doing his Elvis thing at the stag night.' She made a face. 'He doesn't even have the right hair – he has to wear a wig. He isn't a patch on my Andy. But Andy watched him rehearse and gave him some tips. He wasn't going to get paid for doing the stag night, so I suppose it didn't matter so much, and I expect they'd all be too drunk to notice anyway. You know what stag nights are like.'

'So were you and Andy home on Friday night?'

'Yes, and it makes me feel faint to think about it. To think we were up here watching Graham Norton while that horrible man was killing poor Melanie, and we never heard a thing.'

'You didn't hear any sounds of disturbance from downstairs? Anyone come in or go out? Any cars arriving or leaving, during the evening or night?'

'No, Andy came home, oh, about half past

seven, quarter to eight, and we had our meal, and then we settled in to watch the telly. We went to bed about eleven, just after, and that was that. Andy sleeps really heavily, he's that tired at the end of the day. And even if I'm awake, I can't hear anything for him snoring. Mind you, we wouldn't hear anything from up here anyway. We never do. The Beales, *they're* the ones who are always complaining about noise,' she concluded bitterly. 'You can't *move* up here without them moaning. You should ask them.'

'I will,' said Swilley.

But the Beales – whom she had to track down at work – could not help. They were extremely indignant that their lives had been disrupted by the press, and asked, like Sharon Bolton, why Fitton had not been arrested, and how a convicted murderer could be allowed to roam around unsupervised, putting everyone's lives at risk. But they had been out at a friend's for dinner on Friday evening, going straight from work, and had not arrived home until after midnight. They had not seen anyone else around, nor heard any sounds during the night. They had gone out at about half past ten the following morning, to shop and then to lunch, and had not heard or seen anything untoward before leaving. They had not heard the dog barking, though they had heard that creature upstairs moving furniture about, and playing the radio far too loudly. You'd think she was roller-skating on the bare boards, sometimes, the noise she managed to make.

They had known Melanie Hunter only to say

hello to, and had thought her nice, friendly, pleasant. They had spoken to Scott Hibbert once or twice. He seemed a very nice man, too. He worked for an estate agent, but it was an up-market one – was it Jackson Stops? No, Hatter and Ruck, that was it – which of course made a difference. He had a plan for turning the house into two maisonettes by getting rid of the undesirable top floor and basement people. The Beales could have a really nice maisonette if they could incorporate the top floor into their flat. Hibbert had thought the freeholder would be willing, and the top floor were only renting, and he said there were always ways of getting renters out, but that man Fitton actually owned his flat, so he had to be persuaded to sell. Scott Hibbert had raised the matter with him but so far without success. Mr Beale wanted to know what the position would be when Fitton went to prison for murdering Melanie Hunter. Would his flat be seized, and would it go on the open market? He wondered whether the notoriety would raise the price or suppress it. He seemed hopeful it would be the latter. Mrs Beale had doubts about remaining there at all, now this had happened, but Mr Beale thought property was hard enough to come by in this area, and one shouldn't be foolishly squeamish, especially when turning the flats into two maisonettes would considerably more than double the value of each. When would they be arresting Fitton?

The Beales, she told Slider when she reported back, were a charming couple, but cold and ruth-less.

'A sort of Steve and Eydie Amin?' Slider offered.

'But it does at least tighten up Scott Hibbert's alibi, boss,' Swilley said, not knowing who Steve and Eydie were. 'If he was actually doing an entertainment at the stag night on Friday, there was no way he wouldn't be missed. And though he might have a motive for getting rid of Ronnie Fitton and the Boltons, he had none for getting rid of Melanie.'

'Except,' Slider said, 'if he had any reason to expect to inherit the flat on her death, so he could double its value and keep all the profit himself. But that's a meagre sort of motive, and not one I'd like to have to convince a jury of.'

'He couldn't double its value without getting Fitton to sell,' said Swilley. 'But if Fitton went down for the murder, that would get him out of the way.' She was joking, he could see, but there was some serious thought behind it.

'Go on,' he invited.

She smiled. 'And then the other people leave because they don't want to live in a murder house, the price falls because of the notoriety, he snaps up the other flats cheap, and then he redevelops the whole house and makes a killing. Pardon the pun.'

'Ingenious,' Slider said.

'Yeah,' said Swilley apologetically. 'It'd make a good movie. And nobody likes estate agents. But anyway, he loved her – everyone says so.'

'All the same, we need to check up on his movements. Since we don't know exactly what time Melanie was killed, there's still the possibility that he drove home from Salisbury during the night and went back afterwards. And –' he forestalled her objection – 'we can work on the motive afterwards, if necessary.'

Connolly was glad to see the dog perk up as she pulled up in front of the house. There were neighbours and pressmen gathered along the pavement, keeping a respectful but agog distance from the front door where a uniform – Dave Bright – was keeping guard. He came down to the car as she stopped, but recognized Slider and nodded. He was an old-fashioned copper, large, authoritative and serene, and such was his presence that no one moved when he opened the car door for her. When she encouraged the dog out after her, there was a murmur among the neighbours and a stirring, like a wheat field in a summer breeze, among the pressmen, but Bright looked left and right and raised a massive hand, and everyone came to rest again, though there was a frenzied zip-zip of photo-shutters, like a caucus of cicadas. Slider's exit was met with a barrage of questions from the fourth estate, cancelling each other out since he could not hear them over each other – though they seemed to be mostly about Ronnie Fitton. He ignored them sturdily, following Bright, Connolly and the dog up the path, past the family car, to the front door.

In the house of mourning, tea was brewing, as it always was, and a large, spongey woman was ministering to Mrs Wiseman in the sitting room, and was introduced as 'my friend' by Mrs Wiseman and 'Margie Sutton from number forty-eight' by herself. Bethany was in the kitchen with a school friend – 'we couldn't make her go in today, not with all this going on, and reporters everywhere' – and Mr Wiseman was also home, hovering angrily between sitting room and kitchen, his clenched fists shoved into his pockets and his face twitching with tension. He seemed irritated not only by the crowds outside but by the presence of 'Margie' inside.

'My wife felt she needed support,' was all he said, but it was the way he said it.

Slider could see that Margie might come across as irritating, obviously relishing the tragedy and the opportunities it opened up for being sentimental and gushingly supportive.

'Ooh, I *know*,' she crooned to anything Mrs Wiseman said, while urging her to 'put her feet up', 'be kind to herself', and not 'hold it back'. She had soft, moist eyes like over-boiled gooseberries, and such a cascade of chins her fat white face looked like a cat on a pile of cushions.

But there was no doubt Marty the dog was pleased to see them. He strained forward on the leash, wagging his entire back end with gladness, and when Connolly released him, shoved his nose into the crotch of each person in turn, swinging his body round for patting, and panting with happiness. Mrs Wiseman seemed distracted and inclined to weep at him, but Mr Wiseman was hugely glad of the distraction and petted the dog extensively, saying, 'Good old boy. Good old dog,' over and over. Bethany and her friend came to the door to see what was happening, and were easily persuaded to take Marty out into the garden and play with him; which, when a little semaphore between Slider and Connolly had taken place, left the kitchen free for Slider to interview Mr Wiseman, while Connolly worked her magic on the distaff side in the sitting room.

Wiseman seemed relieved to be in the presence of just another man, and his tension seemed to drop back a notch – though he was still wound so tight it didn't make him the king of cool by several nuclear reactors' worth. 'Would you like a cup of tea?' he offered, with a slight awkwardness that suggested he thought this was a woman's opening, and that he only felt constrained to make it because of the unusual circumstances. Slider calculated that Wiseman would not sit down so was better off with something to do, and accepted. It got his fists out of his pockets, at any rate – Slider was worried for his stitching.

He studied the man as he moved about the kitchen, making a fresh pot. Ian Wiseman was not exceptionally tall – about five ten, Slider thought – but there was no doubt he was in shape. His face was lean and tanned, his hair thick and curly and with very little grey in the brown, his shoulders and arms powerful, his body neat and his legs muscled. He was wearing cord trousers and a V-necked sweater over a check shirt, open at the neck – just the clothes Slider would have expected of a teacher off duty. His hands shook slightly as he made the tea, the tendons stood out in his neck and his expression was grim with, Slider presumed, maintaining control in such difficult circumstances. Other-wise, he thought, he would have been quite good-looking, in a dark-haired, blue-eyed, Irish sort of way.

'This must be difficult for you,' Slider said in sympathetic tones, by way of opening the con-versation.

'It certainly is,' he snapped back immediately. 'Crowds out there so we can't get out of our own front door. Our life not our own. We've had to unplug the phone. I had to keep Bethany home from school, and God knows she can't afford to lose any more days. She's already had time off this term with a cold, and with her grades she needs to keep her nose to the grindstone. And then to cap it all my head sent a message to tell me not to come in this week!' He crashed the lid on to the teapot with a kind of suppressed fury. 'Not that I would have been able to go today, the way things are, but to have him write me off, and for the whole week! I've got a hockey team to coach for the play-offs, I've got soccer teams, I've got basketball inter-schools coming up, I've got kids lined up for private coaching – and I'm stuck indoors here. I can't afford to take a week off.'

Interesting approach to bereavement, Slider thought, not without pity. It took different people different ways, and he could see that, for an active man, being cooped up with two dripping females and nothing to do would be trying. Still it was not his job to sympathize.

'And you must be upset about Melanie,' he said.

111

Wiseman's back was to him, pouring the tea. He seemed to pause for a beat, and then said, rather stiffly, 'Of course I'm upset.' He finished pouring and brought Slider's cup and saucer to the table. 'Do you take sugar?'

'No, thanks,' said Slider. 'Are you not having one?'

'I'm up to here with tea,' Wiseman said savagely, and then went and stood by the window with his fists in his pockets again. He seemed to have been working on control, because he said in a quiet tone, 'Look, she wasn't my own child – you know that?'

'Yes,' said Slider. He wished the man would turn round. He liked faces to his words.

'But I did my best by her. Rachel was widowed – you know about that?'

'Yes, her husband died in the Greenford rail crash.'

'That's right. And my wife died suddenly, leaving me with Bethany, who was only eighteen months old. So we were both – we needed each other. I don't say there wasn't a bit of – well, I suppose you don't call it rebound when it's a case of bereavement, but it was something like that. We married very quickly. Graham – Rachel's husband – had only been dead just over a year, my wife a bit less than that. Some people were shocked we married so soon. Well, it was none of their business,' he added in a sort of growl.

'No one else can know what you were feeling,' Slider said, as if agreeing.

Wiseman turned and stared at him intently,

112

perhaps judging his sincerity. Apparently he passed muster. 'You're right,' he said. 'I got sick to death of being judged. We dropped all our old friends – friends, they called themselves. There was Rachel with a teenager at the worst possible age for a thing like that, trying to manage all on her own, and I've got a baby, going on a toddler, and trying to hold down a very demanding job. You may think it's a cushy number being a PE teacher, but I can tell you it's not.'

'I'm sure it's not,' Slider said sincerely. 'It must take a great deal out of you.'

He seemed mollified. 'Well, it's not nine to five,' he said forcefully. 'There's all the out-of-hours coaching, and travelling with teams to competitions, and these days there's all the paperwork that goes with it, too. And one has to keep oneself fit, and that takes time. It was impossible to give Bethany any kind of decent home life. So Rachel and I joined forces, and—' He didn't quite shrug, but Slider got the impression that if he wasn't such a gentleman he would have hinted that the bargain hadn't been evenly balanced. 'I always tried to do the right thing by Melanie. I did my best.'

'Did you and she not get along?' Slider asked neutrally.

Wiseman gave an exasperated sort of sigh. 'Oh, it wasn't that. Not the way *you* mean. But she was sixteen, her father was dead – and she and him were always close. She was bound to be upset and mixed up and so on. She had all the usual teenage problems, only more so – and I wasn't the answer to them, as far as she was concerned. All I could do was give her a stable home and the right influence. I dare say she'd have liked me better if I'd been permissive and let her do whatever the hell she wanted, but that's not how you bring up children. I wouldn't have been doing my duty by her if I hadn't come down hard on certain things. And she thanked me for it in the long run. I mean, she knew I was right, once she got herself sorted out. But for a couple of years it was hard going. And Rachel was no help. Well, she was devastated by Graham's death. I didn't realize until later how much it affected her.' His face darkened, and Slider read between the lines that he wouldn't have married her if he had. 'She would never take any kind of line with Melanie, it was always left up to me. And she wasn't even my child.'

'I can see how difficult it must have been. But your relationship did get better in the end?'

'Oh, we were all right with each other. The last few years – once she'd got herself sorted out. She pulled herself together – got a degree, worked hard and got a good job – and that made all the difference. Once she'd got some self-respect, she knew I'd been right to take a tough line with her. I wouldn't say we were ever really close, not warm, but we respected each other, and that was enough.'

'Did you see much of her?'

'Not really. She had her own life, you know what kids are. She rang her mother often, and she came over for Sunday lunch once in a while. You wouldn't expect more at her time of life.'

'When did you last see her?'

114

'About a fortnight ago, it was; she and Scott came over for Sunday lunch. That would be the last time I spoke to her. Though she rang her mother, I think, on the Friday – on the day.' He stopped abruptly, his face dark, his eyebrows pulled together like storm clouds.

'What did you think of Scott?' Slider said.

'*He*'s all right,' Wiseman said, and Slider thought the emphasis revealing. 'Steady lad, good job, nice manners. He wanted to marry her, you know,' he burst out as though it was impossible to bear, 'but she was the one holding back. I didn't approve of them living together like that. It's not respectable. But Scott was working on her, bringing her round. *He* had the right ideas. It was—' He stopped again, brooding. 'If she'd married, this would never have happened. If she'd listened to me...'

'Do you know if Melanie was worried about anything, the last few weeks?' Slider tried. 'Was there anything you and her mother were concerned about?'

'Apart from her not marrying Scott? No, not that I know of.'

'She wasn't in money trouble?'

'She never said she was. And Scott earned plenty.'

'Or mixing with any unsavoury types?'

'Scott would never have allowed that. No, she was all right, as far as I knew.'

Slider drank off his tea. 'Well, thank you, Mr Wiseman. You've been very helpful. Just one last thing – were you at home on Friday evening?'

Something happened. Slider had been going to ask about phone calls during the evening, but Wiseman stiffened like a fox smelling the hounds. 'What d'you want to know that for?' he asked, suppressed anger all present and correct again.

'Purely routine,' Slider said soothingly. 'We like to know where everyone was at the time.'

'If you're thinking I had anything to do with Melanie's death, just because I'm her stepfather—'

'Not at all. It's just a routine question, nothing to worry about. Where were you, in fact?'

Wiseman scowled horribly. 'I was coaching a school soccer team in the early part of the evening, if you must know, and after I got home I watched television with my wife until bedtime. As she'll tell you, if you can't take my word for it.'

Slider made a placating movement with his hands. 'There's no need for that. I assure you, the question was not meant disrespectfully. We ask everyone, just to clear the field.'

Wiseman evidently liked the word 'disrespectfully' and his hackles slowly went down. Through the kitchen window Slider could see the school friend playing with the dog, but Bethany was nowhere to be seen. He wondered what Wiseman would think of her absenting herself without permission – but there had not seemed anything particularly cowed about Bethany in the brief time he had observed her. More pertinently, he wondered how Connolly had got on; and that, at least, he could do something about.

116

Six

Thirst Among Equals

Margie was hanging around in the hall as he passed through.

'Rachel's gone upstairs to have a lay down. I think that little talk with your lady upset her. I left them to it – private, you know – but I think I'd better stay on a bit in case I'm wanted,' she concluded wistfully.

'Has my colleague left?'

'Oh yes, a few minutes ago. Was – is Ian OK? Such a lovely man. P'raps I'd better go and make him a cup of tea? It can't be easy talking about something like this.'

There isn't something like this, Slider thought. But some malicious sprite prompted him to say, 'Good idea. I expect he needs a cup.' She scuttled off with a new mission in life and Slider escaped through the front door. The first thing he saw was Connolly, down the side of the house, deep in conversation with Bethany, so he turned his back on them and talked to Dave Bright for a bit, to give her space. He'd have gone and sat in the car, but that would have left him vulnerable to the crowd.

* * *

Connolly had been surprised when Mrs Sutton had offered to leave her alone with Mrs Wiseman, levered herself up on tiptoe and crept out: an elephant of tact. She had thought missing the interview would be the last thing Mrs Sutton would want to do, and gave her points for having more depths than was at first apparent.

Mrs Wiseman had been only too eager to talk. Grief had made her loquacious, though rambling. She kept weeping, like a slow bleed, but it did not interfere with her speech.

'I knew, when that other police-lady came, I knew she was gone. I had this premonition, somehow, that she was dead. My Melanie. I can't seem to make it real in my head, d'you know what I mean? I keep thinking she'll ring me any minute. And yet I just knew the moment she said she was missing that she wasn't coming back.'

She wiped at her nose hopelessly with a soggy tissue that was in danger of disintegrating. Connolly passed her another and murmured something about a 'mother's instinct'. Mrs Wiseman jumped on that eagerly.

'That's what it was! That's what it must have been. A mother's instinct. Because Ian's been saying he always knew it would end up like this, but that's not right. It's not right to say something like that, just because she had that bit of trouble. That was years ago, and she's turned her life right round since then. It's not right to keep harping on about it. She was just a girl, and her dad had been killed, and it's no wonder she went off the rails a bit. I said at the time he ought to be more sympathetic, but he's so hard, Ian, he never makes allowances. He thinks everybody ought to be as together as he is. Oh, I know he thought he was doing right by her, being strict and everything, and I expect it did help her, in the long run, but to be saying a thing like that now, all these years later, when she's such a lovely girl, and she's really made something of herself. She's got a lovely job and a lovely boy-friend and there's no reason *at all* to say "I told you so" about something like this. I mean, nobody deserves to have that happen to them, and she was a good girl, a really good girl.'

'What was the bit of trouble she got in?' Connolly asked. 'When her Dad died?'

'Well, it wasn't right away, that's the funny thing. She was wonderful at first, a tower of strength to me – because I just went to *pieces*, I can tell you. It was the most terrible, terrible time; but Melanie was so wonderful, and she really adored her dad, you know, they were so close, but she supported me and did all the things that needed doing, and she was so calm and everything. I suppose in the end it was bound to come out, like a sort of – of...'

'Belated reaction?' Connolly offered.

'That's right,' said Mrs Wiseman. 'Anyway, it all seemed to come over her suddenly, after Ian and I got married.' She frowned. 'She didn't really approve of that, she thought it was too soon, and anyway you know what children are, they think you should never look at a man again, but I was only twenty when I had her so I was much too young to throw myself in the grave with him, so to speak. And Graham – Melanie's dad – well, he was a charmer all right, but he wasn't a good husband. Melanie had no idea, of course – well, that's not the sort of thing you tell your daughter, is it? Especially when she adores her dad like she did. But he was always in and out of different jobs and running up debts, and spending what we didn't have. It was hand to mouth the whole time with him. You never knew where the next meal was coming from. He was the sort of man who'd leave the gas bill unpaid but take us away for a weekend in a hotel. Always bringing home presents and useless things for the house – he was gadget mad, that man. But Melanie had holes in her shoes and no winter coat.' She shook her head at the memory and wiped her eyes again. 'So when Ian proposed to me, I wasn't thinking about it being too soon, I can tell you. A good man – a churchgoer and everything! And with a steady job – *and* ready to take on a stepdaughter just at the difficult age? I'd have been mad not to snap him up. But then Melanie sort of went to pieces. She sulked, and she was rude to me, and she'd barely talk to Ian, and Ian – well, I don't think he had the knack of handling her, not that anything would have helped much, the way she was then. But they were like two cats glaring at each other, and if one said white the other said black and off they'd go. Well, anyway, the upshot was my poor Melanie got into bad company. She started smoking, she was always out late and not saying where she was – you know the sort of thing.'

Connolly nodded helpfully.

'And all the time it was like she was defying Ian to stop her. Oh, he tried, and the rows were terrible, but it just seemed to make her worse. And then she—' She stopped, biting her lip.

'She got into trouble?' Connolly said, to help her along.

Mrs Wiseman nodded her head, lowering her eyes in shame. 'She got pregnant. We didn't know she'd been going with boys. You know – having sex, I mean. Because she was always a pretty girl and naturally boys liked her and we knew she had boyfriends, but not that she was – doing that. Well, it was like the world came to an end. I mean, Ian – he's really strict about anything like that. The rows before were nothing to what happened then. And she wouldn't say who the father was. Ian was raging, he wanted to go round and make the boy face up to it, but she wouldn't say who it was. And then in the middle of one row – I don't know if it was just to wind Ian up, or if it was true – I can't believe it was true – she said she *didn't know who the father was.*' She put a weak hand to her face. 'Ian just went mad.'

Connolly handed over more tissues in silent sympathy. She could imagine the cataclysm. And she could imagine the young Melanie facing her stepfather down, sixteen or seventeen, confused, miserable, pregnant and frightened, having it made clear to her she had nowhere to turn. *I hope he dies roaring for a priest*, she thought with unexpected savagery.

'So what happened?' she asked after a moment, when the mopping was finished. 'With the

121

baby, and all?'

Mrs Wiseman hauled up a sigh from so deep it could have turned her tights inside out. 'She had an abortion. Ian arranged it. I was a bit surprised, him being a churchgoer and all, but he said having the baby would blight her whole life. And ours. I suppose he was right. Well, I know he was, because when it was all over, Melanie sorted herself out, buckled down at school, went to university and everything, and she couldn't have done that with a baby in tow. But I always wondered.' Another sigh. 'Well, you can't help thinking, can you, what if? And it would have been my grandchild. I'll never have one now.'

'But Melanie agreed that it was the right thing to do?' Connolly asked. It was hard not to get sucked into this kind of sorrow.

'Oh yes – she knew it was the only way. And we managed to hush it all up, so that no one ever knew. Luckily it was the beginning of the school summer holidays, so Ian arranged for us all to go away, and it was done at a private clinic. By the time school started again it was all over and done with, and she was fit and well again, so there was no need for her friends or the teachers or the neighbours to know about it. It was like a clean start for her, and to do her credit, she took full advantage. She cut herself off from the bad gang and became, well, a model student. And daughter. And she thanked Ian, in her heart, for putting her right, I know she did. I mean, it wasn't something we ever talked about, not directly, but once or twice when I've said how well she was doing, she's said something like, yes, it was the right decision.'

'And she got on with Ian all right in the end?'

'Oh yes. Like I said to the other lady, I wouldn't say they're all over each other, but underneath I think there's a real respect and affection. She *knew* he saved her from a terrible mistake. Everything she had, really, was down to him.'

Connolly relayed this story to Slider as they walked down to her car, settled in and drove away. 'It accounts for why the best friend Kiera didn't know anything about it – Melanie got whisked away, and came back with her sins scrubbed clean. Everything tidied away under the carpet. After that she put a shape on her life, and ended up on the pig's back, but you can't help wondering if there wasn't some bit of her thought it could have been different ... What was your man like?'

'Mean, moody and magnificent,' Slider said. 'Well, mean and moody, anyway. It's obvious he likes to control. He'd be a strict father.'

'Yeah, I got that. Must a been cat for him, married to that blancmange of a woman.'

'What did you get from the child – Bethany?'

'That one! Eleven going on thirty-five. She waylaid me as I came out the door, couldn't wait to wear the ear offa me.'

Connolly had heard her hiss as she stepped past Dave Bright, and looking back had seen the child standing down the side access, beckoning.

'My dad's mad as fire about all this,' she con-

123

fided as soon as Connolly was close enough. 'Mel getting killed and everything.'

'Why would he be mad?' Connolly queried.

'Cause he thinks it's getting us talked about. He's always going on about what the neighbours think. Who cares what the poxy neighbours think, that's what I say. But he worries about that sort of crap. It's being a teacher. Got to be ultra-respectable if you're a teacher, or it's all over the tabloids. That's why he's a sidesman at church. Thinks it gives him Brownie points.' She snorted in derision. 'Dad thinks I'm gonna be a teacher when I grow up. Catch me! I'm not doing anything where some poxy boss can tell me what I can do and can't do. Dad's mad because Mr Bellerby – he's the head at Dad's school – told him not to come in. Dad thinks he thinks he's letting the school down, or some crap like that.'

'I don't suppose your dad likes you using words like crap,' Connolly said.

Bethany looked surprised, and then narrowed her eyes. 'You're not cool like that other one that came, the tall one.'

'Oh, I'm way cooler than her,' Connolly said. 'What did you think of Melanie?'

Bethany shrugged. 'She was all right. She let me try her make-up and things, when she was a student. But she turned into this boring grown-up with a boring job, just like everybody else. I'm not going to be like that.'

'Did you see a lot of her?'

'She come over every now and then. For Sunday lunch.' She rolled her eyes. 'The burnt offerings, Dad calls it.'

'Isn't your mum a good cook?'

'You kidding? She thinks the smoke alarm's a timer. That's what Dad says. She's not my real mother, but I call her Mum and everything. I don't remember my real mum – she died when I was a baby. Of gusto enteritis. I'm gonna be a doctor when I grow up, but not a poxy GP – a big posh consultant, me, so nobody can tell me what to do. Dad married Mum when I was a baby so he'd have someone to look after me and cook and clean and everything. Good luck with that! He says she's as much use as a sick headache.'

'He doesn't say those things to you?' Connolly said, privately shocked.

'No, course not. I hear them rowing, and he says it to her.'

'Do they row a lot?'

'Yeah. She gets on his nerves. And she snores, so they don't sleep in the same room any more. She wakes *me* up, sometimes. It's like the house is falling down.' She looked troubled for a moment, and said, 'She's all right, really, my mum. I mean, I love her and everything. She's just not very good at "mum" things.'

'Different people are good at different things,' Connolly said, and the child looked relieved.

'Yeah, that's right. She sings nice, my mum. She used to sing to me at night when she tucked me in. Course, I'm too old for that now, but I like it when she sings round the house, when she's on her own and she thinks no one's listening. And when Mel came, sometimes they'd sing together, soppy old songs from the dark ages, but it sounded nice.'

'When did Melanie last come over?'

'Two weeks ago, on the Sunday, but they weren't singing then. Her and my dad had a right old ding-dong. They were in the kitchen making the tea after lunch and I was in the lounge with Mum and Scott, but we could hear 'em all right.'

'What were they rowing about?'

'Oh, the usual – her not being married and living with Scott. Living in sin, Dad calls it – honestly!' She snorted in eye-rolling derision. 'Dad kept saying Scott wanted to marry her and she should be grateful, and she said she didn't have to be grateful to any man, and Dad said she ought to be grateful to *him* for saving her neck, and she said that didn't give him the right to run her life, and he said she was just throwing everything away when he'd worked so hard to make us respectable, and she said *you* can talk and then he slapped her.'

'He hit her?'

'Oh, not hard. Just slapped her face for being cheeky. They didn't talk any more after that and when they came back in with the tea they pretended nothing had happened, but I could see her cheek was a bit red.'

'Does he hit you?'

'He used to, sometimes, but he doesn't now. He got scared of the social lady coming round. He was mad as fire about the government saying you couldn't hit your kids any more. He said the country was going to the dogs. But like I said he's got to be dead careful because of being a teacher, so he couldn't afford to get mixed up with that social lot. They'd send you to prison soon as look at you. That's who I thought the other one was, the other lady policeman who came before. I thought she was from the social at first. But they don't have such nice clothes. It says in the papers a man killed Mel – that man in the basement.'

'I'm sure it doesn't say he killed her, because nobody knows who killed her.'

'Well, it says he was a murderer, he killed his wife, so it's gotta be him, hasn't it? Are you going to arrest him?'

'Not up to me. Anyway, we haven't got any evidence yet. You can't arrest anyone without evidence.'

'You don't know anything, do you? My friend Georgina says her dad said the police are a load of tossers,' Bethany confided pleasantly. 'He says you couldn't find your own arse with both hands and a torch.'

'That's not a nice thing to say,' Connolly said sternly.

'No, but it's funny.' She grinned, and ran off into the back garden.

'So wouldn't you say that was interesting, guv?' Connolly said, heading up the Uxbridge Road. 'Your man's starting to look a bit tasty for it. He's narky as hell, he clatters his kids, he was giving out to Melanie as recently as a fortnight ago. And he was out Friday evening.'

'Yes, he told me. He was coaching a school soccer team.'

127

Connolly took her eyes off the road to give him a level look. 'Mrs Wiseman says he didn't come home until late. She went to bed at eleven and it was after that. Sure, school soccer practice doesn't go on that long.'

'Ah,' said Slider. 'He gave me the impression he was home fairly early – he said he watched television with his wife.'

'He coulda gone for a jar after, I suppose,' Connolly said, to be scrupulously fair.

'But then why wouldn't he have said so?'

'Because he thinks himself fierce posh altogether, and hanging around in boozers is not respectable,' she suggested. 'Or...'

Slider considered, watching the shops lining the street glide away behind them. 'There's certainly a lot of anger in him,' he said. And suppressing it in the name of respectability, when his anger was righteous in origin and ought to be applauded, must be an extra strain, he thought.

'Guv, suppose after praccer he went over to Melanie's to give her another earful about not marrying your man Hibbert? She tells him to mind his business and he goes mental and lamps her.'

'Possible, but there's not enough time for him to get her to Ruislip and be back home by eleven.'

'But he could go home right after killing her, wait'll everyone's in bed and go back and do the rest.'

'Surely his wife would notice if he got up in the middle of the night?'

'No, the kid told me they don't sleep together.

Your woman snores something fierce. So that'd cover any sound he made leaving the house.'

'Ingenious,' Slider said.

'And possible,' Connolly urged.

'You've forgotten one thing, though. The dog.'

'Oh, saints and holy sinners, that dog!' Connolly cried, thinking Mr Porson wasn't so wrong in thinking it was the fly in the woodpile. 'Wait, though. It knows him, the dog. Say it was in another room when he killed her, maybe it wouldn't bark.'

'But he couldn't leave it with the body in the flat while he went home. It'd cut up Cain,' Slider pointed out. They'd reached the station now and she was turning into Tunis Road – going too fast and winding the wheel like a mad mangler. 'You couldn't—'

'No, no, wait'll I think it!' she interrupted urgently, winding again, turning into Stanlake. The gates to the yard slid open and she kept winding. 'I've got it! He could take the dog home with him, leave it in the car while he establishes his alibi, then take it back.' She looked at him triumphantly as she backed into her space. 'We could test his car for dog hair.'

Slider let her have a moment before saying, 'Had we not just taken the dog over there. And even if we hadn't, he could always say the dog had been in his car on another occasion. Why not?'

'Yeah,' said Connolly, deflating.

'All the same,' Slider said, 'he's definitely become interesting. There was obviously a history between him and Melanie, and he's – not

129

exactly lied to me, but he's misled me about his whereabouts on Friday. There's something he doesn't want us to know. I think we must look into him in a bit more detail.'

'Righty-oh,' she said happily.

'But carefully,' Slider warned. 'We don't want to ruin his life if he's innocent. Teachers have to be above reproach, you know.'

'That's what the wean said.' She rolled her eyes as she remembered. 'You'd want to hear the mouth on that kid, guv! Sure, the carry-on of her's so bad, she could end up on the news.'

It was Hollis's birthday, and he had invited the firm for a quiet drink – followed by several noisy ones – at the British Queen, which had become one of their after-work boozers as the poncification of local pubs drove them further and further down the road. Slider said thanks but no thanks – he had a long-standing dinner date with Atherton and Emily – but chipped in to the drinks pot anyway, as guv'nors were expected to; and watched in amazement as McLaren slipped away without saying anything to anybody.

'McLaren not going?' he asked Hollis.

'He said he might join us later,' Hollis said, evidently equally baffled. McLaren never missed a drink, having legendarily no life outside the Job. He lowered his voice. 'Guv, I was taking a leak just now and he was in there, *shaving*.'

'But he was clean-shaven this morning,' Slider remembered. In fact, he had not had to exhort McLaren to stand closer to the razor for weeks.

'Aye, and I know them leccy shavers don't do

the job like the old cold steel, but still...'

'Yes,' Slider said thoughtfully. Twice in one day? McLaren? The man who'd need the full-time attentions of a valet just to achieve the level of *mal-soigné*?

'Guv, I'm wondering if he's poorly,' Hollis said awkwardly. No man likes to talk about his colleagues behind their backs. Especially on sensitive subjects. 'He's lost a bit o' ground lately. Been off his oats.'

Slider nodded. McLaren had never been fat, but there had been the fleshiness of the chip-eater and beer-drinker about him. Now his lines were less blurred. 'Maybe I should have a word with him.'

'Discreet, like,' Hollis added hastily. 'You won't let on—?'

'Of course not.'

Which meant that at Atherton's bijou terraced house in West Hampstead – which he called an artesian cottage because it was so damp – the conversation was, surprisingly, on McLaren rather than the case for the first half hour. Joanna had met them there, having left Slider's father to babysit. Emily was doing the cooking for once, which meant that Atherton was rather distracted in any case, listening – and smelling – for crises in the kitchen. Not that Emily couldn't cook, but she had her ways and he had his; and besides, he had been so famed for his dinner parties before they met, it was hard to give up the tiller to the cabin boy. He occupied himself giving each of them a gin and tonic large enough to have stood in as a water feature in a medium-sized court-

131

yard garden, and fiddled about rearranging the cutlery on the table.

Outside the slicing wind had not let up, and as the glazing was Victorian, the crimson velvet curtains over the windows heaved and struggled like an opera singer getting dressed – much to the delight of the cats, who pretended they thought there was something hiding behind them that needed killing. The sealpoint Siameses, Sredni Vashtar and Tiglath Pileser – usually known as Vash and Tig – were relics of a previous relationship (divorce is so hard on the children, Atherton was wont to say) and had at least two cats' worth too much energy for a house this size. Which was why he and Emily were talking about trying to get a bigger place, with a garden. Slider tried not to let his feelings show when this topic was discussed, because Atherton had never before had a relationship that got that far. For him, commitment had been remembering her name in the morning. But now with Emily ... Slider was so happily married, he wanted the same thing for his friend – like the tailless fox, Atherton said cynically.

Slider had relayed his conversation with Hollis as Atherton went round with nibbles (olives, not crisps – oh, there's posh!).

'There's something up with him,' Slider concluded. 'Hollis thinks he's ill. But why would someone who is ill start to dress smartly and shave twice a day? I can see the losing weight bit makes sense...'

Atherton considered. 'Maybe he was going to see a specialist, and that's why he was posh-ing up.'

'Oh, really!' Emily exclaimed from the kitchen, immediately followed by a crash and an: 'Oh damn!'

Atherton froze. 'Everything all right?' he called.

'Fine!' came the breezy reply. 'Just dropped a saucepan lid. No, seriously, why would someone dress up to see a consultant?'

'People used to tidy up when the doctor was coming,' Slider defended his lieutenant.

Joanna smirked. 'In the fifties, maybe. When Janet and John roamed the earth. You really are a couple of clots. Aren't they, Em?' she called.

'S'obvious!' she called back. 'Plain as the nose on your face.' There were some more noises off, with muffled curses, and then she appeared in the kitchen doorway, holding an empty tumbler. 'What about another of these?'

'Are you sure?' Atherton said. 'I mean, while you're cooking? Kitchens are dangerous places – naked flames, hot superconductive surfaces...'

She stuffed the glass into his hand and kissed the end of his nose. 'Has anyone ever told you you have a cute face?'

'No, but I have acute anxiety,' he responded. But he did another round of drinks. 'So what *is* this bleedin' obvious answer we're all missing,' he asked, tipping gin into glasses with abandon.

'Not all,' Joanna said. 'Just you poor old hairy chaps. He's in love.'

'*McLaren*?' Atherton stopped in the act of uncapping the tonic. The cats had come mincing over, looking for mischief. Tig was trying to get his head up Atherton's trouser leg, while Vash appeared to be calculating whether he could jump straight from the floor to the top of Atherton's head. He'd done it before. It wasn't the process that hurt but the arrival. Heads were slippery and required landing gear to be down.

Emily counted on her fingers. 'Sudden interest in his appearance, stopped stuffing his face, distracted expression, disappearing on his own instead of going for drinks.'

'Yes, but – *McLaren*,' Atherton said again.

'Why not? It happens,' Joanna said. 'To golden girls and lads and chimney sweepers.'

'Love makes the world go round,' said Emily.

'So do large amounts of alcohol,' Atherton retorted, handing her the first glass. She grinned and disappeared into the kitchen.

'It makes sense, I suppose,' Slider said, staring at nothing. 'He turned up at the murder shout before everyone else. I wonder if she lives out that way?'

'Has he never been married?' Joanna asked.

'Oh yes – years ago, before I knew him. I don't think it lasted very long. She left him. Usual copper reasons, I suppose – the unsocial hours, the drinking, blah blah blah. Since then – well, he's not really a ladies' man, our Maurice.'

'More a pie, pasty and bacon sarnie man,' Atherton said, handing Slider his drink.

'Thanks.' He was staring distractedly at an ornate Victorian pot on a tall stand in the corner. 'Didn't you use to have an aspidistra in that?' he asked. It was empty now.

'Aspidistra? You dear old-fashioned thing,'

Joanna said. 'It was a fern, wasn't it, Jim? What happened to it?'

'The kits ate it. FYI, ferns go through cats like the proverbial dose of salts. It took me a while to work out what was causing it, but the results were definitely antisocial. As the saying goes, with fronds like those, who needs enemas?'

'I wonder how serious it is,' Joanna said. 'Not the diarrhoea – McLaren's fancy.'

'I wonder if we'll ever meet her,' Slider said. 'If that *is* what it is, and he's being this secretive ... Is he ashamed of her?'

'More likely doesn't want to be joshed to death by you dinosaurs,' Emily called from the kitchen. 'Dishing up now. A little help?'

Emily's cooking was not as elegantly finished as Atherton's, but it tasted good, and they tucked in happily to a chicken-and-rice dish raised above the everyday by fat black olives and slices of preserved lemon.

Slider recounted the day's advances and Connolly's theory.

'She's an ingenious girl,' Atherton said. 'But you can't get over the dog.'

'That's the same whoever it was,' Slider said.

'He could have put the body in his car boot, driven home to establish his alibi, then gone out again in the middle of the night to dump it. That gets over the dog,' Emily suggested.

'But that would surely have left some sign on her clothes,' Slider said. 'Creases, oil stains. It seems to me most likely she wasn't killed at the flat.'

'You've only got this Ronnie Fitton's word for

135

it that the dog didn't bark,' Joanna said. 'Didn't you say the upstairs people were out all evening? And the top floor ones never heard anything anyway?'

Slider nodded. 'But why would Fitton lie about that?'

'Maybe he didn't lie. Maybe he really didn't hear anything. Which means it could have happened at the flat. Or, if he was the murderer, maybe he wanted to distract attention from himself.'

'But if he was going to lie, wouldn't he lie the other way?' Emily asked. 'Make out that there was a rumpus up there, make you think someone else was there.'

'No,' said Slider. 'Safer not to give false clues that can rebound on you. He wouldn't know what other witnesses might say. Not hearing anything is the default setting – no one can prove you're lying about that. But if you claim to have heard something that never happened, or at a different time from everyone else, questions get asked.'

'So – you think he might have done it, then?' Joanna said, working out his negatives.

'He's the obvious suspect,' Slider said. 'He had a key, he knew the dog, he was on the spot.'

'And he's got a record,' Atherton said.

'Yes, the press have had a field day with that,' Emily mused. She was a freelance journalist. 'Nice people, aren't we?'

'On the other hand, if the deed wasn't done at the flat – what then?' Joanna asked. 'Doesn't that bust it right open?'

136

'Yup,' said Atherton, not happily.

'Well, it's early days yet,' Slider said, though he knew it wasn't, not really. After the first forty-eight hours, it got more and more difficult. And thanks to the 'missing persons' element, the forty-eight had been a diminishing dot in the distance before they were even called to the scene. 'There's got to be evidence out there. All we have to do is find it.'

'And on the basis that it's always the person closest to the victim, it will probably turn out to be either the boyfriend or the stepfather.'

'In fiction,' said Emily, 'it often turns out to be the first person you suspected.'

'Which brings us back to Ronnie Fitton,' said Atherton.

'We're going to have to do something about him,' Slider sighed.

'Ah, but what?' Atherton finished lightly. 'Shall I open another bottle?'

Seven

Deliver Us From Elvis

By the next morning, they had had to close off half of Cathnor Road, to the annoyance of local residents. The crowds were three deep, the press had got themselves all settled in with fleece-lined jackets and telephoto lenses on tripods, and the television news channels all had someone there, wearing a smart knitted scarf with the two ends pushed through the loop, talking to shoulder-cams and trying to make much of little. Add the police cars and forensic vans, and you had a three-ring circus. The only happy people were the upstairs residents across the road who had rented out their windows to paparazzi, and the ingenious downstairs couple who were selling tea and sandwiches to the bored journos.

Because there really wasn't anything to see. The Beales had moved out and gone to stay in their second home, a cottage near Marlow, from which, Mr Beale had told Commander Wether-spoon at some length (it turned out they had met once at a fund-raiser, which was enough of an 'in' to allow him to bend his ear), it was both costly and time-consuming to commute to work. The inconvenience and expense was intolerable

138

considering that the police had the obvious suspect in plain view and could have arrested him right at the beginning and saved everyone a lot of trouble, which was surely what they paid their taxes for.

Slider had been happy for them to go – their alibi had checked out, not that there was any reason to suspect them in the first place, and the fewer people cluttering up the place the better. It was just a pity that out of sight was not out of earshot.

The Boltons had also moved out, to stay with Mrs Bolton's parents in Hayes, because the strain was thought to be too much for Mrs Bolton's condition. And Scott Hibbert had had to give up the flat to the forensic team as soon as the misper case had turned into a murder, and had been provided with a room in an hotel in Hammersmith, where the proprietor was used to such things and was primed to raise the alarm if there were any suggestion of flitting. So there was nothing for the media to observe at the house but the forensic comings and goings, and nothing to hope for but a sight of Ronnie Fitton, who was lying low behind drawn curtains. The old case of his murder of his wife was all over every paper and on every news broadcast, despite anything the Commander and other highups could do. It was in the public domain, and the suggestion that if there ever were a court case, it would be jeopardized by the impossibility of finding anyone for the jury who didn't already think of Fitton as guilty, cut no ice with the media barons.

Porson, having been summoned to an early meeting at Hammersmith, returned to Shepherd's Bush in a fouler. Commander Wetherspoon had that effect on people. He was tall, pompous, blame-allergic, and so ingratiating of those above him, generally all you could see of him was his boots.

'All they care about is it's a good story now,' said Porson of the press. 'And if there's a trial and it goes wrong that'll be an even better story, so why should they care? There's nothing they like better than having a poke at the police – but who do they come screaming to if some punter shoves 'em out the way and they fall down and hurt their little selves?' He rubbed at his jaw, pushing his head sideways to stretch his neck, and then used his other hand to knead his shoulder. 'And to cap it all,' he snarled, 'I got this nostalgia all down one side. It's bloody killing me.'

'Ah yes,' Slider murmured. 'I used to have that.'

Porson straightened up and gave Slider a sharp look. 'There's a lot of pressure on me to arrest Fitton.'

'We haven't got any evidence against him,' Slider said.

'There's more things to consider than evidence. Like it or not, we're engaged in a public relations exercise every time we stick our noses out of doors. Nothing and nobody's sacrospect these days. You got to be seen to be doing something, and if that something is Ronnie Fitton – well, you can't bake bricks without eggs. If we can't keep the press busy they'll be muddying the waters so we can't see the wood for the pile anyway. I got more people on my back than a donkey at the beach, and a bird in the hand's as good as a wink to a blind horse any day.'

When Porson was agitated, his grasp on language became even more random than usual. You could tell how riled he was by the degree of dislocation. Slider put his current rage at around seven-point-five on the sphincter scale.

He had sympathy for the old man – he was always grateful to Porson for standing between him and the PR aspects of the job – but right was right; and he knew Porson believed that too. He maintained a steady gaze and said, 'If we arrest Fitton too soon, it could jeopardize the case against him if we later find we have one to make.'

Porson stared, and then translated his restlessness into pacing back and forth behind his desk. 'I know, I know,' he said more evenly. 'And I said all that to Mr Wetherspoon. But they've got different priorities from us up there in the stratosphere, God help us. And the Police Service isn't a democracy.'

Slider was reminded of a joke of Atherton's: in a democracy, it's your vote that counts; in feudalism it's your count that votes. Definitely feudal, the Job. 'I know, sir. But if we do Fitton we've got to do it right.'

'I know, laddie, I know.' Porson paced a couple of times more, and said, 'I'll hold 'em off you as long as I can. But if it comes to it, we may have to sacrifice the sheep for the goats. Fitton's a big boy. He won't call for his mum if we do give him a tug. But we'll leave him where he is for now. Only for God's sake get yourself in gear and get me something. I can't keep Mr Wetherspoon happy by showing him my legs.'

On this horrifying thought, Slider left.

When he was crossing the squad room on his way back to his own, Swilley called him, waving a couple of forensic reports. Slider eyed the pile of papers on his desk, visible through his open door – frankly, it would have been visible from space – and said, 'Precis them for me.'

'This one's the stomach contents,' she obliged. 'Food was still present in the stomach, suggesting the victim died less than three hours after her last meal. Recognizable elements in the partially digested contents were some kind of fish, vegetables and sponge pudding.' She looked up. 'That accords with the meal she had at the Vic, according to her mates – pan-fried sea-bass with roasted vegetables and sticky-toffee pudding.' She rolled her eyes slightly. 'And if they were eating between, say, eight o'clock and nine, allowing for having drinks first and waiting for service, that means she was probably killed about half ten, eleven o'clock time.'

'So that rules out imprisonment and a later murder,' Slider said. 'Well, it's a relief to get that out of the way. She went home and was killed soon afterwards.'

'Which makes it more likely she was killed at the flat, doesn't it?' Swilley said. 'And that brings us back to Fitton.'

'Or anyone who had a key or she might let in. What's the other one?' he asked, of the paper in her hand.

'Examination of the clothes. Nothing much there: on the back of her coat and her skirt, some traces of earth and partially composted vegetable matter – I think they mean leaves, boss. They match the earth and leaves of the site – big surprise. And some hairs that turned out to be dog hair – no surprises there either.'

Slider nodded. 'Shove 'em on my desk, then. I'll look at them later.'

Before either of them could move, Atherton came in, waving a large paper bag. 'Another day, another doughnut,' he said. 'I stopped on the way. Thought I'd do my bit for the common weal.'

It was amazing. Instantly he disappeared in a passionate press of bodies that had been quietly at their desks the instant before. From inside, his voice emerged. 'What can I say? It's something I've always had.'

When the scrum evaporated, he brushed himself smooth and said, 'So, what's up?'

'The pound, and Mr Porson's blood pressure,' Slider said. 'But not our tails.'

Hollis drifted over. 'What are we on today, guv?' he asked. 'We've still got canvassing to complete – Mackay was supervising that yesterday?' He made it a question and Slider nodded agreement. 'Fathom's on cars – local stolen, parked, and ANPR'd in the area. And McLaren's still trying to trace her route home.'

'Forensic's in the flat and the public areas of

the house,' Atherton added. 'And the garden, such as it is. What else?'

'There's Hibbert's alibi to check. That means going down to Salisbury.'

'I'll do that,' Swilley offered.

'No, I want you and Connolly to keep interviewing her girl friends. And go over her papers. I want to know more about her life. You've read Connolly's report?'

'About her little bit of trouble?' Swilley said. 'Yeah, boss. You think she wasn't as white as she was painted?'

'I'm not making any judgements,' Slider said. 'But she had a secret in her past, and that makes her interesting. Did anyone else know it? And did she have any others?'

Atherton shook his head. 'Three perfectly good suspects and you want more?'

'Three?'

'What about Wiseman? I like him even better than Hibbert.'

'That's because you're an iconoclast. I suppose we'll have to check his alibi, just to be on the safe side. Soccer practice is as good as they get, but he was rather late home.'

'I'll do it,' Atherton said.

'No, I think I'll put Connolly on to it when she's done with the girl friends. It might involve talking to teenagers, and she's got the most street cred amongst us.'

Atherton and Swilley exchanged a rare look of sympathy. 'He's just comprehensively trashed the two of us, you understand?' he said.

'You're always telling me I'm really mumsy

now,' said Swilley, who looked like Barbie made flesh, and was mumsy in the same way that the middle of the Atlantic was really dry.

'But what does that make me?' Atherton enquired querulously.

'It makes you on your way to Salisbury,' Slider said.

'Me?'

'Yes, you. Why not?'

'He was at a stag do with an entire football team's worth of witnesses. What's to find out? Can't I just do it on the phone?'

'There may be things that people will tell you face to face. Hibbert may have the most solid alibi outside tea with the governor in Pentonville, but he might have said something to his friends in a drink-induced open moment that will give us a lead.'

'A lead where?'

'If I knew that I wouldn't need to send you. I need someone with subtlety, perseverance and an enquiring mind.'

Atherton was not beguiled by the compliments. Too little, too late. 'You need me at your side,' he said. 'I don't want to leave you high and dry.'

'I've never been lower or wetter,' Slider assured him. 'Go!'

So when Andy Bolton came in, Slider went down to talk to him himself. He was a short young man, very muscular and fit, good-looking in an obvious sort of way and sporting a tan which, given the time of year, might well have

145

been sprayed on. He had no obvious resemblance to The King other than blue eyes and a thick head of black hair styled in the manner, with quiff, duck's arse and sideburns all present and correct. Perhaps the tan was part of the act, Slider thought. It certainly made his teeth look very white.

'The wife said you wanted to talk to me,' he said amiably, 'but I haven't had a minute to spare before now to get over here. It's a busy time of year, especially with this extra-cold weather. I'm a gas-fitter, you know? And I wouldn't've had a minute now, only I had to take the morning off to move our stuff out to Hayes, to the wife's mum and dad's. Well, she's got it into her head Mr Fitton downstairs is a murderer and there's no talking to women when they get like that. But I'm glad to have her out the way, anyway. It's like a madhouse back there, in Cathnor Road, with all the media and everything, and in her condition it's not good to put a strain like that on her. We're a bit cramped at her mum and dad's, and it's going to take me longer every day getting in and back, but it eases my mind to know someone's keeping an eye on her while I'm out. So what did you want to see me about? Only, I don't know as I can tell you anything more than Sharon – the wife.'

He obviously liked to talk as much as his other half did, but his voice was light and easy on the ear – Slider could tell he was a singer – so it was no great hardship. The rather round blue eyes regarded Slider with friendly openness, and that in itself was a pleasant change from the usual

146

hostility and suspicion. 'It's always good to get another perspective on things,' Slider said.

It was enough to set him off again. 'Oh, I know, you people have got your way of doing things. I'm just the same. When I do a job I have to have my tools set out a certain way, I do things in a certain order, I'm very methodical. Some people make fun of me for it, but that's the way I am. I can't abide messiness or careless-ness – well, you can't take chances with gas. Other people's lives depend on it. So, poor old Ronnie Fitton down in the basement – he's hav-ing a rough old time of it, isn't he? Is that right, he murdered his wife?'

'Haven't you read the papers?' Slider asked.

'Not to say *read*. I've seen the headlines. It gave me a shock, seeing my own house right there on the front page. Some of the others were talking about it, though, at this job I was on yesterday – fitting out a new block of flats. The chippies and plasterers were joshing me rotten about living in "the murder house". But I haven't got time for reading that sort of rubbish. Sharon – the wife – was glued to the telly all evening waiting for the news but I made her turn it off. I said it wasn't fair on the baby to dwell on that sort of thing. I took her down the pub in the end, just to get her out – not that she's a drinker, especially not with the baby coming. She just had a lemon and lime. But it was a change of scene for her. She kept going on about Mr Fitton – he's not really a murderer, is he? He seems like such a nice old boy. Reminds me of my dad, a bit.'

147

'It's true he killed his wife, a long time ago,' Slider said. 'Nothing is known against him since then.'

'Well, I can't believe he'd kill Mel. Just 'cause he killed his wife? Why would he? They were really friendly.'

'Were they?'

'Oh, yes. Always standing nattering – every time I went in or out of the house, it seemed like. And they used to go down the pub together.'

'*Did* they?' This was interesting news to Slider.

'Yeah, every once in a while. They used to go down the Wellington, down Paddenswick Road. Well, that's the nearest. Me, I like the Anglesea Arms – down Wingate Road?' Slider nodded. 'It's quieter, a bit classier. But maybe that's why Mr Fitton liked the Wellington – you wouldn't stand out in there, being's it's so noisy and crowded.'

'More anonymous?' Slider offered.

'That's it.' He shook his head sadly. 'I don't suppose he'll be going for a drink anywhere now, after having his face plastered all over the paper like that. It doesn't seem fair. I feel sorry for him – everyone's got it in for him now.' He thought a moment. 'Unless he *did* kill Mel. Do you think he did?'

'We don't know yet,' Slider said. 'How do you know he and Melanie went for drinks together?'

'Oh, she told me, when I saw her come in with him once. And I've seen them going into the Wellington when I've been passing on me way home. *She* liked him, so he must have been all

148

right, mustn't he?'

'What did her boyfriend think about her going to the pub with him?'

'Scott? Well, I don't know if he knew,' Bolton said. 'It was of a Thursday evening, usually, and that was the night Scott always worked late. So she may have told him or she may not have. I mean, there was no reason he shouldn't know. No reason he should object. It wasn't like she was seeing another man or anything. I mean, Ronnie Fitton – well, he's old. He's not – you know, someone she'd have an affair with. And none of us knew about him being – about him killing his wife and that. But he's never said anything to me about Mel and Ronnie Fitton being friends, Scott hasn't, so I've never said anything to him. You don't go stirring things up, do you?'

'Why do you think it would stir things up? You think Scott *would* object if he knew?'

Andy frowned with puzzlement. 'No, like I say – well, not like that. But he's a funny old geezer, and I know if my wife struck up a friendship with him, to actually going to the pub with him, I'd think it was a bit funny.'

'Did Melanie ever tell you *why* she was friends with Mr Fitton? What the connection between them was?'

'No. I never asked,' Bolton said easily, with his frank, blue look. 'Not my business. D'you think I *should've* said something, then? To Scott?'

Do I look like an agony aunt? Slider retorted silently. 'Tell me about Scott Hibbert,' he said.

149

'Your wife said you and he were friends.'

'Oh, he's all right,' Bolton said, but without great enthusiasm. 'I dunno about friends. We pass the time of day, that sort of thing. And we've gone for drinks now and then. To the Anglesea mostly. He likes the Conningham and I've been there once or twice with him, but it's a Hoops pub and I'm Shed.'

The Hoops were Queens Park Rangers football team; the Shed was Chelsea. No further explanation was necessary.

'Do you like him?' Slider asked.

Andy Bolton seemed to struggle with this idea. 'He's all right,' he said again. 'He can be good company. But I mean – well, he strikes me as a bit...' He stared blankly as he thought. 'I can't say I know anything against him for a fact, but sometimes the way he talks, I get the impression he's a bit of a wide boy. A bit of a wheeler-dealer, you know?'

'You think he's not honest?'

He looked alarmed. 'Oh, like I said, I don't know anything against him. But if someone was to tell me he was up to something a bit shady, I wouldn't be surprised. He's a bit mouthy, you know? Always going on about the important people he knows and the big money he's gonna make. If you've been anywhere or done anything, he's always got to go one better – like if you've had a trip on a hot-air balloon, he's gone skydiving with the Pope.'

'He's a fantasist?' Slider suggested.

'Yeah, like that,' Bolton agreed. 'Not that there's any harm in that. I mean, it's quite enter-

150

taining to listen to him sometimes. But I tell you one thing.' It seemed to burst through his natural unwillingness to speak ill. 'I don't like the way he is around women. He's always looking at them, and making remarks. I don't like that sort of thing. You may think it's funny, but I think women should be treated with respect. And while he was living with Mel, he shouldn't have flirted with other women, and talked dirty to them. Any chance he got,' he went on, thoroughly roused now, 'he'd have his arm round their waist and be whispering and sniggering. One time we went to the Conningham, there was this female, he'd been chatting her up, like I say, and she went off to the loo, and he went straight after, and he was away a long time. When he came back he sort of gave me a wink and smacked his lips. I reckon they'd gone out the back and...' He let the sentence die, and sat for a moment frowning down at his hands.

Well, well, Slider thought. So friend Hibbert is a bit of a Lothario? Somehow he wasn't surprised. Fantasist, Lothario and wide boy. Suspect-wise, what was not to like? 'I understand you were helping him with his Elvis impersonations,' he said, to prime the pump again.

Bolton looked up, startled out of his thoughts, and gave a reluctant smile. 'Sharon told you about that, did she? Well, it's something I've done for years. I know it sounds funny, but I make a bit of money at it. You can, if you work hard, but it's a crowded field, so you've got to be good. Well, Scott was always asking me about it. Just to take the piss, to start with. But when he realizes there's actual money in it, he starts to take it serious, and says he wants to get into it.' He shook his head. 'I always tried to put him off. I mean, I can't see he had any talent for it. And I was worried that what he was really interested in was the girls – you know, you always get some hanging around when you do a stage act, even if it's only in a pub or a community hall. Groupies, he called 'em. He kept talking about them being easy – like fruit falling off a tree, he said. I didn't like that. But he went on and on until in the end, more to shut him up, really, I said I'd help him.'

'He actually had a date – a booking?'

'I don't know if you'd call it that. It was a mate's stag night. They weren't paying him or anything, as far as I could gather. Good thing, too – I know he's a mate and everything, but it has to be said, he's a crap Elvis. Can't sing, can't dance – all he had was the dark glasses, and the white rhinestone suit he was gonna hire.'

'And that was on Friday – last Friday, wasn't it?'

'That's right.' He looked suddenly stricken. 'God, the poor bastard. He must be kicking himself that he went. If he'd stayed home, none of this would've happened. He must be heartbroken.'

'So he did love Melanie?'

'Oh yes. They were besotted – all over each other. I know maybe I've given the wrong impression – he was a bit of a pain in the neck sometimes, but he was all right really, and he did love her. I think he got annoyed with her sometimes because she wouldn't marry him.'

152

'Why do you think that was?'

He made a comical face. 'I know, women are all supposed to be mad to get married, aren't they? But this time I know for a fact *he* asked *her* and she said no – or not yet, anyway – because they both told me. All she said to me was she wasn't ready yet. She said they'd only been going out two years and it wasn't long enough, and she said she'd got enough on her plate as it was. But Scott wanted kids, and the sooner the better. They were already living together, the way he saw it, and he had plans for them to get a house – well, he *is* in the trade – and the next step in his mind was to get married, have kids. But every time he asked her, she said she wasn't ready.'

Slider nodded. 'It's a big step,' he said profoundly. Then, 'Do you know if there was anything in her past that might have made her reluctant to get married?' he tried. He wondered how far the information about Melanie's 'bit of trouble' had gone.

But Bolton shook his head. 'I wasn't that chummy with her, really. We'd have a chat, and she was very nice and easy to get on with, but she never gave anything away. It was just time of day, sort of thing. I never felt – well, I reckon there was another Mel inside the one I knew. Must've been, when you think about it – I was just the neighbour, after all. Scott's the one you need to talk to about that,' he concluded; but with a faintly puzzled air, as if he wasn't sure Hibbert *was* the person to apply to, actually.

Which was interesting for all sorts of reasons.

Eight

Attitude Sickness

Simone Ridware, Melanie's work colleague and friend at the Natural History Museum, was a different prospect from Kiera Williams: older, to start with – late thirties by the look of her – well spoken and obviously educated. What Swilley always classified to herself as a National Trust sort of person – posh and well off – but in this case clever too. She was apparently in the Micropalaeontology Section, and how that differed from the Palaeontology Section Swilley no more cared than she could spell it.

Simone Ridware had offered to take her to the canteen for their talk, but Swilley arranged to meet her in a café nearby, by South Kensington Station. Just going into a museum gave her vertigo.

Despite being called Simone she was not French, even a bit. 'It was a name my mother picked. She just had a liking for it,' she said apologetically. 'I have a brother called Hubert, so I suppose I got off lightly.' She came from Maidstone originally, where her father was a solicitor, had gone to Benenden, then Cambridge, had worked for BP for a short time and

154

then found her home-from-home within the dreaming spires and glazed Victorian tiles of the Nat His Mu. She had married a subsurface geologist she had met at BP (bet *their* conversations at home are exciting, Swilley thought) and had two children, Poppy and Oliver, aged five and seven, and lived in a large Victorian house in the nice bit of Muswell Hill. No surprises there.

She was, however, wearing a very elegant suit on her enviable figure, and Swilley would really have liked a better view of her shoes. Who'd have thought palaeontology was a hotbed of fashion?

They ordered coffee and Danish pastries, and Mrs Ridware opened the batting with, 'You want to talk to me about Melanie, of course. What can I tell you?'

She had short, dark hair, fine and curly, like soft black feathers all over her head, and an averagely good-looking face subtly enhanced by skilful make-up. A geek, but *hardly dull at all*, Swilley paraphrased to herself. To the penetrating eye, she looked a little pale and worn under the make-up, and Swilley wondered if it was on Melanie's behalf, and hoped so. She put aside her chippy prejudices and prepared to listen.

'What was she like?' she asked. 'Did you like her?'

'We were friends,' said Mrs Ridware, as if that said it all. And then, 'I had tremendous admiration for her. She came from quite a difficult background, but she never let it hold her back.

What she achieved, she achieved on her own merits. She was very good at her job, and she had a brilliant career ahead of her.' She paused and, as if realizing that this sounded too much like a press release, added in a different tone, 'Yes, I liked her. We were very close, and I shall miss her very much.'

'When you say she had a difficult background—?' Swilley tried.

'She came from a poor home,' Mrs Ridware said. 'Her father was feckless and her mother was ineffectual, so she was thrown on her own resources. He was often out of work, and I believe he gambled, too, so money was always tight. And her mother was a poor housekeeper. All too often Melanie as a child came home to have to cook supper herself and wash and iron her own clothes for school. She never had the material things other girls had, and I know you may think that's character-building –' she smiled at Swilley, who hadn't thought anything of the sort – 'but girls can be cruel and it's hard always to be an outsider. But despite his inadequacies, she adored her father. I gather he was a charming wastrel.'

Swilley nodded.

'That sort can be the hardest to resist, and do the most damage.'

'Melanie told you all this herself, did she?' Swilley asked.

'Yes, over time. It was hard for her to confide at first – I think she'd held herself back for so many years it had become a habit. But we liked each other from the first moment she joined the museum, and bit by bit the barriers came down – with me, at least. She was always guarded with other people.' She hesitated, and Swilley gave an encouraging nod. 'She developed a technique of getting everyone she met to talk about themselves, so that she wouldn't have to talk about *her*self. To be the listener is always safer – and it makes people like you. Everyone loved her. She had a large number of friends. But I think fundamentally she was a very lonely person.'

'Why was that?'

'Partly her background – her parents, I mean – and partly her father being killed. You know about that?'

'In the train crash – yes.'

'It was a terrible blow to her, and she had to do all the coping because her mother couldn't. She had to suppress her feelings and get on with things. And then her mother remarried a basically unsympathetic man, so the protective shell just got thicker, until it became such a habit she couldn't break it. When she first came to the museum I think she was desperate to talk to someone, but simply didn't know how. Fortunately we struck up a friendship and—' She shrugged, elegantly. 'I was glad to be her confidante.'

'So she didn't get on with her stepfather?'

'She wouldn't have liked anyone who took her father's place. But I gather – I never met him, you understand – that he was somewhat *limited*. No imagination. Everything by the book because he couldn't think further than that. And she might have accepted that – her mother, after

157

all, was no Einstein – except that he gave himself airs and claimed a superiority he didn't have, and used it as the basis for imposing discipline on her.'

Atherton should be having this conversation, Swilley thought resentfully. Or the boss. I'm a solid facts girl. *She didn't like her stepdad, and he tried to make her toe the line.* Why dress it up in all this airy-fairy psychobabble? 'Did he hit her?'

'I didn't mean discipline in that sense,' Mrs Ridware said, kindly enough to get up Swilley's nose.

'But did he hit her?' she repeated stolidly.

She hesitated. 'I think he did, on occasion – but not violently. I don't want you to think he was beating her, or anything like that. Not that Nigel and I believe in corporal punishment – we would *never* hit Poppy or Oliver – it sends all the wrong signals and teaches the wrong values. But many people believe that the occasional slap is justified, and I suppose Melanie's stepfather was one of them. Of course, she was too old by then to do other than resent it, especially as he wasn't her real father. They used to have tremendous arguments, she told me. I think it was a relief all round when she left home.'

'Did she tell you about the trouble she got into?'

'You mean—?'

'Getting pregnant,' Swilley said brutally. The girl was dead, for heaven's sake. The time to be holding stuff back was well gone.

'Yes, she told me about that. How did you

158

know?'

'Her mum told us.'

'Oh. Of course. But I don't think she told another soul about it. Certainly nobody here knew except me. It was a desperately painful incident, and coming so soon after her father dying...'

'Did she resent her stepdad for making her have the abortion?'

'No, not exactly. She knew it was the only thing to be done, and she knew she wouldn't have had the same career if she *had* kept it. I don't think he forced her – of course, there was pressure put on her, but if she'd really insisted...'

Yeah, thought Swilley. That's all right from someone with nice supportive parents who always discussed things rationally with their kids. And where money had never been an issue. She knew what 'pressure' would have meant in Melanie's case, and how there would have been no alternative for a girl with no money and nowhere else to go.

'But she regretted it deeply, all the same,' Mrs Ridware went on. 'She brooded about the child she didn't have. She felt guilty because she hadn't protected it. And she doubted her fitness to be a mother, because she had failed so spectacularly at the first hurdle.' She sighed. 'It was something we talked about often, when we went out alone together, after work. She envied me my children, said how lucky I was to have had a normal life, with everything happening as it should, naturally and in the right order.' She looked at Swilley, her eyes suddenly vulnerable

159

and troubled. 'I know I'm lucky, I really do. I have everything, and Melanie—' She bit her lip. 'Now she's had even her life taken away from her. Whoever did that—' She stopped abruptly and looked away.

She really had cared about Melanie, then. Swilley liked her better.

'What about Scott Hibbert? Did you ever meet him?'

'Once or twice, when he came to meet Melanie after work, and at the Christmas party. They'd only been going out for just over two years. I can't say I knew him well, except for what Melanie told me.'

'And what was that?'

'She was madly in love with him,' said Mrs Ridware, with a sorrowful look, 'but in my view he wasn't right for her. She had real depths and real intellect, but he was just a – a flashy, self-centred nothing. He was so shallow—' She paused, and Swilley finished for her without thinking:

'—it was a wonder he didn't evaporate?'

But she didn't take offence. She gave a small, controlled smile. 'Yes. I must remember that – it's good.'

'But they were living together and he wanted to marry her.'

'Yes, she said he'd proposed more than once. I think he thought she'd be a good corporate wife – an asset to his career. It was all about him. He was an awful snob, you know – still is, I suppose. I don't know why I'm talking about him in the past tense. At the Christmas parties he was always name-dropping, button-holing the most important people, trying to ingratiate himself with anyone with a title. I think he thought Melanie would give him a leg up the social scale.'

'So he didn't love her?'

'Oh, goodness, I didn't mean that. I'm sure he did. He was certainly all over her, embarrassingly so sometimes. But I don't think he ever really – what do they say nowadays? – *got* her. He loved her for the wrong reasons, because he didn't really know her.'

'If he was so unsatisfactory, why did she love him?'

'He was handsome, well dressed, attentive, he loved her. That most of all, I think – she was desperate to be loved. But I think deep down she knew it was no good. Almost the whole time she's been with him she's been unhappy. They moved in together about three months after they met – almost exactly two years ago – and I noticed a change in her at once. Something's been troubling her, something she won't talk to me about, and I don't know what it could be if it's not Scott. And it gets worse the longer it goes on. Just lately she's been really worried, withdrawn and preoccupied. I know he's been pressing her to marry him, because he wants to start a family, and as I said, she has doubts about her fitness to be a mother. But I wonder if underneath she hasn't realized that Scott simply won't do?'

Swilley noticed she had slipped into the present tense. A good sign that they really had

161

been close, and that her testimony was therefore worth something. 'Did she say that to you?' she asked.

'No, never. She's very loyal to him. As I said, these last two years there's been a part of her closed off even from me. But you know...' She hesitated, and went on with an appeal to Swilley, woman to woman. 'You know that women are always supposed to end up marrying their fathers? I think perhaps she'd realized she'd picked a man who, on the surface looked right – steady job, money in his pockets and so on – but underneath was like her father after all – an unreliable charmer.'

Or maybe she hadn't, Swilley thought, resisting the appeal. Maybe it was something else entirely. *All women marry their fathers, eh?* She considered her own Tony. Actually, ghastly thought, he *was* a bit like how she remembered her dad – not to look at so much as in personality – the kindness and patience, the way he'd look at her with that sort of what-are-you-going-to-get-up-to-next wry smile, all up one side ... She jerked herself back from the edge of the abyss.

'What can you tell me about last Friday?' she said, extra sternly to make up for having weakened.

Simone Ridware blinked, but stood up to the question bravely. 'It was just an ordinary Friday, as far as I remember. Let me see. Melanie had a bit of a tiff with Scott that morning, but that wasn't unusual.'

A tiff, eh? How posh, thought Swilley. 'What about?'

162

'Oh, it wasn't serious. Just one of the niggling little did-didn't arguments people have. He was going away for the weekend to see some of his old friends from home, whom Melanie didn't like: they were rather noisy and vulgar. Words were had; but she was over it by mid-morning. She said it was her fault – nobody likes to think their partner despises their friends. And she was going out herself that evening to meet some of her old friends from home, and Scott probably didn't like any of them any better. She was a very balanced person in that way – always able to see the other side.'

'So when she left work, she was in a normal mood, going out for a drink with the girls? Not unhappy or worried or anxious or anything?'

She frowned. 'I'm – not sure. She did seem very quiet that afternoon. Preoccupied. When I spoke to her just before she left, she was smiling and cheerful, but then she was always a good actor. I did feel there was something on her mind, something hanging over her. But it could just have been Scott's weekend away. Or I could have been imagining it.'

'You don't know of anything specific she might have been worried about?'

'Beyond her relationship with Scott – no.'

'She didn't have money worries?'

'Not as far as I know.'

'Health problems?'

'She never mentioned any. She seemed well.'

'Did she have a drug habit?'

'Good heavens, no!'

'And was that the last time you spoke to her?

163

Friday going-home time?'

'Yes. Sometimes she would ring me at home in the evening for a chat, but as she was out with friends I wouldn't have expected that, on that Friday. And she didn't ring. So the last words I spoke to her were, "See you on Monday."'

She relapsed into a very despondent pose, looking as if she might cry. But Benenden girls don't cry in public. They breed a gritty sort of chap down there.

In fairness, Swilley suspended her automatic hostility to privilege for long enough to acknowledge that she really had cared for Melanie, and to be glad that *someone* had.

Atherton's idea of a trip to Salisbury would probably have featured a stroll through the cobbled streets looking in the antique shops, a glance round the Cathedral, and possibly tea in Ye Olde Precinct Tea Rooms if the time was right. It wouldn't by any stretch of the imagination have involved his standing in some very chilly rain on the edge of an arterial road (along which the traffic, suspiciously, was all heading *out* of the city at great speed, buffeting him in passing and dashing dirty spray at his back in the process) looking enquiringly into the Stygian shadows of an independent garage workshop. His nostrils flared at the smell of oil. There were oil patches on the floor and oily pictures of large-busted women on the walls. A red Ford Focus was up on the lift and dripping oil into the lube pit. Oil, he fancied he could say with some assurance, was the motif *du jour*.

A man emerged from the depths of the cavern, wearing oily overalls and wiping his hands on an oily rag. He had a puggily good-looking face, liberally streaked with yes-you've-guessed-it; his gingery fair hair was cut into a halo of spikes and – Atherton would have thought it unnecessary given the prevalence of freely-available dressing, but there you go – waxed to keep them in position. He said, 'Can I help you?' but without notable friendliness.

'I'm looking for Paul Heaton,' Atherton said.

'That's me,' said the man, with a slight increase in latent hostility as his eyes raked Atherton, in his well-fitting coat and expensive shoes, trying to guess who he was.

Fortunately, Atherton had spotted, lurking in the shadows, something a bit more interesting than a Focus. *Like* the Aston,' he said. 'DB6, isn't it? Not as pretty as the five, but it handles so much better. Is it yours?'

'Yeah,' said Heaton, all resistance seeping away like water down the plug hole. 'I'm rebuilding it.'

He led the way over and a satisfactory conversation followed as they examined the car together in every aspect and Heaton described the condition he had bought it in, the processes he was going through to restore it and what he planned to do with it when it was finished. At the end of which Atherton was no longer a snotty-looking stranger and possible trouble but a fellow DB-lover, and was offered a cuppa. The tea came in a mug decorated with oily finger-marks (Atherton noted them professionally –

165

you'd get beautiful lifts off those) and had a faint fragrance of Castrol about it, but he sipped it bravely and brought the conversation round to the wedding and Scott Hibbert.

Paul Heaton had been the best man – in the absence of the groom on honeymoon, the closest Atherton could get to the horse's mouth. And subtlety and perseverance turned out not to be needed. To a fellow DB fan, Heaton was happy to spill everything, and at once, no questions asked.

'Oh, he was at the wedding all right, but he never turned up to the stag do. Dave was pissed off about it, but what can you do? Scott's like that – unreliable bugger.' It was said without heat – blokes who'd been at school with each other accepted each other's little peccadilloes.

'Called off, did he?' Atherton asked, trying not to sound as if that was very, *very* interesting.

'I don't know about called off. He just never showed. Typical, when he was the one who'd made all the fuss – there *had* to be a stag night, and *had* to be done a certain way. He was the one who made all the arrangements, booked the place and phoned everybody up, and then *he's* the one who doesn't turn up.'

'But wasn't he supposed to be doing the entertainment?'

'Eh?'

'He was going to do his Elvis impersonation act, wasn't he?'

The pale-blue eyes under the raised sandy eyebrows were genuinely puzzled. 'Elvis act? What are you talking about? Scott doesn't do anything like that. He organized a strippergram – she came dressed as a postman, because Dave's with the Royal Mail. She was good, too,' he added with reminiscent relish. Then came back to the present. 'What you on about?'

'He told a friend back home he was doing an Elvis impersonation at the stag on Friday,' Atherton said.

Heaton shrugged. 'That's Scott all over. He's a bit – you know.' He made the 'mouthy' gesture with the hand that wasn't holding the mug. 'You don't want to take any notice of half he says. He was always like that – at school he was always on about stuff he'd done, and you knew it was all bullshit. Like, he's driven his dad's car when he was ten, and gone all the way with a girl when he was twelve, and he'd done this, that and the other. Showing off, you know. But that's just his way. He's all right, really. Elvis impersonations!' He shook his head in amused wonder. 'What'll he come up with next? He's a joker!'

'So,' Atherton said, getting down to business, 'he didn't come to the stag, but he did come to the wedding?'

'Yeah, he turned up at the church, but he was like a cat on hot bricks. He was on the end of the pew behind me, and I could see him fidgeting about all the way through. Then as soon as the photographs were finished, he comes up to me and says he's not going to the reception – asks me to apologize to Dave. Says he's got a really important piece of business for his firm he's got to see to. Says it's a massive deal and worth a big bonus and a promotion if he pulls it off. Then

167

off he goes.' He shrugged. 'I didn't say anything to Dave right then – no point in upsetting anyone. But later on Dave comes up to me and says, where's Scott, I haven't seen him, so I tell him then. Well, he shrugs and says, same old Scott, but I could see he was a bit pissed off, when he'd missed the stag as well.'

'Did he say why he'd missed it?'

'I never got the chance to ask. He arrived at the last minute, and you can't chat in church, can you? Then there were the photographs, and time that was all over, he'd gone again. I suppose he wanted to get back to his bird. All that about a big deal going down – that's just the sort of thing he says. He's only an estate agent, for crying out loud. You'd think he was doing oil deals with Arab sheikhs.'

He swilled down some tea, and then a frown came over his well-lubricated face. 'Why are you asking me all this, anyway?' Awareness dawned. 'Oh Christ, I forgot about his bird – his girlfriend getting killed. Poor old Scotty – but you don't think he had anything to do with it? That's not why you're asking, is it?'

'It's just routine,' Atherton said soothingly. 'We have to establish where everyone was, whether we suspect them or not. It's like a pattern, you see – only if you know where everyone was, can you see who's missing.'

Heaton looked baffled, as well he might, by this piece of hoo-ha. 'I see,' he said doubtfully.

'So, have you any idea where he might have been on Friday night and Saturday morning?'

'No,' Heaton said, as though that were obvious. 'Why don't you ask him?'

Atherton dodged that one. 'Was there anywhere you know that he went when he was down this way? Where he might go? Other friends? Hobbies, sports, clubs?'

'No. I mean I don't know. He's lived here all his life, till he went to London, so it could be anywhere, couldn't it? Anyway,' he concluded with an air of relief, 'wherever he was, he couldn't have had anything to do with – with the murder.' Like many people, he found the word odd on his lips when it was real life and not fiction or the telly. 'He was dead keen on her. Always talking about her – how smart she was, how posh she was, what a good job she had, how she was nuts about him. They were going to get married in September.'

'Is that what he said?'

'Yeah, September. I remember because I usually have me holiday in September and he said I'd have to change it this year because of his wedding. He was going to fly everybody out to St Lucia for a week. Well –' he shrugged again – 'I took *that* with a pinch of salt. But it sounded good when he said it. This resort with all tropical flowers and a pool with a free swim-up bar, and they were going to get married on the beach at sunset, and Mel was going to arrive on a white horse, riding through the surf.'

'Romantic.'

He smiled unwillingly. 'Oh yeah, he can spin a tale, old Scott. You'd go to him every time for romantic. But whatever, he was dead keen on Mel.'

'Did you like her? You'd met her?'

'I can't say I *knew* her. He'd brought her down a couple of times, weekends, to see his mum and dad, and they'd come to the pub Saturday night, where a bunch of us get together. She was nice, but quiet, you know? You couldn't get much of an idea what she was like. She was very nice, though,' he said again, helpless to offer more insight. He fidgeted, some thought obviously bothering him, like a raspberry pip between the teeth. Atherton looked receptive, and finally he said, 'The second time I saw her, in the pub: that night Scott was a bit, well, bumptious. Going on about how much money he was going to make and the big house him and Mel were going to have and all that kind of stuff. Showing off, you know? And I think she felt a bit embarrassed. Well, *I* was embarrassed, and I know him! And it has to be said a lot of pints went down that night, and we probably all got a bit noisy. Anyway after that, she didn't come out with him again, down here, with our lot. I think that's why she didn't come to the wedding. He said it was because she was working, but maybe...' He stared a moment at nothing, ordering his thoughts. 'Course,' he concluded in fairness, 'it's not really a women's night out. There's eight or ten of us, all went to school together. We don't usually bring our birds, and if one or two of 'em does come, they sit off on their own and talk to each other. But o' course, she didn't know anyone, Mel. And then Scott going on about how much money he's making and the big car he's getting and all that. It was probably uncom-

170

fortable for her.'

He sniffed, finished his tea in one gulp, wiped his nose on the cuff of his overall, decorating it with another hydrocarbon smear, and said, 'That your Astra? VXR, innit? What is it, two litre? What's it drive like?'

Thus the two chaps were able to wade safely back before the incoming tide of psychoanalysis and – *aargh!* – 'relationships' to the safe, dry shore of car ownership, and parted in good humour with each other. Atherton even shook his hand, and nobly waited until he was out of sight before getting out a handkerchief to wipe it.

Bob Bailey, the SOC manager, tracked Slider down in the canteen where he was having a very late lunch – so late he had had to have a leftover portion of macaroni cheese heated up for him in the microwave, and he only got that because the canteen staff liked him, and it was a crusty bit from the corner of the dish that no one else fancied. He had quarantined himself in a far corner with a heap of reports to reread. On the other side of the room, nearer the windows and a watery bit of sunshine that was attempting to creep in through the soot of ages on the panes, various uniforms were having their afternoon tea break, with a buzz of chatter and the occasional burst of laughter.

Bailey eyed the congealing remains on the plate – Slider wasn't getting on with it very well – and thought the bad news he was delivering might usefully serve as a counter-irritant.

'I was passing,' he said, 'so I thought I'd come and report to you in person.'

Slider pushed his plate away with every appearance of relief, and said, 'Judging by your face, it isn't good news.'

'Depends on your point of view. I should think Scott Hibbert's dear old white-haired mother would be very pleased.' He sat down. 'We've gone over every inch of the flat, the stairs and the common parts, and there's nothing to suggest Melanie Hunter was killed there. We've also looked at her car, and though she was obviously in there alive, there's no reason to think she was restrained there or transported dead. In fact, the back seats are so pristine I wouldn't think anyone's ever ridden in them. I think you can take it as read that she left her own premises alive.'

'I don't know that I'm surprised,' Slider said. 'It was always a possibility that she was killed elsewhere, and there were always problems about her being killed in the flat – the dog being the main one.'

'Yes, most dogs would go nuts in a scenario like that.'

'But if she left the flat alive, why would she leave her handbag and take the door keys? Leaving the handbag looks like coercion, but taking the keys looks like a voluntary action.' None of the evidence made a lot of sense. 'Never mind.' He pulled himself together, and managed a polite smile. 'Not your problem.'

'Thank God for that,' said Bailey.

Nine

Lynch, Anyone?

'So,' Atherton said to his assembled colleagues, 'wherever Hibbert was on Friday night and Saturday morning, it wasn't where he said he was. And I checked the hotel he was supposed to have been staying in, and guess what, folks?'

'Why wasn't he staying with his parents?' Connolly asked.

'So as not to disturb them when arriving home drunk in the small hours from the stag do,' Atherton said.

'It doesn't follow that he didn't change his mind,' Norma said.

'I know,' said Atherton, 'and we'll have to check that.'

'Or he could have gone to a different hotel,' said Hollis.

'Rather than check them all,' Atherton said with irony, 'why don't we ask him? But it's my bet that, if he wasn't at the stag, and hardly at the wedding, he probably wasn't in the area at all. He was off doing something nefarious, and the wedding was just his alibi.'

'Not much of an alibi,' Connolly said derisively, 'when ya could bust it that easy.'

'He probably thought no one would check,' Atherton said. 'Swaggering over-confidence doesn't usually go with painstaking analysis.'

'But he'd told her well before the date that he was going to this wedding. Told Andy Bolton, too,' said Mackay.

'The wedding was fact, not fiction,' Atherton said. 'What's your point?'

'Well, are you saying he planned to kill her as soon as he got the invitation?' Mackay asked. 'Or was it just lucky chance, he killed her spurathemoment and happened to have this alibi set up?'

'Lucky?' Connolly protested.

'For him, not for her.'

'There must have been a degree of planning,' Atherton said, 'because we know she was killed that evening, so he must have come back from wherever he was to do it. I can't see him plotting far ahead, but maybe it gradually grew on him he could make use of the occasion, if he was getting fed up with her for some reason.'

'Yeah, but what reason?' Mackay said.

'Never mind that for the moment. From our point of view, he's good because he's got all the time in the world to take the body out to Ruislip, do any cleaning up that's needed in the flat, and get back to Salisbury for an eleven o'clock wedding. He wouldn't be likely to interfere with her sexually. And he knows the dog, and it knows him. Did you notice how he didn't seem to want anything to do with it afterwards?' he added, looking round them.

'What does that prove?' Swilley asked.

'Well, I'm just thinking, if he had a bit of trouble with it at the time – and why wouldn't he? – he might have been very glad someone had taken it away when he got back. He might well be scared of seeing it again, in case it attacked him.'

Connolly said, 'But if it was him – and fair play to ya, he's a big enough thick to think no one would check the stagger alibi – why would he leave the wedding early? Why not stay on for the rest of the day?'

'Maybe he didn't want to be around his mates answering questions about why he'd missed the stag,' Atherton said. 'Maybe he was too shaken up by the murder to be around people at all. It takes a cool head to behave as if nothing's happened when you've just killed someone.'

Connolly nodded. 'And didn't we think it was queer he didn't know she was missing – that he hadn't rung her all Saturday? Well, why would he, if he knew she was dead?'

But why,' said Norma, 'if it was Hibbert who killed her, would he take her door keys? He had keys of his own.'

Atherton declined to be dampened. 'To make it look as if she'd gone out on her own two feet.'

'But then wouldn't he have taken her whole handbag?' Norma said.

'That would just make more things to get rid of. Keys are easy to drop down a drain, but a handbag the size of Belgium, like you women all carry these days...'

It was at this point that Slider came in, just in time to save Atherton from being lynched for the

175

'you women'. Atherton told him about the busted alibi; Slider told them about the clean flat. 'So whoever killed her, it wasn't at home.'

Atherton was not downcast. 'Never mind, it still makes it Hibbert for my money. Who else could so easily lure her into his car and drive off without her putting up a fight? He only has to pretend it's something romantic – let's look at the lido by moonlight, something like that.'

'At that time of night?' Swilley objected.

'Best time for romance. Get Tony to explain it to you. Anyway, we know for a fact that he's lied about his alibi, and there must be a reason for that.'

'I agree that Hibbert's got some explaining to do about where he spent the night,' Slider began.

'If he was killing her and dumping the body,' Hollis said, 'he'd have been too late to drive to Salisbury and check into an hotel. More likely he just got changed at the flat and went to the wedding from there.'

'He'd have had to leave early, anyway, not to be seen,' Mackay said. 'Maybe slept in his car in a lay-by or something.'

'At least it gives us something to check,' Slider said. 'Whatever he was doing, there must have been some car movements. Fathom, put his reg number into the ANPR and see if you can find out where he was at any point between Friday morning and Sunday morning. I'd sooner have something concrete to face him with than just asking him blind where he was and having a whole lot of new lies to disprove.'

'You'll get them anyway,' Atherton said.

'At least we can narrow the field if we know whether he was in Maidstone, Maidenhead or Middlesborough.'

'I've got something else, boss,' Swilley said. 'This Hibbert talk's all very well.' She gave Atherton a look so cool you could have kept a side of beef on it for a week. 'But everybody agrees he's a prime plonker and about as subtle as a hand grenade. Plotting cunning murders and carrying them out—'

'Not that cunning,' Atherton protested.

'Not that obvious, either, or we'd know all about it.'

'A person can pretend to be more gormless than they are.'

'Oh, is that your excuse?'

'What's your point, Norma?' Slider intervened hastily.

She turned to him. 'I've been going through Melanie's papers, and I started off with her bank statements and so on. Well, she was doing all right, just about breaking even, like most of us with a mortgage. She and Scott bought the flat between them and they were paying half each, and I suppose the same went for the bills – I haven't got that far yet, but it's fair to assume. But the thing is, a couple of years ago she had a decent amount in savings, but it's been going down steadily. She's been drawing out sums of money in cash – five hundred, a thousand, two hundred – at irregular intervals for the last two years. Ever since she moved into that house. And Simone Ridware said that for about the same length of time she's felt Melanie had

177

something on her mind, was worried and anxious about something. She thought it was to do with Scott, because she reckoned Melanie knew subconsciously that he wasn't good enough for her.'

'Makes sense to me,' said Atherton. 'The man's a tool.'

Swilley shook her head. 'That's crap. She'd only just met him – they'd only been going out for three months when they got the flat together, so they must have decided to live together almost from day one. Which means she was head over heels in love with him. That doesn't wear off in an instant. Two years ago she'd have been happy as Larry setting up home with her new bloke. But from the time she moves into *that house*, she's anxious, and lumps of cash start disappearing from her savings.' She looked at Slider. 'What does that add up to, boss?'

'I don't know that it adds up to anything more than her salary not quite being enough, but you're thinking blackmail?' he obliged.

'Right. And who in the house made mysterious hints about her having secrets no one knew? And went out to the pub with her but never saw fit to tell us? And has a criminal record?'

'Not for blackmail,' Atherton objected.

'No, for murder,' Norma said triumphantly.

'Why would he blackmail her?' Hollis asked, after a short silence paid tribute to the idea.

'For money, of course,' Swilley said, witheringly. 'He can't get a job, he's living on benefits – why not?'

'He owns that flat,' Connolly added, with a

178

shade of reluctance. 'He doesn't rent it. How'd he afford it, on the broo?'

'No, I mean, what'd he blackmail her *with*,' Hollis said.

'I dunno. Maybe that abortion thing – maybe she didn't want Scott to know about it. Or maybe she'd done something else. We don't know – her mum said she got into bad company at one time, so she may have been hiding some other secret.'

'But then why would he kill her?' Hollis persisted. 'You don't kill the person you're blackmailing – that cuts off the supply. It's the other way round. The victim kills the blackmailer out o' desperation.'

'Well,' Swilley said, thinking, 'maybe she did get desperate – she was near the end of her savings. Maybe she finally stood up to him and threatened to go to the police. Fitton couldn't allow that. He'd be finished – he's out on licence, he'd have gone straight back inside so fast his head would swim. No, in the end he had more to lose than she did, and maybe she finally realized it. So then he realized she'd have a hold on him for the rest of his life, and decided to get rid of her.'

'*If* she knew about his past,' Atherton said. 'No one else seems to have.'

'Well, we don't know, do we?' she snapped. 'We can't ask her.' She appealed to Slider. 'It's just that it looks like a coincidence, boss, the timing. As soon as she comes into contact with Fitton, she starts shelling out cash, and goes round being anxious.'

Slider nodded reluctantly. 'There may be something in it. And I know Mr Porson would like to get Fitton in and sweat him a bit. There are unanswered questions.'

'And he has the mark o' Cain on his brow,' Connolly concluded disgustedly. 'Sure, give a dog a bad name...'

Slider looked at her kindly. 'We're just going to ask him some questions. He might even find it a relief – it can't be nice for him cooped up in that flat with the media howling for his blood. He might like a nice, quiet cell for a change. Get a good night's sleep.' Connolly looked at him reproachfully, but he wasn't joking. 'And a square meal,' he added. 'He probably hasn't eaten in days – can't get out to the shops, can he?'

'But guv,' Atherton said, 'what about Hibbert? Alibi blown, lies all round, absent without leave for the very time we're interested in?'

'Fathom can look for his car on the ANPR, and then we'll see. Don't look at me like that. We can always do him later. He's not going anywhere.'

As Slider predicted, Porson was thrilled with the new evidence, if that's what it was, against Fitton. *'That's* more like it. A nice juicy blackmail to get our teeth into.'

'It's only a suggestion, sir. We haven't got anything concrete to go on.'

'Except that he never told us about going out for drinkies with the girl, did he? That's enough concrete for a dam. Besides,' he added, his brows converging like animals round a water-hole, 'it's getting a bit ugly out there. Bloody lunch mob it's turning into. We don't want some bright spark chucking a rock through his window or pouring petrol through his letterbox. Better get him in. Poor bastard might even be grateful,' he added, echoing Slider. 'Get it over with. He must know we're going to have to tug him sooner or later.'

'It will give us a chance to go over his flat,' Slider said.

'Right. If he did kill her, it'd make more sense to do it in his flat, out of the way of the dog. Ask her to come down for a minute, boom. Then straight into her car and away.'

'Her car was clean.'

'He could have wrapped her in something.'

'And apparently, he can't drive,' Slider mentioned. 'He's certainly never had a licence.'

'Easy to pretend you can't drive when you can,' Porson dismissed the quibble. 'If it was the other way round ... Anyway, bring him in. But not right now. Don't want to start a riot. Make it a dawn raid – snatch him in the early hours when there's nobody about. Try and get him out without any photos. Did you see this morning's effort? Photo of Melanie Hunter right next to that old one of Fitton's wife they used at the time. Talk about conflagatory! Might as well put "He Done It" in big letters right across the headline.'

Inflammatory and confrontational enough to create a conflagration, Slider thought as he went away to set things in train. There was economy in Porson's madness.

McLaren appeared in Slider's doorway. Slider was on the phone, and held up his hand while he finished the call, which gave him a moment and an excuse to study his detective constable's amazingly changed appearance. McLaren had had his hair cut, which was unusual enough – it was habitually on the shaggy and collar-brushing side – but it looked as if it had also been *styled*, which was weird in the extreme. As against that, he had definitely lost weight – his cheeks looked quite sunken – and today there was none of that sappy air of dreamy satisfaction. He was leaning against the door frame with a disconsolate look about him.

'Right,' Slider said into the phone. 'Thank you.' And put it down.

McLaren eased himself upright. 'Guv, I got something.'

Slider almost said, I hope it's not catching. But baiting this new McLaren wasn't so much fun. 'Let's have it, then.'

'I found out where she was, that missing ten minutes on her way home. I been doing all the shops up and down Uxbridge Road. First of all she parks up and goes to the ATM, takes some money out. I checked – it was two hundred quid. I got her on the ATM camera. And then, a couple of doors down, there's this Chinese place, the Golden Dragon Pavilion. It's a takeaway.'

'I know it.' It used to be called the Hung Fat. Perhaps they finally realized the name was not working for the English clientele.

'It's a family business – well, they always are,

aren't they? Mum and Dad, couple o' young cousins in the back, and the eldest son on the till. Well, I shows 'em the photo, and they all say no, no, never seen, the way they always do. But I see the young lad clock her, so I hang about outside till mum and dad goes in the back, then I goes back in for a crafty word with him.'

'Does he speak English?'

'Oh yeah. He was born here. His mum and dad was, too. It's just the cousins that are over from the old country. But they all pretend not to speak English. Stops 'em being bothered.'

Slider knew this was a perennial problem with the Chinese community – the linguistic equivalent of the Great Wall. He had come across it in his Central days, when investigating anything in the Chinatown section of Soho had been a specialist job with its own unit. Mostly they just gave you the Look that said no understand, but if pressed they would burst into floods of hysterical-sounding Chinese, with hand gestures and deep scowls, to drive you away. But out here, away from the centre, they lived a quietly separate life and caused no trouble, so leaving them alone worked well both ways.

'So, did you get anything out of him?'

'Yeah, once I got him on his own he said he'd seen her face in the papers and recognized her. Course, he wouldn't come forward, but now I was asking – she come in that night, Friday, and bought a takeaway.'

'Did she, indeed!'

'Yeah, and they cook everything fresh, so it took eight, ten minutes – they had telephone orders to do before hers. She sat down in the corner to wait, and he said she stared at the telly for a bit, then she got out a pen and paper. He said she seemed to be working out sums, something like that – said it looked like numbers, not words. Anyway, then her order comes out. Sweet an' sour pork balls, spicy chicken with bean sprouts, and crispy fried noodles. She pays, and then goes off. That's between twenty and twenty-five past ten, he says. Which makes it right for her getting home around half past.'

'Which means she didn't go anywhere else or meet anyone else,' Slider concluded. Well, that was one thing cleared up. 'Did anyone come in while she was there?'

'Yeah, a couple of people come in for their telephone orders, but Lee says they never spoke to her. Didn't even look at her. Just come up to the counter, took their orders and left. But we can check that for ourselves, guv, because they got a CCTV camera. When he said she'd been in I said we've have to have the tape, and he said his mum and dad would never allow it. So I had to lean on him a bit. He went in the back and I could hear this almighty row going on – all scribble-talk, y'know? – but in the end he comes back with the tape.'

'Good,' said Slider. 'Even if she didn't speak to anyone, it's possible someone noticed her and followed her home.' Though that had always been a possibility, with or without a Chinese takeaway. But that scenario presented its own problems, because either she would have had to invite them into her flat to get murdered there, or have got into a car with them – theirs or hers – to be driven away and murdered somewhere else. And why would she do that? Being snatched between her car and the flat didn't work because she parked right outside Fitton's window and he would have heard the struggle; and there were no signs on the body of her having been restrained.

'Well, let's go and look at it,' he said. He followed McLaren to the tape room and watched over his shoulder as he ploughed through fast-forward until the right time cue came up and he pressed play. There was nothing much to it. The camera was above the television, so it showed anyone coming in the door three-quarter view, anyone at the counter side-on, and anyone on the chairs full face. But since everyone at some point had to look at the screen – the human who could be in the same room as a television and not look at it once had not been bred yet – there was at least one full-face of everyone.

Slider saw Melanie Hunter walk into the otherwise empty shop and up to the counter. She gave Lee the order – she didn't seem, interestingly, to study the menu on the wall behind him, but gave the order at once as if she had decided before she came in. She smiled at him, and he smiled back and said something – presumably something on the lines of 'it'll be ten minutes'. Then she went and sat on the plastic chair in the corner, at the end of the row of four, and gazed idly into the camera for some time.

It was a chance for Slider to study her face. People don't look at their best staring blankly at the idiot box, but he could see that she was pretty, and she looked tired. It was poignant for him, because unlike the people she had known, whom they had been interviewing, this was the first time he had seen her alive, so from now on it would be his only living memory of her. He looked at her, knowing that the sand was running rapidly out of her glass, that she was living the last minutes of her life without knowing it. To her it was just the end of another day. He saw her rub an itch on the end of her nose, push her hair back from her forehead: unconscious, natural movements that would always be part of his knowledge of her now. His life was so intimately bound with hers, for this intense period, he felt anguished and guilty that he could not tell the girl in the grainy grey-scale picture what he knew, and save her. *Don't go home tonight*! But if it didn't get her tonight, would death come for her anyway, tomorrow, or next week? How determined was her murderer that she should die? And *why*? That above all.

She seemed to think of something. She pulled her handbag over on to her lap and rummaged in it, came up with a pen and a piece of paper – it looked like a till receipt – and began writing on the back. That Lee was a smart fellow, he thought: it *did* look like numbers rather than words. But it was not possible to read it. She jotted, totted, and thought; and meanwhile other customers came in, walked across to the counter, looked at the television, received their orders and went out. None seemed to notice the girl in the corner – certainly no one looked at her directly or addressed her.

Finally Lee came out with a stiff paper carrier bag and said something and she looked up. She balled the paper she had been writing on in her hand. Slider became tense. *What happened to that paper?* He watched it, rather than her, as she put away the pen and got out her purse, went to the counter, paid, received change, put away her purse and took up the handles of the carrier. At that point she seemed to become aware of the paper in her hand, and dropped it with the utmost casualness into the carrier. Slider let his breath out.

'Wonder what was on that bit of paper,' McLaren said, breaking the silence, and proving himself more of a detective than was often apparent.

'Whatever it was, it's with the rest of the rubbish now,' Slider said. 'Wherever that is.'

Melanie said goodnight, with a smile, to Lee, walked to the shop door, opened it and turned right, disappearing out of camera range.

'Can't see her motor,' McLaren said, 'but she parked outside the ATM, which is that way.' And a moment later, 'There. That's her.' He ran the tape back and watched again, slowing it as a small car, which could have been a Polo, and could have been green, went past in the road outside, just visible to the camera. 'You can't see the driver, but I bet that's her.'

'It doesn't really matter,' Slider said. 'We know she went home and she must have gone straight there because of the time.' The time cue in the corner was showing 22.25. She had driven away to her appointment with death, and there was nothing he could do to change it.

As they walked back to the main office, McLaren said, 'Guv, I been thinking.'

'I tried that once,' Slider said. 'Didn't take to it.'

'About that takeaway,' McLaren went on. His only defence against Slider's more inexplicable remarks was to ignore them. 'That's a meal for one. Not enough there for two.'

'I take your word for it,' Slider said, and meant it. McLaren was the oracle when it came to junk food. He had never met a ready meal he didn't like. Or, at least, that had been the case up until whatever epiphany had recently struck him.

'Well, then, what happened to it?' McLaren asked.

'You're right. We know she didn't eat it,' Slider said, 'because we have the forensic report on her stomach contents. If she'd eaten it so soon before she was killed, it would still have been in the stomach and recognizable.'

'Anyway, she'd just had a big dinner,' McLaren said.

'And she couldn't have bought it in a fit of absent-mindedness, since she had ten minutes to sit and think while it was being cooked. So, we have to conclude...?'

'That she bought it for someone else,' McLaren said. 'But who?'

'And then there's the money. I can't remember offhand but I'm pretty sure there wasn't two hundred pounds in her purse.'

'No, guv,' McLaren said. 'Forty pounds and

188

some change. And she didn't spend a hundred and sixty on a takeaway.'

In the office, Hollis was still at work and Atherton and Swilley were back. They gathered round and Slider explained about the tape and Melanie's takeaway purchase.

'Not for herself, obviously. But who do you buy a takeaway for?' Atherton said. 'Someone you know. Someone you live with.'

'Hibbert was away,' said Hollis.

'Or was he?' Atherton countered. 'With Melanie dead, we've only his word for it. We certainly know where he wasn't. Suppose when he rang her at the pub that night he told her he'd seen the error of his ways and was on his way home?'

'And asked her to get him a takeaway?' Norma said scornfully. 'When he was on his way to murder her?'

'You don't know what the habit was between them,' he reasoned. 'She didn't know she was for the chop. Maybe it was customary after his nights at the pub. Maybe she asked him, "Shall I get you a Chinese as usual?" and he said yes rather than arouse her suspicions.'

'The person she lived with is the most likely person she'd buy a takeaway for,' Hollis allowed. 'But what happened to the containers?'

'Yeah,' said McLaren. 'Connolly was in there Saturday, and she looked round and in the bin in the kitchen, and there was nothing like that there. And they weren't in the dustbins, either.'

The contents of the household dustbins were secured on Monday – that was SOP – and since

189

collection day was Tuesday, anything thrown in there over the weekend would still have been there.

'He could have taken them out and disposed of them,' Atherton said. 'He had plenty of time. They could be in any bin between here and Salisbury.'

'That's true,' Slider said. 'But why would he bother?'

'To hide the fact that he was there,' said Atherton. 'If we'd found the debris, we'd have got DNA out of the saliva traces and identified him as being at home when he was supposed to be at the wedding.'

'But would he think of that? This is the man whose alibi was cracked at the first question,' Slider said.

'You just don't know what he might think of. Or maybe he killed her first, then took it with him and ate it in the car,' Atherton said impatiently.

'It'd have been well cold,' McLaren said scornfully. 'He had to get rid of the body first.'

'You know who else she could have bought it for,' Swilley said. 'That she was friendly with. Who had time to get rid of the rubbish. And I bet he eats a lot of takeaways. And there's the money, too. If it wasn't in her purse, where was it?'

'Most likely Hibbert took it,' said Atherton.

'No,' said Slider. 'She means Ronnie Fitton.'

190

Ten

The Son Also Rises

Slider was holding down the fort at home that evening, as Joanna had a recording session, and for a wonder Dad had a date as well. Since selling up his home and coming to live with them, he had been available night and day, and Slider had often told him that he ought to go out more, get some interests of his own. It was said as a sop to Slider's conscience, not for his father's benefit, since he knew, deep down, that what his father liked best was being at home and looking after George; but it seemed that at last Mr Slider had heeded him and gone and joined a club. A Scrabble club, of all things.

'I didn't even know you played Scrabble,' Slider had said.

'Everybody plays Scrabble,' Dad had said. 'T'isn't difficult. Anyway, it's company. Gets me out o' the house.'

Slider had started worrying on a whole new level. 'Those dedicated Scrabble players can be peculiar people. Fiercely competitive. They know words all made up of Qs and Ks, and they're scornful of anyone who doesn't.'

Mr Slider had been untroubled 'It's not like

that in this club. All amateurs – just nice people wanting a quiet game. You wanted me to go out,' he pointed out.

'I want you to be happy, though.'

'Your trouble is you never have enough to worry about. You're an addict. Even when you got plenty, you keep looking for more. Anyway, if I don't like it I can always leave, can't I? I got to go once, because I told someone I'd give it a try.'

'Oh? You've made a new friend?' Slider didn't know why he was surprised. It's just he never visualized his father outside the home, talking to anybody.

There was a gleam in Mr Slider's eye, as if he read this thought quite plainly. 'Not deaf and dumb, am I? I see people in the street, talk to them in the supermarket. Quite a friendly old place, this. Anyway, you needn't worry about me. I had half an hour with the dictionary while my boy was taking his nap, and I'm all primed up.' He patted his forehead, as if it were a willing horse. 'Quassia, quern, quincunx. Kukri, kowtow, kumis. Want to test me on the Js and Zs?'

It was odd, though, to see his father off and close the door, leaving himself in a silent house, empty except for George, asleep upstairs. He went up and had a look at him, just for the pleasure, then came down, feeling at a loss, and realizing how comfortable his life had been of recent months – always a fire lit and a meal ready when he came home, and sympathetic company to tell his day's experiences to. Ah well. He drifted into the kitchen, where his father had left him half a shepherd's pie in the oven, warming on a low light. There were vegetables, cut and ready to cook, but even as he looked at them he knew they were doomed to lie there undisturbed, and that when the moment came he would eat the shepherd's pie straight from the dish with a spoon. He was not a man who had been designed ever to live alone.

He thought he'd have a small malt whisky before eating, took time over choosing, and carried his Scapa into the sitting room. He intended to spend the evening doing some heavy reading and some even heavier thinking. He had the uneasy feeling he had missed something, or forgotten something – that someone had told him something important that he had put aside in his head and now couldn't lay his hand on. It was not unusual when he was involved in a complex case – probably just part of the way his mind worked – but it was uncomfortable all the same.

He decided to look at the paper first, while he drank his whisky, to see if leaving it alone would make the missing thing pop up of its own accord. That sometimes happened. He took a sip, put down his glass, took up the paper, read the first paragraph of the first story, and passed out, sandbagged by sheer exhaustion.

He woke an unknown time later with a stiff neck and a thumping heart as George's cry pierced the fog. He was on his feet and moving before he'd even opened his eyes, so he knew, as he hurried upstairs towards the sobbing, that it was the first cry he had heard. George was on his feet, clutching the side of his cot, his face contorted with grief and swimming with those great, fat, somehow extra glistening tears babies could produce as though their tear ducts were primed with glycerine. His hands went out with the familiar snatching gesture as soon as Slider appeared, and he swooped the boy up to his shoulder, felt the wet cheek against his neck, and the hands gripping his clothes with the ferocity of the bad dream that had wakened him. He was going through a phase of being woken by nightmares that he hadn't the vocabulary to explain, which was distressing to everyone.

'Was it a bad dream?' he asked, holding the tight little body close.

Nod.

'Never mind, it's all gone now.'

The hands clutched harder.

'What was it about, do you remember?'

Shake.

'Do you want to come downstairs with me for a bit?'

Nod.

So he carried him downstairs to the lighted room, where the fire had sunk, but was still giving warmth. He sat on the sofa and held George in his lap, and George stuck his thumb in his mouth and stared at the fire glow.

After a bit he unplugged and said, 'Story, Daddy.'

Slider embarked on the story of the ugly duckling from memory, adding in extra characters and action to pad it out, to give George time to get sleepy again. When the boy finally dozed off, Slider stayed put, to make sure he was really down before moving him again. He sat with the lovely weight in his lap, staring at the fire and not thinking of anything in particular.

And that was how Mr Slider found them, both asleep, when he got back from his Scrabble evening. The smell of the forgotten shepherd's pie was strong on the air. Good job I put it on low, he thought, with a fond and exasperated shake of the head.

Despite not having done any industrial-strength thinking, it was probably a good thing he'd had that extra sleep, Slider reasoned the next morning, when he went in to work feeling rested and firing on all cylinders. He stopped off to talk to Paxman, the duty sergeant downstairs, who told him that the operation had gone off smoothly, and Ronnie Fitton was safely banged up in the cells awaiting his fate.

'Did he give any trouble?'

'No trouble at all,' said Paxman, a large, heavy-built man, with stationary eyes and tightly curly hair that gave him a faint resemblance to a Hereford bull. 'Fact he seemed to be expecting it. Resigned. He got a couple of hours' kip once we'd processed him, and he's had a good breakfast, so he's ready for you any time.'

'Any trouble with the press?'

'Nah. Too cold for 'em to hang about all night on the off-chance. The one in the house across the road's the only one still around, and he missed his chance. Musta been cooping. The story's in the paper, but there's no picture, only of the forensics going in.'

'Oh, they're in already, are they? Good.'

Slider was about to pass on, when Paxman retained him with a large, beefy hand on his arm. 'Bill, are you sure about this one?'

'Sure? I'm not even close. Why, what's up?'

Paxman shook his head slowly, as if goaded by flies. 'I dunno. I've got a feeling about this geezer. There's something about him.' He waited for thought to develop. 'He's too quiet,' he concluded, as if that was not really what he meant, but was the closest he could get.

'He's the best suspect we've got,' Slider said. 'And we had to do something.'

Paxman nodded. He understood that. 'Just be careful. He could be trouble.'

'What sort of trouble?' Slider asked.

'I dunno,' Paxman said. 'Wish I did. Just – be careful.'

'I will. Thanks, Arthur.' Paxman was long on the job and old in the ways of men. Slider always took him seriously.

Slider had studied Ronnie Fitton's file, and there was much about him that did not fit the usual criminal profile, and some features that did. He was born to an ordinary working-class family in West Acton. His father worked for British Rail as a ticket collector and station attendant; his mother worked part-time on a supermarket checkout. They lived in a small terraced house, privately rented.

There had been another son, Keith, two years older than Ronnie. He had been killed by a train

196

when he was fourteen: he and some friends had been trespassing on railway property and Keith and another boy were playing 'chicken'. The other boy survived; Keith was killed instantly, tossed up on to the low embankment between the lines and the back gardens like a stringless marionette.

That must have had the hell of an effect on Ronnie, aged twelve, Slider thought. It was the sort of thing that could turn a boy to the bad, but it seemed to have had the opposite effect. Defence counsel at his trial had made much of the fact that after his brother's death he had never been in trouble, had worked hard at school and got three GCSEs, and had gone to a vocational college and got himself a trade qualification in graphic design. After working for various printing firms, he had ended up as manager of a sign-making company, earning a good salary. He had married a girl he had been dating for a couple of years, and bought a house in North-fields not too far from the business. Then, two years into the marriage, he had come home unexpectedly early and found his wife in bed with another man, and killed her.

It was the first break in the pattern of exemplary behaviour, and on the surface it was inexplicable. He had no history of violence: friends and neighbours agreed the couple had been on good terms and there was no suggestion he had ever raised a hand to her. But it was possible to imagine that he had been affected by the shock and horror of the brother's death – they had apparently been close – which had been brought upon him by his own wrongdoing. Had young Ronnie buckled down and behaved all those years, done the right things in the right order, and at least subconsciously expected his reward to be that his life would be blessed? – only to be betrayed by the person closest to him. Slider thought there could well have been deeply suppressed emotions – grief and rage – from the time of his brother's death which broke through in that moment of betrayal and caused him to lash out. The trouble was that he did not say of himself that he had snapped, lost his temper and lashed out. He had refused to say anything other than that she had deserved it, thus portraying it as a calculated act and not subject to mitigation.

What Slider came away with was a sense of a frightening degree of control, which in turn suggested a frightening amount of something underneath to need controlling. It would make him a dangerous man, as Paxman hinted. You would never know what he might do, or when he might do it. It was over twenty years since he had killed his wife; the safety valve on the pressure cooker might have reached its limits. And if it was Fitton who killed Melanie, it would make sense of the no-sexual-assault aspect. It was love and betrayal that had sparked him to kill his wife. Had he loved Melanie? And had she betrayed him in some way? Not sexually: Fitton's would have been a secret and suppressed love, perhaps an idolization. She would only need to do something he regarded as betraying his image of her, something he thought beneath her.

Or, of course (he had to admit to himself) that

fierce control could have been simply covering up a series of criminal deeds. He could have been a 'right wrong'un' all along, but with the mental acuity not to get himself caught, and it was blackmail after all. One thing you could be sure of – good man or bad, he would not have wanted to go back inside.

Fitton seemed very calm. He sat in a relaxed attitude on the chair in the interview room, his lean legs in the paper overalls crossed, smoking a cigarette. His face showed nothing, not fear or apprehension or even interest in what was happening to him, but Slider felt that there was a point of carbon steel somewhere in the middle of him, like the tip of a whipping top. He might appear to be motionless, but that was only because he was spinning so hard.

Slider took his place on the opposite side of the table. Atherton came in behind him and sat by the tape machine. Fitton did not look at either of them. He took a drag on his cigarette and blew upwards, watching the smoke and the ceiling.

'Cup of tea?' Slider offered.

Fitton shook his head.

'Are they treating you all right?'

'No complaints,' Fitton said.

'You've had breakfast?'

'Full house. You do a good one here.'

'Thank you. I'll mention it to the Michelin inspector.'

Fitton gave no reaction to the pleasantry.

'Have you had your phone call?'

'I've got no one to ring.' He said it as a plain statement of fact, not an appeal for sympathy.

'Solicitor?'

'Don't want one.'

That was usually a bad sign – the guilty man calleth his brief when no man pursueth, as the proverb had it. But in Fitton's case you couldn't read anything into it. He hadn't wanted anything to do with his legal team the first time round, either. He seemed to have a robust contempt for the profession.

'You're sure?' Slider said.

Now Fitton looked at him – and the level eyes were not calm, like the rest of him, but hard, with a spark in them like a glimpse of fire deep down in a fissure in the earth. There was a volcanic eruption somewhere being suppressed; molten magma was flowing along `secret channels far below the surface. He said, 'I don't need one because I'm not answering your questions.'

'Why is that?' Slider asked.

'Don't try and make friends with me,' Fitton said. 'I didn't kill her and you can't prove I did. You're wasting your time.'

'If you didn't kill her, you must want to help us find out who did.'

'I don't care if you do or you don't. It won't bring her back. Time to help her was when she was alive.'

'Did you try to help her?'

'Not my business,' he said briskly. Then he paused, seeming, curiously, not to like the sound of that answer when he heard it out loud. He added, 'She knew where I was.'

Not the same, Slider thought. Not the same at all. He said, 'Well, then, you must at least want to see justice done?'

The spark flickered brighter for an instant. 'Justice? You talk about justice? You're all in hock to the press, the lot of you. You only arrested me because the newspapers kept demanding why you didn't, and your PR department told your bosses they had to do something about it. Bad press is the only thing that matters to you bloody lot these days. The press could get the Home Secretary and the Commissioner the sack if they put up a campaign against 'em, so the shove goes in, all the way down the line until it ends up with you. And you just have to do as you're told, whether you like it or not. So you pull me in because I've got a record. You call that justice?'

'You've obviously thought about it a lot,' Slider said evenly.

'Had a lot of time for thinking, didn't I?' He turned his head away again, drawing on his cigarette.

'Do you think justice was not done in your own case? Do you feel aggrieved about that?'

'Not much good at this psychological bollocks, are you?' he enquired of the air. 'I killed my wife. I never denied it. I was punished. I never complained about that. But justice had nothing to do with it. It was retribution.' He finished the cigarette and stubbed it out in the tinfoil ashtray on the table.

'In what way was justice not done, then?'

He looked at Slider with a sad shake of the head like a teacher dealing with a very thick pupil. 'It's *called* the Justice System. That's just its *name*. Don't get sucked in by fancy language. Crime and punishment, that's all it is. I killed my wife. That's against the law. I was punished. End of.'

'Very well, then, don't you want the person who killed Melanie to be punished?'

'Not interested. I'll have that cup of tea, now. Two sugars.'

Slider sighed inwardly, and nodded to Atherton. Depriving him of tea or cigarettes was not going to make any difference to a tough nut like this. But he had proved he liked to talk. The only chance was to build an atmosphere where he would sound off on his pet themes and perhaps let something slip.

While Atherton was at the door, talking to the constable outside, Fitton looked at Slider with a marked drop in attitude and asked, 'How's Marty?'

'We took him to Melanie's parents.'

'Who took him? That girl you sent round? The Irish one?'

'Yes. She said he seemed happy to be there.'

'I hope they treat him right.'

'Why wouldn't they?'

He looked at Slider thoughtfully for a moment, and then said, 'You know as much as I do. You work it out.'

Slider tried, 'You're fond of him? Marty?'

'I like all dogs. They don't mess you around. They can't lie to you. I'm glad that pillock Scott didn't take him back. He doesn't deserve a nice dog like Marty.'

'Did you have a dog when you were a kid?'

Fitton eyed him sidelong. 'I said, don't try to make friends with me. I don't like lies, and pretending is lying. You're not interested in me. You just want to get enough on me to charge me so you can get your pat on the back from the bosses. It's all political with you coppers nowadays.'

'I'm not like that,' Slider said, mildly but with truth. 'I saw her body. You say you hate lies – well, I hate waste. And no one had the right to take her life away from her.'

'People take other people's lives away all the time – not by killing 'em, but by crushing their spirit, brutalizing 'em, denying 'em education, chances, bottling 'em up in a ghetto of ignorance and hopelessness. They're as good as dead. A life like that is worse than death.'

Slider couldn't decide whether this was a deeply felt socio-political view or simply smoke being blown in his eyes to keep him from asking any more pertinent questions. Long winded discourse was a funny way of not answering, he thought, and he was glad other arrestees didn't resort to it. Policing was exhausting enough as it was without being lectured into the bargain.

The tea came. Fitton blew on it, sipped it, put it down, asked for another cigarette. He was the king of the custody suite, his attitude said. *I've done time for murder – this is kiddy league stuff in comparison.*

Slider decided to go for specifics. 'You gave us

203

the impression that you knew Melanie only casually. But in fact you knew her quite well. You went out for drinks with her quite often. Why didn't you tell us about that?'

'That's my business.'

'No, it's ours now. Everything about everyone who knew her is our business.'

'That's your bad luck, then. I'm not answering your questions.'

'If you're innocent, why not?'

'Because I don't have to tell my business to anyone.'

Crap, Slider thought. 'You know, don't you, that murder always leaves forensic traces, which we will find. Sooner or later, the truth will come out. Why don't you make it easier on yourself? You chose the hard line the first time round, and where did that get you? There may be mitigating circumstances that can be taken into account. There may—'

'Don't make me laugh,' Fitton interrupted, with no laughter anywhere in sight. 'Mitigating circumstances! If you charge me I'm back inside for the rest of my kip. They'll throw away the key. I don't fancy that, thank you very much. My flat's not much, but it's mine, and I don't have to share it with some farting, snoring, nose-picking Neanderthal with stinking feet.'

'Then help us.'

'Help yourselves. I had a reasonable life, until you lot sold me out to the papers. All I wanted was to be left alone. Fat chance of that, now.'

There was a knock, and Atherton went to the door, conducted a whispered conversation, then said to Slider, 'Mr Porson wants you.'

Slider got up. 'I'll be back,' he told Fitton.

'Take your time,' Fitton replied.

Porson was looking worried, which was so unusual it gave Slider a qualm. Fierce or impatient were Porson's normal expressions, along with any degree of either in-between. The old man didn't do worried. He flung himself headlong at problems, sword in hand, slashing away – less in Zorro than in anger, Slider always said.

'Getting anywhere?' was Porson's first question.

'Like Bank Holiday Monday on the A303.'

Porson grunted. 'Being abstrapalous, is he?'

'Refusing to answer questions. He's too calm and a lot too cocky for my liking – but there's a lot of anger there, underneath. I can see him doing it. On the other hand, I don't get the feeling he's a bad man, basically.'

'You can be a good man right up to the moment you're not,' Porson said. 'But I had a phone call this morning that complicates matters.'

Oh joy, Slider thought. My life was too simple. There was just no challenge.

'In fact, it's chucked a bit of a spaniel in the works,' Porson went on. 'It was from the director of Stamford House.'

Stamford House, the secure home for violent young offenders. They had forgotten about that, Slider thought. Or had put it to one side, rather. 'Don't tell me they had someone over the wall on Friday?' Slider asked. 'We didn't think this

205

looked like something one of them would have done – hiding the body and so on. They'd have had to have a car to—'

'No, no, it's nothing like that,' Porson interrupted. 'No, it was about Fitton.' He picked up a rubber band from his desk and stretched it round his fingers. 'He knows him, you see.'

'Personally? Or in a professional capacity?' Slider asked.

Porson began stretching and easing the rubber band. Slider took a surreptitious half step backwards. He could see it flying off Porson's fingers.

'Both. You see, it turns out he's been helping over there, with the kids.'

'*Fitton* has?'

Porson nodded unhappily. 'Started off with coming in to give 'em a talk about what it was really like in prison – explode the myth, show there was nothing glamorous about it, put 'em off it for life.'

'How did that come about? How did the director know about him?'

'He didn't. It was the other way round. Fitton volunteered. Said he wanted to help. Couldn't stand seeing those young kids going to the bad, like the ones he met inside. If he could save a single one, his suffering wouldn't be in vain, sort of effort.' Porson's eyebrows went up like a pair of herons taking off from a pond. 'Apparently he was very eloquent. Anyway, the director bought it. They've got a hell of a tough ask in there; anything and anyone that might help is welcome. After all due checks and percautions, they let him come in and do his talk, and a Q and A afterwards. The kids were well impressed. The staff even more so. He handled their questions with tact, didn't let them get purulent about the murder or make him some kind of hero, and they obviously related to him, gathered round when it was over, started talking about themselves, asking his advice.'

The rubber band flew across the room, just missing Slider's ear. Porson didn't even notice it was gone. 'Thing is, it's hard to reach these kids. Most of 'em view all grown-ups as the enemy. They desperately need guidance but won't let 'emselves take it. So someone who could talk to 'em, who they'd talk to, is worth his weight.' He shrugged. 'He's been going in a couple of times a week, taking groups sometimes, talking to individuals other times. Advice, information, sometimes just a shoulder to cry on. Doing good work, apparently – good results. Some real little nut jobs have calmed down a lot. So when it said in the papers we'd arrested him – well, the director was agog, the staff were up in arms. As far as they're concerned he was from the planet Krypton. Couldn't do wrong.' Porson raised sorrowful eyes to Slider's. 'He was in there Friday. All afternoon.'

'Ah,' said Slider. 'He told us he was out, but wouldn't say where. Said it was his business.'

So,' said Porson. It wasn't much, but his expression was eloquent. They were silent a moment.

'It doesn't necessarily follow—' Slider began.

'No, but it's a hell of a good indicator,' said

207

Porson. 'It'd look good in court. Stand up on its own like a pair of soldier's socks.'

'He had good character the last time,' Slider pointed out.

'Last time he never denied it. Put his hand up right off. I think we got to tread careful. Don't want the press saying we're hounding a man who's doing his best to pay his debt to society.'

'They're the ones doing the hounding. They've been shouting his guilt ever since they discovered his record.'

'Well, you don't expect them to be rational. No, it's our nuts on the block here. We'll keep him until the forensic comes back on his flat, and then if there's nothing there, let him go. I still think he's tasty, but without evidence ... He won't be able to go anywhere. Everyone in the country knows his face now.'

And Slider experienced a pang of sympathy for Fitton, which really, really annoyed him. He went back to the interview room feeling distinctly narked.

'Why didn't you tell us about your work at Stamford House?' he asked trying not to show it.

Fitton gave him that same darkly calm look. 'How many times do I have to say it? It's my business.' Slider took a breath to reply and he went on in a different tone, more conciliatory. 'Anyway, I don't want you bothering those kids. They've got enough on their plates, without the Vogons clumping all over 'em, asking 'em questions. You leave 'em alone. You could knock 'em back months, just when they're making some progress.'

'I'm not going to ask them anything. There's no need. The director told us about your involvement with them.'

'Oh, did he?' Fitton commented, and did a bit of a brood.

Slider tried to capitalize on the new mood. 'So what was the nature of your interest in Melanie Hunter?'

'Who said I had any interest in her?'

'Was it because she'd been in trouble at one time?'

He looked up at that. 'Criminal trouble?'

'No, not that. But she'd been a bad girl, and pulled herself round. That must have taken courage. Was that why you admired her?'

'I didn't know she had,' he said slowly, staring at some inner landscape. 'But I guessed there was something. There's a sort of look about girls who've been through the mill ... She never said anything to me,' he added sharply. 'And I would not ask. But I told your girl – the Irish one – there was more to Mel than met the eye. She was in some kind of trouble, but she never told me.'

'So why did you go for drinks with her? To try to help her? Did she see you as some kind of father figure?' He was seeing the edge of a scenario he really didn't want to contemplate, in which Fitton, driven to megalomania by his success with disturbed children, felt obliged to put the girl out of her misery – another crime which was no crime in his eyes, like the justice delivered to his erring wife. No one came out of prison after fifteen years entirely sane.

Fitton was silent a long moment, and Slider

209

didn't think he was going to answer. Then he said quite abruptly, 'She wanted to help me.'

'Help you do what?'

'With the kids. She wanted me to get her into Stamford House. I told her it was way too dangerous. Those kids may be under sixteen but they're violent criminals. She thought she could help some of the girls. I see now, if you say she'd been there herself, why she thought that. But she had no idea. It wasn't on. Still, she kept asking, and even when she stopped asking, she liked to ask me about what I'd been doing and how they were getting on, the ones I was mentoring. And I—' A long pause, and then, almost sub voce, 'I enjoyed telling her.'

Yes, Slider could see that. A man so cut off from all normal discourse; the interest – the admiring interest – of a pretty young woman in the most important thing in his life. Very understandable; but also, given the nature of the pressure cooker, a potentially combustible situation. If something had threatened to take her away from him ... Or she had said the wrong thing, lost interest in his mission, dissed his protégés, or appeared to...

A thought occurred to him. 'Did she ever give you money to give to them – to help them through a difficult patch, for instance?'

Fitton looked surprised, and then angry. 'I didn't take money from her. And I didn't give money to the kids. D'you think I'm some kind of amateur? If you want to know anything about them, go to the director. I'm done talking to you.'

Slider ended the interview; Atherton turned off the tape and called in the constable to return Fitton to his cell. As he passed him, Slider asked casually, 'Do you like Chinese food?'

But there was no reaction from Fitton's set face or grim voice. 'I can take it or leave it,' he said.

Slider and Atherton trod upstairs. 'It could still be him,' Atherton said. 'He obviously had feelings for her. And he's more than a little nutty.'

Slider nodded. 'In fact, I'm feeling bad, now, about sending Connolly round there. But this helping with the disturbed kids is a powerful thing on his side. Unless we get some real evidence from the flat, or an eye witness, we can't even hold him. But he's still got the best opportunity to get rid of the body and the takeaway cartons.'

'Unless he really can't drive.'

'And in any case, *what* would he drive? So far we haven't got her car logged anywhere on Friday night after she left the pub, and we don't know about any other car he has access to.'

'Right,' said Atherton cheerfully, 'so we'd better leave him to one side and concentrate on the person who had equally good opportunity, even better access, who could have been spending her money hand over fist for two years for all we know, and who's lied to us about his whereabouts and has a busted alibi. Do you like Chinese food, indeed! Let's ask Scott Hibbert the same question.'

'I suppose you're right,' Slider said. 'As soon

as Fathom gets his report in, we'll reel him in for a chat.'

They reached the door of the office, and Hollis came towards them, looking like a worried peperami stick, with Mackay eager at his elbow.

'I was just going to ring down to you, guv,' Hollis began.

Mackay couldn't wait. 'Hibbert's had it away!'

'What?'

'On his toes.'

'Done a runner,' Hollis amplified.

'See?' Atherton said in triumph. 'I told you so.'

Eleven

That Bourne to Which No Traveller Returns

Fathom was looking worried. He wasn't one of the very brightest: if brains were air miles, he couldn't have got further than Birmingham. But stick him in front of a computer with a well-defined task and you couldn't go wrong. So as he loomed in Slider's doorway with his forehead resembling the winning entry in a drunken ploughing contest, Slider was alarmed.

'Guv, I've tracked Hibbert's motor last weekend. He's got a silver Ford Mondeo – well,' he sidetracked himself, 'it's reckoned an OK car now, since James Bond's drove one in that film. I mean, it used to be really boring, but now all the reps want one, even the ones that used to drive BMWs—'

'Hibbert's movements?' Slider prompted him gently.

It was like watching an oil tanker doing a U-turn. The turbines thrashed painfully for a moment before he righted himself. 'Oh, yeah. Well, I've picked him up on the Watford Way, the A41, at Fiveways Corner.'

'He said he was going to Hendon on Friday morning,' Slider said, 'so that fits.'

213

'Yeah, guv. That ping's Friday lunchtime, ha'pass twelve time. Then he's took the M1, M25, round to the M3, and I've got him filling up at the Fleet Services, westbound.'

'So it looks as though he was heading down to Salisbury,' Slider said. 'But leaving early in the day – I wonder if his employers knew he was taking the afternoon off?'

'Dunno,' Fathom said. 'He didn't go to Salisbury, though – not right away. He's stopped on the M3. I've picked him up Winchester, Eastleigh, then he's took the M27, A31, I've caught him at Ringwood, then he's on the A338 towards Bournemouth. I've lost him after that. There's not so many cameras down that way as there are in the London area. But I reckon he must have stopped somewhere in the Bournemouth area, because the next time he's pinged is at Ringwood again, going north this time on the A338, which takes him to Salisbury. That's half ten-ish Saturday morning.'

'Which looks like heading for the eleven o'clock wedding,' Slider said.

'Yeah, guv,' Fathom said, with an anxious look. 'So how did he get from Bournemouth to Shepherd's Bush to murder Hunter without getting pinged?'

Slider glanced at the paper in his hand. 'What are the rest of his movements?'

'Back to Bournemouth straight after the wedding. Then Sunday morning I've got him on the A303, M3 back to London. He stops on the motorway all the way to Sunbury, then I've got him Richmond, Barnes, and Hammersmith

214

Bridge at ten to ten. Which is right for him getting home at around ten, like he said. So if that's the way he went home Sunday, how'd he do it Friday?'

Slider shook his head. 'There are ways, I suppose. Not every road has a camera on it by a long chalk. He could have gone a roundabout route, by the back roads—'

'Yeah, guv, but how would *he* know where the cameras were?'

'Or even that there are cameras,' Slider completed. Few people did, and even if they knew, or suspected, driving habits were so ingrained it was hard for them to keep the idea in mind when going from A to B. A man with no criminal background would be unlikely to govern his movements by fear of being caught by the ANPR. 'However,' he said in a comforting tone, for Fathom was looking as bereft as if his puppy had been taken away from him, 'there is another possibility – that he did the journey in a different car.'

Fathom's face cleared. 'Oh, yeah!' That was altogether more explicable. A man might not know about the cameras, but he might just grasp that if his car was spotted in the wrong place at the wrong time it could spell trouble.

'What's exercising me more is what he was doing in Bournemouth.'

'The Bournemouth area,' Fathom corrected. 'There's a lot of places he could have gone from there, if he didn't go on the main roads.'

'Let's say that when I say "Bournemouth", I mean the Bournemouth area,' Slider said.

'Maybe it was something for his firm after all,' Fathom said. 'He went straight there from London. And didn't that bloke, the best man, say he was talking about doing a big deal?'

'True. And I suppose even a liar and fantasist might tell the truth sometimes, by mistake. Well, you've done some good work here, Fathom.'

'Thanks, guv.'

'And given me lots of questions to ask Mr Hibbert – as soon as we find him.'

'Yeah,' Fathom said, his momentary pleasure at being praised flagging. An all-cars, all-areas general shout had gone out for Hibbert. He had achieved fugitive status, and other eyes than Fathom's would be scanning the ANPR for the silver Mondeo now.

Slider gave him a consolation prize. 'I'd like you to get on to his employers – Hatter and Ruck – and find out if he was doing anything for them in Bournemouth, and whether they've had any contact with him since Friday. And if he wasn't on company business in Bournemouth, whether he's ever mentioned the place or has any connection with it.'

Porson had been talking to headquarters at Hammersmith, as was apparent from the redness of his right ear and his air of restrained frenzy. 'Mr Wetherspoon first, and then the PR girl – woman – person.'

'Lily Saddler,' Slider offered her name, to get Porson out of the PC mire. It was no wonder he had difficulty remembering it. She was the third in two years – it was a job no one stayed in

216

very long, largely, Slider thought, because of Mr Wetherspoon, whose tact, sensitivity and sweetness of nature made him about as popular as Hitler at a bar mitzvah.

'Saddler, that's her,' Porson said. He gave a sigh that would have registered on seismographs all round the world. 'Bloody PR again! I don't know why we don't just get Saatchi and Saatchi in to run the police and have done with it. Anyway, the upshoot is they've decided there's no harm in letting the press have Hibbert doing a runner. They'll get on to it sooner or later, and Mr Wetherspoon thinks it'll be good to have something else already on the go for if and when we have to let Ronnie Fitton out, so they can't say we've been wasting our time chasing our own tails while the real villain gets away.'

'It's a point,' Slider conceded.

Porson eyed him. 'I can see through you like a book,' he said. 'You think Fitton's a washout, don't you?'

'I wouldn't go that far, sir. I certainly think he's capable of it. I'd even say it looks like his kind of murder – done in a moment of rage, the hands round the throat and the single blow to the head. But I also think, who better than him would know how to cover his tracks? If he did do it, we may never be able to put together a case against him. Unless they find some blood in his flat. Just evidence of her being there won't do, because they were friends, there's no reason she shouldn't go in there.'

'You're full of bloody sunshine, you are,' Porson said disconsolately. 'When are you expecting the forensic report?'

'Some time today. They finished the site examination yesterday – the flat's so empty it was relatively easy – so we're just waiting for the swab analysis. Unofficially, Bob Bailey isn't hopeful. But that doesn't mean he didn't kill her elsewhere, of course.'

Porson grunted. 'Trouble is, elsewhere's a big place. I'm going to have to get on to Mr Fox, see if we can widen the search area, look around those woods for some blood, or some bloody clothes. I'd be grateful,' he said with an air of pathos, 'for a nice pair of discarded surgical gloves.' He pulled himself together. 'Meanwhile, we'll have to pin our hopes on Hibbert. One thing, getting the press involved will find him quicker. If he's gone to ground, once his picture's in the papers, someone will recognize their new next-door neighbour.'

Connolly was waiting for him when he got back to his room. 'Boss, I know we're all off our heads about your man Hibbert doing a legger—'

'It doesn't mean we can't keep our eyes open in other directions,' Slider said.

'That's what I was thinking.' She was wearing smart grey slacks and an enormous reddish-coloured shaggy sweater with one of those roll-necks that didn't fit closely, so her neck and head rose from it like something growing in a flowerpot. She had recently had her hair cut shorter so it was a flower with the petals furled, he thought.

218

'There's something here,' she said, waving the papers she was holding. 'I was going over the interviews with the friends Hunter went for a jar with on Friday. You know one of the questions we asked them was if she had any phone calls? Well, this one, Leanne Buckley, said she had a phone call from her dad.'

'But when I spoke to Ian Wiseman, he said he hadn't spoken to her for two weeks,' Slider remembered. 'He said she'd spoken to her mother on the Friday.'

'Yeah, boss. Her mammy said she'd phoned her in the afternoon, from work. So he wouldn't have been around. He couldn't have just taken the phone from her for a quick hello, and then forgotten it.'

'So what's your point?'

'I went back to this Buckley female, just to check, and she's quite sure about it. She said she was sitting next to Hunter when the call came in, and she seemed upset by it. Didn't say much, just yes and no and I see, that class o' caper. But whatever was being said was annoying her, and finally she said, "Yes, all *right*, Dad," really narky like. And here's the best bit, boss –' she forestalled his comment – 'this was around ten o'clock, and soon afterwards Hunter says she's feeling like shite and wants to go home, and she breaks the party up.'

'I always felt it was a bit early,' Slider said.

'Yeah, me too, boss. When you get together with your mates for a crack, especially on someone's birthday, you don't hang up your boots while the trains are still running. So I'm think-

219

ing, what if Wiseman asked her to meet him somewhere?'

'Given that they had a row last time they met, why would she go?' Slider objected.

'Well, he is her dad. Even if she didn't like him, you kind of do what the owl ones ask, don't you? And say he said he wanted to make up with her? He was sorry for giving out to her, and wanted them to be friends. So she thinks better get it over with, and says OK.'

'She might perhaps want to do that for her mother's sake.'

'Yeah, boss. It'd be uncomfortable for her mammy with the bad blood in the house, so she could think, I'll do it for her, sure the owl man's making the effort, have to give him the benefit of the doubt.'

Slider thought about it. 'And the Chinese takeaway?'

Connolly frowned. 'Well, to be honest with you, that has me a bit confounded. But I suppose he might have said, I'm just coming from praccer and I've not eaten, could y'ever get me a takeaway on your way home?'

'But he could have got his own takeaway, if he was going over there by car.'

'I know. I haven't quite worked that one out. But the fact is –' she stared at him earnestly, like someone trying to persuade through Pelmanism – 'he said he didn't speak to her and he did, and she got upset and left early. That's got to be worth something, hasn't it?'

'Yes,' said Slider. Besides which, Wiseman was good for villain. Quite apart from his being her stepfather – most murders were done by someone close to the victim – there was his disposition, his disapproval of Melanie; the fact that he had rowed with her in the recent past, *and* hit her; his daughter Bethany's evidence that he spoke contemptuously of Melanie's mother (though of course what children said always had to be taken with a pinch of salt).

And his conflicting testimony about his alibi. 'He told me he got home in time to watch television with his wife before going to bed, but Mrs Wiseman told you he got home late, after she was in bed,' he said.

'But if he went to see Melanie after footer, and ended up killing her...'

'That would account for it,' Slider finished for her. He thought for a moment. 'All right, this is how we'll do it. You find out what you can, discreetly, about the football practice – where, how long, when it finished. See if you can get hold of some of the kids to ask. I'd sooner not go to the school authorities yet – they'd be bound to refer it to him and I don't want to spook him if he is guilty, or have a lawsuit brought down on us if he isn't. And try and find out if he was accustomed to go for a drink anywhere after school or after practice. You can find out a lot more about a person in a pub than anywhere else.'

'Right, boss,' Connolly said. 'Leave it to me.'

'If he does frequent a pub, let me know. I might send in Mackay – sometimes a man's better in that environment than a woman.'

'Depends on the boozer,' Connolly said, and she wasn't wrong.

The ANPR did not take long in picking up Hibbert's car on the same route down to Bournemouth that it had traced on the Friday. They remained on alert for any further movement, but as long as he was thought to be in the Bournemouth area, the actual searching for him on the ground had to be handed over to the local police, leaving Slider's hands tied.

Fathom meanwhile had interviewed the staff at Hatter and Ruck and learned that Hibbert had indeed been going to Hendon that morning, to look at a large house that was going on the market. He was then supposed to call in at the Hampstead branch on internal business, but had phoned them to say he had been delayed and was running late and would not be coming in after all. He was supposed to be working at home in the afternoon. They had not seen or heard from him since Friday, but of course they had not expected to once the murder became known. They had sent him a text of condolence, saying he should take leave of absence for as long as necessary. He hadn't responded to that. It had been quite awkward because he had some papers with him which they needed, and they'd had to do a lot of the work again, but you couldn't go bothering someone at a time like that, asking them for documents, could you?

As far as they knew he had no business down in Bournemouth, and had certainly not told anyone that he was going there. They had a branch in Dorchester that dealt with Bournemouth and all places west, in any case: it would not go through Knightsbridge, unless it were something very big, like a major development, which would require the services of their specialist commercial section. Scott Hibbert was not involved in commercial property. He was purely residential. They had no complaints about his work. He had so far proved reliable. And he was *quite* well thought of.

'They didn't rave about him, guv,' Fathom reported. 'They're a right nobby lot in there – real Eton-and-Oxford types, with posh accents – and I kind of got the impression they thought he was all right for a chav, know what I mean? This bird Belinda something said something about him I didn't catch, and the others kind of smirked behind their hands.' He looked indignant. 'And him just widowed and everything! Though I s'pose,' he added, in fairness, 'that they probably don't reckon he deserves so much sympathy, now he's scarpered.'

Connolly was reliving some of her worst nightmares. Though she had been a moderately sporty child, and had enjoyed gymnastics, tennis and some athletics, she had hated outdoor team games, especially muddy ones. The agonies of school hockey were burnt into her memory. The mist of a chilly winter afternoon with the sky going pink behind the bare trees, the pitch frozen harder than iron, the grass frosted to cutting sharpness; the encroaching numbness of feet, the blue and crimson knees and knuckles, the breath smoking, the way the voices bounced on the winter-hard air, echoing like a swimming

223

pool; the agonizing, bone-deep pain of a whack on the shin, the way cuts wouldn't even bleed until you got back in the pav and started to thaw out; the maddening, burning itch of reviving skin...

This wasn't hockey, but soccer, but all the other elements were there. Still, it was a job to be done. She hunched deep into her coat, woolly hat on head, muffler wound round her neck and chin, and watched the poor eejits running up and down with blue noses, steaming like horses into the icy air. There were two matches going on on two pitches, one big guys and one medium. A lot of kids and a handful of adults were scattered around the touchlines watching. She didn't feel she stuck out too much. The referee in one match was a short, bandy-legged older guy, scurrying about with a whistle in his mouth. In the other, supervising the bigger guys' game, a young man, tall, hunky and fit, in shorts and a dark-blue rugby shirt, was a bit of a ride.

She idled along towards where a group of girls was sitting on a couple of benches watching the senior game. She strolled casually behind them and paused, listening to their chatter. Two of them on the farther bench had their heads together and were texting and giggling in tight, breathless bursts. The other three, on the nearer bench, their hands in their pockets, their jaws moving ruminatively like cows round their chewing gum, were having a 'she said, and then I said, so she said' kind of conversation. She took them to be about fourteen.

She moved slightly, coming forward at the end

of the bench so that she was in their sight line. They all looked at her and then away without interest, which was good. One of the boys on the pitch went down to a tackle, to a combined groan from the onlookers, the whistle was blown, and the ridey feller ran over to adjudicate, disappearing into a small knot of vehemence as both teams protested.

'You're rubbish, Jackson!' one of the girls shouted, and they all giggled. 'Sanchez never even touched him.'

'God, I wouldn't be them,' Connolly commented. 'That ground's hard. And why do they make 'em wear shorts on a day like this?'

The one who had shouted, who had so many freckles it looked like a skin disease, said, 'Where there's no sense, there's no feeling,' and they exchanged sly grins.

'D'you go to this school?' Connolly asked.

'Yeah,' said Freckles, and rolled her eyes at the others. Read the uniform, dork, said the gesture.

'We wouldn't be sitting here if we didn't,' said the smaller, darker one with curls.

'Oh, I dunno,' said the third, podgy and fair, with the sort of pink face that always looks sticky, and shiny lips as if she'd been eating boiled sweets. She threw a glance at the boys playing, and they all giggled. 'The view's not bad.'

'Yeah, some of 'em are well fit,' said Curly.

'Except for Jackson,' said Freckles. 'Remember that time his shorts come off and he wasn't wearing any underpants?'

'I bet you all laughed like drains,' Connolly

said. 'Poor guy.'

'What are you, his mother?' Freckles said, with routine rudeness. It was not a question.

They all watched for a moment, then Connolly asked, 'Did you see the game last Friday?'

'What game?' Podgy asked, blowing out and snapping her gum like a professional.

'Here, after school.'

'Oh, I thought you meant on telly,' she said, losing interest.

'Thursday, you mean,' said Curly. 'Thursday nights after school.'

'Oh, I thought it was Fridays.'

'Nah,' Freckles said scornfully. 'The teachers wouldn't stay late on a Friday night. They all bugger off home as fast as they can, soon as ha'pass three comes.'

'Don't blame 'em,' said Podgy. 'Get enough of this dump the rest of the time.'

'Oh, look, there's Freya,' said Curly, looking along the line at another group of girls.

'Lets go and see if she's got any fags,' said Freckles, and they all got up and hurried away, hunching together like a many-legged single entity, whispering and giggling. Apart from the fag remark, which Connolly guessed was a show-off for her benefit, they had shown her so little interest she was sure she and her questions would be forgotten within seconds. That was the beauty of that age. And grown-ups asked stupid questions all the time, so you got used to it.

Connolly moved to a different part of the touchline, watching the good-looking teacher so intently that at one point, when he ran near her,

226

he glanced over and met her eyes. She smiled, and he gave a brief half smile in response, earning Connolly a bitter look from two sixth-form girls huddled together and presumably on the same mission.

When the games finished, the older man headed straight to the changing block with his team, while the younger teacher gathered his boys round him for a debriefing talk that went on until it seemed he suddenly noticed it was getting even colder (can't *believe* it's April!) and they were hopping on the spot and rubbing their own arms. He went off with them without a glance around, so Connolly had no chance to talk to him. Well, you just have to *make* a chance, she told herself. There was a small parking area beside the changing block which she assumed was for the teachers. Beyond that was a small flight of shops, and she went and bought a newspaper and then sat on a bench on the far side of the parking area and watched.

She was in luck. In ones and twos and groups the boys came out and hurried off; some adults retrieved their cars and left; the little bandy man got in a Fiesta rust bucket and disappeared; but the ridey teacher was still inside. She got up, stuck her paper under her arm, and began to wander towards the remaining cars, pretending to rummage in her handbag while watching the door under her eyebrows.

It took a degree of skill to extend the rummaging the required length of time and still make it look natural; it took skill and a certain gymnastic agility, when the man came out (alone, thank

God, in a cosy-looking padded jacket with a large Adidas bag on his shoulder) to wander into his path at just the right moment and allow him to knock her over.

'Oh, God, I'm so sorry!' he cried, swinging his bag to the ground to offer both hands for her assistance.

'My fault, I wasn't looking,' she said. She had managed to spill a few things from her handbag, and when he had pulled her to her feet he crouched and gathered them up, while she brushed down the back of her coat. 'Thanks,' she said, as he restored the items to her cupped hands.

'Are you all right?' he asked. 'Not hurt?'

'No, no, I'm fine. Only me dignity's smarting.'

'I'm so sorry. Clumsy of me.'

'T'wasn't your fault. I wasn't looking where I was going.' She looked up and directly into his eyes. Good, he was interested. 'I saw you taking the game with the boys. You wouldn't be Mr Wiseman, would you?'

'No, I'm afraid he's not here.'

'But he'll be here later, will he? For the late practice. Don't you have practice after school on Fridays?'

'No, Thursdays,' he said. 'Never on Fridays.'

'Oh – I thought there was something last Friday, after school.'

'No, we've never had after school games on a Friday.' He gave a rueful smile. 'Too many of the parents want to get away for long weekends.'

'Oh, so I've missed Mr Wiseman, then.'

'Is it anything I can help you with? My name's

228

Rofant. Simon Rofant. I'm the other games teacher at the school. Um...' He hesitated. 'I'm afraid Mr Wiseman probably won't be in for a while. Something rather awful happened. His daughter got killed.'

'That's terrible! The poor guy. What happened?'

He hesitated again, and said, 'Look, it's too cold to stand here. Do you fancy a cup of tea? There's a café just along there.' He gestured along the line of shops.

'That'd be nice, but don't you have to be somewhere?'

He raised his hands, almost in a 'guilty' gesture. 'Nope. Footloose and fancy free. But what about you?'

'Same here,' she said, and smiled. He smiled back. Bingo, she thought.

In the café – very small and functional, six Formica tables with tubular chairs and counter service of tea and coffee, cakes, sandwiches, and an all-day vat of soup that smelled like unwashed bodies – there was a diminishing knot of schoolchildren, buying sweets and snacks with agonizing indecision. But they were gathered at the counter, and left with their purchases without sitting down, though not without giving Rofant and his companion a long, interested look followed by head-together sniggering. One table was occupied by schoolgirls, but they were all texting away, heads down, and nothing, Connolly thought, short of the Last Trump would draw their attention away from their little screens.

Rofant ignored them all magnificently, insisted on buying her a tea ('It's the least I can do after knocking you down'), and when they were seated, told her all about the Melanie Hunter murder – from the point of view of the general punter, which was interesting. Connolly explained her ignorance of the matter by saying she'd only just come over from Ireland and had been so busy with the moving the last few days she hadn't had time to read the papers or watch the news.

'Poor guy,' she said. 'What a terrible thing to happen. He must be really cut up.'

'Yes. The head told him right away to take the week off. I must say our head's decent like that. But I don't suppose he'll be back next week either. I mean, apart from what he must be feeling, and his wife, you don't want to expose yourself to the kids at a time like that. Staring eyes and prying questions. Curiosity always overcomes tact.'

'Not just with kids, either,' Connolly said. 'It must be really hard to get away from it, even for a minute. I suppose he can't even go down to his usual pub for a bit of relief.'

'No, especially not in his case. He's famously teetotal,' Rofant said. 'Disapproves of pubs and the demon alcohol.' He said it lightly, seeming to think, even as he said it, that it was a bit disloyal. He looked uncomfortable for an instant and then said, 'What was it you wanted to see him for, anyway? Perhaps I can help.'

This was always going to be the danger moment. 'I heard he did private coaching – out of school hours, I mean.'

230

'I think he does. Who told you that?'

'A neighbour of mine knows someone who knows someone he's coaching. I think she's in the sixth form,' Connolly said vaguely. The coaching would have to be for herself – she didn't want to have to invent a child.

'Oh. That must be Stephanie, I suppose. Stephanie Bentham. Small, fair girl – lives in Boston Manor somewhere?'

'I've never seen her. But I think that was the name. Well, I suppose he won't be doing any coaching for a long time now – if ever, poor guy.' She finished her tea, and made leaving movements, eager to get away now. 'Well, thanks a heap for the tea. That's warmed me up. I can't believe it's so cold – you'd never think it was spring.'

'My pleasure,' he said, standing too, his eyes on her. 'It's been nice meeting you. Would you – I wonder, would you like to go for a drink sometime?'

She would, she definitely would, but that was the trouble with what she did. You couldn't start a relationship with a subterfuge; now she had fooled him, she could never get to know him. Besides, it was near impossible to go out with any man who wasn't in the Job. They just didn't understand. While men in the Job understood too well, and were all neurotic bastards anyway. She'd had two bad relationships with coppers that ended in heartbreak and that was enough for one lifetime. As long as she remained a copper, she would have to remain alone.

'I'd really like to,' she said, putting sincerity

231

into her eyes, 'but I'm kind of half seeing some-one else. I came over here to see if we can make a go of it. Well –' she shrugged – 'you know. But thanks for asking.'

'That's me all over, wrong place at the wrong time,' he said self-deprecatingly. 'Well, if it doesn't work out, you know where to find me.'

'You've got it,' she said with a smile, and they parted on a handshake.

Isn't that just like bloody life, she thought, heading for her car. You meet a total ride, who's interested in you, who's also available – and how often does that happen? – and you can't do anything about it. Not because you've already got someone, oh no, that'd be too easy, but because you've been forced to make up some-one in order to get out of going out with a bloke you *want* to go out with. God was just a big, bloody tease, so he was, and it wasn't *fair*.

Twelve

Crowd Cuckoo Land

'But if there was no soccer practice on Fridays, why wouldn't Mrs Wiseman know that?' Atherton asked. 'She's been married to him long enough.'

Connolly counted on her fingers. 'She's confused, she's not that interested, he's told her and she's forgotten, or he's just not told her. You don't get the feeling there's much communication in that marriage. "I'm off out, dear." "All right, dear." And she sees he's got his bag with him, so she thinks, oh, he's off to football. Sure, she's not going to say "Where the hell have you been?" when he comes in, not her, not to a man like him.'

'Yeah,' said McLaren, who had been just waiting for her to finish this, which, to him, was the uninteresting part of the problem. 'But then where was he Friday evening? Even if it was him phoned Hunter at ten o'clock and arranged a meet, he wasn't with her from after school till then.'

'He wasn't where he said he was,' Atherton replied, 'and that's enough for us. Maybe he was driving about, working himself up into a rage, or

233

planning how he was going to do it.'

'Maybe he was doing private coaching,' Connolly felt obliged to offer.

'But then why would he lie to his wife about it?'

'We don't *know* he lied. She's not that bright or on the ball. She maybe just got the wrong end of the stick. Or like I said, he never told her and she just assumed.'

'Well,' said Slider, 'we'll have to ask.' He shook his head. 'Two suspects with stupid, easy-to-bust alibis.'

'They weren't stupid alibis as long as no one checked,' Atherton said. 'They were very good, solid as the Bank of England alibis. A stag night and a soccer match – dozens of witnesses to prove you were there. Much better than Fitton's "I was alone at home all evening".'

'Right up to the point when it wasn't. What's the world coming to, when villains can't even be bothered to construct a decently professional lie?' Slider complained.

'What about Fitton, guv?' Hollis asked. The forensic report had come back negative – no traces of blood or tissue in the flat, on any of the objects confiscated, or down the plugholes or in the drains. Nothing to say Melanie Hunter had been murdered on the premises. There had been no large sums of cash knocking about, and Fitton's bank account showed nothing but his benefits going in each month and coming out week by week, so nothing to suggest blackmail. That was not to say he could not have killed her outside the house, or indeed have hidden money elsewhere, but you could only go on what you had evidence for.

'We let him go,' Slider said. 'And keep an eye on him. Release him later tonight, when it's quieter around the house.'

'Ironic, isn't it?' Atherton said. 'Fortunately we've got another suspect to take attention away from him. Unfortunately, they both live in the same house.'

'There'll be plenty in the papers tomorrow about Hibbert. They'll have had time to do their homework. Let's hope all the attention will flush him out,' Slider said. 'Meanwhile, we keep our eye on Fitton. And there's going to be a fingertip search of the woods as soon as it gets light tomorrow, in the hope that, if she wasn't killed at home, she was killed there, and there's something to find.'

'And what about Wiseman, boss?' Connolly asked.

'We bring him in and ask him some questions. I'll talk to Mr Porson about it now. I think it would be nice to take him late tonight, give him a night in the cells to unsettle him, and have a go at him in the morning when he's had time to think about the error of his ways. And while he's in here, one of you can go and offer his wife a shoulder to cry on, see what comes out.'

'And the kid,' Connolly added. 'Bethany. That one'd have you mortified, the language on her, but she has a useful habit of eavesdropping. You never know what she's found out about her dad.'

It turned out to be an exciting night, not only

235

with the arrest of Ian Wiseman, who was not pleased about it and made his feelings known as vocally as a cat on the way to the vet's, but because late that evening the Bournemouth police found Scott Hibbert.

'What was it, a tip-off?' Slider asked. He had not been home yet. He was downstairs talking to Paxman about the treatment of Wiseman when the news came in, and hurried upstairs to find Mr Porson in the office, along with Atherton, and Hollis, who was night duty officer and the only one of them who was actually supposed to be there.

'Better than that,' Porson said. 'The woman he was lying low with gave him up. She sneaked in the kitchen while he was watching telly and told 'em to come and get him. They went straight round there. Found him in his underpants.'

'I wonder why they didn't think of looking there first?' Slider murmured. Atherton shot him a look. He shouldn't, he really shouldn't.

Fortunately Porson didn't catch it. He was too full of the wonder of Hibbert. 'He was watching himself on telly, the dipstick. On the twenty-four-hour news. No wonder she wanted rid of him. He burst into tears, apparently, when the Bournemouth plod came in. Anyway, they're wrapping him up and sending him over to us right away. They've got the woman in, giving her statement, pending our decision whether we want her banged up for obstruction or not.'

'We'll want to question her, won't we?' Slider said.

'Got to think of the practicosities,' Porson

236

said. 'We can't clutter up our cells with all these bodies at the same time. You've already got Wiseman, Hibbert's coming, Fitton's going – it's getting like a murderers' convention in there. Anyway, I want you to have a crack at Hibbert tonight, while he's off balance.'

'Yes, sir, but I'd still like to get the woman's side of it while it's fresh.' He turned to Atherton. 'You'd better get down there and interview her first thing tomorrow.'

'I'll have to have a word with Bournemouth, then, grease the whales,' Porson said, and stumped off to his own room.

'Why are you here, anyway?' Slider asked Atherton when they were alone. 'Haven't you got a home to go to?'

'Emily's in Ireland, covering the euro crisis,' he admitted. 'I didn't fancy going home to an empty house.'

Blimey, he did have it bad, Slider thought. Atherton had always been the cat who walked alone; now he was so much a part of the Jim-and-Emily combo, the house didn't feel right without her. 'I wouldn't have thought the house would feel empty with those hooligan cats of yours,' he said.

'Not the same,' Atherton replied. 'A cat does not keep you warm at night. Well, it does, but – you can't cuddle a cat. Well, you can, but—'

'I get the picture,' Slider said hastily. He didn't like to think where that litany was going. 'Hadn't you better go back for a bit of shut-eye before Bournemouth?'

'I'd sooner see how Hibbert turns out,' said

Atherton.

But in the end, they didn't get to have a crack at Hibbert, because he was in too bad a state when he arrived. He had been in tears all the way up, according to the stone-faced Dorset coppers accompanying him; and as soon as he walked in from the dark to the brightly-lit station he started shaking, and rapidly got so bad they had to get the surgeon in to give him a tranquillizer. After that he got a lot happier but it was impossible to interview him properly – his responses had slowed down so much it was going to take them most of the night to process him – so Slider gave it up until the morning. 'Get the woman's end of it first, then we can tackle him tomorrow from a position of strength.'

'Tomorrow's getting to be quite a day,' Atherton said as they trod out into the darkness.

'Today, now,' Slider said.

'So between Hibbert and Wiseman, which do you fancy more?' Atherton asked. 'Or is it still Fitton?'

'*I* don't know. There's something to be said for all of them.'

'All of them? You mean some kind of *Murder on the Orient Express* scenario?'

'Each of them, then, if you must be pedantic.'

'Why are people who are just trying to be accurate always called pedantic?'

'Beats me. God, I'm hungry.'

'Fancy going for a curry?' Atherton suggested. 'I know one that's still open.'

'At this time of night? You're so young.'

238

'All right for you,' Atherton grumbled. 'You have got a nice warm wife at home, who'll probably leap out of bed and cook you bacon and eggs. All I've got is the sound of my own broken sobbing.'

'Oh, go on then,' Slider said. As it happened, he felt wide awake and didn't want to go home yet. And it was ages since he'd had a curry. This marriage lark certainly put paid to a lot of the old social habits. 'We can talk some things through.'

'Good. There's a question that's really been bugging me,' Atherton said as they turned towards the Uxbridge Road.

'What?'

'Who on earth thought of putting an "s" in the word "lisp"?'

In the end, Atherton didn't go to bed: it probably wasn't a good idea to try to sleep on a substantial curry anyway, and he thought he might as well get the journey down to Bournemouth done in the early hours when the roads were quiet. So he had a shower, shave and change of clothes, played for half an hour with the cats, who were querulous about not having seen anyone All Day, and was down in Bournemouth well before breakfast time.

The first thing he learned at the station was that the woman, Valerie Proctor, was no longer there.

'She insisted on going home,' said the duty officer, one Kevin Bone. 'She'd come in voluntarily so we couldn't stop her unless we arrested her, and we didn't want to do that, because she'd have clammed up right away and asked for a brief. She's a bit of a stroppy cow, and I reckon you'll get more out of her if you don't rile her.'

'She's at home now?' Atherton asked. 'How do you know she won't do a runner?'

'In her mind she's got nothing to run from. She's turned him in, she's the good guy,' said Bone. 'Anyway, we've got a uniform on her door. To protect her from the press, we told her, but it cuts both ways, o' course.'

'Excellent,' said Atherton. 'Well, if she's safely confined, I've got time to read the reports and have breakfast before I go over.'

'We do a cracking bacon sarnie up in the canteen,' said Bone.

A female uniformed officer, Hewlitt, drove Atherton to the house and would sit in with him at the interview. 'You don't want to take chances with this one,' Bone had said.

'You think she'll jump me?' Atherton had asked. 'I know I'm generally considered irresistible, but...'

Bone, of course, did not know Atherton, and his way of talking was evidently unfamiliar down in Dorset. He had given him a very odd look, cleared his throat, and said carefully, 'She's the sort who might make an accusation against you, so you'd better have a woman PC with you, for safety's sake.'

'Thanks,' Atherton had said, chastened. No more jokes for you, my boy, he had ordered his overactive brain.

But in the car, Hewlitt, who was evidently a

brighter spark, wafted her hand about in the air after driving for a few minutes and said, 'Phew! Are you planning to gas her and get her to confess while she's under the influence? Cos I have to tell you, that's against the rules.'

'Ripe, is it?' Atherton said with a grin.

'Eight hundred on a Geiger counter, at least,' she said. 'Evacuate the reactor building without delay.'

'Sorry.'

'I don't mind. I love curry. But she might claim it was cruel and unusual. There's some Trebors in the glove in front of you. Better suck a couple.'

Mrs Proctor lived in Winton, which Hewlitt explained was a bit of a mixed area, on the edge of the classier Talbot Woods, and with some nice houses, but some not so nice.

'And what's she like?'

Hewlitt flung him a sidelong look. 'I don't want to sound bitchy.'

'Oh go on – treat yourself.'

'You're funny, you are,' she said, almost in wonder. 'Well, she's not Talbot Woods, I'll say that. And if I hadn't sworn never to be mean about other women, I'd say she was mutton dressed as lamb.'

'Good job you did swear, then,' said Atherton. 'Nobody likes catty females.'

The house, when they came to it, was a meanly proportioned, yellow-brick modern one in a small estate of identical raw new buildings, each functionally square, with the sort of porch tacked on that was a flat concrete canopy supported

241

at the front by two metal poles from which the paint was already peeling. Each house stood at the back of a small unfenced front garden which was half unsuccessful grass and half hardstanding for a car. Each house owed its upward-mobility credentials to having a garage, and a three-foot-wide strip of separation on either side between it and its neighbours. Atherton couldn't help thinking that an extra six feet of room inside would have been a better use of the space, but for reasons no one could explain the word 'detached' had mysterious magical powers over the asking price of a house.

There was a car on the hardstanding in front of the garage, a sporty-looking red Zetec S-Max.

'Menopause car,' said Hewlitt, who seemed to have forgotten her pledge.

Atherton made a note of the number and made a quick call to Hollis, to have it ANPR'd. Then they went in.

Atherton's first thought was that if Mrs Proctor hadn't turned Hibbert in, he probably would have surrendered himself in a short time. The inside of the house was decorated with so much exuberant bad taste he thought for a minute he had wandered into a traveller wedding. Mirrors, chandeliers, ornaments, pelmets; gilt, onyx, Dralon; huge vases of artificial peonies and roses; reproductions of classic paintings in gaudy gold-coloured frames crammed together in the spaces between the tassel-shaded wall-lights; a life-size china greyhound sitting in the hearth of the modern gas fire which, on this chilly day, was alight behind its glass panel and showed realistic flames licking up, inexplicably, from a heap of pebbles. There was so much bling and so many conflicting patterns, within seconds he was getting an ice-cream headache.

Atherton's second thought, which arrived on seeing Valerie Proctor, was almost as unallowable as Hewlitt's. Though nowhere near menopausal, she was obviously quite a bit older than Hibbert, at least in her late-thirties, more likely early forties. She was trim and well corseted, and had evidently redone her make-up and hair as a priority when she got back from the station, for both were impeccable. She must have changed, too, for she was wearing a smart suit. Though more subdued than her decor, it was still bright yellow trimmed with black and rather shorter in the skirt than was strictly necessary; and she was wearing very high heels, and a great deal of costume jewellery. But despite the effort she must have put in, she looked worn underneath the maquillage and somehow – to Atherton almost touchingly – even mumsy.

His momentary softness passed as she tottered towards him like an infuriated giraffe. 'I want to make a complaint, a serious complaint, about the way I've been treated,' she snapped, skewering him with a look you could have barbecued king prawns on. 'I went to the police voluntarily, doing my civic duty, and I've been held at a police station all night answering questions and now I've got you bursting in to harass me all over again. It's no wonder everyone hates the police when you treat honest citizens the way you do. You ought to try getting out and catching

a few criminals for a change, instead of per-
secuting people who are trying to help, hanging
about motorways stopping people who just
accidentally creep a couple of miles over the
speed limit, when the road was practically
empty, there was no one else about, it wasn't
doing the slightest bit of harm to a soul. It's a
disgrace the way you persecute motorists, just
because you can, and particularly women because you know they won't cause trouble. It's all
about the money, just like the cameras. You're
not really interested in road safety, you just want
the fines.'

From the seamless segue from the general to
the particular and back, Atherton surmised she
had recently been stopped for speeding in her
sporty red car and hadn't managed to talk her
way out of it. He dialled the charm up to blatant,
smiled at her admiringly, and said, 'I think it's
wonderful the way you've come forward to help
us, at considerable inconvenience to yourself,
and I'm sorry I have to ask you to go through it
all again for me, but from my own point of view
I can only say it's a privilege to have the chance
to visit you in your lovely home. If you wouldn't
mind me just asking a *few* more questions, I can
take myself out of your hair as soon as possible.
Where *did* you get those beautiful flowers at this
time of year?'

The needle was quivering on the edge of the
red zone, and he could sense Hewlitt staring at
him with her mental mouth hanging open like a
door. For a breathless moment of silence he
thought he had gone too far; but then Mrs Proc-

tor almost visibly dismounted from her high horse and said with something close to a dimple, 'They're artificial. You can't get peonies like that in April, silly. But they're very good, aren't they?' A little laugh. 'I sometimes think they're real myself, for a moment, when I catch sight of them out of the corner of my eye.'

And so it was all right. Tea and 'something stronger' were offered and refused, and in short order Atherton found himself sitting on the sofa, with please-call-me-Valerie in the armchair almost knee to knee with him and ready to tell him whatever he wanted. He was glad of the presence of Hewlitt, who sensibly removed herself out of Valerie's line of sight, but remained on hand in case of trouble. He had a feeling he was in for the long haul, and was only glad, from the way Valerie leaned forward as she spoke, that either she had no sense of smell or was particularly fond of curry and peppermint.

Wiseman knew about his rights and insisted on them, refusing to answer any questions until he had seen his solicitor, and since the one he requested couldn't at first be contacted and then took some time to arrive, a good part of the morning had worn away before Slider actually faced him over the table in the tape-room.

The solicitor, Drobcek, a small and swarthy man with an amazing crop of black curly hair, turned out to be one who had advised some pupils at Wiseman's school who had got into trouble with the law. He had a substantial criminal practice in Hayes and Southall, but he specialized in juvenile, and seemed a little puzzled that Wiseman had called on him. But he was prepared to do his best and got the first punch in, complaining that there had been no call to drag Wiseman in in the middle of the night.

'My client had made no attempt to abscond, and he is a pillar of his local community. You could just as easily have *asked* him to come in voluntarily to answer questions, which he would have agreed to do. Or if you *had* to arrest him, you could have done it at a more reasonable time, not dragged him from his bed in that ridiculous, melodramatic way, upsetting his wife and child.'

'Your objection has been noted,' Slider said, studying Wiseman's face. He looked more drawn than he had on Tuesday, as if he had not had much sleep between then and now; but the suppressed rage in him seemed to have been turned down a notch, as though some of it had been replaced with some other emotion. Apprehension, perhaps? But he still had enough anger for two normal people, and his fists – which looked very hard, on the end of extremely whippy arms – kept clenching and unclenching, as though he'd really like to smack his way out of the trouble he had found himself in.

'But as you are here now,' he went on to Wiseman, 'perhaps we should get the questions over with as quickly as possible, for everyone's sake.'

'I've nothing to say to you,' he snapped. 'You came to my house, I talked to you then, openly and freely, and nothing has changed. Don't you

246

realize the effect arresting me is going to have on my career? There are always people who say things like "there's no smoke without fire". Isn't it bad enough that we've lost our beloved daughter, without you ruining my livelihood as well?'

'She was your stepdaughter, not your daughter,' Slider said, the better to goad him.

He was goaded. 'Oh, is that what this is about? You've been reading too many fairy stories about wicked stepmothers. I always looked upon Melanie as being as much my own daughter as Bethany.'

'Even if that were true,' Slider said, 'she didn't look upon you as her father, did she? She resented your marrying her mother, and wouldn't accept your authority. You had a hard struggle with her from the very beginning.'

'All I ever tried to do was my best, to bring her up properly,' Wiseman said, his face tight with emotion. 'But it seems these days people who try to do the right thing are mocked and abused. There's no reward or admiration for virtue any more.'

'Did Melanie mock and abuse you?'

He was about to reply, but caught himself up. 'I don't have to answer your questions. I'm not saying anything to you.'

'I don't want you asking my client any leading questions,' said Drobcek.

'We're not in court,' Slider said. 'I can ask him what I want. You're right,' he addressed Wiseman, 'you *don't* have to answer my questions. But you must think of the impression it gives if you won't. It's true, isn't it, that Melanie refused from the beginning to accept your discipline? A young girl, who'd recently lost the father she adored – it wasn't surprising if you had difficulty in taking his place.'

'I never tried to take his place,' Wiseman said, provoked. 'He was a lazy, shiftless, work-shy, spendthrift waster and the world was better off without him.'

'Rachel Hunter in particular was better off without him. You were a much more satisfactory husband – one who knew his duty towards his wife and family.'

Wiseman looked put out, as if he couldn't be sure praise really was praise and suspected a trap. 'The facts speak for themselves,' he said stiffly. 'I've supported my wife and the girls properly through my own efforts right from the beginning.'

'So it must have been extra frustrating when you found you couldn't guide Melanie along the right paths for her own good.'

Wiseman glanced uncertainly at Drobcek, who gave a small shrug, indicating that there was nothing wrong with the question. 'I – did my best,' was all he said.

'And when she defied all your attempts to guide her, she got into trouble, and *you* were the one who had to bail her out of it.'

'I don't want to talk about that,' he said through rigid lips. 'It's all in the past.'

'Unfortunately, all of Melanie's life is now in the past,' Slider said, and saw the words give Wiseman a jolt. 'Isn't it true that you have something of a hasty temper?'

The fists clenched. 'I do *not*—' he began angrily, and then controlled himself with an effort. 'I won't answer any more questions.'

'And that you have hit both Bethany and Melanie on more than one occasion?'

'My client is not to be asked to incriminate himself,' said Drobcek.

Slider ignored him. 'And that in fact you hit Melanie on the last occasion you saw her before the night of her death? When she came to Sunday lunch a fortnight before, you had a blazing row with her and hit her across the face.'

Wiseman went white. 'Who told you that?' he asked furiously; and then: 'It's a lie! Who told you such a monstrous lie?'

'Your house doesn't have very thick walls. Several other people were in the next room,' Slider said, and added conversationally: 'It's curious how far the sound of a slap travels – I suppose it's the pitch.'

'I tell you it's a lie!' Wiseman said vehemently. He leaned forward, fists on the table. 'People are out to blacken me. You tell me who told such a lie about me, and I'll—'

'You'll kill them?' Slider finished for him unemphatically.

Wiseman blenched and fell back.

'Lies *have* been told,' Slider went on, 'but not about that. Not about you, but *by* you.'

'I think this has gone far enough,' Drobcek said, and Wiseman threw him a glance of relief. 'If you have evidence against my client, you had better produce it, and stop all the innuendo.'

'Very well,' Slider said. 'Where were you on

Friday night, Mr Wiseman? From the end of the school day until you got home?'

'I've already told you, I was taking soccer practice,' he said.

'And there's the lie,' Slider said calmly. 'From your lips, before witnesses and on tape. There was no soccer practice on Friday. There never is soccer or any other game after school on Fridays. The teachers are always in a hurry to get home.'

He blinked. 'I—' he began. He looked at Drobcek.

Drobcek shrugged. 'Better clear it up,' he said. 'Otherwise it does look bad.'

'It wasn't an official, school practice,' Wiseman said, thinking hard. 'It's a scratch team – local kids – I help out. We meet every Friday after school. Keeps them out of trouble. It's – a sort of voluntary work I do, to help the community. A thing I do out of the kindness of my heart.'

'Give me the names of the boys involved.'

'I ... I can't remember.'

'Give me one name.'

No answer.

'You can't remember the name of a single boy? Even though you see them every Friday?'

'I'm – under a lot of stress at the moment. I can't think clearly when I'm being attacked like this.'

'I'm not attacking you. I'm trying to get at the facts. How long did this football practice go on?' Slider asked.

He must have sensed the trap. 'I don't remember. We play until they've had enough. It goes on longer than a school practice would.'

'As much as two hours? Three?'

'Easily that. They're very keen.'

'And where did you go afterwards?'

'Home, of course.'

'So you'd have been home by – what – half past seven? At the latest. School comes out at half past three. It would hardly have gone on longer than four hours.'

Wiseman stared, his eyes desperately trying to strip meaning out of Slider's face.

'Half past seven? Would you say you got home by then?'

And Wiseman said, in a strangled voice, 'Yes.'

'And there's another lie,' Slider said. 'Your wife said you weren't home until late, until after she went to bed. Something like half past eleven.'

'She wouldn't know,' he cried. 'She's confused. She's thinking of another night. She never knows what day it is anyway. You can't take her word for it. Woolly-minded. Hopeless. You can't rely on her for anything.'

'Then *you* can't rely on her to give you an alibi for Friday night, can you?' Slider said, while Drobcek gave Wiseman an exasperated look, and Wiseman stared from one to the other, his lips moving as if there were words somewhere, but he wasn't managing to capture them.

Atherton was working his way patiently through Valerie Proctor's life story towards the part of it that interested him. He could see she was enjoy-

251

ing herself, and little as he wanted to afford her the satisfaction, he knew from the gleam of self-righteousness in her eye that she was the sort of person to whom umbrage was not something you took but something you were born with a right to. In the long run it would be quicker to let her do it her way than put her back up and have to deal with the consequences.

So he went through her childhood ('I was such a talented child. I could have gone on the stage but Daddy wouldn't have it. I sing, you know, and play the piano'), and her marriage to Proctor ('My maiden name, Critchfield, was a much better one – *and* a proper Dorset name – but Steve insisted I change, and once you have it's too much hassle to change back'), and the divorce ('I hope I'm a fair-minded person, but I'm sure I put more into this house than ever he did, so why should he have it, just to make a pigsty out of it, the way he did everything?').

She told him how she had gone into the estate agency business straight from school. 'It was always what I wanted to do – well, once I gave up wanting to go on the stage, which was never really a possibility once Daddy put his foot down. I mean, that's something you have to have support to do.' She had started as an office junior and worked her way up. 'I have a qualification, you know – NFPP.'

'NFPP?' Atherton enquired, and then wished he hadn't.

'The National Federation of Property Professionals,' she explained. 'The Technical Award in Residential Letting and Property Management is an important qualification. I mean, it's equivalent to an A-Level, you know.'

They did a brief résumé (though not brief enough) of her career through various estate agents, finishing with the Hatter and Ruck branch in Poole ('dealing with all the really expensive properties, five and six million, swimming pools, boat houses, you name it'), marrying and divorcing Steve Proctor on the way, and came at last to meeting Scott Hibbert.

'It was at an IREA – the International Real Estate Alliance – trade show. The London Property Exhibition at Earl's Court. Scott was on the Hatter and Ruck headquarters stand. I was divorced by then, of course, and – well, it was attraction at first sight. We had such a lot in common – you know, both being in the business and everything, and both being forceful, go-ahead, ambitious people. But I won't deny there was a definite animal attraction between us. A sort of mutual magnetism we simply couldn't resist. It was as if we were meant for each other. Of course,' she added, with a descent into bathos, 'I had a hotel room – it was a two-day show – which was a definite advantage.'

'I can see,' Atherton said patiently, 'that it would be.'

Thirteen

Discomfort Zone

After a break, requested by Drobcek to consult privately with his client, and the bringing of tea, which Drobcek drank and Wiseman didn't, Slider, with Mackay as his assistant, went back in and the taping was resumed.

Drobcek opened the batting. 'My client wishes to say that he was mistaken in his previous statement about taking soccer practice last Friday. His state of emotional turmoil and grief left him confused. I'm sure you will understand that.'

Slider understood, all right. 'So where were you on Friday evening, Mr Wiseman?' Drobcek opened his mouth and Slider forestalled him. 'I would like to hear it from Mr Wiseman himself.' Legally it was no less valid if Drobcek said it on instruction, but Wiseman was a self-proclaimed virtuous man and a churchgoer, and if another lie was coming Slider knew instinctively it would make a difference to *him*. He wanted to make him say the words and face the shame.

Wiseman gave him a look that could have charred a thousand-acre forest, but he seemed to have himself under control. His arms were folded so tightly across his chest it was a wonder he could breathe, and his face was rigid, but he said in a calm voice that sounded almost normal, 'I was doing individual coaching. I have several young protégés who I see privately for one-on-one coaching.'

'And which one, or ones, did you see on Friday night? Names and addresses, please.'

'I am not going to give you any names,' Wiseman said. 'It would be quite wrong to expose them to this unpleasantness.'

Ah, that was the way he was going, was it? That accounted for his air of serenity. He thought he'd found a winning formula. A glance at Drobcek showed him worried, but hopeful.

'I'm afraid I must insist,' Slider said.

'And I'm afraid I must refuse,' Wiseman said with an air of moral superiority that got right up Slider's nose. 'I am in loco parentis to these young people, and I could not betray their confidence, or do anything to expose them to unpleasantness. It would be quite wrong of me to sacrifice their privacy simply to convenience myself. I must hold to what I believe is right and face the consequences, even if they are unpleasant to me personally.'

Ooh, don't you just hate it when that happens? Slider enquired of himself ironically. Wiseman was looking at him now, satisfied he had got the upper hand, and the longing to wipe that smug look off his face was strong.

'Never mind,' said Porson. 'We'll see. He who last laughs, lasts longest.' He paused a fraction of a second, as if aware that hadn't come out right, shrugged, and went on. 'I'm not bothered about upsetting his sacred bloody young people. Flaming Nora, the stuff they watch on telly and see on the Internet these days, *I'm* more sensitive than they are! We'll find out who he coaches, if he does coach anyone. And appeal to their parents to let them come forward. It is a case of murder, after all. No sympathy to be had in that. And in the end, it's up to Wiseman to prove his alibi.'

'Yes, sir,' said Slider, comforted but not entirely cheered by Porson's confidence. 'But it's up to us to prove he killed her, even if he hasn't got an alibi.'

'Ah well. Can't make cakes without straw,' Porson said. 'We'll get him, laddie, one way or another.'

'Did you know he was involved with someone else?' Atherton asked. As it was turning into a long session, Hewlitt had gone to make tea, and Valerie kept casting nervous glances in that direction – not, Atherton surmised, because she was afraid he would jump her without supervision, but because she was afraid Hewlitt would mess up her kitchen. But the question brought her attention sharply back on him.

'Of course not. What do you take me for?'

'Did you ever get invited to his place in London?'

'No,' she admitted. 'But he told me he only had a little bed-sitter. It wasn't nice like my place. And he said it was a treat for him to get away from London, so we always met down

256

here. If I'd known there was another woman on the scene, I'd have made him sort it out double quick, believe you me. I don't share. That's what I told Steve. I said you choose, right now, because I don't share with anyone. And when he dithered about it, that was that. He was out on his ear.' She gave him a nod, her lips tight closed, the meat of her face trembling a little with the emphasis.

'Quite right too,' Atherton said, still buttering her. 'So how often did you and Scott meet?'

'Oh, every couple of weeks, I suppose. We were both busy people, and the time just flies by, doesn't it?'

'And this has been going on for...?'

'A year. A bit over a year. The London Property Exhibition was February.'

'And I read in the transcript of your statement last night that you had a business relationship with Scott, as well as a personal one.'

Surprisingly, she went red, visible even under the several layers of make-up. 'We did – he did – there was...' She didn't seem to know how to phrase it. She looked at him appealingly, opening her eyes wide and leaning forward a fraction more. 'Look, I'm not going to get into trouble, am I?'

'It depends what you've done,' Atherton said, but with an easy, I'm-relaxed-about-minor-infractions smile.

'Only,' she said, 'I did come forward and turn him in. At considerable inconvenience, not to say danger, to myself, and if there was a bit of – let's say – irregularity about our business deal,

257

well, no one was hurt by it. It goes on all the time, believe you me, but one's bosses can be a bit strict about it – well, they're bound to be, really, I suppose – but if everything was always done strictly by the book—'

'I'm only interested in the murder,' Atherton said. 'Anything else that went on is not my business.'

She looked relieved. 'So I don't need to tell you. Only, I wouldn't have said anything at the station, but I was flustered and it sort of slipped out.'

'I said it wasn't my business, but I do need to know the exact nature of your relationship with Scott, so I'm afraid you will have to tell me what you and he were doing. It could have a profound effect on the case.'

She was not fetched by the waffle. 'Does that mean I'll have to stand up in court about it?' she asked sharply.

'It probably won't come to that.'

'Will you give me your word?'

He gave a stern look. 'I'm afraid I can't do that. You will have to do your duty, whatever that turns out to be. But I know a woman of your strength of character will meet that challenge head on, with the same courage you've shown in your actions so far.' She didn't quite buy it, tilting her head a little to one side and eyeing him speculatively, so he went on in a quiet, firm tone. 'Tell me what you and Scott were doing – besides your private relationship.'

She made up her mind. 'Well, it was just a matter of bringing client and vendor together and adjusting the price between them. Which is what we do all the time anyway, estate agents. Only,' she sighed, 'when the circumstances were right, Scott would come in and convince the vendor to drop the price, and the purchaser would split the difference with us. It was a win-win situation – nobody was hurt.'

'Except the vendor,' Atherton suggested.

'Well, not really, because we'd do the sale privately so he wouldn't have to pay the agency its commission.'

'Ah,' said Atherton. Yes, he could see it all. The real victim was the agency, but as that was a company and not an individual, people like Valerie and Scott wouldn't regard harm to it as any harm at all. It came under the heading of making private calls from your company phone, stealing stationery from work or adding a new carpet to the insurance claim – a victimless crime.

'Anyway,' she went on, 'if the vendor looked likely to be difficult, I'd just stop them getting any other offers, so then I could tell them it was because the price was too high, and if they dropped it they'd be able to sell all right. And then, of course, when they dropped the price and the offer came in, I was proved right, so *they* were happy.'

'Wouldn't they wonder why other people's houses were selling for more?'

She looked dismissive. 'You can always find *something* about a house to bring the price down. The punters don't know any better.'

'And presumably you'd only be doing it on

really top price houses,' Atherton said. 'So a small percentage worked out at a nice commission.'

She seemed to take this as a criticism. 'We didn't do it very often,' she protested. 'It would've been too risky to chance anything but the occasional property. And the circumstances had to be right – the purchaser had to be on board. But Poole being what it is...' She shrugged.

Yes, thought Atherton – the most expensive real estate in the country, hitched on to a top-whack marina.

She looked unhappy. 'But just lately I'd been feeling that the risk wasn't worth it. I was on at Scott to stop while we were ahead, and for him to make the break with London, move down here. I wanted us to set up as independent estate agents. We had all the skills between us, and the contacts, and I couldn't see why Hatter and Ruck should get all the benefit from our hard work and expertise. With the money we'd already made we could cover set-up costs, and there's plenty of scope for a new player in the field. Frankly, Hatter and Ruck are a bit stodgy and old-fashioned. I mean, they're OK for selling Georgian vicarages, but for the new sort of client that's coming into the market now, people with lots of cash money to spend, especially for the newer properties, places like Poole, and the luxury flats that are going up in Bournemouth...'

'And Scott wasn't willing to go along with your plans?' Atherton asked sympathetically.

'Oh, it wasn't that. But he wanted us to do one

last job, a big one, make a big killing before we stopped. And I was a bit nervous about it. It was outside my comfort zone, if you want to know. But he said he'd be doing all the hard work and taking all the risk. Well, I didn't quite see it that way. But anyway, I said that if we were going to do something like that, he should make the break with London, he should move in to my house, we should get married.' She looked to see if he understood.

'You wanted some kind of assurance that you were in it together?' Atherton said.

She looked relieved. 'Yes, right. Well, even though we'd been going out for over a year, we didn't see all that much of each other, and I didn't feel I knew everything about him. Which proved to be true,' she added bitterly, 'because when I said that about getting married, he told me about being involved with someone. Actually living with her.'

'How did he explain that away?' Atherton asked.

'He said it was all over between them before he met me. He said he'd been going to leave her for a long time, but she was very neurotic, and he had to pick the right moment because she might self-harm. He said she was anorexic and she'd been having psychiatric treatment so he had to be careful. He promised he would sort it all out and we would get married, but he couldn't control the timing.' Now she lifted to his face eyes that were haunted. 'I never knew,' she said, 'I swear to you I never knew that he was going to kill her. That wasn't what I thought

261

he meant. If I'd had any idea, I'd have gone straight to the police. That poor girl...' She shuddered.

'But you'd seen in the papers and on television that she'd been murdered?'

'I'd seen it, yes, but I wasn't that interested. I mean, there's always someone being murdered, isn't there? I don't read the gory stuff, I just skip over the headlines. And of course, I never knew her name, so I never connected it with Scott. Why would I?' she appealed for forgiveness.

'He hadn't contacted you, then, since the weekend? Not to tell you she was missing or anything like that?'

'No, I never heard from him – but that wasn't unusual. He wasn't a great one for talking on the phone. Usually I'd just get a call when he was planning to come down again. I never even knew when he turned up here Thursday night. I mean, he looked terrible – unshaven, dirty, smelling of drink. He'd just really let himself go to the dogs. Obviously something bad had happened.'

'Didn't you ask what?'

'I started to, but he said, "Leave me alone. I can't talk now," and I could see he was in a real state, so I thought I'd leave him alone till he was a bit more together. To be honest, I thought he'd finally broken up with this other woman and it had been a bit difficult, so I thought a bit of sympathy on my part would—'

'Point up the contrast,' Atherton supplied.

She looked a little reproachful, but didn't contradict him. 'But then he started watching the

262

news all the time, and I saw the police were looking for him. I said, "What have you done?" and he said, "Nothing." But then he said, "They're after me for Mel's murder." *Then* I got the connection. Well, then I knew what I had to do. I gave him a lot of scotch, to try to make him fall asleep. But he just wouldn't go off. But he was so into the telly and looking at himself on the news, I thought he wouldn't notice anyway. So I told him his clothes needed washing – which they did – and took 'em away so he couldn't make a run for it. And I phoned the police. And they came round and took him away.' She looked distressed. 'You should have heard his language! And then he started crying. I didn't know where to look, I was that asham-ed.' She shook her head, musing. 'I don't know how I could have been so wrong about him. I should've known from the beginning he was no good. When I first met him, at Earl's Court, and we went to my hotel, instead of his house.' And she added in a burst of angry frankness. 'Going up to my room, he farted in the lift.'

'That's wrong on so many levels,' Atherton murmured.

Mrs Wiseman was beyond being of any help to anyone. She seemed to have sunk and spread into the armchair she sat in, like a jelly on a plate beginning to melt. It was Bethany who answered the door, and hurried Connolly into the living room as if she hoped she could save them both; and she hung around the back of her mother's armchair looking by turns scared and defiant.

263

'D'you want to go and make your mammy a cup of tea?' Connolly urged, to get her out of the way.

'She's not my mammy,' Bethany objected, 'she's me mum. You don't half talk funny. And she's had cups of tea all morning.'

'I bet she could do with another,' Connolly said.

'You want me out of the way so you can talk about Dad killing Mel,' Bethany said. 'Well, he never. He wouldn't do that. My dad's the best, and when he gets out he's gonna sue the lot of you for false arrest, then you'll be sorry.'

Connolly looked at her kindly. 'I know you're upset, and no wonder, but we're not going to hurt him. We just want to ask him a few questions, that's all.'

'Then why d'you have to arrest him for? That's like saying you think he did it.'

'Not a bit. We arrest a lot o' people. It's a process we have to go through. We ask them questions then they're free to go. We only want to find out the truth about what happened to Melanie. You must want that too.'

'I don't care,' Bethany said, close to tears. 'She's dead. I just want my dad back.'

'Well, hop and make your mum a cuppa, and let me ask me questions, so. The sooner that's done, the sooner we can sort it all out. Ah, g'wan, that's a good girl.'

She extracted herself by unwilling inches, and all this time Mrs Wiseman had been sitting staring at nothing, only her fingers moving as they screwed and shredded a damp tissue between

264

them. Connolly hunkered down by the chair so that she was at face level, and said, 'Mrs Wiseman, it's me, Detective Constable Connolly. Rita. We talked before, d'you remember?' There was no response, and no eye contact, but she thought the woman was listening. 'I just want you to cast your mind back to that Friday, the day Melanie disappeared.'

'The day she was killed,' Mrs Wiseman amended harshly. So she was listening.

'Your husband was out all evening, is that right? Until what time?'

'I don't know. I don't know anything any more. What does it matter anyway? Mel's dead. She's not coming back.'

'But you still have Bethany,' Connolly said. 'You've got to be a mother to her, poor wean. You've got to make the effort to hold on.'

The tortured eyes came round, red-rimmed and exhausted. 'You think Ian did it? You think he killed her?'

Connolly had to take the opportunity. 'Do you think he could?'

'I don't know.' She stared, her mind revolving like something trapped in a space too small. 'He was out that evening,' she said at last. 'But he was often out, after school. Only, he was later back that night. He didn't come in until after I was in bed. That couldn't have been school stuff, could it?'

'Where did he say he'd been?'

'He didn't say. He didn't speak to me. I was in bed. I heard him come in and go straight to his bedroom.' She shook her head wearily. 'We

265

never talked about his work any more. In the beginning he'd sometimes tell me what he'd done at school that day, but not lately. Not for years.'

God, what a sterile life, Connolly thought. 'Could it have been private coaching he was doing that night? Did he do private coaching?'

'No. I don't know. Maybe,' she said. 'He never said he did.'

Connolly tried, 'Could he have gone out again after he'd gone to bed? Would you have heard him if he did?'

'I'm a sound sleeper. I wouldn't hear.' Still she stared into the mid-distance, but not in the dazed manner of before, but as if she were watching something unfolding, a movie of events being replayed for her private torture. Her eyes widened as if she saw a new scenario she had not yet contemplated. 'A father wouldn't kill his own child,' she said, almost in a whisper. 'It's not possible.' Suddenly she gripped Connolly's forearm with fingers that hurt. 'Did he do it? I have to know. Did he kill my Mel?'

Connolly tried gently to unlatch the fingers, but they were like steel bands. This poor tormented woman deserved the truth, but what was that? Connolly didn't know. 'I can't tell you. I don't know. We're trying to find out, that's all.' She put a bit more effort into prying the fingers loose as her arm was going dead under the pressure, and the next moment something flew at her and hit her round the back of the head, not hard, but heartfelt.

'Don't you hurt my mum!' Bethany cried as

Connolly, her arm released, fell awkwardly on her behind on the carpet. 'I'll kill you! Don't you touch her.'

'I didn't hurt her,' Connolly said, wondering whether to rub her arm or her head. It was only the rolled-up *Radio Times*, she saw, in the child's hand. If she'd come from the kitchen, lucky it wasn't a knife. Did homicide run in families?

'You get out! I knew I shouldn't leave her alone. You get out now!' Bethany shouted, elevated above the childish by her furious defence of her stepmother. Connolly moved towards the door, with Bethany ushering her like a sheepdog. Connolly almost expected to have her heels nipped. At the front door she paused with her hand on the latch and said, 'Bethany, we have to find out where your dad was, so that we can cross him off. There has to be someone who can say where he was. Only, he wasn't at soccer practice, you see.'

'If you knew where he was, would you let him go?' she asked, suddenly sharp.

'Yes, if we can find someone who can swear to it. Did he have private pupils? You know, for sports coaching?'

Bethany suddenly looked very young, and frightened. 'I don't want to get into trouble.'

'You won't, I promise.'

'But you won't tell Dad I told?'

'No, pet, I won't.'

Bethany chewed her lip. 'Only, my friend Georgia's dad does some work in the evenings he doesn't want anyone to know about, 'cos of the taxman, and she says he'll go to prison if

267

anyone finds out. You have to tell the taxman everything you do, and he doesn't.'

'So your dad is teaching private pupils in the evening, is he?'

'I dunno. I think so. Only, you won't tell him I told you? And you won't tell the taxman?'

'Neither one nor t'other,' Connolly swore solemnly. 'How d'you know about it?'

'I heard some sixth-form boys at our school talking about someone seeing one of the teachers after school, and then one of them said my dad's name, and one of them said, "He's working on her forehand grip," and then they laughed. I don't know why – it wasn't funny.'

'No, *alana*, it wasn't. Is her name Stephanie?'

'I don't know. I never heard. It was me dad's name that made me listen. He must be giving her tennis coaching.'

'Is that where your dad was on that Friday?'

'I don't know. But this time, Georgia was in her mum's car coming home from her gran's, and they passed our car on the A40, and there was a girl sitting beside me dad, like, older than me. He never looked round so he didn't see, but Georgia said it was definitely him but she didn't know the girl. And that was a Friday night.'

'Did Georgia's mum see him and the girl?'

'No. She was looking at the traffic lights, saying, "Don't change, you bastards, don't change." Dad doesn't let me say bastard. He says it's swearing. But Georgia says it isn't really, it just means someone you don't like.'

'Well, you'd better not say it if your dad doesn't like it,' Connolly said judiciously, glad the child had calmed down. She didn't like to leave her all alone with a whacked-out mum. 'Would your mum's friend not come in and mind yez both?' she asked. 'That Mrs Sutton? She seemed nice.'

'She's all right,' Bethany said listlessly, and then thought of something. 'Would she cook us some dinner? We haven't had anything to eat today, except cornflakes, cos I can do those.'

'I bet she would,' Connolly said with utmost sincerity. 'Wait'll I ask her. Number forty-eight, isn't it?'

She was eager to get away and track down Stephanie Bentham, but she could not in conscience leave this waif to cope alone. But she felt sure that Margie would be only too willing to get back on stage, and negotiations would take only as long as it took her to grab her handbag.

Slider left Wiseman to stew for a bit, and went to see if Scott Hibbert was back from the land of the fairies. He looked terrible, and didn't smell any too good, either. Obviously his stay first at the hotel, and then at Valerie's, with no work to go to and nothing to take his mind off his sins, had sent him on a downward spiral, for he was sporting several days of beard and did not seem to have bathed for the same length of time. He was wearing a nasty pair of sweat pants and a zipped fleece top over a T-shirt, his hair was matted and his feet were shoved bare into a pair of battered-looking trainers that were adding something of the ripe Gorgonzola to the olfactory mix in the cell.

Slider looked at him through the wicket. His eyes were inflamed and rather crazed-looking, and he sniffed constantly and wiped his nose on his cuff. 'Is he all right for interviewing?' he asked O'Flaherty, the sergeant on duty.

'If y'ask me,' O'Flaherty said without sympathy, 'him and reality's never been on first name terms. But he's no worse than the average headbanger we get in here. Sure, you can talk to him if you think it'll help. The doc's signed off on him, and he's about as able for't as he'll ever be. Tape Room One?'

'Trot him along. I'll be there in five minutes,' Slider said, and went to collect Norma, so as to have fresh ears on the case.

Hibbert scrambled to his feet as soon as Slider entered, and was gently pushed back down by Gostyn, the uniform minding him. 'Are you the boss around here?' Hibbert asked, his eyes flitting nervously to Swilley and back. 'I want to talk to the boss.'

'I'm the investigating officer,' Slider said, and introduced himself and Swilley. 'Are they treating you all right?'

'Yes, yes, but I want to talk to you,' he said urgently.

'You can, son, just settle down. I'm going to ask you some questions and I have to ask you if you want a solicitor to be present.'

'They've already asked me that,' he said almost petulantly. 'I don't want a solicitor. I just want to talk to whoever's in charge.'

Slider managed to shut him up for long enough

to get the tape rolling according to protocol, and then he was off.

'You've got to understand, it wasn't the way it looked. Valerie. It was just a business arrangement. Of course I had to keep it secret from Mel because she wouldn't have understood. Women never do. But Val was good, the best in the business, and she had the contacts, so I needed her for that end of it. And she was – well, you saw her. She's not a bad-looking woman but she's a lot older than me, and a bit desperate. Anyway, she made it clear enough I was going to have to give her a bit more than just money to get her on board with it. What was I to do? I had to keep her sweet or she could have blown the whole thing and landed us both in trouble. She wasn't that bad, actually,' he said, his mind wandering. He stared vacantly at Swilley, who stared back blankly, not to disturb him. 'I mean, she knew a thing or two – you know, in bed – and I'm not saying I'd have needed my arm twisted in normal circumstances. But I didn't set out to be unfaithful to Mel.'

'What was the nature of this business arrangement you had with Valerie?' Slider asked, to get him back on track.

Hibbert explained it pretty much as Valerie had to Atherton, but with a lot more detail. 'But the thing was,' he went on, 'she was obviously more interested in me than the job, and she'd started hinting about me moving down there with her. Then she started talking about marriage. So I knew I didn't have much longer before I was going to have to dump her. But we had this really big job coming up. It was a developer thing, the biggest job I'd ever had a hand in. This row of houses with big gardens. The developer wanted to pull 'em down and put up blocks of flats. He didn't mind saving a bit of money wherever he could. If we could get the owners to sell, and get the prices right, we were sitting on a million quid for our trouble – and all cash, tax free. You don't get chances like that every day of the week. So I had to keep her sweet, Valerie, until it was done. I had to pretend it was her that mattered to me. I even had to pretend I might marry her. But I never *wanted* to be unfaithful to Mel. It was just business.'

He looked to them for sympathy for his predicament.

'Tell me about that Friday, the weekend of your friend's wedding.'

'Well, I was down there, of course. Doing this deal. Val and me had to wine and dine the developer and get it all tied up. The wedding was a blessing, because it meant I could get away on Friday. There was a stag night thing going on, so I said I was going to that. Saturday I had to go to the wedding, but I got away as quick as I could, and Val and me pretty much worked through the night putting it all together. Then she started on about our marriage plans again, and saying we could have a lovely Sunday together, just her and me, so I thought it was a good idea to get out while I could. So I went back to London Sunday morning.'

'So it wasn't the case that Melanie was the

one thing standing between you and your new life down in Bournemouth, making lots of lovely money in a hot housing market?' Slider said.

Hibbert looked stunned. He licked his lips. 'I know you think I killed her. I've seen it in the papers, and on telly. You think I did it. Well, maybe I did. She was a cracking girl, Melanie, but she was too good for me. All her friends thought so. She was smart and clever and educated and everything, and all I had was – well, I don't know what she saw in me. I'm good at what I do, that's all. I'd got this plan to turn the flats in the house where we live into two maisonettes. Would have made a lot of money. But I don't think she liked it, because it meant getting that old fool Ronnie out of the basement, and he didn't want to go. She liked him, God knows why. I think,' he said, with a hint of anger, 'she liked him more than me, sometimes. It was always waifs and strays with her. Anyone with a hard luck story. She didn't appreciate someone who got on and got ahead through their own efforts. She just didn't appreciate money, thought it didn't matter, though she didn't mind spending mine. It was a good job I made good bread because she never had a cent. Dunno what she spent it on. But I still think she'd have loved me more if I was an ex-con like Ronnie or a waster like her father.'

'It's hard not to be appreciated,' Slider said.

'Yeah,' said Hibbert. He flicked a look at the impassive Norma, then returned his congested eyes to Slider. 'Maybe that's why she had to go,

273

so I could start a new life with Val. *She* appreciates me. She knows she's lucky to get me. I'm good-looking, I'm young, I've got a nice car, I've got what it takes to make money. What more does a women want? She made me mad sometimes, Mel, the way she was always so much better than me. I couldn't drop my socks on the floor, had to put them in the laundry basket. It's my bloody floor, just as much as hers! Bloody laundry basket – who has one of those? And the way I held my fork – that didn't please her. And she was always correcting my grammar. How d'you think that makes me feel? She didn't like my ties. She didn't like my signet ring – *her father* never wore jewellery, she said. And everything in the house had to be done the way *she* liked it. I brought her home this ornament once – kind of like a fairy, with wings and everything, holding some flowers – china you know. Well, Val's got one, and she likes it, and I saw one like it in a shop, so I brought it home, a present for Mel, and you should have heard her! Well, she didn't actually *say* anything, I mean she said thanks and everything, but you could see she didn't like it. Practically put gloves on to touch it. And you know, that fairy never made it to the mantelpiece. I never saw it again. I reckon she must have put it in the bin when I was out of the way.'

'She didn't like your friends, either, did she?' Slider suggested.

He glared at Swilley, who seemed to be becoming a substitute for the absent. 'No, she bloody didn't. She thought she was too good for

274

them. She said they were boring. That's why the wedding was such a good excuse, because I knew she'd never want to come.'

'So it served her right, really, that it *was* just an excuse.'

'Yeah!' Hibbert cried. 'Stuck up, snotty cow! Served her right! You're all the same, you bitches, think you're better than us!' And he flung himself across the table at Norma, trying to grab her by the throat.

Norma moved like lightning, catching his wrists and slamming them down on to the table with a strength hard-won in endless arm-wrestling bouts since she first joined the Job. Slider and Gostyn were round the table and got a grip on his elbows, but in truth Swilley could have held him on her own. Motherhood had taken none of her edge, Slider thought with satisfaction.

But Hibbert didn't struggle. He'd cried out in pain when his wrists hit the table, and yielded as soon as Slider and Gostyn grabbed him. When they let him go, he collapsed slowly forwards on to the desk, cushioning his head in his arms, and sobbing brokenly. 'I killed her,' he wept. 'I really, really loved her. I don't care if Dave said she was a snotty cow. I loved her, and I killed her, and now I've got nothing. I wish I was dead!' He finished on a howl, and said nothing more coherent.

Slider watched him dispassionately, knowing there would have to be another visit by the doctor to make sure he was not hurt – his cry of pain was on the tape, and the sounds of scuffle –

and that if another tranquillizer was administered they wouldn't get to interview him again for hours, by which time the impetus would be gone.

Fourteen

Virgin Athletic

When Connolly finally tracked down Stephanie Bentham, she was with a bunch of other youngsters in typical Saturday afternoon mode. There was a patch of green with a bench and a bus stop beside it, and they were hanging about there, some sitting on the bench, some standing, one sitting, arms crossed, on his bicycle, pushing himself an inch forward and backward monotonously with his foot. They were chatting, laughing, texting, two of the girls were smoking with faint defiance, and the atmosphere was so heavy with teenage hormones it could have triggered a Control Order under the Clean Air Act.

Stephanie was a little apart, sitting on the rail surrounding the green. Connolly thought she had never seen anyone look so unhappy. She was hunched, her hands between her knees, and when Connolly stood before her she raised wide desperate eyes like a cornered hind staring at the hunter.

'Are you Stephanie?' Connolly asked, showing her brief, but discreetly, shielded by her body from view of the others.

Stephanie nodded.

277

'I need to talk to you. D'you want to walk along with me? No need for them to know your business, is there?'

She seemed beyond being grateful for that, but she hitched herself off the rail and fell in beside Connolly, walking away from the group, some of whom, Connolly noted from her eye corners, looked their way, but not with great interest, God love 'em. Ah, the self-absorption of youth!

'I've me car round the corner,' she said to Stephanie when they were clear. 'We can sit in that for a chat if you like.'

Stephanie looked a moment of alarm. 'No. Not in the car,' she said quickly; then seemed to collect herself and said: 'Can't we just walk? There's the park down there.'

The car, Connolly surmised, was playing some leading part in the feature movie going on in the girl's head; or maybe she was afraid of being abducted.

'Walking's fine with me,' Connolly said cheerily. 'Sure I don't get out in the fresh air enough.'

She thought she would wait until they were in the park to begin, to build up some trust between them, or at least let her get used to her, but before they reached the gates Stephanie made the first move. 'It is right?' she asked, without looking at Connolly. 'Did – Mr Wiseman – did he really kill his stepdaughter, like they're saying?'

'Who's saying that?' Connolly asked.

'The others.' She gestured backwards. 'Everyone at school. They say that's why he's not been in. They say the head's sacked him, and now

278

you've arrested him.' Now she looked at Connolly, appalled. 'If he's a murderer...'

'We arrest a lot of people,' Connolly said for the second time that day. 'It's what we have to do sometimes to question people – it's a technical thing. I won't bother you with it, but it does not mean they've done anything, necessarily.' Stephanie was staring at the ground again, trudging miserably. 'You care about him, don't you?' Connolly said gently. A startled look. 'Ah, g'wan, I know all about it. You can tell me.'

The head went even further down. Her next words were so tiny they were almost indecipherable. 'Will my mum and dad have to know about it?'

'It may not come to that,' Connolly said. 'You're seventeen, right?'

'Last December,' she confirmed.

'I can talk to you without your parents, so. Look, pet, if I can keep it quiet I will, but it's not entirely in my hands. But you've got to do the right thing. You know that, don't you?'

Nod.

'Did you know Melanie Hunter?'

Shake. 'Only what's in the paper. My mum reads every word, she's obsessed with it. Knowing that – Mr Wiseman's one of our teachers makes her more interested. If she knew – you know – she'd go mad. My dad'd kill me. And the others – they wouldn't understand. They think he's just a boring grown-up, a teacher. They don't know...'

'The other side of him,' Connolly suggested. Pass the sick bag, Nora.

279

Stephanie looked up, eager and hopeful of understanding. 'He's not like he seems in school. He's different. More – gentle, and – he talks to me, like a real person. Not like Mum and Dad. They just, like, issue orders, and when they ask you questions they don't listen to the answers. But Ian – Mr Wiseman—'

'You can call him Ian to me,' Connolly said.

Stephanie looked doubtful.

'You're quite close to him, aren't you?' Connolly went on. Anyone who could think Ian Wiseman was a fluffy bunny-rabbit must be pure dotey on him. It'd sicken you, she thought, but she kept her face kindly and interested. Plenty of time to throw up later. 'You're fond of him?'

'I love him!' Stephanie burst out. Evidently the pressure to tell had overcome the dam of fearful restraint. 'And he loves me! I know he's married, but he doesn't love his wife. How could he? She's old and fat and dull and – and she doesn't understand him! She's not interested in anything he does, just sits at home watching TV all the time. He's a wonderful person, and she just doesn't get it, how lucky she is. And now he's in trouble, and he needs me, and I can't see him! *She* won't be any use to him. He's all alone, and I can't help him!' Huge tears formed in the doe eyes.

Connolly hastily thrust a tissue at her. Love a' God, she'd want to listen to herself! 'Come on, Stephanie. Cool the head, now. Sure, nothing's happened to him. He's just answering some questions for us. And you *can* help him.' A blurry look of hope. 'Stop the crying, now, blow your nose, and talk to me like a sensible woman.'

They had come to a bench, fortuitously empty, and Connolly thought it better to sit down while Stephanie got herself together. She provided a couple more tissues, and mopping up was soon achieved. Stephanie stopped crying as easily as she had started, but she still looked miserable – and why not? Connolly thought.

'So tell me about Ian,' she said. 'He's coaching you, is he? What is it, tennis?'

'No,' Stephanie said. 'That's just the excuse. Someone saw us together and one of the other teachers asked him, so he said he was coaching me. It kind of spread, a bit, and a few people at school think I'm getting coaching, which is a laugh really, because I'm no good at sports. If it got to my mum and dad they'd go mad, because they'd know it wasn't coaching, cos they'd have to pay for it, and they're not, so you won't tell, will you?'

'So what *do* you do together?' Connolly asked, leaving that one.

'Go out in his car, mostly. Go for drives. We stop somewhere and sit and talk, and—' Suddenly she blushed, richly, and Connolly felt a quickening of pulse. 'We go to the pictures sometimes,' Stephanie went on quickly, as if to avoid the subject. 'And for meals, or we get a takeaway and eat it in the car. When the weather was nicer we sat outside, like on Horsenden Hill or somewhere like that.'

'It's been going on for a while, so?'

'Since September. When we came back to

281

school. I bumped into him the first day back and dropped my books and he helped me pick them up and kind of touched my hand accidentally and we sort of smiled at each other. And then he said, "Glad to be back?" and I said, "Yes," and he said, "Me too," but I knew he meant something different by it, from the way he was looking at me. And I started hanging about after school to see if I could catch him coming out, but he's got games a lot after school. So I started staying to watch and he saw me and one day after a match when he came out from the changing rooms he saw me and said I must be frozen and would I like a cup of tea.' Her eyes were misty with rapture. 'So we went to this café out Uxbridge way, where nobody'd know us, and we talked and talked. And that was the start of it.'

'So you've been meeting regularly since then?'

'Whenever he can. It was awful over Christmas because there was no school and he was with his family and I was with mine and all I could think of was that we ought to be together. I couldn't wait to get back to school. And the minute I saw him—'

'Great,' Connolly said, to forestall any more syrup. Gak! That muscle-bound, narky little eejit? The girl was a looper. 'Did you have a regular day you met?'

'No, it was any time we could manage, but it was often a Friday evening because there are no games after school on a Friday. Weekends were harder, because of our families.'

'What about Friday week past? Did you see him then?' Connolly asked, as casual as open-toed sandals.

Stephanie sighed like a high-speed train going into a tunnel. 'That was the last time I saw him.'

'Tell me about it.'

She seemed only too glad to – a chance to discuss her beloved? Bring it on! 'We met straight after school. I walk up to the main road and there's a place where I wait for him, where there's never anyone around, and he comes along in the car and picks me up.'

'And what did you do then?'

'We went to the pictures,' she said.

'Where?'

'The Royale Leisure park. You know, on the A40, by Park Royal station. It's big enough so no one'd see us. We went to the four fifteen show, then when we came out we got something to eat.'

'In a restaurant? Or a pub?'

'He doesn't go into pubs. He doesn't drink. He says it rots your brain and ruins your body. We went to cafés sometimes, but more often it was takeaways.'

'And that Friday?'

'He took me to Starvin' Marvin's – you know, that American diner, sort of opposite the Hoover building?'

'I know it,' Connolly said. Your man's a prince, she thought. It sat beside the A40 trunk road, a silver Airstream caravan-type construction, decorated inside with chrome and neon and boasting of real American diner food of the nachos, wings, ribs and burgers type. Reviews Connolly had heard of it were mixed, though the malted milkshakes were supposed to be good. McLaren had been an occasional customer before his recent epiphany, but as McLaren would famously eat a dead pony between two baps that didn't necessarily count as an endorsement. But romantic candlelit tryst it was not.

'Let me see,' she said. 'You went to the four fifteen show, so you'd be out o' there, what, half six?'

'Quarter to seven,' Stephanie said.

'And you'd be in Marvin's an hour, maybe?'

'I don't know. I wasn't watching the clock. About that, I s'pose.'

'So call it eight-ish. What did you do then?'

'Went for a drive. It was a lovely night – cold, but kind of icy-clear, you know? Ian said we should go somewhere out in the country where we could see the stars. You can't see them where there are street lights. So we did.'

'Where did you go?'

'I don't know. We drove for a while. Where we ended up, it was kind of hilly, and there were a lot of trees, and not many houses about. Something Woods, I think he said. Ash Woods, was it? I dunno. But we ended up in this car park on top of a hill, with, like, all trees round it, and in front it kind of dropped away down the hill. And you could see millions of stars up above. It was beautiful.'

'And you did what there?'

'Talked,' she said. She blushed again.

'And? Did he kiss you?'

284

She looked mortified.

'More than that?'

Hurt and angry eyes in the blazing face met Connolly's. 'We were lovers! He was my first ever. We'd been lovers all along, nearly since the first time! You think I'm just some stupid kid with a crush on my teacher, but you don't know! We loved each other! We were going to get married!'

'Did he tell you that?'

Amazingly, the blush intensified. She was so red you could have stuck her on a mast to keep aircraft away. 'We talked about it that night. He said how unhappy he was with his wife. He said he was going to leave her as soon as he could find the right time to tell her. Then we'd be together. We'd get married. He said he'd probably have to leave his job, but he'd soon get another one. And we'd have to move away somewhere people didn't know us. And he said he'd have to find a way to tell his daughter, because she wasn't that much younger than me and she'd find it hard to accept. But he said all problems were there to be solved, and we'd solve them.'

Connolly didn't know what to make of this. Was he flying a kite, or shooting a line? Did he really want to cut loose with a wee teeny-bopper, or was he just saying it to keep her sweet? Or – the idea came to her with a sudden rush of blood to the head – was he planning his post-murder escape, and thinking he might as well have some company along for the ride? The bit about having to leave his job ... moving away ... Another thought occurred to her, unwelcome

285

and shocking, but it would explain some things, notably Stephanie's deep unhappiness.

'You're not pregnant, are you?'

She couldn't get any redder, but her eyes filled with tears. 'No,' she said. 'Course not. We do all about that at school. But I wish I was! Then I'd have something of his. I don't care what you say, I don't believe he's a murderer. You don't know him like I do. He could never do that. He'd never lift a finger to a soul.'

Connolly thought of telling her that he hit his daughters, but didn't. Sure, the whole thing was blown now and she'd probably never see him again, so what harm? 'So how long did you stay there, makin' love and gazin' at the stars?'

Her eyes narrowed. 'Are you making fun of me?'

'Far from it. I see no fun in the whole caper. Did you not think he was spinning you a line? You'd want to cop on to yourself, a nice bright girl like you. Men like him don't leave their wives.'

'They do! All the time!' she cried passionately, but in her eyes was the bitter knowledge that Connolly was right.

'Listen, willya – men that are going to leave do it right away. The ones that talk about waiting for the "right time" never do it. Ah, c'mon, I'm not givin' out to ya. We've all gone through it, fallen for the wrong geezer and made a holy show of ourselves. You're not the first and you won't be the last. But this time it's important, because other things hang on it. So I need you to tell me how long you were up this hill, wherever it was, and what time you came home.'

'I don't know how long we were there,' she said, half sulky, half passionate. *Sure if she tells me love knows no time I'll be forced to clatter her,* Connolly thought. 'It was hours, anyway. We didn't want to leave each other. But my dad goes mad if I'm out after midnight – honestly, he's such a dinosaur! – so we had to go. Ian drove me home and dropped me at the end of my road, like usual, and when I got in it was a quarter to twelve.'

Ah, thought Connolly. Another grand theory down the Swanee. 'You're sure about that?'

'Yeah. Course. I looked at the clock to make sure I was all right.'

'So you'd been with Ian the whole time, every minute, from around four o'clock until a quarter to midnight? Every moment?'

'Yeah,' said Stephanie, looking vaguely proud of her prowess as Ian-time-consumer; until something else occurred to her, her eyes widened and her jaw dropped like the temperature on a Bank Holiday. 'Is that – does that mean – is it his alibi? Am I his alibi? Does it mean he didn't kill her after all?'

'If you're telling me the truth,' Connolly said.

'I am! I am! I swear it! Oh, I knew he didn't do it! He couldn't!' For a moment euphoria reigned, and then drained slowly from her young little face. 'But – it'll all come out now, won't it? I'll have to go in court and swear it, and my parents'll know, and everyone at school. Will he get into trouble? I mean for – for me? I'm over age, but...' Her face had sunk to misery level

287

again. 'But he's married, and he'll have to take care of his wife and kid. He'll go away and I'll never see him again. It's all over,' she concluded with absolute certainty.

'Yeah,' said Connolly. She could say no less; but she said it with sympathy. The poor kid had got it bad, and she wasn't one to dance on the body, even though this was one wake that should be welcomed by all. Stephanie'd had a lucky escape, though she was too dumb to see it. But she'd only want a run-in with Mr ClearBlue to put sense on her.

'So when someone was killing Melanie, Wiseman and Stephanie Bentham were in a car park somewhere wearing the head off each other,' Connolly told Slider on the phone. 'She says he left her home at a quarter to twelve.'

'That's too late for him to have got over there and murdered Melanie before the food left her stomach,' Slider said. 'Which means he's in the clear. Unless she's lying?' he added.

'She's knickers mad about him, and she'd tell a lie at the drop of a hat to save him, but I don't think she is. She told me all that before she realized she was givin' him an alibi. I think it's gospel, all right.'

So Slider went back to Wiseman, who was looking worn now, more than angry: worn and depressed. Probably the realization of the complete destruction of his life either way had arrived in his brain.

'Do you want to tell me where you really were on Friday night?' Slider asked.

'I've told you,' he said, with an effort at a snap. 'I have nothing more to say.'

'Even if I tell you I *know* where you were, and with whom?'

Wiseman flinched.

'And it was nothing to do with coaching – or not coaching of any sport known to the Olympics board, anyway.'

'How *dare* you make jokes—' Wiseman began, mottling.

'I truly don't think it was very funny,' Slider said seriously. 'You're lucky the girl was of age, or you could be facing very serious charges.'

'I never—' He swallowed. 'I don't know what you're talking about.'

'Oh, must I spell it out for you?' Slider said wearily. 'The girl has told us everything, voluntarily. You've been having an affair with one of your pupils, a seventeen year old called Stephanie Bentham, and at the time of Melanie's death you were with her, having sex in your car in a car park. A very shabby figure you will cut if that comes out.'

'She – I never taught her. She wasn't my student,' Wiseman said feebly.

'I don't think that is going to make any difference, do you? So here's the thing – this brave girl is willing to risk her reputation and face angry parents and the ruination of her hopes and future to give you an alibi. Unless, of course, you want to confess to murdering Melanie, and tell us where you really were and exactly what you did that night.'

'But I didn't! I didn't kill her! I *was* with

Stephanie. Now you know I'm innocent, you'll *have* to let me go.'

'You're going to rely on Stephanie, are you? Let her sacrifice herself for you? Hasn't she sacrificed enough already?'

'What do you want me to say? I *was* with her. She's telling the truth. I was with her all evening. I can't tell a lie, can I?'

'It hasn't bothered you before,' Slider said.

Drobcek objected, but his heart was no longer in it. There was going to be no brilliant defence of a murder charge to make his name after all. He was back to juvenile shoplifters on Monday.

'But I couldn't contradict Stephanie and call her a liar when she's telling the truth,' Wiseman said. 'You have to let me go now, don't you? Doesn't he?' he appealed to Drobcek.

'Do you have any other evidence against my client?' Drobcek asked.

'Hold your horses,' Slider said, though it was mere endgame flourishing. 'We have to check the alibi first.'

'It sounds as though he's covered, then,' Porson said with disappointment. He had wanted Wiseman ever since he heard about him hitting Melanie. He didn't like hitters. And the nature of this new evidence made him unhappy. He doodled a series of ducks on his phone pad. He liked ducks. They always sounded as if they were laughing. They took your mind off things. When he retired, he was going to find a house with enough room for a pond and get some. 'What about this girl? Is she pukka?'

'Connolly believes so. We can check the early parts of the alibi, but the important part, covering the murder time, is down to her alone.'

'What do you think?' Porson asked sharply, looking up.

'My gut instinct is that she's telling the truth, and therefore that it wasn't him.'

'Hmm,' said Porson.

'And we don't have any other evidence against him. If we let him go, and it was him, it might put him off his guard. Then if anything turned up, we could catch him unawares with it.'

'Suppose he scarpers?'

'I don't see him as the type, sir. He sets a lot of store by respectability. Once he's free, he'll want to re-establish his reputation.'

'And what about the girl? She'll be in a shed-load of trouble.'

'Unless we charge him, her evidence needn't become public. If she keeps her mouth shut, and Wiseman does, it may all blow over for her.'

It was the best they could hope for. Porson nodded. A big pond. With a little island in the middle, so they can sleep safe from foxes. 'He's ruined anyway. He wasn't wrong about that. The school won't want him back.'

'But he's been vindicated. They'll have to take him, or disparage the rule of law. And that will be good reason for him to keep his mouth shut about the girl, because he'd certainly lose his job over *that*.'

'Why should he get away with it?'

'He shouldn't. But if he doesn't, she doesn't.'

Maybe a duck house – just a plain one. A little

wooden cabin. He sketched straight walls and a sloping roof. 'I suppose you're right,' he said. He thought of the girl infatuated, and Wiseman debauching her, and Melanie still dead, and sometimes he felt the whole weight of human nature on his neck, crushing him down. He *needed* ducks. The simplicity of them. And the quacking.

'Let him go,' he said. 'Warn him to keep his mouth shut about the girl. And get after Hibbert. Half a confession's better than no bread.'

'Yes, sir.'

Slider was at the door when Porson said, 'What's that poem? Learnt it in school. About bees, or beans, or something, and living on an island, and a cabin, or some such?'

Slider, who had long ago given up being surprised by anything Porson said, dug through his brain. 'Do you mean "The Lake Isle of Innisfree", sir?' He quoted, '"Nine bean rows will I have there, and a hive for the honey bee."'

'Sounds like it. Mention a cabin?'

'Yes, sir. "And a small cabin build there" – that's the second line.' He waited for enlightenment.

Porson grunted. 'Any ducks?'

'Ducks? I don't think so. But to be honest, I only know the first verse. I suppose there might be ducks later.'

'Have to be later,' Porson said. 'Retirement plan.' Slider was looking at him, just faintly puzzled. 'Well, what are you standing there for? Get on with it!' he barked.

Slider got.

As he reached the office on his way to his room, Norma was on the phone saying, 'He's in with Mr – oh, no, here he is, just walked in.' She held out the receiver to Slider. 'Atherton, boss.'

'I'll take it in my room,' he said.

Swilley looked at him with motherly affection as he trudged past thinking vaguely, though she knew it not, of ducks and beans and sex in cars. 'You look cream crackered, boss. Shall I get you a cuppa?'

'Would you? I need one before I go and tackle Hibbert again. He's all we've got now.'

'Bad news on Wiseman?'

'I'll tell you when I've taken this call. Maybe it'll cheer me up.'

But Atherton, always cheery, said, 'It's bad news. It looks as though Hibbert's a washout.'

Slider whimpered. 'But he's confessed.'

'Really?'

'Sort of.' Of course when a man was in the emotional state Hibbert was – and particularly if he's a self-obsessed, grandstanding sort of bloke with a taste for fantasizing – there was always the danger of false confessions. But hey, when you got nuthin you got nuthin to lose. A man can dream, can't he? 'And Wiseman's no good. We found his alibi.'

'You had to go looking! So – what? He was doing private coaching?'

'Of the carnal sort. Nice young sixth-former says he was with her all evening, and at the crucial time they were testing his car's suspension in a deserted car-park, somewhere, we

293

guess, in the Chilterns.'

'No wonder he lied about it. And didn't tell his wife,' said Atherton. 'Instant dismissal for that. But it lets him out?'

'Unless she's lying, but we don't think she is. And now you're telling me Hibbert's no good?'

'I've been running the marathon with Valerie Proctor,' Atherton said wearily. 'It seems—'

'I've heard all about the scams and the doinking from Hibbert,' Slider forestalled him. 'He was only servicing her to keep her on side, according to him.'

'She didn't know about Melanie, according to her. What a prize pair!'

'We can compare notes later. But what's this about an alibi?'

'On Friday evening, when he wasn't at the stag, Valerie says they took a developer out to dinner at a posh restaurant in Christchurch, to discuss Hibbert's idea for a big scoop. There were delicate negotiations to be made, feelers to put out to see if the developer was crooked enough to go along with it, so oiling the wheels was considered a good idea.'

'You keep saying "the developer". Doesn't he have a name?'

'She didn't want to tell me that, and I didn't press, because she says they'll certainly remember them in the restaurant. Apparently merry was made and the festive board groaned. The bill came to over six hundred quid, and restaurant staff tend to remember that, especially in Bournemouth – on the subject of which—'

'Which?'

'Bournemouth – can I come home now? I promise to be good.'

'Don't you like it? Jewel of the south coast, I've always heard.'

'Valerie's interior decor's given me a migraine. And it's not good for me to mix with people who think dishonesty is just fine, as long as they're the ones doing it.'

'You're too delicate to be a policeman. Remind me again how you got into the Job.' It was a famous mystery, long disputed in the canteen, but Atherton had always liked to be enigmatic and had never told, not even Slider.

'Nice try, guv,' came the reply, 'but no banana.'

'So what time did the party leave the restaurant?' Slider asked, going back to work. Not that there was any urgency about it, if Hibbert was blown and his confession just self-indulgent hysteria.

'Close to midnight, she says. A fine cognac was going round – and round – and round. Then Valerie and Hibbert went home for a celebratory two-step – I don't even want to think about that – after which he passed into a heavy sleep. She slept too, but she said when she woke at eight on Saturday morning, he hadn't even changed position, and he didn't surface until after ten.'

Slider sighed. He'd sighed so much lately he was going to have to replace his battery. 'I suppose she could be lying to cover him.'

'Two chances – fat, and slim. Now she knows about Melanie and thinks he killed her, she's desperate to be rid of him. She turned him in, remember.'

'She could just be trying to save her own skin.'

'But she doesn't know how the murder was done, or when, so she didn't even know she was giving him an alibi until I showed an interest in the detail. She seems to think 'e done 'er in on Saturday, when he left her ostensibly to go to the wedding. Now she knows Saturday night was important I think she'd like to take it back, but she can't.'

'Always the problem,' Slider said. 'You can't ask people questions without warning them about what you want to know.'

'Fine, fine, but can I come home now?' Atherton asked impatiently.

'You have to visit the restaurant first,' said Slider sternly. 'We've had enough of people giving us alibis they think we won't check up on. Go and be diligent. And quick, because if he didn't do it, I want to get rid of him. I don't like the bugger, not one little bit.'

'Valerie's a hero, really,' Atherton remarked.

'All women are heroes. There's not one man I know that I'd want to put up with on a domestic basis.'

'Except your dad.'

'Well, of course. Now stop stalling, and go.'

'So why did you run, you dipstick?' Slider asked Hibbert, who looked so unappealingly crusty a public health inspector would have closed him down.

The restaurant had amply confirmed the alibi – one of the waiters even knew the developer and was eager to tell them his name, address in a glamour-pad in Poole, mobile phone number and the identity of his mistress, a former beauty queen who had been Miss South Coast Resort two years earlier and was installed in a glass-and-chrome 'luxury' flat overlooking the sea on Overcliff Drive. And the ANPR had not found any movements of Valerie's car between Bournemouth and London, so even if everyone was mistaken about the time, he'd have had to go and murder Melanie by train. He was as clear as it was possible to be in this naughty world.

Hibbert was massively deflated. Out from under his latest trank, he had got a severe lungful of cold reality. He was not Cap'n Jack Sparrow, swooping up doubloons from under the noses of his fat corporate bosses. He was not Heathcliff, driven to noble madness and murder by over-mastering love. He was a bloke with a job at an estate agent's (which he might well lose, if his scams came to light) and nothing to show for his life but a few flashy suits and a motor he still owed payments on. And no girlfriend. When he went home, Melanie was not going to be there. The house would be cold and smell funny and the washing wouldn't have been done. And he really had loved Mel. She had been part of his grand design, the top wife enhancing his status as he climbed to higher things. And she had adored him. Now she was dead. He stared at Slider in abject misery.

'I knew you lot were after me,' he said. His voice was hoarse from all his recent troubles. 'I thought you were going to frame me for Mel's murder.' His lower lip trembled. 'I didn't want to go to prison. I was scared. Terrible things happen in there. Ronnie told me once. About these big boss cons who run everything, all muscles and tattoos, and when someone like me comes in they—' He gulped and squeezed his eyes shut. 'I don't even want to think about it.'

Slider could imagine Fitton, who didn't like Hibbert and thought him a big soft ponce, indulging in a little light blood-curdling as they passed in the dustbin area of a Monday night.

'Then why did you say you killed her?'

Hibbert's frightened eyes were those of a small boy who had been egged on to something too serious for him by bigger boys. 'I – I s'pose I sort of got carried away,' he confessed abjectly.

Slider almost felt sorry for him. 'It happens a lot,' he said.

'And then there were none,' Porson said disgustedly. 'A week on, and we've got nothing. Unless Ronnie Fitton still comes up trumps.' He brightened slightly. *'He's* got no alibi, anyway, good or bad.'

'But we've no evidence against him.'

'I know that!' Porson snapped. 'Blimey, I wouldn't have thought you'd want to boast about your incomptitude at a time like this! Your job is to *get* the evidence. The press is going to be all over this by Monday.' He stamped about a bit, and Slider understood that his anger was not against him, but the perversity of fate and, most importantly, the pressure put on them all by their bosses' fealty to the press. He turned to Slider,

steam now vented, and said quite kindly, 'You look all in. Go home. There's nothing more you can do today. They're going on with the finger-tip search tomorrow, and maybe something'll come up. Take tomorrow off, do some thinking, come back fresh on Monday.'

'Yes, sir,' said Slider.

'Don't look so blue, laddie,' Porson said. 'We've come back from the brink before now. I had one case in Finchley where we didn't even have a single suspect until nearly three weeks in. Keep plugging away. Slow and steady wins the race.'

Likewise, Slider thought as he trudged away, if at first you don't succeed, don't try skydiving.

Fifteen

Tough On Crumbs,
Tough On the Causes of Crumbs

'I'm so glad to see you,' Joanna said, meeting him in the hall. His heart rose for a fraction of a second before she went on, 'You did remember your dad's out tonight, then.'

'Tonight?' he said, bleary-minded.

'It's Saturday, honey. Scrabble club, Wednesday and Saturday.'

'And you've got a concert.'

'You know I have. Festival Hall tonight and repeat in Croydon tomorrow. Paris Symphony and Mendelssohn Italian. More dots between 'em than a Seurat mural. Oh my achin' fingers.' She eyed him warily. 'You *didn't* remember.'

'I'm sorry,' he said. 'But I'm here now. Dumb luck.'

'Just as well. I've got to get going.' She patted his arm. 'Don't look like that. I had a back-up plan. If you didn't arrive, I'd arranged with your dad that I'd ring him on his mobile and he'd come back.'

'He doesn't have a mobile.'

'Fat lot you know about your own household! He bought himself a pay-as-you-go last week for

300

this very reason. He said with two of us on impossible schedules, he had to make sure he was reachable at all times.'

'That man's a marvel. A giant of conscience.'

'He's a lot like you,' Joanna said, leading him towards the kitchen. 'Or you're a lot like him.'

'And you're a giant of understanding,' he said. 'I don't deserve you.'

'Yes you do,' she said easily. 'Because I'm going to leave you to finish Georgie while I get ready.'

'We're not going to be calling him "Georgie" are we?' he asked anxiously. 'It sounds like the fat spoiled boy in a *William* story.'

'Oh, get on with you! He's just a little lad. He'll have a dozen names before he settles into one.'

George lifted a beaming face to his father, a smile that washed away all the day's miseries and the sins of the Hibberts and Wisemans of Slider's world. 'Daddy!' he said, as if it was the best thing that had happened to him all week.

'How's my boy?' Slider replied. He was sufficiently devoted to family life not to blench at the quantity of mashed food spread around George's face and the immediate vicinity. The only good thing you could say about it was it gave purpose to the sea of crumbs underneath it.

'Can you finish giving him his supper, and then he'll need a bath before bed. You needn't wash his hair, though. I've got to hustle now. There's roadworks in Earl's Court *and* on the Embankment, so it doesn't matter which way I go.'

'Fine, hurry along. I'll hold the fort.' He drew up a chair beside his son and peered into the plastic bowl. 'What is that you're eating?'

'Cabbot, Daddy,' George said, digging his spoon into the orange gloop. Mashed carrot, one of his favourite things. And the other stuff was avocado. 'Green!' George called it, digging in his rusk with the other hand. And chopped chicken, Slider recognized.

'Yum yum,' he said encouragingly.

'Yum,' George agreed. 'More now.' He was pretty efficient with the spoon, as long as he concentrated; though he had to be supervised or he often reverted to his hands; and if he grew bored he had learned a lot of interesting things you can do with purée, a spoon, and human bodily cavities – not necessarily his own.

'Let's see some action, then, son. Lock and load,' Slider urged.

George obliged, glad to show off his prowess before the other half of his parent, but he wasn't really eating. It was the mechanical process that interested him, and after watching for a bit Slider took the spoon from him and despatched the rest in a few swift scrapes.

Having wiped the slurry from his son's face and hands, he said, 'What's next? Is there pudding, boy?'

'Puddie! Yogog!' George said. And, as his father approached with it, 'New spoon.'

'You're getting very dainty in your old age,' Slider remarked. 'Speaking of which do you know how old you are?'

'Two o'clock,' George answered.

Slider was impressed that he knew a numerical answer was required. 'Not yet you're not,' he said, and spooned yoghurt into him. Usually George was determined to feed himself, but he was tired now, and allowed himself to relax and be serviced by the Big Stoker.

Joanna came back in, looking gorgeous, as always, in her Long Black. She didn't like changing at the Hall, and travelling in her black meant she could make a quicker getaway at the end. Slider gave her a wolf whistle and she smirked self-consciously. 'You watch it, or I'll make you put your money where your mouth is,' she threatened.

'Oh yeah?' Slider sneered back. 'My dad can beat your dad.'

'I haven't a doubt. I'm going to leave a bit early, if you're OK, because of those road works. Has he eaten everything? You are good! You and your dad are much better with him than I am.'

'But he only has one mother.'

She stooped to kiss him. 'Bless your heart, I'm not jealous. Listen, I can see you've had a hard day and I want to ask you about your case, but I just haven't got time now. If you can stay awake, shall we talk when I get home?'

It was only after he heard the front door slam behind her that he realized he hadn't asked what was for supper. Never mind, he'd find out sooner or later. He went through the pleasant, laundry-scented, life-affirming rituals of bathing his son, putting him to bed and reading his story with his mind idling in neutral; kissed the rose-petal cheek, and went downstairs to the kitchen

303

to feed the inner beast. He was hungry now.

But for once the system had broken down: nothing had been prepared for him. Nothing in the slow oven, nothing in the fridge, no little billy-doo anywhere explaining what had been planned. Homer, i.e. his perfect wife, had nodded. Probably she had thought Dad was doing something and Dad had thought she was. Well, it just showed how lucky he was to be catered for every other evening, like someone out of a 1950's Electrolux advert. Anyway, the fridge wasn't bare. There were eggs, there was cheese, there were tomatoes and – treasure trove – some cold potatoes. With a few herbs and a dash of Tabasco he knocked up a handsome big omelette – well, big, anyway – and ate it at the kitchen table with the newspaper open and unread beside him. His eyes might focus on the Middle East or the latest MP sex scandal, but his mind wouldn't. It wanted the evening off.

Joanna rang during the interval. He could hear the thunderous murmur of voices and the clinking of glasses behind her. 'I forgot to get you any supper!' she wailed.

'I managed. I'm not helpless, you know.'

'That's my seven stone weakling! George go off all right?'

'Couldn't keep his eyes open. How's the concert?'

'I can't tell you here – far too public.'

'Oh, like that it is? Conductor woes? Or too much scrubbing?'

'Both. In spades. How well you know me.'

'I'm a fully paid-up orchestra husband. Good

audience?'

'Is this you chatting to me on the phone, like you used to before we were married?'

'Romantic, isn't it? Reminds me of those heady days when—'

'Be careful how you end that sentence. If you were going to say "when we were in love"...'

'No, when we couldn't see each other whenever we wanted.'

'I wouldn't call them heady, then. Anyway, we still can't see each other whenever we want. Little thing called work, remember that? Listen, gotta go. The Leader wants to use the phone. *Jawohl, mein führer. Zu befehl,*' she said aside, and then to Slider: 'He loves all that kind of thing. You should see him puff up ... Ow! Ow! Not the hair!' And she was gone.

She got back tired, but not terribly late, and not yet 'down' from the performance, so he easily persuaded her into a large g-and-t on the sofa with him before the fire.

'Dad in?' she asked.

'About ten minutes ago, but he went straight to his own rooms.'

'Did he say anything about his Scrabble-fest?'

'Like what? I don't think winning is the primary reason for going.'

'Of course it's not. I think he's got a girl-friend.'

'What? No. Not Dad.'

'Why not?' she said with vicarious indignation. 'He's a very attractive man. You're not one of those people who think your parents can never love again once they're widowed?'

Despite himself, Slider thought of Melanie. He said mildly, 'He never has, all these years.'

'Well, he probably didn't have much chance,' Joanna said, 'stuck out there in carrot country, a hundred square miles of mud in every direction. Doesn't mean he's not a man all the same.'

'Well, what makes you think there is some-one?'

'Woman's instinct,' she said mischievously.

'Don't give me that baloney.'

'You don't really think he's developed a craze for little plastic tiles in his old age? And what about the new trousers and jumper he bought? And the aftershave he wears when he goes to "Scrabble night"?' She did the inverted commas with her fingers, ludicrously exaggerated.

'All circumstantial,' Slider said. 'Give me one piece of firm evidence.'

'Well, oh mighty detective, it so happens I saw him outside that mini-mart on the High Road when I went past in the car on Thursday, talking to a very nice-looking lady of mature but well-preserved aspect.'

'I dare say he talks to a lot of people. He's a friendly person.'

'Believe me when I tell you, they weren't just discussing the weather. There was body langu-age going on. Possibly hand-touching, couldn't swear to that, but definite, incontrovertible body-language.'

'And you saw all that while whizzing past in the car?'

'Who said anything about whizzing? The

lights were red and I was slowing down for them.' She looked at him over her tumbler. 'You're not jealous, are you?'

He rearranged his face. 'No, of course not.'

'You sounded cross. And looked it.'

'Oh, not about Dad. I'd be delighted if he had a new—' He couldn't think of the word.

'Amour?' she supplied facetiously. Then, 'It's the case, is it?'

'Yes. All our suspects have turned out not to be, and after a week of grind we've got nothing at all.'

'Do you want to talk about it?'

He looked at her for a long moment, his brows furrowed in weariness and trouble. But he said at last, 'Not really. Not now. Or I'll never sleep. Tomorrow morning, if you're up to it, I'd love to dump all my problems on to your shoulders. You haven't got a rehearsal, have you? It's a repeat?'

'Just a seating rehearsal in the afternoon, so I'm all yours for the morning. We'll get your dad to take George out somewhere for an hour, and have a nice heart-to-heart.'

'That'll be nice.'

But he was still furrowing, so she said, 'Would you like to hear my troubles? Like a nice go of toothache to take your mind off your dicky tummy?'

He roused himself. 'Have you got troubles, my love?'

'Boy, howdy! This cold weather is terrible for us fiddle players. Makes it impossible to tune. You're up and down like the Assyrian empire. And I'm terrified the old girl will crack with it, and then what'll I do? Even if the insurance is enough to replace her, I'd have a whole new fiddle to get used to. And coming in from the cold and having to start playing right away is the worst thing for the old tendons. And my neck's been killing me for weeks now – I think it's partly because the boy's getting so heavy, but it's probably mostly from playing. It gets us all in the end, you know – the unnatural position, sitting for long hours, the tension of performance.'

'Have you—' he began, but she was off and running.

'Patsy's left and I've got a new desk partner. Kid called Ravi Shukla – nice lad, but still wet behind the ears, good technique but he hasn't learned yet to be a section player. And he comes in late *every single entry*. It's driving me mad. And he keeps forgetting to turn – seems to think that because I'm a woman, it's my job. I've told him the inside player turns, and he just smiles with those perfect bloody white teeth and says sorry and lets it drop clean out of his mind. Next time I'm going to kick him, hard, and he'll probably put in a formal complaint and get me sacked.'

'Couldn't you—'

'And to crown it all, we've got Daniel Kluger conducting us for a whole season. *Kluger*! With his curly bloody hair and his perky little bum and his teenage groupies hanging round him, and his press conferences, and the media think the sun shines out of every orifice, but he *can't conduct for toffee*, and we're the poor schmucks who have to pick up the pieces when he carves up – which he does with monotonous regularity. But he's got recording contracts so we have to have him, and we have to suck up to him, and say *sorry maestro* when he tries to bring us in a bar early and we ignore him for the sake of the bloody music.'

She stopped, drew a breath, smiled, and said, 'That's better.'

'Is that it?'

'That's it. Just about. For now.'

He leaned across and kissed her. 'Thank you,' he said humbly.

'For what?'

'For reminding me that I'm not the only person on this planet with problems. I tend to get immersed to a state of blinkeredness. I'm sorry if I've been selfish. As soon as I can get out of the other side of this case, I'll make it up to you.'

'That'll be nice.'

'Think about something I can do for you, to make you happy. When the case is closed.'

'Oh, there is something. And it doesn't have to wait until then.'

'What's that?'

'Finish your drink and I'll show you.'

Slider lay awake, the darkness pressing on him soft and unpleasant, like a fat person sitting on his face. The wind had gone round and the iron grip of the cold had loosened at last – the temperature must have gone up ten degrees since they went to bed. He had to slip his feet surreptitiously out from under the duvet to cool off.

Beside him Joanna was full fathom five, down

deep where the busy and good go by night; but he had known as soon as they turned out the light that he would not sleep. Somewhere in the darkness, untouchable and near, Melanie Hunter waited, creeping towards him in encroaching tendrils like grave-damp. She was dead; nothing for her now but decay and oblivion; nothing of her but the faint whimperings of her ghost.

But what had she been? She had lost her father when she was hardly more than a child; had lost her own child soon afterwards. She had gone to the bad, then had tried to make good. Her child taken from her – she had always been more sinned against than sinning. She had done her best to be what she had been expected to be, worked hard, succeeded, got a career, helped others, tried to love Scott Hibbert – tried so hard, because you have to love someone, don't you? And good boyfriends are hard to come by. But she had not wanted to marry him, not dared risk a child. How far had she really consented to the abortion? How deep did the guilt run in her?

He heard her in the darkness, but could not hear her words. *Tell me who did it*, he begged her. He felt around restlessly in his mind for the end of a thread to catch on to. He had spent the evening, before Joanna came home, reading through his copy of the notes, which he had brought home; but they refused to fall into any pattern, just whirled about like leaves blown by a gusty wind.

She had tried to be good, make something of herself, had succeeded pretty much. But something was wrong somewhere. Ronnie Fitton had said there were things no one knew about her. She had a secret. Was it the secret that killed her?

Fitton said she wasn't a happy person; that everyone fed off her and no one cared how *she* felt. Life and soul of the party – the smiling clown, sad under the paint, that old cliché. But clichés became clichés because they were true. She was loved by many – but not enough. And then, perhaps, someone had loved her too much?

Wiseman and Hibbert, both so tempting, but both out of the frame. So unless it was Fitton after all ... Say, for the sake of argument, it wasn't Fitton. We're back where we started; clean slate. Begin again, forgetting surmises. Begin again with what we know.

She went home, stopped off for a Chinese takeaway – but it wasn't for her. She'd just had a big meal; and she didn't, in fact, eat it. She must have bought it for someone else. But who would you buy a late-night takeaway for? A flat-mate, your boyfriend, a housebound neighbour just possibly. Someone close.

She parked the car and went into the flat, but came out again with only her door keys. And, presumably, the takeaway. So it must have been almost immediately or the takeaway would have gone cold. Came out with only her keys, so she had expected to go back, and soon. Just pop out and back again. To deliver the food? Where? A neighbour? But then why hadn't they come forward?

She came out with just her keys but she didn't go back in. She wasn't killed in the flat or anywhere in the house. She left the area – but not in her car. So: someone else's car. She got into someone else's car and drove away with them, despite having only her keys with her. If she wasn't coerced, it must have been someone she knew and trusted – like Hibbert. But it wasn't Hibbert.

And the takeaway – she must have taken the takeaway out with her. So could it be that she had bought it *for* the person in the car? But why, then, drive off with them? And if they had a car, why couldn't they get their own takeaway?

Because they had no money? There was the missing two hundred quid. Hibbert could have taken it, of course. But maybe it was the takeaway person. But they had a car. Yes, but you can have a car and be strapped for cash on a short term basis. But who would she do such a thing for? And even if she gave them money and food, *why did she get into the car*?

Hibbert worked because he was the person closest to her; Wiseman worked because of his temper and because he had spoken to her on the phone just before she left the Vic and bought the takeaway. Why had he denied that, by the way? But it wasn't either of them.

Something happened in his mind, a click and thunk, of things shifting and falling into place. It was like the bit in an Indiana Jones film when a lever is pulled and massive blocks of stone re-arrange themselves to reveal a secret door. It couldn't be, could it? He felt the blood running under his skin as the excitement of ideas increased his heart rate. It seemed unlikely; there

312

were large problems in the way; and yet it answered many other questions.

At all events, they had nothing else to go on; it was worth a shot. And he knew that now he had thought of it, he would never rest until he had made the enquiries. He oozed carefully out of bed, gathered his clothes and took them to the bathroom to dress, went downstairs and put the kettle on. He couldn't go yet, not at this time of night. He would spend the rest of the time, until it was a civilized enough hour to leave, reading the file again.

If it were true, would she have told Fitton? No – and Fitton said he didn't know. But might he have guessed? Possibly. Possibly. He was a man who had had more to do with sudden death than your average punter. And he had loved Melanie.

Joanna came downstairs with George who – Slider realized belatedly – had been bouncing and chuntering up there in his cot for some time, possessed by the urgency of his usual early morning hunger.

'Couldn't sleep?' Joanna asked. She put George in his chair and located and delivered a rusk to his grasp almost without opening her eyes. She yawned mightily and George stared at her with huge eyes, David Attenborough encountering a new species.

'Sorry if I disturbed you,' Slider said.

'You didn't, this time. I was out to the wide.' She rubbed her eyes, and only then registered what he was wearing. 'You're going out? she said, and didn't manage to disguise her disappointment. Well, she was only human. And she'd planned a lovely leg of lamb.

'I'm sorry,' he said abjectly.

'It's because it was a girl, isn't it? You're never like this when the victim's a man.'

'Not true. I always feel responsible.'

'All right, but it's worse when it's a female. Especially a young one.'

'I can't help it,' he said unhappily. 'Men are supposed to protect women and children. That's what we're for.'

She softened. 'You're a dear old-fashioned thing.'

'Don't mock me. Not you.'

'No, I wasn't. You're right. So, can you tell me about it?'

He hesitated.

'OK, I know.' He never would articulate when his thoughts were only half formed, in case speaking drove essential links away. 'But you're going out,' she said.

'I'm sorry,' he said again.

She shrugged. It was only what she had come to expect. Unlike Irene, his first wife, she didn't resent him for it. But then she had a job that took her away at unreasonable hours, too. Perspective made all the difference to a marriage. 'Just tell me this – you're not going to do anything dangerous, are you? There won't be guns? Or knives?' she added. Knives were almost worse. For while a bullet might go anywhere, a knife was almost sure to go somewhere.

His face cleared and he smiled; like one of those April days when the clouds suddenly part

314

and for an instant the sun belts down as if it had been doing summer up there all the time. 'I'm just going to look at some records,' he assured her.

It was definitely milder. The wind, he discovered as he stepped from the house, had backed westerly, bringing with it an unbroken grey cover of cloud, too high for real rain, but dispensing the sort of fine mizzle you don't even realize is there until you turn your face upwards and feel it prickling your skin like tiny insect feet. Haar, his mother had used to call it. She said it always came when you'd just put your washing out. The absolute disproof of the adage it never rains but it pours.

Greenford came under Ealing police, and he went first to their headquarters in the hope that they had kept copies of everything, because otherwise it was the Home Office or the Department of Transport, neither of which was likely to be welcoming, let alone accessible on a Sunday. The previous boss of the Ealing CID, Slider's old nemesis Gordon Arundel – a serial womanizer known behind his back as Gorgeous Gordon, who had also been notoriously unhelpful to coppers outside his own borough – was no longer there, having been promoted suddenly up and sideways like a lamb snatched by an eagle. Rumour had it that he had been doinking the borough commander's wife and daughter at the same time, unknown to any of the three of them, or his own wife, until one exquisitely embarrassing Christmas party when a social collision took

315

place that would have seen the Hadron physicists drooling with envy.

On the other hand, DC Phil Hunt, the rhyming policeman, who had once been one of Slider's firm, was still there, and as luck would have it was on duty that day. Hunt was easy to manipulate: chit-chat a few minutes, reminisce a few minutes, hint that they could do with his unique qualities back at Shepherd's Bush (with fingers crossed behind his back that he didn't take him at his word and put in for a transfer) and Hunt was ready to move heaven and earth to prove to Slider that he *could* move heaven and earth. The crash records? Yes, no problem at all. Yes, they had everything, except the papers from the subsequent public enquiry – all the original records from the time of the crash and the immediate aftermath, certainly. He would take Slider down to the records room personally and make sure he had everything he wanted.

The records clerk was a young female uniform who looked at Hunt as though she had just found him on her shoe. Hunt, however, had always been as perceptive as a box of rocks when it came to women, and said in a proprietorial manner, 'This is Mo Kennet, the wizard of the records room. My old boss, DI Slider, Mo, all the way from Shepherd's Bush on an important mission. The lovely Mo will see you get everything you want, guv. Just leave it to her.'

Hunt loitered as though he intended to stay and officiate, and Kennet and Slider stood locked in a bubble of embarrassment, until she roused herself to say, 'Thanks, Phil. I'll take care of it.

Hadn't you better get back and man the phones?'

He beamed nauseatingly. 'Always looking after my welfare, is Mo. Famous for her kind heart – isn't that right, love? When are you going to come for a ride in my car? I know you like motors.' His voice changed from crass suggestiveness to pure love when he went on, 'I've just had this new exhaust kit put in – cost over a hundred quid just for the parts, but it was worth it. You should hear her now – purrs like a big kitty till you put your foot down, and then—'

Hunt always had been able to bore for England about his cars, which Slider had believed had taken the place of a sexual partner in his life. He intervened while he and Kennet still had the use of their faculties. 'Thanks a lot, Hunt. I appreciate it. I can manage from here.'

Kennet made an eloquent face at Hunt's departing back, but became completely sensible when she turned to Slider to ask him what he wanted. In ten minutes he was sitting at a reading desk with the first of the files, while she brought in more and dumped them on the neighbouring desk to leave him room.

'That's the lot, sir,' she said finally, brushing her hands off. She looked at him curiously. 'If there's anything I can do to help...? I mean, it was before my time, of course, and I only know what I remember from the news, but I'd be happy to trawl for you if there was anything in particular you were looking for?'

'Thanks, that's very kind. I'm on a bit of a fishing expedition, but I'll give you a yell if I need help.'

317

'Okey-doke. I'll just be through there.' She gave a rueful smile. 'Nothing much on today, so I'd be glad of something to do. Get you a coffee or anything?'

'No, thanks, I'm fine. Thanks a lot.' He smiled at her kindly and she obediently removed herself, though curiosity was sticking out all over her like boils. A good girl, that, he thought. She could go far.

He began to read.

Sixteen

Sleight of Hand

It had been a terrible incident, with a hundred and eight killed and two hundred and twenty-four injured: the second worst rail accident ever in England, surpassed only by the Harrow crash of 1952 which involved three trains, two of them expresses. The Greenford incident was a head-on crash between a passenger express out of Paddington, diverted from the fast rail because of engineering works, and an eastbound local train that had just left Greenford Station. The subsequent long and costly public enquiry had finally blamed driver error, which was easy to do since both drivers had been killed; but badly placed signals and lack of sufficient training had also been cited, management of both the train and track companies had been obliged eventually to resign, and compensation claims had dragged through the courts for years.

Slider read the general reports from police and fire brigade to get the overall picture, and then went on to the medical records. Yes, here it was at last: Hunter, Graham Dennis Ormonde, aged forty-two. Dead at scene on arrival of medical personnel.

His head had been crushed by falling debris, which had also almost decapitated him, severing the neck almost to the cervical spine. Death would have been instantaneous. A very quick glance at the photographs were enough for Slider. Hunter had been identified on the scene by paramedics going through his pockets, who had discovered a wallet in his inside jacket pocket containing business cards and credit cards, and in another pocket a letter addressed to him from an individual in Bristol, and several bills.

His wife had also subsequently identified him at the temporary morgue from these documents and from his clothes, wrist watch and signet ring. She had had to be given medical treatment for shock and distress and had been referred to her own GP for ongoing sedative prescriptions.

There was no doubt about it.

He read through it again, the back of his mind imagining the scene, the smoke, the fires, the vast mangled engines flipped outrageously on to their sides like dying dinosaurs, the debris, the bodies, the wounded moaning, the trapped crying out for help, the stunned survivors wandering in shocked silence until they bumped into the helpers scrambling down the embankment from nearby houses, almost as shocked themselves. And then the emergency services arriving...

He had been at one or two major incidents in his time – what copper hadn't? None as bad as this, thank God. The newspapers always talked of screaming, chaos and panic – well, they had to sell copies. But in his experience there was never panic, just empathy and selflessness. The walking wounded always went immediately to the aid of the worse hurt, and the latter waited with a bitter patience and courage for the 'authorities' to arrive. As for screaming – the overall impression was always one of an eerie quiet, murmuring voices usually accompanied by background hissing and metallic ticking from whatever machines had been involved. The 'chaos' lay in the physical appearance of wreck-ed artefacts: the human element were always stunningly calm.

The official reports were equally lacking in hysteria. They didn't need any more drama – they had enough of their own to last a lifetime. He read on, through all the deaths, impelled by a terrible pity to absorb them all: each one a cataclysm for its own small universe. Then, in a groove, he went on through the injuries. Some were horrific, and subsequently added to the final death toll; others were lifelong crippling. And at the end were the minor injuries treated at the scene by medics. Not all such were, of course. Some people would have just tied a handkerchief round the cut and carried on, or were patched up with an Elastoplast by the locals coming down to help.

Near the end, a name caught his eye. Bad gash across the left palm. Paramedic had found him trying to bandage it with a handkerchief and had taken him to the aid station, where the doctor had put three stitches in it and given him a tetanus injection. William McGuire, age 55, hospital porter, Flat 2, Brunel House, Cleveland Estate, W2. He knew the Cleveland Estate – they were 1930s council flats, very like the White City ones on his own ground; a smallish estate within a short walk of Paddington Station. You could see them from the elevated section of the motorway as you headed westwards, facing the multiplicity of railway lines disgorged from the terminus.

So McGuire had been in the Greenford crash as well. Of course the medical reports did not say which train any of the victims had been travelling on, let alone why. And it could be nothing but a coincidence. But Hunter and McGuire were both injured in the same train wreck, one of them fatally, and ten years later Hunter's adored little girl was murdered and her body was discovered by McGuire. It made you uneasy, to say the least.

It made you think.

He went to Walpole Park and walked there for a long time, thinking things through. The haar had stopped and the park was quiet, nobody around but pigeons and squirrels, going about their daily business, bothering nobody. The humans were not up yet: enjoying the Sunday lie-in; the early dog-walkers would have come and gone already. There had not been enough water in the haar even to drip from the trees, but the grass was wet underfoot, and smelled green and damp and springlike. That was the worst of prolonged cold spells that extended winter – no smells.

He had a new theory, now the old one had been

dismissed, but there was one big problem with it, one thing that made it impossible in execution, so impossible that it would never get past the planning stage. The planner would look at the problem and say, 'Oh, forget that, then.' But the maddening thing was that it felt right to him.

Back at his car he rang Mrs Wiseman. The child answered, and when he identified himself, she volunteered the information that her dad was out, watching the Sunday league down at the Rec. He felt a surge of relief, and said it was her mother he wanted to talk to, and could he come round right away. He heard her shrug, even over the phone. 'If you ask me, she's going a bit dippy. But you can try.'

'I'll be there in five minutes,' Slider said.

Mrs Wiseman was sitting in the same armchair where Connolly had last interviewed her. In fact, she might not have moved since then, for she looked definitely *mal-soigné*, and there was a selection of untouched drinks and snacks on plates and in mugs on the various surfaces around her. The child, Bethany, greeted Slider with a mixture of aggression and relief that told him she had been left to cope more completely than she ought, or than she was capable of. And the dog, coming straight to Slider and putting its head into his hands, tail wagging pleadingly, told him most clearly of all that the ship had become rudderless.

'She's hardly eaten anything,' Bethany told him almost in the first breath. 'I keep bringing her stuff, but I can only do sandwiches and cornflakes really, and Dad keeps going out all the time so *he's* not cooking. I think Mum's going a bit la-la with all this stuff going on, but I don't know what to do for her. She slept in the chair last night. Wouldn't go up to bed. And when Dad tried to talk to her she just screamed at him to leave her alone.'

'Well, let me have a talk with her, and I'll see if I can help.'

She looked anxious. 'You won't hurt her, will you?'

'Of course not. I'm a police officer.'

'But I've heard some policemen are bad.'

'Well, I'm not one of those. Look, see how your dog likes me? They always know.'

She looked at the dog, which was leaning against Slider's legs with its eyes shut in bliss while he massaged its scalp, and said moodily, 'He's not my dog, he's Mel's. Wish he *was* mine.'

'It seems to me,' Slider said judiciously, 'that he is yours now. Your mum and dad won't want to be bothered doing things for him, will they?'

She brightened. 'No. They're too old. They don't even remember to feed him.'

'And dogs need a lot of attention. He'll need someone to play with him and take him for walks. Dogs have to go for walks every day. Tell you what, why don't you take him out for a walk now, while I talk to your mum? He'll need about twenty minutes. Have you got a watch?'

Her eyes narrowed. 'You just want me out of the house so you can talk to her without me hearing.'

324

Slider didn't try to deny it. 'That too. Grown-ups sometimes have to talk privately. You know that. But the dog does need a walk.'

Suddenly she was close to tears. 'Marty. Don't call him "the dog" like he wasn't a person. His name's Marty.'

He hunkered, and she was in his arms, straining her rigid little body against him while he folded his arms round her, and the dog licked whatever portions of her bare arms it could reach. How long was it, Slider wondered, since anyone had held the poor child? He didn't imagine Wiseman was a huggy sort of dad at the best of times, and Mrs W had been out of it since Melanie died.

It only lasted a moment. She pulled herself free and dashed away with her sleeve the few tears that had managed to squeeze out. 'All right, I'll take him out. But don't upset my mum,' she said, roughly, to prove she was not a soft touch.

He saw her off, with the grateful dog on a lead, and then went in to Mrs Wiseman.

She was staring at nothing, her hands folded in her lap, still as death. He drew up a leather pouffe and sat so he would be as near as possible to her face-level, and said, 'Mrs Wiseman, it's Bill Slider from Shepherd's Bush police. You remember me. I came once before. I want to talk to you about your husband.'

'Ian's out, at the football,' she said automatically in a toneless voice.

'No, not about Ian. About your first husband. About Graham Hunter.'

325

Now her eyes came round to him, examined his face for a long time. He looked back steadily, and saw a trembling begin in the rigid facade. 'He's dead,' she said at last, faintly.

'Is he?' he asked with the same steady look, though his heart was thumping with the urgency of the moment. If she didn't tell him, he had nothing.

And slowly her eyes widened and her mouth crumpled. 'You know,' she said. He saw how afraid she was.

He nodded, trying to project sympathy. 'Tell me about it. The train crash. That day, when you had to go to the morgue – no one should have to go through that, identifying a body. That was a terrible thing you had to do.'

She nodded, her eyes held by his as though fascinated. 'But there were lots of us, all together. That helped a bit. We sort of hung on to each other. Some of them were crying, but I couldn't.'

'Shock takes people different ways,' he said.

She nodded. 'Those of us who weren't crying sort of helped the ones who were. And they called us in, one by one, to look at the bodies.'

'They told you they had found your husband's wallet in the inside pocket, and other things with his name on – a letter, some bills?'

Her mouth turned down at the mention of the bills. 'It was always bills. Gas, electricity, telephone. Everything. He'd open them and take them away without showing me. I'll pay them, he'd say. You don't have to worry about things like that. But the first thing I'd know, a man would come to cut us off. It was humiliating. And right there in the morgue they showed me bills with Final Demand on them in red. And betting slips – must have been a dozen. Right in front of all those people, doctors and policemen and such. I was so ashamed.'

'But they were his things all right,' he said. 'His wallet – credit cards and so on.'

'Oh yes. Everything he had in his pockets – even his hanky. I ironed them often enough, I knew all his hankies.'

'But,' Slider said, inwardly holding his breath, 'it wasn't him.'

She looked away into history. 'They'd covered his head with this green cloth thing, like in an operating theatre, so only his body was showing,' she said tonelessly. 'They said his head was too crushed to recognize, but I'd have known him by something – his hair, his ears, something. I loved that man for a long time, more than I can tell you. The real reason they covered him up was because they thought I wouldn't be able to stand it. And they were sure who he was anyway, because of the things in his pocket. It was just a formality. But I knew right away it wasn't him. They weren't his clothes, to start with.'

'A person can change their clothes.'

'Yes, but why would he? And he'd never have worn horrible cheap things like that. He had fancy tastes. Pity he never had the money to go with them. Besides, I could just see it wasn't him. This man's body was a different shape, he was older. It wasn't Graham's hands. I'd know his hands anywhere.' She shivered.

327

'But you told them that it was him anyway.'

Her eyes returned to him, to the present. 'It came to me, all of a sudden, what had happened. He'd been there, he'd seen this poor man, who-ever he was, swapped the contents of his pockets with him, and walked away. He'd walked out on me. I'd been afraid all along he'd do that one day – he wasn't the sort of man to stay put for ever. But doing it this way, it was obvious he wanted to get away completely, not just from me but from everything. Start a new life with a new identity. And my first thought was, what an idiot! He must know I'd know it wasn't him. So I thought I'd denounce him, tell them what he'd done, have him hunted down and punished for – whatever crime it is to do that. Interfering with a body, or something. It must be a crime, mustn't it?'

'Yes,' said Slider. 'What changed your mind?'

'It all happened in a second, you understand,' she said, looking at him anxiously. He saw that it was a relief to her to tell someone after all these years, but she wanted to be forgiven, too. 'As soon as I realized what he'd done, and I saw how stupid it was, how it couldn't work, I saw how, if it was a way for him to leave me, it was a way for me to be rid of him, too.'

'And you wanted to be rid of him?'

'Oh!' An indescribable sound of pain and longing. 'I loved him, I always loved him, but he was impossible to live with. You don't know what it was like. The lies, the bills, the stupid big ideas that were going to make him a millionaire, the let-downs. I'd save and save and scrape a little bit of money so Melanie could have something she needed, or a little treat, or a birthday present, and then he'd find the money and blow it on some stupid "investment".' She said the word as though it were a sleazy night with two prostitutes and some furry handcuffs. 'The drinking – he wasn't a violent drunk, but he was a *silly* drunk. Oh, he made Melanie laugh with his clowning, but I hated the smell on him, and it made me mad that he was throwing away our money on drink when there was so much we needed. He humiliated us, week after week, time after time. I couldn't hold my head up around the neighbours. And Melanie was like an orphanage kid next to those rich girls at school. I half wish she'd never won the scholarship, then she could have gone to an ordinary school and not stuck out so much. But she was always bright – and Graham was so proud of her.' A bitter look came over her face. 'That was the thing, you see. She loved him. They loved each other. No matter what he did – and I tried to keep the worst of it from her – she adored him, much more than she ever did me. I was just the one who worked and slaved to keep food on our plates and clothes on our backs. He was the fun one. He was magic. She never saw what a lousy husband and dad he really was.'

Slider nodded sympathetically. 'So it's no wonder, when you saw a chance to be rid of him...'

'I thought, if he wants to go, why stop him?' she said bitterly. 'So I said it was my husband. I said I knew his wrist watch and his ring – though

Graham would never have worn a ring. He hated jewellery on men.'

It was what Slider had picked up on in the records office. 'And they were satisfied with your identification.'

'Along with everything else – why not? And once I'd said it, I couldn't go back on it.'

'Did you want to?'

'Often and often. I still loved him. And whatever you think, when you're married, about being rid of him, it's different when you're all alone and you've got to face up to looking after yourself and your child with no help. But you see –' she met his eyes now with misery and a plea for forgiveness – 'there was a life insurance, and for a miracle he'd kept up the payments. It wasn't much but we desperately needed it, Melanie and me. And once I'd taken the insurance money, I could never tell. And so I never did.'

'You never told Melanie?'

Shake of head.

'Do you think she guessed?'

Another definite shake. 'Not then. She believed her daddy was dead. I can't tell you what that was like. I told myself she was better off without him, but to hear her crying, night after night...'

'And then you got married again.'

'Don't look at me like that!' she cried, though Slider was sure his expression hadn't changed. The blame was in her own mind. 'I was desperate by then. I couldn't cope on my own, and Melanie was having to do too much, and the insurance money was all gone and I didn't know

330

which way to turn. Ian was my only chance. And I sort of convinced myself that Graham really was dead, that I'd been mistaken at the morgue that day. After all, I'd been upset. I was on tranquillizers for ages afterwards. So obviously I must have imagined the whole thing. That's how I fixed it in my mind. All his things were in the pockets, so it must have been him and he really was dead. So I married Ian and – that was that.'

'Except,' Slider said, and now he really was punting, 'Graham didn't stay dead, did he?'

She looked wary. 'Why d'you say that?'

'Oh, come on, you've told me the worst, no point in holding back now. Did he contact you?'

'No,' she said definitely. 'Never. I was always scared he would, but I suppose he had as much to lose as me. He'd have gone to jail. No, he never contacted me.'

'Melanie, then? He contacted Melanie.' She didn't want to answer, and he added, 'About two years ago.'

She shuddered and looked down. 'I don't know. She never said anything to me, but I guessed something was up. It was just after she and Scott got together. I was so glad she'd got a nice boy at last, one who wanted to marry her and everything. And she was so happy at first. Then they moved into that flat together, and soon afterwards she started acting strangely. She wasn't happy any more – not the way she used to be. I think she tried to tell me a couple of times, but she never managed it. Then one day, when we were washing up after Sunday lunch, she asked me about her dad dying, asked me

331

about identifying him at the morgue, and I just knew she knew. And how could she, unless she'd seen him, unless he'd told her?'

'What did you say to her when she asked that?'

'I just told the lie again. What could I say? I couldn't tell her he'd been alive all that time and I'd let her grieve for him for nothing, could I? That I'd committed bigamy? Not to say insurance fraud. She'd have hated me. So I let her think I didn't know, that I really thought he was dead, and after that she got sort of – strained with me. I suppose it was always on her mind, wanting to tell me but not daring to.'

'For all the same reasons.'

'Yes.' She brooded a moment. 'He should never have done it. But he loved her so much, I suppose he couldn't keep away. *Me* he could leave and never see again, but his little Mel ... And he was always a selfish man. He wouldn't leave her alone for her own good. It would be *his* wants he'd be thinking about.'

'But you never actually knew anything about his whereabouts? Or that he had definitely contacted Melanie? It was just surmise on your part.'

'I didn't know anything. But I *knew*, if you understand me.' She looked up at him sharply. 'How did *you* know?'

'I guessed. A couple of things. The ring, for instance. And the fact that she bought a take-away meal for someone that night – it had to be someone close to her.'

She was struck by that. 'God, was he making

332

her buy him food? I suppose he was broke again. What was it, Chinese? He loved Chinese. I can't stand the stuff.'

'And then there was the fact that Melanie had a call from someone that evening, someone she called "Dad". But you'd said she never called Ian "Dad".'

'No. She never did. Not once that I remember, ever.'

They had come to the place of dread.

'And then you said to my colleague, "A father wouldn't hurt his own daughter, would he?" She thought you meant Ian, but when I read it in her report, I wondered.'

'You don't think,' she began, and it was a plea rather than a question, 'that he had anything to do with it, do you?'

'I don't know. I have to find out. But to find out, I had to know the whole story.'

'But why would you even think – I mean, apart from Melanie, nobody knows where he is, even what name he's living by.'

'I think I do,' Slider said. 'I think he's the man who found her body.'

All the implications seemed to fall on her at once like a rock slide. She gave a terrible cry – not loud, but agonizing – the like of which Slider would be glad never to hear again.

'Did you ever hear her mention a man called William McGuire?'

'No,' she said. 'Never. Is that him?'

'I don't know. It's possible.'

She twisted her hands together and rocked in her agony. 'If he killed her, it's my fault, for not

333

telling her, for lying to her all these years. If she could have told me he'd contacted her, I could have protected her.'

'I don't know—' Slider began, but she was beyond reaching.

'I've killed my own daughter,' she said. And she rocked, silent and dry-eyed, in a place of unimaginable nightmare.

It took some nifty telephoning and hard talking back at the office to get in touch with the head of the Parks Department, who was extremely miffed about having to go in on a Sunday to access the employment records of one of his very minor minions. Slider was preparing to go and meet the man himself, there being no one in the Sunday-slim department to send, when Atherton walked in.

'Why aren't you at home?' Slider asked him.

'Why aren't you?' he countered.

'I've been following up something that occurred to me—'

'In the stilly watches of the night,' Atherton finished for him. 'Whereas I have been reclining on the sofa all morning with two cats sitting on me, watching *Chitty Chitty Bang Bang* until I'm ready to kill myself.'

'Why watch it, then?'

'I wasn't watching it – I said the cats were. It's one of their favourite films. Vash's got a *thing* for James Robertson Justice. Emily's not back until Tuesday and my mind is racketing itself to pieces, so I thought I'd come in. And here you are. What's the panic?'

'I'll tell you in the car,' Slider said. 'You can come with me. I'll need you there for the last bit, anyway.'

'So,' said Atherton, some time later, as they trundled towards Uxbridge, 'you were going entirely on her calling someone "Dad" over the phone? You didn't think it could have been a misspeak?'

'Anything could be anything. But remember, less than a week before, he had slapped her face. I don't think the word "Dad" would have leapt to her lips for Ian Wiseman at that point. But there was also the takeaway. Who do you buy food for? It's either charity, or love. No one's come forward to say she brought them a lifeline of Chinese food that evening. I'd have bet on Hibbert—'

'But he's out of it.'

'So who else did she love? And there was another problem. If she bought Chinese for someone, and then got into their car and drove off with them, there must have been a reason. It wasn't exactly closing time, but—'

Atherton got it. 'He was drunk? Turned up drunk in his car to collect the grub, and she thought, oh bugger, I'll have to drive him home?'

'He was a drinker in his previous incarnation. And there was the matter of her savings going missing over the past two years, and the two hundred on the Friday. Who was she giving that to?'

Atherton thought he'd spotted a flaw. 'If she drove him home, how was she going to get home

335

herself?'

'My guess is that she'd drive herself home in his car, and then either he'd come and collect it the next day, or she'd take it back to him and come home by bus or taxi. It would be a Saturday, remember, so no work. And Hibbert was away, so there'd be no complications from that direction. And if she was worried about Fitton seeing her drive in in a strange car, she could have always parked it round the corner. But as it happened, the need didn't arise.'

A silence fell between them on that thought, which lasted all the way to the council offices, where a very annoyed Trevor Parrott was waiting to give them his full and generous cooperation on this matter of importance.

'I can't see why it couldn't have waited until tomorrow,' he grumbled. 'Then you needn't have bothered me. One of the girls could have given you the information you wanted.'

'Operational reasons, I'm afraid,' Slider said smoothly. 'I can't tell you more.'

'Well, if this man is a dangerous criminal, you ought to arrest him, not leave him running around loose to endanger other people. And you should have warned us about him so we could dismiss him. What did he do, anyway?'

'He's a gardener, I believe,' Slider said.

Parrot mottled. 'You deliberately misunderstood me. I meant what *crime* has he committed, of course.'

'I don't know yet that he has done anything.'

'Then why on earth did you have to drag me out on a Sunday?' Parrot cried in frustration, back at the front of the loop.

'We won't keep you long,' Atherton said soothingly, seeing that all the soothe seemed to have leaked out of his boss for the moment. 'It's good of you to help us out. We wouldn't ask if it wasn't important.'

It didn't take long. William McGuire had joined the department two years ago as an under-gardener, after a short spell on benefits. Before that he had been self-employed, a minicab driver, for eight years, first for Remo's Taxis, Fulham, then Magic Cabs of Shepherd's Bush. Previous address in Fulham. And there was a note that, in view of the location of his work for the council, he had been offered a council-own-ed one-bedroom maisonette in Lakeside Close. No black marks against him since he took up employment. His wage, Slider observed, was minuscule, which accounted, he supposed, for his being taken on with no previous parks and gardens experience. Probably no one else had wanted the job. It was hardly worth coming off benefits for. And he had been absent from work for the past week without notice.

'So that closes the last gap,' Slider said as they walked back to the car. 'The less fussy minicab firms – and I know Magic Cabs – will take on anyone with a clean driving licence, no ques-tions asked. And a short spell on benefits gave him an insurance number to take to an actual employer. All we don't know is why he changed from being a driver to being a gardener.'

'If you think that's all we don't know, you must be on something,' Atherton observed.

337

'Whether he came back into Melanie's life; why he did; whether he killed her, if he did; why he "found" the body – not to mention that we don't actually *know* he's Graham Hunter at all. That's just a guess on your part. You'll look a right wally when it turns out he isn't.'

'Thank you for that comforting thought. But McGuire's record only goes back ten years, to the time of the Greenford crash. Before that he was a hospital porter living in a council flat in Paddington. Why the sudden break?'

'He might well have wanted a complete change after the trauma of the crash. Why not?'

'And there's the fact that he and Hunter were both in the crash, and he's the one who found Hunter's murdered daughter ten years on. That's one hell of a coincidence.'

'Ah, well,' Atherton admitted lightly, 'there you have me. I'll go for a coinkidink every time over hard fact. Makes life so much more interesting.'

'You're supposed to be polite to me and flatter me. You seem to forget I'm your boss,' Slider said, plipping open the car and climbing in. 'I should hate to see you throwing everything away when the world is at your feet.'

'Usual place for it,' Atherton observed, getting in the other side. 'Where are we going now?' he asked, as Slider started the engine.

'Where d'you think?' said Slider.

'Oh boy,' said Atherton. 'I feel a lawsuit coming on.'

'There's something else,' Slider admitted after a silence, 'and it's my fault.'

338

'What?'

'When Norma brought me the forensic report on the clothes, I was busy. I told her to precis for me. I didn't read it until last night.'

'And?'

'The dog hair on her clothes wasn't black, it was white. And Marty doesn't have a white hair on him.'

Atherton wrinkled his nose. 'McGuire had a white dog,' he admitted, 'but it was the dog that found her. The hair could have got on her clothes then.'

'She was found lying on her back. The hair was on the seat of her skirt. So unless the dog managed to turn her right over and sit on her—'

'Ah, I'm with you now.'

'Every dog owner has the dog in the car at some point, and dog hair is the devil to get off the upholstery. So if we can DNA match McGuire's dog's hair to the hair on her skirt—'

'We've got him. Hallelujah, some firm evidence at last.'

'But we won't tell him that to begin with. If I'm right, I think he may confess.'

Seventeen

Dieu Que Le Son Du Cor Est Triste
Au Fond Des Bois

There was no answer from McGuire's half of the maisonette. 'I hope he hasn't skedaddled,' Slider said.

'Or done himself in,' said Atherton.

'Thank you for that cheery thought.' He rang again. 'The dog's not barking,' he observed.

'So he probably has flitted,' Atherton said.

'Or he's taken it for a walk.' He tried one more ring.

A window upstairs opened and a woman stuck her head out. 'He's prob'ly down the pub. The Bells. Round the corner. Why don't you try there? I can't hear the telly for your ringing.'

They left the car and walked round. The Six Bells, like most pubs since the smoking ban came in, had to use food to entice the customers in, and most of it was laid out for restaurant purposes, though there was a small bar area in the back. They strolled round the whole premises but there was no sign of McGuire. The bar and waiting staff were all young, mostly East European and temporary, and even when you could get them to stand still for a minute, they had no knowledge of the customers. But there was one older woman, smartly dressed from the Valerie Proctor catalogue, who came out from the back just as they were admitting defeat. She clocked them at once for what they were (*what was it? The suits? Slider wondered. Or did they have 'policemen's eyes'? Horrible thought*), backed them into a quiet corner and said, 'Looking for someone? What's he done?'

'Why does everyone always ask that?' Atherton said plaintively. 'As soon as we want to talk to someone...'

'He's just a witness,' Slider said. 'Or we hope he might be.' He described McGuire.

'Oh, yeah, Old Bill we call him. His name's Bill,' she added helpfully. 'Got a little dog. We don't mind dogs if they're well behaved. Not in the restaurant area, of course.'

'Of course not,' Slider agreed kindly. 'Has he been in tonight?'

'Not been in – ooh – a while. Quite a regular usually. Weekends, mostly, though he does come in of a weekday night, but he doesn't drink then – has something soft. Very strict. Says he'll never put his job in jeopardy. Mind you, Friday nights and Saturday nights he tanks it a bit. But he's never any trouble. Have to stop him singing sometimes. Got quite a nice voice, but we can't have the punters singing. Gives the wrong impression.'

'Can you remember when you last saw him?'

'No, not offhand. It's been a while, though. Couple of weeks, maybe.'

'Can you remember Friday week past?' Slider

341

asked. 'Was he in then?'

'Dunno. Maybe. Probably – Fridays are his big night. Wait a minute, was that the night he ran out of cash?' She screwed up her face with effort. 'I think it could've been. It was a Friday, anyway. He tried to get credit, the cheeky bastard. I told him to sling his hook.'

'Do you know what time that would have been?'

'Are you kidding? I can't remember stuff like that from weeks ago. It was before chucking out time, I can tell you that, though. I only remember it was a Friday because he was back in the next night – Saturday being his other drinking night – and I told him no credit before he could open his mouth, and he got out his wallet and showed me cash.' She frowned again. 'Now I think about it, he wasn't his usual self that night. Usually he's the life and soul of the party, laughing and joking and trying to sing, like I told you. But that night he just sat down at the end of the bar and threw 'em back, not a peep out of him. I think that might've been the last time I saw him, come to think of it. Has something happened to him?' There was an eagerness for disaster in her voice that Slider didn't want to feed.

'Not that I know of. I just want to talk to him about something he might have seen.'

'Well, if he comes in, I'll tell him you're looking for him,' she said.

They walked back to the car. 'Ran out of money on the Friday, got chucked out early,' Atherton said. 'That fits. A phone call to Mel-

anie – "Can you lend me some money, pet?"
And when she agrees to meet him outside her
flat with the cash, "You wouldn't get me a
Chinese on your way, would you?" And she
says, with a degree of irritation, "All *right*,
Dad." As per report.'

'And on Saturday night he's drinking to
forget.'

'He'd got some balls going to the pub at all. If
it was him.'

'If it was him, he might feel he had to stick to
his usual pattern. But couldn't quite hack the
bonhomie.'

'Well, I like him better for that, anyway,'
Atherton said. 'If there's one thing I hate, it's
a cheerful murderer.' They reached their car.
'What now?'

Slider was looking past him, towards the Lido.
'Here he comes,' he said quietly. 'He must have
been taking the dog for a walk. Why didn't we
think of that?'

McGuire was shuffling along, hunched into his
clothes, the little dog trotting at his side, looking
subdued, glancing up at his master from time to
time in that anxious way dogs have when something doesn't feel right. He didn't seem to see
the two men waiting for him until he actually
reached them, and then he stopped and looked at
them with an appalling resignation, and so much
pain, if he had been an animal Slider would have
wanted to put him down right there and then.

'Mr Hunter,' he said quietly, 'can we have a
word with you?'

He showed no surprise. He just looked old –

343

his face lined, his eyes bagged and raw, his skin slack and grey. It was as if all the lost years of William McGuire had been added to his own, a terrible reverse Dorian Gray of a punishment. The dog watched them warily, nose working hard, waiting for a cue from its master as to whether to wag or growl.

At last McGuire said, 'You'd better come in.' His voice was different from the way Slider remembered it, from their first interview: lighter, his accent posher, more suited to an educated man rather than a manual labourer. So he had been a bit of an actor as well, Slider thought as they followed him to his door. Well, that was no surprise. There was always a bit of an actor in the man who lived by his charm. But there was no sign of that charm now. This was a beaten man; the spark had gone out.

There was no smell of drink in the room, or from McGuire. He let the dog out into the back garden, and came back, caught Slider sniffing, and said, 'I'm not drunk. I haven't touched a drop for five days. I'm never going to drink again.' He sat down heavily in an armchair whose seat bore the impression.

'You didn't react when I called you Mr Hunter,' Slider said. 'For the record, you are Graham Hunter, aren't you?'

He seemed to think about it for a moment; or perhaps he was choosing his words. 'If you've got as far as asking me that question, I suppose there's no point in denying it. I've gone all these years wondering when it would come, but after a certain point, you think it's all been settled in your favour, and you stop worrying. Yes, I'm Graham Hunter – or at least, I was once. I feel as if he died a long time ago. I wish he had,' he concluded bitterly.

'Tell me about the train crash,' Slider said. 'What do you remember about it?'

'Not much about the actual crash. I was going down to Bristol to see a man about a business proposition.' He made a wry face. 'Importing edible insects from Latin America – cicadas, beetles and ants. Dried, and mixed in small bags. He said it would be the next snack food craze – eat them at the bar instead of peanuts or pork scratchings. Seen any lately in your local?' he enquired ironically. 'I remember there were engineering works and the train was quite slow to start with. Men in red safety jackets beside the line as we went slowly past. Then not long after we speeded up—'

He paused. The dog came in, flip-flap, from the garden, and looked at them, then sat on the invisible frontier between the sitting room and the kitchen.

'It's funny,' Hunter went on, 'I don't remember a noise. There was a terrific bang, but it was a feeling rather than a sound. The train was packed and I hadn't been able to get a seat, which probably saved me. I was standing in the space by the door between two carriages with a lot of other people. Then came this bang. I remember feeling as if all the breath was pressed out of my body. Then I hit the ground, or the ground hit me, and there were bits of debris

345

falling all around me. A twisted piece of metal fell on my outstretched hand. Cut my palm. I was lucky it didn't sever it completely. I was bruised and breathless, but otherwise I wasn't hurt. I just lay there thinking, what happened? It seemed like ages, though I suppose it couldn't have been more than a minute, before the power of thought came back to me, and I said to myself, "The train crashed."'

Slider guessed this was the first time he had told this story – who would there have been to tell it to, after all? – which was why he had it all honed and ready. He must have gone over it in his mind a thousand times. All he and Atherton had to do was sit still and listen.

'I sat up,' Hunter went on, 'and looked around. There were the trains. The express had ridden over the top of the slow train, so there were three carriages sitting on top of it. Both engines had derailed and were on their sides and one of them had caught fire. Some of the carriages were catching, too. And there was debris everywhere. And bodies.' He stopped. 'Well, I suppose you've seen pictures of it.'

'Yes,' said Slider.

'I got up. I was a bit dazed, I think. I wandered around a bit, just looking, unable to take it in. Then I thought about seeing if there was anyone I could help. The first person I came to was obviously beyond help. A massive great metal thing – looked like a cast-iron water tank – had landed on his head. He was dead as a nail. I didn't even think about moving that thing – I didn't want to think what was underneath. But as

I knelt there looking at him, I saw the blood dripping from my hand, and realized it was quite badly cut. I couldn't find my handkerchief for the moment, but I saw one poking out of the dead man's pocket, so I pulled it out, and it looked clean, so I thought, "He won't want it any more," and I tied my hand up with it. And that was when it came to me.'

He looked at Slider, as if to check that he really knew.

'The idea of swapping identities,' Slider supplied.

'It was the maddest thing. I think it was a symptom of shock that it even crossed my mind. But I thought, here was a way to start again, a clean slate, leave all my troubles behind. My life was a mess, my marriage was on the rocks, I had debts from here to Timbuktu. If I could just walk away from the lot, I could start a new life, all clean and clear. Like a snake shedding its old skin. I went through his pockets. He didn't have much, poor bugger. I found a driving licence with his name and address on it, a cheap wallet with a few quid and a Blockbuster card, and one of those plastic name badges on a lanyard – a hospital pass for Queen Mary's isolation annexe in Greenford – the old fever hospital. Given that, and the fact that his address was in Paddington, I think he must have been on the local train. Well, it was the work of a moment to switch what was in his pockets with what was in mine. And then I walked away. I had a bad moment when a paramedic grabbed me and insisted on looking at my hand – the handkerchief had

347

soaked through and I was fiddling with it. He made me go to the first aid tent they'd set up, and a young doctor stitched it for me. I remembered to tell them my new name for the record, but I couldn't remember the address. I looked dumb and gave them the driving licence, and I suppose they decided I was in shock. Anyway, they took down the information from that, even worked out I was fifty-five. It was a funny thing – I felt a sort of pang about that. I thought I'd lost thirteen years of my life. But then I was free to go. They were giving out cups of tea and sandwiches in another tent nearby and I got something and sat down for a bit – I was starting to shake with the reaction. But I didn't want to hang around – I was afraid someone would find out about the switch, God knows how – everyone had too much to do. So I walked to the nearest bit of civilization, which turned out to be Greenford, and got myself a bed in a cheap hotel for the night, took the aspirin the doctor had given me, and slept like the dead.'

He sighed and looked down at his hand, flexing it absently in the manner of someone who has grown used to the ache and stiffness of age. Slider thought he saw, among the natural creases, the faint scar of an old wound across the palm. The dog thought the movement was for him, and trotted forward, and sat hopefully at Hunter's feet, but he didn't notice it.

'Of course,' he resumed, 'in the morning I realized what a stupid scheme it was. There was no possible way it could work. My wife would be called to identify the body, and she'd know

348

right away it wasn't me. I haunted the papers for days, expecting some outcry. When I finally saw my own name on the list of casualties – well, it gave me a jolt, I can tell you. That's a strange thing to read. And then there was a notice of my death in the deaths column, and the date of my funeral.' He looked at Atherton as if anticipating the question, though Atherton had not made a sound. 'No, I didn't go. I wasn't quite that mad. By then I'd realized what had happened. Rachel had decided that if I wanted out, she was going to let me. She must have known the body wasn't mine, but she'd gone along with it anyway. And then I remembered the life insurance. I was more use to her dead than alive. So I stayed dead. I didn't blame her. Life with me wasn't a bed of roses for her, poor bitch. If she preferred the money to my company, who's to say she wasn't right?'

'What about William McGuire? How did you go about becoming him?' Slider asked.

Hunter sighed with a sort of weariness, settling back in the chair as if he needed help to get to the end. The dog, seeing the movement, and tired of waiting, jumped up on to his lap, and he moved his hands automatically to accommodate it. 'I went to his address the next day. It was a council flat.'

'Yes. I know the estate,' Slider said.

'I watched the place for hours to see if anyone would go in or out. Then I thought, this is stupid, bucked myself up and went and knocked. When there was no answer I used the key from his pocket. It was a grim sort of place. One bedroom, small and very dark, sitting room with a kitchen area and a tiny bathroom. Hardly any furniture or belongings. Hadn't been decorated in an age. Smelt funny, too. But right away I could see he'd lived alone. There was no woman stuff there, no women's clothes in the wardrobe, no make-up or anything in the bathroom. And the cooking arrangements were primitive. Sliced bread and a tub of Flora in the fridge. A few tins of baked beans in the cupboard. Dirty plates in the sink. I never saw such a bleak place in my life – well, I hadn't then. I have since. I know a lot about the William McGuires of this world now. But it was just my dumb luck that it was him. A fifty-five-year-old bachelor, works as a hospital porter, lives in a council flat: a person like him disappears, and no one will even notice for weeks. And when they notice, they won't care. I don't know if he had any relatives. There was nothing in the flat to suggest it. Maybe he had some, far away and out of touch. I still sometimes wonder if anyone ever asked themselves what had become of old Bill.'

'Did you stay there? At the flat?'

'God, no! That would have been too weird. And maybe dangerous. Once I'd had a look round, I just left, and never went back. I had to find a room to rent and a job. I had five hundred quid in cash with me – it was going to be a down payment to the man in Bristol, to get me in on the scheme – but that was all, and I couldn't use my credit cards. I needed some way to support myself with no questions asked. Poor old William didn't have much, but the one thing of value he left me was his driving licence. I went to the library and went online, found a ten-year-old Nissan saloon in decent condition, well looked after, with eleven months MOT, for three-fifty. I got myself a room, from an advert in a newsagent's, in Maida Vale, and went along and signed up with a minicab company. Within a week, I had my new life all set up. I moved around a good bit for the first year, to foil the scent, in case anyone was looking for me. But in the end, I concluded that old Bill hadn't had any friends in the world, and I settled down in Fulham.'

'Why Fulham?' Slider asked.

'Oh, it was as good a place as anywhere,' he said listlessly. 'A man I knew, one of the other drivers, said Remo's in Fulham paid more than where I was, so I drifted that way. It didn't matter to me where I lived by then.'

'You were unhappy,' Slider suggested.

'It's strange,' Hunter said reflectively. 'At first I found it exhilarating to be someone else. And being someone like McGuire was such a relief – no one expected anything of him. He had no responsibilities, no standards to live up to, nothing in the world to do beyond turn up at work long enough to earn the cash and not piss off the bosses. I played to my new role. I was dumb but reliable. A loner. A very, very dull person. No hobbies, no habits, no friends. I drove my car, in the evenings I watched telly. At the weekends I got drunk. When I was flush, I went down the betting shop for a flutter on the ponies. When I was broke, I worked overtime. Once I went to

the pictures, and bought fish and chips afterwards and ate them out of the paper.' He paused.
'I think that was what finished me, that night,
going to the pictures on my own.'

'Finished you?'

'I ended that night lying on my bed staring at
the ceiling and thinking, "What have I done?"'
He lifted haunted eyes, tired to death. 'You can't
imagine what a life like that is like. The utter
pointlessness. The tedium. The loneliness. I'd
done the best bit of acting of my life, I *was*
William McGuire, but what was the use? I could
never go home again. I could never see my
daughter again.'

Now they had come to it, Slider thought. 'You
missed Melanie?'

'So much,' he blurted. 'I can't tell you. It was
like a gnawing in the guts, longing for her; day
after day, and it got worse all the time. It was
worse than if she'd died, because then I'd know
she was beyond reach. But I knew she was there,
somewhere, and I could go and find her and see
her and talk to her – only I mustn't, not ever.
That's why I drank so much, to try and keep it at
bay. In the end, I lost my job. I went in to work
still under the influence and they told me to sling
my hook. That was the one thing they couldn't
allow – that and stealing.'

'So what did you do?'

'I saw an advertisement for an under gardener
for the Parks Department in Ruislip, and I
thought a change would be good – the outdoor
life might soothe me. And the word "Ruislip"
reminded me of the Lido. I used to bring Mel

and her little friend here when she was a kid, on fine Sundays – cheaper than the seaside. She loved it. They were happy times. I never thought I'd end up living right next to the Lido, but when I said I lived in Fulham, they told me I could have this place, to be on hand. Sometimes there's emergency work, if a tree blows down or a bank collapses, and I have to turn out. So I moved here. I thought, this time I'll be happy. I even got myself a dog.' He looked down at the terrier, which had curled itself up on his lap, as if noticing it for the first time. He caressed its ears, and it waggled its stump tail without waking up.

'But you weren't happy,' Slider said.

He shook his head. 'Living here only made me think about her more. The longing for my old life was terrible. One day I went to the Natural History Museum, because it was another favourite place of hers when she was a kid. And I saw her.' He seemed to be staring at his memory now, as if at a movie. 'It was a long time – eight years – and she'd grown up a lot, but I knew her. I'd have known her in the dark. She was walking away down a corridor. I followed her, just in time to see her go in through a door marked "Private, Staff Only". She'd used the security keypad by the door, so I knew she must work there. It was a funny thing, just as she was pushing in through the door she paused and looked round, as if she felt me watching her. I jumped back behind a pillar. She didn't see me. She wouldn't have known me anyway – I'd grown this beard. But I think somehow she'd felt my presence.

'After that, I couldn't keep the feelings down. I was drinking more than ever – weekends only. I didn't want to lose this job. But it was no good. I had to see her. One evening I waited outside the museum and followed her home.'

'Did you speak to her?'

'Not then. It took a lot of nights, standing across the road from her house, watching her go in and out, before I could pluck up the courage. Then one night she came out alone and walked off along the street. She looked so happy and busy, living her life, I followed her, really just to see where she was going, maybe to suck in some of that happiness. I don't think I meant to speak to her. But when she stopped at the pedestrian lights, waiting to cross the road, I just walked up to her and before I could stop myself, I said, "Melanie?"'

'She looked round. She was scared for a second – there was this bearded old man who knew her name – and then there was a sort of dawning in her face, and she said, "Dad?"'

At that point, he flagged so alarmingly with, Slider supposed, sheer emotional exhaustion that he looked for a moment as though he was having an attack of some sort. He slumped back in the chair, his face drawn and putty-coloured, breathing through his mouth.

'Take a breather,' Slider said. 'Do you want a drink? Is there anything in the house?'

'No,' he said, a protest, though a feeble one. 'I'm not drinking, never again.'

'Tea, then?'

'A cup of tea,' Hunter agreed weakly. He licked his lips. 'Mouth's dry.'

Slider got up before Atherton could move. 'I'll do it,' he said. The dog lifted its head sharply at the movement. Slider went into the kitchen part, took the kettle to the tap, and leaned against the sink for a moment, his eyes closed. He found his hands were shaking. Emotional draining didn't only happen to the narrator, he discovered, but to the interlocutor too.

It had been wonderful at first. Of course, she had been shocked at what he had done, and it had taken a lot of explaining before she could accept that he had done it for her and her mother's own good. Then she had had to tell him about her life, and there were some painful parts to that, too. And her mother's remarriage, to Ian, who she didn't like one bit. And Scott, whom she adored: Hunter had had to grit his teeth against the jealousy.

They couldn't meet very often, because no one could know about him, and the secrecy was wearing on them both. She would meet him somewhere, a café, or just a bench, in her lunch-time usually. Evenings and weekends were difficult. Mostly it was snatched meetings just to catch up, though they talked on the phone when they could. But of course, the problem for any addict is that having a little bit only makes you want more; and he was addicted to Melanie.

He hadn't meant to ask her for money. But she had been shocked at the way he lived, and how little he earned, and the shabbiness of his clothes. She had given him money, against his protests, the first time, so he could buy himself a new jacket. The next time, he asked her. The strain of the situation meant he was drinking and gambling more at the weekends, and that went through the money more than anything. She didn't like giving him money just to waste it, but she never refused him.

But then she started urging him to put things right. She wanted him to tell her mother he was alive. It was cruel, she said, to leave her in ignorance. He'd told her that revealing himself would make her a bigamist, and then she'd got angry. He had to do the right thing, she said. He must go to the police and make a clean breast of everything. They couldn't go on like this.

'I think in the back of her mind,' he said sadly, 'she had the idea that if only I would do that, everything could go back to the way it was. Ian would somehow disappear, I would come home and live with Rachel, and we would be a family again. She was a bright girl, but when it came to that, emotionally she was just five years old. I tried to explain to her how impossible it was, but she persisted with the idea that if only I would confess, everything would be forgiven, just like that.'

And so they came to the Friday night. The tea had been drunk, had revived him a little, but he still looked ghastly. Slider felt exhausted; Atherton looked apprehensive. Only the dog slumbered comfortably on his master's lap. Hunter stroked it slowly, over and over, as he told the last part of the story.

He had gone for his Friday night drink at the Six Bells. It had been a hard week, he'd had words with his immediate superior, and there had been hints that departmental cuts might lose him his job, despite the fact that there was too much work for the staff they had. He had gone to the pub determined to tie one on, only to discover, before he was drunk enough for oblivion, that he had run out of money. He'd asked for credit – he was in there often enough, for God's sake – and the barmaid, the snotty one with the voice like a bandsaw, had given him short shrift and long contempt. He was furious and humiliated and wanted nothing more than to get back at her – turn up with enough cash to flash at her to make her sorry she'd been sharp with him.

Outside, he'd rung Melanie. She was out with friends – he could hear the sounds of people having a good time in the background. A wave of self-pity had come over him. He'd told her he was in a bad way for cash and spun her a story which he could hear she didn't believe, but she'd agreed to meet him at her house with funds as soon as he could get there. And he'd asked her to get him a takeaway as well – he hadn't eaten since breakfast – and she'd snapped at him. It hadn't boded well.

When he arrived at her house she'd come down with the carrier bag in her hand, and got in beside him to talk to him. But right away she'd peered at him and sniffed and said he was too drunk to drive home, and insisted on switching places with him and driving him back.

When they reached Reservoir Road she'd

driven to the Lido car park and pulled up there 'so I can talk to you'. It was a long harangue, on much the same lines as before, about him 'doing the right thing'. She'd been doing some sums while she waited for the Chinese food, and realized how much of her money he had gone through in the last two years. It had to stop, she said.

He'd eaten the food while she talked but he hadn't enjoyed it, which annoyed him. He tried to tell her all over again how it was impossible for him to go back, and how it wouldn't help anyway. The harangue had turned into an argument. He'd got out of the car to escape it, but she followed him. He tried to get it through her thick skull that if he went to police it would end up with him and her mother in prison, but she persisted in assuring him that wouldn't happen.

She got angry with him, about having left her all those years thinking he was dead, about his drinking and his poor little bets on the ponies, called him a coward for not facing his responsibilities, told him if he didn't put things right she'd stop seeing him.

He got angry too, and accused her of emotional blackmail, and of being a silly, naive little prig.

And in the middle of all the anger, he had grabbed her by the neck and shaken her.

'Not hard. I didn't grab her hard. Even losing my temper, I was enough her father to check myself, not to hurt her. But she was shocked. I'd never laid a rough hand on her before. She jerked away from me, just as I let her go. She lost her balance, her foot skidded on the mud, and she went over backwards, hitting her head sharply on the edge of the car roof.

'I didn't mean to hurt her,' he said in a faded voice of horror. 'I would never hurt my little girl. I knelt beside her, slipped my hand under her head, felt the blood. I called her name, and I thought she looked at me, but then she was limp and her eyes weren't looking anywhere. Just staring. But I never meant to hurt her, I swear to you. If I could have died instead...'

'But you didn't,' Slider said.

Eighteen

The Devil Wears Primark

'That's a terrible story,' Joanna said. 'That's the worst thing I've heard. The poor man.'

Slider had rung her on her mobile to say he didn't know what time he'd be home, and she had diverted after the concert and come to the station to hear about it first hand. She was sitting on his desk now, still in her long black, a breath of fresh air from the outside world – the real world, if you wanted to look at it that way, in which people lived their lives without ever murdering or being murdered.

Sitting as he was in his normal chair behind the desk, he was looking up at her. He admired her almost painfully. She had just been engaged in something of extraordinary, unimaginable skill – playing the violin before an audience of thousands, recreating great music from tiny, random-looking dots on a page – something so beyond his comprehension that it stood in his mind like a conjuring trick in a child's: genuine magic. She was a hummingbird, a kingfisher – airborne, delicate, a jewel of brightness and a quicksilver of movement. He was a humble duck, patiently drudging about in the weed.

360

She was also his wife, which was a pretty damn fine thing, whichever way you looked at it.

'But,' she said, 'if it was an accident, why didn't he just go straight to the police?'

Atherton, sitting on the cold radiator as usual, answered. 'Because of this whole identity swap thing. He was afraid it would all come out and he was terrified of going to prison. So he carried her into the woods and laid her half under a bush. He had to make it look as though she'd been concealed, but he wanted her to be found, so he chose a place not far off the path. Then he went home and waited.'

'It must have been hell,' Joanna observed.

'Yes,' said Atherton, 'particularly when she *wasn't* found. Saturday went past and Sunday went past, and all the usual visitors and dog walkers kept going in there and nothing happened. He didn't want to be caught, but he couldn't bear to leave her lying out there any longer. I mean, not just the agonizing suspense, but what with foxes and stoats and such—'

'Don't.' Joanna winced.

'So on Monday morning he finally broke, and "found" her himself. He was in a terrible state when we interviewed him, but then, finding a dead body is not a nice thing for the ordinary punter, so we didn't think anything of it. And then, when we didn't come back for him...'

'I suppose he was on tenterhooks, wondering if, and whether, and when,' Joanna said thoughtfully. 'A whole week of it.'

'Yes, I think he was just glad in the end, when

361

we did come for him, that it was all over.'

'Hardly that,' Slider said. They looked at him. 'Not all over by any means.'

'Well, no, there's all the mess to clear up,' Atherton admitted. 'And *what* a mess he's made of everything! His daughter's dead. His wife's marriage is bigamous.'

'That's easily remedied, surely? Divorce and remarriage would fix that,' Joanna suggested.

'It was still knowing bigamy on her part, which is a crime. Not to mention the insurance fraud. She could do time. And the marriage is ruined anyway. Ian's not going to want her back. And his life will never be the same, either. He'll have to change his job – if he can get another one after being a suspect. Though it's hard to feel sympathy for him, given the Stephanie incident. There's the child, Bethany – she's bound to find out everything sooner or later, and it's not a pretty story. What will that do to her? And then there's Toby.'

'Who's Toby? Joanna asked.

'Hunter's dog. It was the one thing he asked as we arrested him – what's going to happen to Toby?'

'Well, what does?'

'A local dog charity took him. We have an arrangement with them for such eventualities. They'll keep him for a bit, and if Hunter ends up going inside they'll rehome him. That was the one thing he talked about in the car on the way here. He said, "Toby'll be dead by the time I get out." We could have given him – the dog – to Mrs Wiseman-stroke-Hunter – Marty could do

362

with a brother – but with the chance she'll be going away at Her Majesty's pleasure as well, we couldn't risk it.'

Joanna contemplated for a bit. 'You're right. It is a mess. What must he be feeling?'

'At the moment, he just wants to die,' Atherton said. 'He's killed his darling and there's nothing left for him. He'll have to be put on suicide watch, which is a great nuisance to everybody. Then, of course, there's William McGuire to consider. We'll have to try and track down his relatives, if any, and tell them. We haven't yet checked with MisPer whether he was ever reported missing. If he was, that'll make it easier.' He rolled his eyes. 'Just the paperwork of undeading Hunter and redeading McGuire is a nightmare.'

'And then there's the case to prepare,' Slider said. Joanna noticed that he had been curiously silent all through this. Usually the relief of getting to the end of a case made him talkative. But he was sitting with his head bent in a dejected attitude, twirling a pencil round and round in his fingers.

'But if it was an accident, not murder, what case is there?' she asked.

'Failure to notify a death. Interference with a human corpse. Concealing a crime. Impeding a police investigation. Plus the original identity swap fraud, and complicity in insurance fraud,' Atherton enumerated.

'If it was an accident,' Slider said. They both looked at him. 'We have no evidence about the death. No evidence either for him or against

363

him. No evidence at all.'

'But – he confessed,' Joanna said.

'Confessions can be retracted. We get false confessions all the time. He can go back to saying he only found the body, that it had nothing to do with him. Claim he was upset and didn't know what he was saying.'

'But there's Toby's hair on her clothes,' Atherton objected.

'A good counsel will get over that, given he and Toby found the body.'

'The wound could be matched to the roof edge of his car.'

'It's a common make and model. Without any traces of her blood on it ... And he was a minicab driver. One thing he knows how to do is wash a car. There were no witnesses. We've got nothing but the coincidence of her being his daughter.'

'But she was *there* – only yards from his home!' Joanna protested. 'Doesn't that mean something?'

He shook his head. 'He used to take her to the Lido when she was a kid. Who's to say she wasn't just having a nostalgia trip and got killed by a nutter walking in the woods? We can't prove he knew she was there. She didn't tell anyone he had come back into her life, and we don't know that they were ever seen together. The CPS would never go on a confession alone, particularly one like that, made under emotional strain, if it was retracted. No, if he thinks better of it, there's nothing we can do.'

'Well, perhaps losing his beloved daughter is punishment enough,' Joanna said, and then caught up with something he'd said. 'What do you mean, "if it was an accident"?'

'He said her foot skidded in the mud,' said Slider. 'But the ground had been frozen hard for weeks. There was no mud. I noticed myself when we arrived on the scene, because I was thinking about possible footmarks.'

'Maybe she skidded on something else,' Joanna said reasonably.

'Maybe,' Slider said. 'But someone falling backwards against a car like that – you wouldn't expect the blow to be hard enough to kill. But if, being drunk and furious *and* afraid, he dashed her backwards with all his considerable strength – he was a manual worker, so he was pretty sinewy...'

'But it would still be an accident,' Joanna said.

'The law wouldn't see it that way,' Slider said. 'Intent to hurt someone, if it ends in killing them – especially with the deliberate cover-up afterwards. He tied her scarf round her neck to make it look as if she'd been strangled. He must have been afraid his hands would have left a mark. That's quite calculated, you know. Not the action of a man in a blind panic. It would weight the evidence against him. If...'

'If?' she asked.

'If the CPS decided to go with it.' He gave a shrug, 'Not my problem, fortunately. Those of far higher counsel than me will go through it all and decide what to charge him with and why. And there's plenty to play with, so they'll get him for something. And as you say, maybe losing her will be punishment enough.' He

365

thought of Ronnie Fitton and his crime and punishment speech. It was never enough, was it, for those who cared?

'Surely your opinion will be taken into account,' Joanna said, concerned for him now, rather than the unknown and now unknowable Melanie.

'Me? I don't have an opinion. I'm just the meek ass between two burdens. More than two, it generally feels like.'

'Issachar was a strong ass, not a meek one,' Atherton said, to lighten the mood. 'I don't usually get to correct you on the Bible, but if you're going to quote...'

'All asses are meek,' Slider said.

'Ah, well, there I have to disagree with you,' Atherton said. 'What about McLaren?'

'Oh, poor McLaren,' Joanna protested. 'You're always picking on him.'

A twitch of a smile moved Slider's mouth. 'One thing I will say about him: he may be weird, but at least you know he probably won't reproduce.'

Some time later, after Joanna had gone home to relieve his father, Connolly brought him a cup of tea. There was so much to do that several of the team had been invited to come in and do some overtime, and she was one of those who had accepted.

She found Slider surrounded by young sky-scrapers of documents, but staring at the studio photograph of Melanie Hunter. He didn't look up as she placed the tea gently on his desk, but he said, 'Now it's just The Melanie Hunter Murder – a shorthand reference in books and papers, coupled in the minds of those who remember at all with this picture.'

She sought for something to say. 'But you got a result, boss. That's something.'

'Not to her,' he said. He put the picture down with an air of squaring his shoulders. 'Thanks for the tea.' She gave a little *you're welcome* gesture, and as she didn't immediately turn away, he said, 'You're glad it didn't turn out to be Fitton, aren't you? I think you had a soft spot for him.'

'Not exactly soft. Just not desperate hard. I think he cared about Melanie.'

'Not to the extent of finding out what was going on in her life,' Slider said, thinking of that *Not my business*. 'I don't think anyone cared that much about her, poor girl.'

'Marty did,' said Connolly, and then wished she hadn't, because far from giving him any comfort, she'd clearly just given him someone else to worry about.

Eventually they had the firm's traditional celebration drink at the Boscombe Arms. So far, Hunter had not retracted his confession, and the mess of possible charges was under consideration. Slider's worry was that the CPS would end up thinking it was not worth the money it would cost to take it to trial, especially as the story was such a good one it would probably get the jury's sympathy. But Porson had said they would have to move on the 'tampering with a body' side of it, at least, *pour decourager les autres*. 'Can't have people faking murders to cover up accidents,' he had said, with no apparent sense of irony. And Paxman, meeting Slider in the canteen one day, brooding over mulligatawny soup, had said that if they went on the tampering bit, it would make no sense without the rest. 'He'll be jugged, good and hard, don't you worry,' he had concluded with unusual sympathy.

It was good that they had found out a little bit about William McGuire. According to MisPers, an elderly aunt from Colwyn Bay had reported him missing, but two months after the train crash, and only because he had missed sending her a birthday card, which he always did, and had not responded to a letter she had sent asking why. He had no other relatives. Nothing much was done about it at the time. As Hunter had said, when someone like McGuire goes missing, no one is very surprised. The old aunt, now 87 and in a home, but still with all her marbles, was contacted and told that he had died in the Greenford rail crash, and it was reported to Slider that she had been glad to know at last what had happened to him, having long made up her mind to it that he was dead.

The superintendent of the home sent Slider a photograph which the old lady had asked to have 'put in his grave with him'. It was of McGuire, in palmier days, standing with his elder brother Robert, whom he had hero-worshipped. Robert was in uniform – he had been an NCO in the Welsh Guards, one of forty killed in the Falklands. Their parents had died when they were in

368

their teens and Robert had always looked out for William. William had wanted to follow Robert into the army, but wasn't bright enough – he could barely read and write. 'He was a little bit simple, poor lamb,' the Colwyn Bay auntie was reported as saying, 'but always ever such a good boy.'

Quite how you put a photograph 'in a grave' Slider wasn't sure; finding the grave at all would be an extra, time-consuming task he could well do without. He was glad, at least, that what with all the other wrongs done him, McGuire had not been murdered. And for the sake of closing files in his mind, he was glad to discover what he had been doing on the train that day – the auntie had said he was on night duty at the annexe, so he would have been on his way home. He wasn't just fulfilling his meeting with destiny.

And so to the celebration, and the astonishing fact that McLaren had sidled to Slider's door shortly after it had been announced and asked, with a casualness that would have fooled nobody, whether they were 'bringing people'.

Slider hadn't got as far as thinking about that – there was so much stuff in his in-tray by now, the bottom layer had turned to coal. Traditionally the celebration had been for the firm only, but Joanna had sometimes come, and though that was probably a special dispensation for him as the big boss, there was no stated rule against it. What was far more interesting was that McLaren wanted to bring 'somebody', which presumably meant a woman, and Slider knew he would lose his place in his team's heart if he denied them the chance to see what sort of woman would go out with McLaren.

So he said yes, and as soon as McLaren had gone, hastened to telephone Joanna to tell her to come.

He didn't say a word to anyone else, but perhaps McLaren himself had mentioned it. At any rate, tension grew through the day, and when they finally decamped for the pub, you could have sliced it, buttered it, whacked a slice of corned beef between and sold it on a sandwich stall. When they got to the Boscombe and secured their usual corner, there was no sign of any extraneous bodies, but McLaren had an air of nervousness, and the usual loud conversation was curiously muted as everyone watched the door while attempting to appear not to.

The publican, Andy Barrett, brought the pints and some grub. It had gone upmarket a bit of late, and instead of the lopsided doorsteps and pork pies of yore there were three sorts of sandwiches in neat triangles on a big salver, with salad garnish; nachos and salsa; and a selection of Indian snacks – samosas, bhajis and pakoras.

Joanna came in. Everyone hitched up a bit and she squeezed in beside Slider.

'What's all this?' she asked, indicating the snacks. 'Posh grub?'

'The clientele is getting younger,' Atherton said across the table, with a touch of moodiness. Emily was away again. 'An effort has to be made.'

'I miss the old days,' Joanna said. 'Those

370

fluorescent-orange Scotch eggs. The Barbie-pink pork pies.'

'That's just colour prejudice,' said Atherton.

'So when's the main event coming off?' she asked.

Slider made a shushing face, but Connolly, who had heard, had no shame, and turned to McLaren and said, 'Yeah, right, Maurice, where's this bird of yours? Sure I'm starting to think you've imagined her.'

'She should be here any minute,' he said, with what Slider would have sworn was a blush. 'She's coming from work.'

Every ear was pricked. 'What's she do, then?' Connolly asked. 'Nurse, is she?'

Joanna exchanged a private smile with Slider. Male musicians often went out with nurses for the same reason – they understood impossible schedules.

'No, she's a beauty therapist,' McLaren said.

Everyone was too stunned to lay tongue to the obvious retorts, which was probably just as well.

'At the Jingles Sports and Beauty Club – you know, down Chiswick, by the river. That big white building.'

'Yes, I know it,' Joanna said, to rescue the poor mutt from the prevailing shock and awe. 'I've gone past it a few times going down to Barn Elms, to the recording studios. That must be an interesting job.'

'Yeah. She's the senior consultant,' he said with pride. He met Joanna's eyes and said, with an air of flinging himself off a cliff, 'She's been giving me a make-over.'

The explosion of suppressed derision from around the table was fortunately masked by the door opening again and McLaren saying with rather touching eagerness, 'There she is.'

Atherton, who had been fiddling with his mobile, wondering whether it would seem too needy to ring Emily again, looked up, and felt his jaw drop like rain in Wimbledon week. McLaren's girlfriend stood framed in the doorway, looking around for a friendly face. She was a good deal older than him, for a start, but seemed to have forgotten to take that into account when getting dressed. Her skirt was short and black, her shoes vertiginous and strappy, her top was clinging and fuchsia pink, and displayed a cleavage Carter and Caernarvon would have felt compelled to stick their heads down. 'I see wonderful things!' But more Tooting Common than Tutankhamen. Her make-up was blatantly professional, her hair brazenly highlighted, and her costume jewellery so bright it could have been used to signal aircraft. All she needs, Atherton thought in astonished awe, is a pimp and a lamp post.

McLaren had lurched to his feet, and Atherton, turning his gaze that way, saw Maurice's face so soft and marshmallowy and eager and proud, it would make you vomit if it didn't touch you to the quick.

'Everybody, this is Jackie. Jackie Griffiths,' he said in a voice of wonder. And suddenly Atherton could not bear to see him kicked, even in a friendly manner. He was getting to his feet, but Slider was ahead of him, and because they had

372

both risen, oddly everyone else did, too, and a kindly formality came over the party, keeping those who might have mocked silent.

'Good to meet you, Jackie,' Slider said, reaching out a hand across the table.

'This is the boss, our guv, Mr Slider,' McLaren babbled.

'Pleased to meet you,' Jackie said, shaking the hand. Her nails were long, square cut and French varnished. She smiled a professional smile. 'Maurice has told me a lot about you. About all of you.'

Was there a hint of threat in that? Slider wondered vaguely. The introductions went round, a chair was brought, Jackie sat down, and the moment for ribaldry was safely past. McLaren went to the bar to get her a drink, and she looked round them all, beamed, and said, 'What d'you all think of Maurice's new look? I think it's an improvement, don't you? I said to him, you're a nice-looking chap, but you don't make the most of yourself.'

Slider had never considered McLaren as being nice-looking, or indeed anything-looking. He was just McLaren, the food disposal system, the man for whom the question had been coined, 'Are you a man or a mouth?'

'We all noticed the difference,' he said.

She turned to him happily. 'Well, I'm glad my hard work wasn't all for nothing! D'you like his new hairstyle? I'm not sure I've got it quite right yet, but I'll have to wait a few weeks before I can cut it again. Lucky it grows so fast. He's got lovely thick hair. I told him—' McLaren returned with a gin and tonic to place before her, and she looked up at him. 'I told you, didn't I, you've got lovely hair, but you don't do anything with it.'

'You live somewhere out Ruislip way, don't you?' Slider asked, to settle at least one question in his mind.

'Northolt,' she said. 'How did you know?' Luckily she didn't wait for the question to be answered. 'It's a bit of a trek out to Chiswick, where I work now. I was thinking of moving when I got the new job, and it'd be nice to be a bit nearer to Maurice, but you've got to think of house prices. Of course, they do say two can live as cheaply as one. Maybe I could get someone to share with,' she concluded with a gay laugh and a roguish glance at McLaren, who only gazed back at her, obviously entranced by her vivacity. Slider had never known him so silent.

Mind you, Jackie talked so much there was no need for anyone else to do a thing. It occurred to him sadly that there might now have to be a rule about bringing people in future. But he couldn't feel anything but kindness towards someone who was willing to go to so much trouble to bring happiness and an appearance of living in the twenty-first century to someone like McLaren, the man civilization forgot.

On the way home, Joanna said, 'It didn't feel much like a celebration.'

'I'm afraid she did talk a lot,' Slider said. 'But there's no harm in her.'

'I didn't mean that,' she said. 'It's just that

there's usually a certain elation because you've got your man. The Mountie syndrome. But everyone seemed a bit subdued.'

'It's the uncertainty, I suppose. Not knowing what Hunter will be charged with or whether it will go to trial.'

'But you solved the problem. The mystery. You started off knowing nothing, and now you know it all. That must be a satisfaction. Intellectually, at least, if not emotionally.' She looked at him, at his face waxing and waning as they passed street lamps. 'And Auntie McGuire knows what happened to her Billy at last.'

He smiled. 'All right, I give in. It's a triumph of sorts, and I'll accept the bouquets and put it behind me. Now what shall we talk about?'

'We could talk about my troubles.'

'Have you still got troubles? Oh yes, you're stuck with Daniel Kluger for the rest of the season. Can't you just rise above him?'

'That's the trouble. It might just be possible. There's a job being advertised – co-principal in the LSO. More status, more money, a chance to get away from Kluger. And my laggard desk partner.'

Slider was alert. 'Are you thinking of going for it?' he asked carefully.

'Maybe,' she said. 'They don't mind women any more. Jack – our leader, I mean, Jack Willis – thinks I could get it. But.'

He waited a bit and then said, 'But what?'

'It would be more work – which is great, more money – but I'd be away a lot more. Concerts, recordings. Travelling. Not being there to put

Georgie to bed. All the babysitting problems that come with it.'

'Luckily, we've got Dad,' he said.

'George needs his parents too.'

'I can be fairly regular when there isn't a big case on.'

'Hmph,' she said. And then, 'Not seeing so much of you. Is it worth it?'

'I can't answer that,' he said. 'It's your career. It would be a big step up for you, wouldn't it?'

'Yes. Different pieces, different artists, different style of playing. Exciting. Challenging. Living on my wits – even more than I do now.'

'But you love all that, don't you?' He glanced at her sideways. 'Or don't you? You don't have to do it, you know, if you don't want to.'

'I *do* want to! Of course I do! But it's the old dilemma, isn't it? I'm a married woman with a child. I can't give my all to my career without failing the other side.'

'And vice versa,' he said quietly.

'Oh, blast you, why must you always see both sides?' she said, with an exasperated sort of laugh. 'You men just don't know what it's like. You *can* have everything.'

'Well,' he began.

But she said, 'There's something else.'

'Yes?'

'If I do go for it, and I don't get it – I don't know how I'll cope with that.'

'Why shouldn't you get it? You're good enough, aren't you?'

'It isn't always a matter of that. There's style, too, and personality – getting on with people.'

'You get on with everyone.'

'And age.'

'Ah,' said Slider.

'Music's getting to be more and more a young person's field. They don't value experience and knowing the repertoire and all the rest of it. Not above youth and looks, anyway. Suppose I went for the audition, and I didn't get it. You know how I hate to fail.'

'You can't let that stop you trying things.'

'Yes, that's the point isn't it?' she said, giving him another amused and rueful look. 'Would I feel more of a failure for failing, or for not trying?'

He made a helpless gesture with his hands. 'I can't tell you that. How can I tell you that? You really want Atherton for these abstruse, philosophical discussions. I'm just an ordinary, common-or-garden copper.'

Another silence. She resumed: 'I'll tell you one thing, though.'

'What's that?'

'It made you forget Melanie Hunter for a while, didn't it?'

He looked indignant. 'Was that what it was all about? This whole job thing was just a ruse?'

'Wouldn't you like to know?' She grinned.

What was it she had said – toothache to take your mind off stomach ache? And yet...

While he was still thinking it out, she said, 'Those snacks weren't very substantial, I must say. Fancy some fish and chips? It's not too late, is it?'

'Never too late for fish and chips,' he said.

377